THE CRIME OF WORLD POWER

FOR

MRS. G.
E. J.
R. J. A.

THE CRIME OF WORLD POWER

POLITICS WITHOUT GOVERNMENT IN THE INTERNATIONAL SYSTEM

By Richard A. Aliano

Capricorn Books

•

G. P. Putnam's Sons, New York

 Published simultaneously in Canada by Longman Canada Limited, Toronto.

SBN: 399-12027-0 hardcover
SBN: 399-50371-4 softcover

Library of Congress Cataloging in Publication Data

Aliano, Richard A
The crime of world power.

Includes index

1. International relations. I. Title.
JX1395.A39 1978 327 77-25866

PRINTED IN THE UNITED STATES OF AMERICA

CONTENTS

PART I

OVERVIEW

My father is a businessman. . . . What you have to understand is that he considers himself the equal of all those great men like Presidents and Prime Ministers and Supreme Court Justices and Governors of the States.

—Michael Corleone, in Mario Puzo's
The Godfather

Chapter 1

Politics Without Government

> There is more money potential in narcotics than in any other business. If we don't get into it, somebody will, maybe the Tattaglia Family. With the revenue they earn they can amass more and more police and political power. Their family will become stronger than ours. Eventually they will come after us to take away what we have. It's just like countries. If they arm, we have to arm. If they become stronger economically, they become a threat to us. . . . I think we have to have a piece of that action or we risk everything we have. Not now, but maybe ten years from now.
>
> —Hagen, in Mario Puzo's *The Godfather*

AMERICA'S POST-WATERGATE, POST-VIETNAM ERA

Politics is not quite what it used to be—or so it seems. Not since Dwight Eisenhower finished his second term in office in 1961 have we had a President relinquish power normally. We have lost one chief executive to assassination in 1963, another a half-decade later to an unpopular and tragic war, and yet another to domestic scandal in the shadow of impeachment. The American people have been subject to a decade and a half of riots, assassinations, racial confrontations, the rebellion of their youth, unending war and seemingly pervasive corruption. The culmination of this series of traumas has been the most painful twin disillusionment of all—the forced resignation of Richard Nixon and defeat in Vietnam. Within a few months, one helicopter whisked a fallen and disgraced President from the White House lawn and another plucked the American proconsul in Saigon from the roof of his embassy as enemy troops approached. An era seemed at an end. We are now in the post-Watergate, post-Vietnam era. If the post–World War II period was characterized by American ascendance abroad and self-confidence at home, the new era is one of growing challenge and declining influence beyond the water's edge, and lack of direction and consensus in domestic affairs.

Revelations of wrongdoing continue to dominate our attention. The excesses of the Central Intelligence Agency have been so consistent and bizarre as to defy the imagination. According to a report by the select Senate Intelligence Committee, the CIA was implicated in assassination plots against five foreign leaders; the committee heard evidence of involvement in plans to murder two other Third World political figures: In late 1960 President Eisenhower authorized CIA director Allen Dulles to conceive a plan to eliminate Patrice Lumumba, premier of the newly independent Congo, now Zaire (several months later, Lumumba was killed by a rival Congolese faction apparently without United States involvement). At about the same time, the CIA collaborated with and supplied arms to Dominican dissidents who killed long-entrenched dictator Rafael Trujillo. In the month that President Kennedy was shot to death in Dallas, South Vietnamese President Ngo Dien Diem was killed in a coup inspired and supported by the United States. In the early 1960s, the CIA hatched at least eight schemes to do away with Cuba's Fidel Castro, in all likelihood with the approval of John Kennedy. In one case, the agency actually conspired with major underworld chieftains and promised them $150,000 and protection against FBI investigation of their criminal activities in the United States if they would poison Castro. As recently as October 1970, the commander-in-chief of Chile's army was killed while resisting kidnapping, part of a coup supported by the United States government against the Allende regime. Finally, the committee heard testimony suggesting CIA complicity in plots to assassinate President Sukarno of Indonesia and Haitian dictator "Papa Doc" Duvalier.

The Central Intelligence Agency has not been alone in abusing its legal mandate in the name of national security. Prior to Watergate and Vietnam, no institution was more revered in the United States than the Federal Bureau of Investigation. Then it was discovered that President Nixon had consistently used the FBI to carry out domestic surveillance of political enemies and cover up the bugging of the National Democratic Committee. Now it has been revealed that the bureau has been violating civil liberties at least since Franklin Roosevelt ordered the electronic monitoring of defense-establishment critics in 1940. Under director J. Edgar Hoover, the FBI complied with improper requests from Presidents Roosevelt, Kennedy, Johnson and Nixon and offered political intelligence to Truman and Eisenhower as well. Moreover, Hoover directed a personal crusade to discredit civil rights leader Martin Luther King, Jr., which included the use of unauthorized telephone taps, assorted bugging devices, forgery and blackmail.

Not surprisingly, not only government has been found guilty of a long train of abuses. Apparently corruption reigns in the private sector as well. In both their domestic and foreign operations, large corporations have institutionalized a system of political payoffs. In 1973, the Watergate special prosecutor found that the Gulf Oil Corporation had illegally contributed over $150,000 to the 1972 campaigns of domestic political figures. Subsequently, several other corporations were found to have engaged in similar activities. Even more recently, there have been numerous revelations about bribery of foreign officials by American companies, which had attempted to hide these illicit activities from their stockholders. For example, the Northrop Corporation funneled nearly a half-million dollars to a Saudi Arabian middleman for the express purpose of bribing two Saudi air force generals. In Honduras, the United Brands Company made a $1.25 million payoff to that republic's president in return for favorable government treatment. Scores of American politicians and officials in at least four foreign countries were on the gift list of Ashland Oil, including the president and prime minister of Gabon, who received $150,000 each for the protection of oil concessions in their country. Gulf Oil has admitted making over $12 million in political contributions over the last decade and a half to domestic candidates and to government officials in Italy, South Korea, Bolivia and Lebanon. In Japan, Lockheed secretly spent more than $12 million in the two decades after the end of American occupation in 1952, with an alleged $1.67 million bribe going to former Prime Minister Tanaka. In the Netherlands, a major scandal developed about the behavior of Prince Bernhard, who was accused of having been subsidized by both Lockheed and Northrop. In short, American firms have made payoffs to princes, presidents, prime ministers and generals throughout Europe, the Middle East, Latin America, Africa and the Far East to protect their corporate interests.

All in all, corruption seems to be the norm, not the exception, in America's post-Watergate, post-Vietnam era.

POLITICS AS USUAL?

The serious student of politics must grapple with a perplexing question: Is politics any different today from politics fifteen years ago? Or fifty years ago? Or, for that matter, five hundred years ago? To be sure, the world today is very different from the world of only a few decades ago, let alone centuries past. The indexes of dramatic change are readily apparent. For the moment, let us consider just three: the population explosion, the struggle for the planetary product and the revolution in weapons technology.

The present rate of world population growth is unprecedented. It took from the beginning of time until 1830 for the number of human beings on this planet to reach one billion. Now it is four billion. By the year 2010, it will have doubled to eight billion, and additional billions will be added every five years or less. There is a disparity in growth rates between geographical regions. In the Southern Hemisphere, where three-quarters of mankind lives, the population will double in about twenty-five years, and no developing country can stabilize its population at less than double its present size. These countries constitute the poorer portion of the world, so the global poor are multiplying more rapidly than the relatively well-off. This high rate of population growth in less-developed countries (LDCs) must be considered in relation to both the process of development and the ecological system (ecosystem): It hampers economic development, siphoning off up to two-thirds of the annual growth in national product. Coupled with growing industrialization, it is placing a severe strain on the environment's capacity to supply food and raw materials and to absorb wastes and pollutants.

The planetary product (gross world product, or GWP)—the total value of goods and services produced annually by the human race—has more than tripled during the last twenty-five years. The per capita GWP has nearly doubled to about $1400—approximately that of the United States in 1890. However, distribution of global wealth is unequal. The GNP of the United States in 1975 was $1.52 trillion; that of India, $100 billion. The discrepancy is even greater for per capita income: $7,115 for the United States, $162 for India. (Because inequality of income is greater in India than in the United States, the disparity in individual income is even larger than these figures suggest.) Real distribution of the planetary product is skewed in favor of a small minority. The 25 percent of the world's people who live in the developed countries produce and consume nearly 80 percent of the planetary product, while the 75 percent who inhabit the less-developed areas account for 20 percent. The United States, which accounts for some 5 percent of the world's population, produces over one-quarter of the global product; the combined share of China and India (which together make up nearly 40 percent of humankind) is less than 7 percent. With per capita income growing faster in the developed part of the world than in the less developed, the rich are getting richer and proportionately fewer, and the poor are getting poorer and more numerous. What is truly revolutionary for world politics (mere inequality in wealth is nothing new) is that the poor countries are demanding a redistribution of the planetary product and are organizing among themselves to that end.

The third index of change is the revolution in weapons technology. Since the Second World War, there has occurred a quantum leap in the speed and destructiveness of military weaponry, brought about by the cumulative effects of three technological revolutions. The first, the nuclear revolution, began with the devastation of Hiroshima in August 1945. The weapon used was in the 13-kiloton range (that is, its destructive force was equivalent to 13,000 tons of TNT) and was more than one thousand times as powerful as the largest conventional bomb dropped during World War II. The thermonuclear revolution followed in 1953. The hydrogen bomb was in the 20-megaton range (the equivalent of 20 million tons of TNT). Now a single aircraft can rain more destructive force than all the bombs dropped during the Second World War. The third revolution, in delivery capability, occurred with the development of intercontinental ballistic missiles (ICBMs) in the 1960s. It takes between thirty and forty minutes for a strategic missile to travel between the United States and the Soviet Union, and even with the most sophisticated radar or satellite systems, not much more than twenty minutes' warning of impending attack can be had. With the deployment of multiple independently targeted reentry vehicles (MIRVs) in the 1970s, one Poseidon missile launched from an American Polaris submarine was capable of destroying ten cities in the U.S.S.R. In short, the weapons of mass destruction in the hands of the superpowers are more than enough to destroy all life on this planet. Moreover, with the proliferation of this weaponry, the danger of nuclear war due to accident or calculation has been greatly enhanced.

POLITICAL CONTINUITY AND SOCIAL CHANGE

All three of these fundamental alterations in man's environment have been fostered by the general revolution in man's knowledge. The scientific revolution that began several centuries ago in the Western world has provided people with radically new means of controlling their physical and social landscapes. The principal cause of the accelerating growth in world population has been the sudden decrease in the death rate (especially in developing countries), brought about by the introduction of modern sanitation and public-health programs. With the mortality rate spectacularly cut during the last half-century, but with traditional birth rates remaining high, we have removed nature's primary check on population expansion. The population explosion is therefore a by-product of the process of modernization and man's control over the constraints of nature. Similarly, the unprecedented growth of the planetary product is a direct result of the rationalization of production stemming from the Industrial Revolution. Harnessing the power of coal to produce steam married the technological genius of humans with nature's abundance and produced an era of material affluence in the developed world. Now the unchecked exploitation of the ecosystem is leading nature to rebel, and the less well off mass of humanity is pressing for a reallocation of material benefits.

The revolution in man's control over the environment has led to unforseen and formidable problems. That the revolution inherent in modernity has given with one hand and then threatened to take back with the other is nowhere more evident than in weapons technology. Modern science's unraveling of the secret of the atom provided humankind with a new source of energy, which was promptly placed at the disposal of political authorities for the purpose of mass destruction. Yet again, scientific genius threatens to outpace political capacity to control destiny.

There is little doubt, then, that our physical and social environment has been subjected to constant change and is still in a state of flux. Yet to what extent has politics also changed? To what extent have political relationships lagged behind in the overall process of modernization? How great is the gap? What means exist to bridge this gap between political and social developments? These questions, as fundamental as they can be, are not easily answered. Indeed, no real answers have yet been found. But we must realize that the essential starting point of the learning process is the identification of relevant questions.

Is the political process today fundamentally different from the one that existed before Watergate and Indochina? Is the behavior exhibited by our national leaders at home and abroad qualitatively different from the activities they engaged in previously? Is it different in kind from that of leaders of other societies today? Even a superficial survey of recent history suggests a negative response. If the American Central Intelligence Agency is guilty of having plotted the assassination of foreign leaders, so is the Soviet KGB. At least two instances are documented of the KGB planning the murder of foreign statesmen. Immediately after World War II, Stalin sought the elimination of Czechoslavakian foreign minister Jan Masaryk and Yugoslavia's Marshal Tito in order to consolidate his hold over eastern Europe. Masaryk was killed during the 1948 Soviet-inspired coup which toppled the non-Communist government; Tito, of course, escaped assassination. Only recently, three Cuban agents expelled from Paris for their role in a political assassination were believed by French authorities to have been controlled by the Soviet secret police.

Political assassination has a long history in international affairs. The murder of foreign officials was institutionalized in Renaissance Italy, where the elimination of leaders of rival city-states was so commonplace that ruling families regularly employed tasters to sample their food, and adventurers who made political assassination a vocation were called bravos (a term of approbation). Moreover, it was well known that the prince's ministers could be expected to supplement their income with regular annuities from foreign rulers. The interrelationship of diplomacy and assassination was still pronounced enough in the early nineteenth century for Talleyrand, upon hearing of Napoleon's murder of the Duke of Enghien, to remark flippantly: "It's worse than a crime; it's a blunder." With a good deal more finesse, the Senate Intelligence Committee concluded its investigation of CIA involvement in foreign assassinations by noting that not only does political murder "violate moral precepts fundamental to our way of life," but also, because such activities "almost inevitably become known," they do "damage to American foreign policy, to the good name and reputation of the United States abroad, [and] to the American people's faith and support for our government and its foreign policy."

As for American-based multinational corporations engaging in bribery and chicanery overseas, a similarly long established tradition can be cited. The practice existed at least as far back as the seventeenth century, when the British East India Company won preferential treatment from Mogul rulers in exchange for various bounties. Moreover, other countries with enterprises doing business abroad take it for granted that their businessmen are making payments to foreign leaders. And we must bear in mind, as one observer notes, that "bribery abroad is not exactly the corruption of innocents," and that some incidents "smack more of protection and extortion than simply bribery." [1] Far from being mere instruments of American foreign policy, multinational corporations pursue their own interests overseas, which sometimes conflict with those of the mother country. The major oil companies, for example, helped carry out the Arab oil embargo against their home countries in 1973/1974. In 1975, while the CIA was providing financial support to two anti-Soviet factions in Angola, Gulf Oil gave three times as much money to the pro-Soviet faction in return for oil concessions.

Governments have an even longer history than do corporations of bribing foreign leaders. Indeed, the early versions of foreign aid were nothing less than dynastic payoffs on a grand scale. The French under Cardinal Richelieu gave subsidies to the kings of Denmark and Sweden during the Thirty Years' War in the seventeenth century so as to whittle down the power of Austria. Only when the recipient countries were defeated by Austria after a dozen years of warfare did France engage in hostilities itself. In like manner, the British paid substantial sums to continental European states during the Napoleonic Wars to get them to help in the struggle against the French. The United States did the same in both world wars in this century and continued the policy during the cold war that followed. Aiding dissidents in insurrection against their government falls into the same category and may be traced back in history at least to the ancient Greeks. Since 1945, both the United States and the Soviet Union have supported coups against a number of countries. The CIA's operations against Guatemala and Iran in the early 1950s, Cuba and South Vietnam in the early 1960s and Chile in the late 1960s and early 1970s are well documented. Similarly, Soviet aid to indigenous pro-Communist elements in foreign lands (only recently in Portugal and Angola) are well known; there have even been charges that the

U.S.S.R. paid a $50 million bribe to an African leader in return for recognition of the Marxist faction which has set up a government in Angola under Soviet sponsorship.

All this is by no means intended as a rationalization or whitewash or cover-up. In fact, it is interesting to note that until recently, there was little in the way of systematic attempts by governments to either justify or conceal such activities. Today governments feel they must justify them if they cannot conceal them, and the public is outraged when they are revealed, which indicates that it is our perception of political reality that has changed and not reality itself. In its essence, politics has changed little over the years. It is our awareness and acceptance that have changed. The present period is characterized by what former Vice President Agnew in his resignation speech called the "post Watergate morality." How long it will last is another matter, but there is little doubt that the public is currently directing its rage and indignation against all types of political actions judged to be "corrupt."

The judgment that a variety of behavior is corrupt is essentially subjective and reflects changing social standards. Criminal behavior is easy to identify, for, by definition, it violates the laws promulgated by duly constituted authority. Corruption is at once broader and more vague. It suggests deviation, especially on the part of agents of the state, from the public's conception of acceptable behavior. When they are judged to have violated prevailing norms or rules of the game (a notion broader than the law), they are condemned for debasing the political process. That which is corrupt may or may not also be a crime. For a government official to accept a bribe is both. He has committed an illegal act (that is, he has violated a self-imposed restraint—self-imposed in that the state has set rules for its own behavior and that of its agents). He is also guilty of corruption, for the norms established by society as a whole demand that he serve the public good and not his own interest at the public's expense. Then again, an act may be within the limits of permissible behavior as defined by the law (especially if the law is stretched) and yet be considered a corruption of the public trust. When an American secretary of state declares at a press conference that a particular accord with a foreign power contains no "secret agreements," and then is subsequently compelled to admit that there were indeed certain "understandings" which were not made public, he might be judged to have perverted his duty concerning public accountability. By the same token, what is deemed corrupt in one society, or in one historical period, may not be judged corrupt in another. The amount of corruption present in any particular political process ultimately depends upon prevailing values and expectations.

DOMESTIC VS. INTERNATIONAL POLITICS: THE FALSE DICHOTOMY

Reflecting upon the newly discovered corrupt (and, indeed, often criminal) behavior of certain national leaders and institutions, a number of commentators have suggested that the entire Watergate syndrome in our domestic political life has been a logical if deplorable byproduct of our machinations abroad. The perversion of our moral values at home is said to be the result of the consistent and progressive deterioration of ethical standards in the conduct of our foreign policy since World War II. Immoral actions overseas justified under the banner of national security inexorably lead, so this line of reasoning maintains, to a gradual but insidious corrosion of the democratic fiber of the domestic political process. It is a small step from clandestine interference in the electoral procedures of foreign countries to a callous disregard of the basic democratic norms of our own society. Watergate (and all that has been associated with it in the popular mind) becomes the culmination of two decades of dubious foreign ventures. The deceptions and indecencies associated with the war in Vietnam and committed in the name of the national interest are soon transformed into the moral turpitude of Watergate—similarly rationalized in terms of the general welfare and the defense of the Republic. The link between foreign affairs and domestic freedom was noted nearly a century and a half ago by that astute French observer of American society, Alexis de Tocqueville:

> No protracted war can fail to endanger the freedom of a democratic people. . . . War does not always give over democratic communities to military government, but it most invariably and immeasurably increases the powers of civil government; it must almost compulsorily concentrate the direction of all men and the management of all things in the hands of the administration. If it does not lead to despotism by sudden violence, it prepares men for it gently by their habits.[2]

As recent history has demonstrated, this was an accurate warning. Engulfed in a cold war with a mortal enemy (defined in the late 1940s as international communism emanating from the Kremlin), Congress and the American people have been willing to allow the further growth of Presidential primacy and numerous infringements on individual liberties. The consensus that developed after the Second World War allowed for preoccupation with foreign enemies at the expense of vigilance over liberty at home. Certain of our leaders were themselves aware of the dangers inherent in the nation-under-siege mentality. At the height of the cold war, President Eisenhower warned that the regimentation of society that is the necessary concomitant of perpetual mobilization for war and the quest for security abroad would bring with it "all the grim paraphernalia of the garrison state." But he was quick to add that "as long as there is a threat to freedom, they [the free nations] must, *at any price,* remain armed, strong and ready for the risk of war." [3] Thus, a delicate balancing act was necessary to provide for the external security of the United States and maintenance of democratic values internally. By the late 1960s, this precarious balance of values had collapsed.

Yet to assume that domestic politics has been corrupted by the world of international relations reflects a naive conception of the nature of politics. Our domestic politics has never been as pure as we might like to think, and though we became more deeply involved in world politics after 1945 than ever before, no qualitative change in our behavior in the international systems has occurred. Much of our disillusionment stems from our false conception of the difference between national and international politics. We have adopted a consensus model of politics within the United States and a conflict model of international politics. This has led us to the erroneous conclusion that politics within our borders is different in kind from the behavior we have come to expect from countries in their mutual relations and led us to the expectation that the domestic system can be insulated from the evils of interstate rivalry. In fact, there is no wall separating the domestic political system from the international system, and politics in the two tend to differ in degree rather than in kind.

The Consensus Model of Domestic Politics. The misleading consensus model explanation of politics within the United States begins with the premise that there is an underlying harmony in the domestic political system. It is assumed that the small amount of conflict which does exist takes place on the margins of society and never calls into question the fundamental political order and structure. For example, though labor and management may lock horns periodically, they do so within the rules of our pluralist democratic system. Both the National Association of Manufacturers and the AFL-CIO accept the existing constitutional order, and though they may bargain over wages, working conditions and fringe benefits, neither calls for the overthrow of the government or demands revolutionary change. Similarly, basic agreement on values is supposed to be reflected in the two-party system. Neither the Republicans nor the Democrats espouse programs of radical change, and the differences in their party platforms are nominal, revolving around differing emphases within broad areas of conformity. Both major parties (like labor and business) accept the fundamentals of American society: the liberal democratic political framework and the free enterprise or capitalistic economic system. The loss of a presidential election does not lead to riots and insurrection, and those who voted against the winning ticket reluctantly accept the outcome because they accept the electoral process. They take comfort in the conviction that the rules that caused them defeat today may bring them victory tomorrow. For the interim, they can await the next test of strength with the assurance that their opponents share with them basic beliefs about what constitutes a just society. Conflict, then, is always muted and moderated by the shared consensus on norms and values.

The definition of politics that best characterizes the consensus model has been made by political scientist David Easton: "A political system can be designated as those interactions through which values are authoritatively allocated for a society."[4]

Let us take a close look at the implications of this description. When we say something must be allocated we are indicating that it is in short supply. Bear in mind that when we talk about the supply of something, it makes sense to do so only in terms of the demand for it. Something that is in short supply (for example, gasoline during the Arab oil embargo of 1973/1974) is in short supply only because the demand for it is great; more of it is wanted than can be provided readily. Some method must be devised to apportion or ration or allocate the limited supply among those who want it. Again, take the gasoline shortage as an example. One way to ration gasoline would have been to have allowed service-station owners to decide who would get their particular supplies. The Happy Motorist station might decide to sell gasoline only to customers over six feet tall; the Honor Thy Octane garage across the street might choose to service only Cadillacs; the nearby establishment owned by Friendly Freddy might opt to serve only those aggressive and strong enough to fight their way to the pump. Each of these arrangements is an allocative mechanism. For these allocation decisions to be authoritative, two elements would have to be present. First, our service-station owners would have to have the ability to enforce their decisions (either alone or with the help of the state); second, the vast majority of potential buyers must accept those decisions as legitimate. Without the second factor, the first would be extremely difficult if not impossible to obtain. Those under six feet in height would in all likelihood find it difficult to acquiesce to the decision of the Happy Motorist station, and Volkswagen owners would be unlikely to accept the policy of Honor Thy Octane. Under such conditions, both businesses might find themselves besieged by irate motorists. (Luckily, the federal government did not rely on this method of allocation. Though it could have rationed motor fuel much as it had during World War II, it chose to rely on the price mechanism of the market to adjust demand to available supply. By deciding not to ration formally, the government did indeed select an allocation mechanism.)

All political systems must allocate values. Values may be defined broadly as all those things that people desire: wealth, status, education, influence, and so on. These values must be allocated because they are scarce. Take status: By definition, not everyone can be high man on the totem pole; without low men there are no high men. Or wealth: If everyone could satisfy all his material desires, there would be no need to apportion wealth; however, though people may have virtually infinite material wants, society's ability to satisfy these wants is limited. A decision must be made on allocation. The constitutional order (defined broadly to include societies with both written and unwritten constitutions) determines how these allocation decisions are to be made and who is to participate in the decision-making process.

The consensus model assumes that these procedures are legitimate—that is, the vast majority of the citizenry accepts them as just and proper. It also assumes that the greater the legitimacy of the system, the less government needs to enforce its decisions through coercion. Thus the domestic political system is seen as fundamentally harmonious, with conflict existing only on the periphery. Yet this is a misconception, which leads to a distorted view of national politics. Though it may be true that there is fundamental agreement on political procedures, there may be intense conflict over the choice of allocation mechanisms or policies. While the system itself may be considered legitimate by the citizenry as a whole, specific outcomes (or allocation decisions) may not. Large segments of the population may, on the contrary, feel disadvantaged by national policies and even alienated from the body politic. Let us return to the government's decision on gasoline allocation. The decision not to institute a formal rational system and to rely instead on the price mechanism worked to the advantage of some groups and the disadvantage of others. In fact, all governmental decisions tend to benefit certain segments of society at the expense of others—or, at the very least, to benefit some more than others. The consensus model of domestic policies, then, tends to gloss over real and intense conflicts within national societies.

The Conflict Model of International Politics

While the consensus model of politics has dominated our perception of domestic affairs during the last several decades, a totally different conception of politics has predominated on the international level. We have assumed that politics among nations is fundamentally conflictual, lacking as it does either governmental structure or common commitment to a universally accepted notion of justice. Conflict is seen as central in the international system, with harmony the aberration.

Scarcity of values is operative in both the domestic and the international environments. But whereas it is assumed that a generally accepted method of determining allocation of benefits in national society exists, in the world of independent states, there is no legitimate allocation mechanism; moreover, there is no central political authority (or world government) to legislate and enforce decisions on allocation.

The Easton definition of politics cited in the previous section best fits a well-integrated political system supported by broad agreement on values and expectations. Politics as it is conducted among countries has no such qualifications. However, there have been frequent attempts to employ the consensus model as an explanation of international affairs. In the first part of this century, prior to the Second World War, international relations were studied and examined in terms of the criteria developed for domestic political analysis. A college course in world affairs was likely to focus upon the content and evolution of international law as well as the theory and performance of the League of Nations (the predecessor of the United Nations), which together were seen as the twin pillars of a developing world constitutional order. If only states had the means to settle their disputes peacefully, it was maintained, then international politics could be tamed. If a system of laws and a system of courts capable of adjudicating disputes arising under it are the essential causes of domestic stability and tranquillity, then surely relations among nations could be domesticated and civilized by means of analogous international institutions. World public opinion would provide the legitimacy and international organization the means to enforce the decisions of the global body politic. When the international order suddenly collapsed under the weight of the Fascist challenge of the 1930s, and when it became apparent that World War II was but the second phase of this century's own Thirty Years' War, the consensus model of world politics collapsed with it.

Students of international relations, disillusioned with what they termed the utopianism and idealism of the interwar years, attacked the consensus model as fundamentally erroneous in its assumptions. It was claimed that the idealists had placed the cart before the horse: They had assumed that international law and organization would create a global community of values, whereas, it was argued, a real legal and political order would follow only the evolution of an international consensus concerning the just order. The League of Nations system lacked the crucial elements of a viable and stable political order—namely, underlying legitimacy for post–World War I settlement of conflict and executive power to enforce the contemporary distribution of values. On the one hand, there were major states (the Axis powers) who rejected the international status quo and sought to reallocate power and wealth radically. On the other hand, the league proved powerless to enforce that status quo. When the Japanese conquered Manchuria in 1931, committing aggression against the international status quo and flagrantly violating the covenant (or constitution) of the League of Nations, the league failed to undertake any enforcement action. Four years later, Mussolini invaded Ethiopia (one of the few remaining independent states in Africa), and again the league proved unable to intervene effectively, limiting itself to largely symbolic economic sanctions against Italy. By 1938 and the German occupation of Austria, the league was effectively defunct.

In place of an international version of the consensus model of politics, adherents to the new school (who termed themselves realists) embraced a conflict model of world politics. In this view, the essence of politics was the conflict of interests resulting from scarcity of values. Without scarcity, there would be no conflict. Without conflict, there would be no politics. Politics, then, was the study of conflict and the resulting competition for power on the part of rivals seeking to prevail over their opponents and attain their goals. Hans J. Morgenthau, father of the modern realist school, has defined the conflict-model approach best: "International politics, like all politics, is a struggle for power. Whatever the ultimate aims of international politics, power is always the immediate aim."[5]

Emphasis on power and conflict in political affairs, and criticism of the "impossible dream" of idealists, has a long tradition in political thought. This line of thinking can be traced at least as far back as the ancient Greek historian Thucydides, who, in his famous narrative of the Peloponnesian War between Athens and Sparta, wrote: "Our opinion of the gods and knowledge of men lead us to conclude that it is a general necessary law of nature to rule wherever one can."[6] However, it is Machiavelli whose name has become synonymous with the amorality of power politics. This Renaissance Italian thinker maintained that the acquisition and exploitation of power was the state's first law of motion, and that in the imperfect real world, leaders were justified in all activities that served the interest of the national community, regardless of their immorality as judged by individual ethics. Indeed, the standards of behavior for individual citizens and for statesmen were different. The individual was to be judged on his intentions, the statesman by the consequences of his actions. Thus a prince could behave admirably in terms of individual ethics and disastrously in terms of his responsibility for the well-being of the state. For example, British Prime Minister Neville Chamberlain may have had only the purest of intentions when he devised his policy of appeasing Nazi Germany during the 1930s. Indeed, the realist would reason, could anything be nobler than the desire to secure "peace in our time"? But when Chamberlain claimed he had secured it after the Munich Conference, waving a document containing the worthless pledges of Adolf Hitler, he was guilty of an irreparable political miscalculation. In his motives, Chamberlain may have been noble; but the fruition of his ill-conceived policies was nothing less than global disaster. For those who bear the responsibility for the welfare of millions, it is only consequences that count, not intentions.

According to the realists, the conflict inherent in international politics is accentuated by the very nature of its context. Interstate relations are carried on in an environment lacking all the essential attributes that we associate with a well-ordered domestic policy. First, there is no community of values to moderate conflict. Not sharing the same opinions concerning what is just and unjust in the allocation of values among societies, states compete to impose their versions of the just order. Not surprisingly, each state's conception of the just international society presupposes a disproportionately large share of the global pie for itself. Both the United States and the Soviet Union seek to impose their notions of just world order, and each envisions itself in the position of deciding exactly what is a just distribution of benefits internationally. Second, there is no centralization of legitimate authority in the international system; international politics is politics without government. Unlike citizens in a stable domestic society, states have little expectation of receiving their "just" share unless they have the power to seize it. Self-interest can be served only by self-help.

Let us use a brief example to illustrate this important difference between politics at the national and at the international levels. John Smith, driving his car north on Elm Street, collides with a car driven by Joe Doe, who is traveling east on Main Street, at the intersection of the two thoroughfares. We can expect the two men to exchange the pertinent information (and perhaps even a few insults), drive away and report the accident to their respective insurance companies. But why is this the result of their encounter? Because both have been socialized into channeling their conflicts through the regulatory instruments provided by the state. Each has some faith in the procedures established by government to reconcile different versions of justice; both recognize the authority of the state to compel them to submit their disputes to the proper authorities. But what if there were no such underlying consensus? What would happen if no government existed capable of maintaining allegiance and enforcing decisions? In such a case, quite a scene would occur at the corner of Elm and Main.

For the realist, international politics takes place on the corner of Elm and Main. Without world government to restrain conflicts, or even a community of shared values, each state must rely upon its own capabilities to enforce its own conception of justice. The type of behavior likely to occur in such an anarchic environment was aptly characterized by the seventeenth-century English theorist Thomas Hobbes:

> During the time men live without a common power to keep them all in awe, they are in that condition which is called war, and such a war as is every man against every man. For 'war' consisteth not in battle only or the act of fighting, but in a tract of time wherein the will to contend by battle is sufficiently known . . .[7]

Thus, for the realist, international politics is characterized by a perpetual state of war.

POLITICS: WITH AND WITHOUT GOVERNMENT

It is apparent, then, that we have two opposing views of the political world. More than this, in effect we have descriptions of two different worlds: One is the world of domestic politics, supposedly characterized by fundamental harmony concerning ultimate values and goals and a legitimate structure for apportioning benefits among citizens; the other is the world of international politics, where the struggle for power reigns in an anarchic environment devoid of any system of ethics save that of the national interest. Given such a distinct dichotomy, it would be logical to conclude that a porous national political system might be subject to contamination from its external environment. However, the boundary between the two "worlds"—or levels of politics—is not simply porous. It is artificial.

As we have discussed, the consensus model of national politics falls short of a valid explanation of the domestic system. Conflict is a crucial aspect of politics on this level as well, and it cannot be glossed over without doing severe damage to an understanding of the real world. By the same token, world politics is not altogether summarized by reference to the law of the jungle. Certainly the nature of the international system ensures that the shotgun will always be kept in the closet, but it is not always high noon or the gunfight at the O.K. corral. As we shall see in subsequent chapters, there are at least rudimentary values and expectations shared by members of the state system and certain structures and processes which tend to ameliorate competition and rivalry. Both varieties of political behavior have much in common—including flagrant disregard of certain ethical norms.

Politics Defined

It is possible to distill from our two contrasting models a functional definition of politics that is valid at all levels of social interaction. First we must bear in mind that politics is a variety of social behavior. It exists in all human societies and at all stages of historical development. Indeed, political behavior can be discerned even among lower forms of animal life, where we often observe pecking orders and similar hierarchical arrangements—that is, relationships of subordination and superordination. Politics involves influence or control over the behavior of others, and as such is found not only in formal governments but in business firms, universities, churches, peer groups, fraternal organizations, labor unions, families and virtually every group consisting of two or more people who interact on a regular basis. When we speak of "office politics" or "campus politics," we are referring to a type of behavior by which individuals (or groups) vie for positions of influence. Politics is therefore purposeful activity and includes a conscious design to manipulate others—to get them to do what they would not otherwise do (or prevent them from doing what they would otherwise do). Because politics means effecting a change in another actor's behavior, it involves conflict of wills and exercise of power.

Though we will discuss power at greater length in Chapter 3, suffice it to say for now that power is the ability to affect another actor's behavior. Ultimately, it is a psychological relationship, in which A convinces B that it is in B's interest to conform to A's demands. Whether I persuade, cojole, beg, bribe or threaten another party is immaterial; as long as I eventually get my way, it may be said that I have exercised power. Whether it is my respect for the expertise of a physician that persuades me to follow his medical advice, or my fear of the gun in the hand of a mugger that persuades me to hand over my wallet, my calculation concerning self-interest is being affected by the wielder of power. To get me to behave in a certain manner, I must be persuaded that it will be in my interest to do so. If I am offered a bribe, I am being told that my compliance will bring material reward; if I am threatened, I am promised that noncompliance will adversely affect my interests. In both cases, someone is seeking to make me an offer I can't refuse.

People seek power for what it can bring. Power, therefore, is instrumental—a means to an end. Except for the power-hungry deviate who seeks power as an end itself (like a miser who seeks to amass wealth as a final goal), most political actors desire power to either protect or change a certain distribution of benefits. Some forty years ago, Harold Lasswell, one of the pioneers of contemporary political science, described politics as the study of "who gets what, when, and how."[8] The "who" are those with power; the "what" represents values, or all those things people desire (e.g., income, deference, safety); the "when" and "how" is what politics is really all about. From what has been said, it should be apparent that neither the consensus-model definition of politics (Easton) nor the conflict-model definition (Morganthau) is incompatible with this view. Because the study of the domestic political system has tended to deemphasize conflict, it focuses on the ends of politics (that is, allocation of values); the study of international politics has focused upon means (that is, the struggle for power). Fusing the two, we can define politics—all politics—as *competition for power to effect the allocation of values in a given society.*

Politics Without Government

International politics is one case of politics in general and one (and no doubt the most important) aspect of the interaction of national societies. Strictly speaking, international politics might be considered a subdivision of international relations, a concept encompassing all contacts across state boundaries including economic, cultural, technical and political. However, because virtually all social interactions among governments and societies are molded by the nature of international political arrangements, we will use *international relations* and *international politics* interchangeably. (Neither will we quibble over the sometimes subtle differences in meaning assigned to similar terms such as *world politics* or *international affairs.* For our purposes, all these terms refer to the same variety of political behavior.)

International politics is distinguished from other types of politics neither by the persistent conflict among state actors nor by the perennial competition for power in which they are engaged. As we have seen, all politics involves conflict of interests (resulting from scarcity of values) and quest for power. By the acquisition of influence over the behavior of opponents, each competitor seeks a resolution of conflict (and a concomitant distribution of values) from which it will benefit. In its essence, then, international politics is hardly unique. Its novelty is to be found not in the variety of behavior, but in the peculiar context in which it is conducted. Max Weber, for many the father of modern sociology, defined the state as "a human community which (successfully) claims the monopoly of the legitimate use of physical force within a given territory." [9] In this light, international politics may be considered politics in a stateless environment. This remark may well seem peculiar given the existence of over 170 independent states in the present international system. Yet it is an essential attribute of politics among these 170 states that each ultimately reserves to itself the decision of whether to resort to force in defense of its interests. This means that there is a decentralization of the legitimate use of force in international relations.[*] As opposed to the situation in domestic societies, in which each citizen at least theoretically surrenders to the state his right to resort to force, the state in its relations with its peers jealously guards this prerogative. There exists no world state, or international government, capable of determining or enforcing an allocation of values. The distribution of benefits among states is the product of the distribution of power among them.

The conflict of power and interest in the international system is hardly pathological, but rather is inherent in its very nature. The

[*] The extent to which the existence of international law and the United Nations affects this observation will be discussed in Chapter 5.

idealist who seeks to cure the body politic of the disease of conflict operates under an erroneous conception of the reality of politics. Power and conflict cannot be eradicated without abolishing politics itself. However, the quasi-anarchic nature of international politics accentuates conflict. (The phrase "quasi-anarchic" is used purposely to indicate that while international relations do indeed lack an overall structure of government, there are structures and processes for peaceful competition.) Given the decentralized nature of the international system, the environment in which states are compelled to interact virtually ensures the existence of what one observer has termed the "security dilemma."[10] We are all familiar with the motion-picture scene of an isolated farmhouse and the approaching stranger on horseback; almost reflexively, the farmer reaches for his rifle and stands guard at his front door in anticipation of trouble. The stranger may have only peaceful intentions, but he is armed and therefore capable of inflicting harm on the farmer and his family. Preoccupied with his own safety and security in a perpetually hostile world, the farmer is bound to view the physical capabilities of the intruder (even if these capabilities were originally devised for purely defensive purposes) as an indication of potentially hostile or aggressive designs. The logic of the frontier is evident in international relations. An anarchic environment leads to the never-ending quest for and fixation on self-preservation, and is pervaded by suspicion and mutually reinforcing threat perceptions. Indeed, fear is an inevitable ramification of international politics.

The absence of world government to ensure the security of states and provide a legitimate mechanism for the apportionment of values leads to the principle of self-help. Each state recognizes that the sole agent of its interests is itself. It must ultimately be prepared to press for its version of distributive justice and secure the means necessary to overcome the resistance of others. International politics, then, is the competition for power in a quasi-anarchic environment to affect the global distribution of values.

THE "GODFATHER" IMAGE OF WORLD POLITICS

Much of what goes on in the international system would be blatantly illegal by domestic political standards. Indeed, much of what goes on in the international system is probably illegal judged by its own standards. The Charter of the United Nations specifically requires all members to "settle their international disputes by peaceful means" and in effect forbids "the threat or use of force" against any state. And yet over fifty major military engagements and many more threats of war have occurred since these prohibitions went into effect in 1945.

Within its domestic jurisdiction, the state declares homicide to be a public offense subject to extreme penalties. But at the same time, the state regularly endorses the mass killing of foreign nationals by its citizens when conscripted into military service. The first is condemned as murder, the most heinous of crimes; the second is praised as patriotism, the highest service to the community. The murderer finds himself in prison or on death row, while the patriot is decked with medals. If a certain type of behavior is judged a crime if it is undertaken by an individual in defense of his interests at home, and yet the state commits the very same acts abroad in defense of its interests, it becomes evident that "crime is not inherent in behavior, but is a judgment made by some about the actions and characteristics of others." [11] Law itself may be viewed as the instrument of those who control public policy to protect their social interests. Crime is, therefore, ultimately a political definition intended to protect the status quo.

Less than a century ago there existed in this country a number of rising centers of economic power which sought to appropriate larger and larger shares of the rapidly expanding social product. As industrialization grew, great financial entrepreneurs such as the Rockefellers, Harrimans, Carnegies and Du Ponts maneuvered to outflank their competitors and monopolize power in their respective spheres of the new industrial economy. In the course of their struggle for primacy, these self-styled captains of industry (whom their critics later termed robber barons) engaged in all sorts of unethical and even illegal activities: They negotiated treaties among themselves dividing up markets and sources of supply; they infiltrated state legislatures through political payoffs and managed even to secure their own representatives in the United States Senate; they hired private armies (corporate "muscle") such as Pinkertons to intimidate opponents and break up labor unions; they condoned inordinately long working hours, inhuman factory conditions, child labor, subsistence wage scales, deceptive advertisement and the packaging of contaminated foods.[12] Yet within a generation, these robber barons had solidly established themselves and their heirs as part of the Establishment—the defenders of the nation's moral fiber and constitutional order. Names that were the object of the scorn and contempt of social reformers only a few decades ago now populate the rolls of the country's ambassadors, cabinet ministers, governors, and legislators. In the end, the robber barons succeeded in undermining the old status quo and replacing it with another more to their liking and then proceeded to cap the new order with the legitimacy of law and morality.

But today there is a new and even more ruthless generation of robber barons operating outside the legitimate social order. Superimposed on American society is a network of crime syndicates which are similarly organized to maintain large-scale business enterprises. This underworld is composed of approximately two dozen independent kingdoms, or families, each ruled by an absolute monarch, or Don. The head of each of these autonomous organizations surrounds himself with a handful of trusted ministers or advisors, as well as a small but loyal palace guard responsible for his personal safety. The next layer of the organization is composed of the territorial governors, or heads of the regimes, each responsible for a region of the Don's empire. Each of these lieutenants maintains an army of soldiers, or henchmen, who enforce the Don's administration in his particular area. The bottom layer of the syndicate is made up of those who deal directly with the public—the bookies, pimps, runners and dope peddlers. The lords of the underworld progressively branched out from their traditional preserves (bootlegging, gambling, prostitution, protection and, later, narcotics) to infiltrate and eventually take over legitimate businesses.

We must bear in mind that these "states within the State" could not survive without a certain immunity from the law. This is acquired from persons not directly involved in the "mob," but who nonetheless provide it with the essential protection it requires to prosper. Organized crime is deeply embedded in our society through its contacts with police officials, judges, prosecutors, legislators, party leaders, newspapermen, labor organizers, bankers and businessmen—all receiving regular payoffs or some other type of benefit from the association. Without this official sanction, the underworld could not survive. As one sociological study notes: "The interdependence of the underworld of crime and the upperworld of business assures the maintenance of both systems." [13] Or as another critic puts it, the only difference between the "criminal" world and the "legitimate" sector of society is "a lag in respectability." [14]

The new robber barons who operate on the fringes of the social order utilize many of the techniques developed by their now-legitimate predecessors, and their policies bear a striking resemblance to those employed by countries in their mutual relations: bribery, political assassination, systematic deception and denial, and force. Moreover, the numerous crime syndicates populating the country operate from territorial bases and thus are compelled to compete and cooperate with one another in their attempt to allocate the benefits society permits them to have. In their struggle for power, the families have developed an elaborate system of interaction which includes spheres of influence, negotiation, alliances, wars, peace treaties, summit conferences and even instruments of mediation and collaboration, which resemble, in a rudimentary way, international organizations like the United Nations.

Organized crime syndicates are thus engaged in a political system of their own, albeit a rather primitive one. A primitive political system is characterized by the absence of formal government, the principle of self-help, the pervasive threat of or use of violence and the existence of rudimentary institutions and customs for the mediation of conflict. By these standards, the international system is certainly also of a primitive nature.[15]

Indeed, as one reads Mario Puzo's novel *The Godfather,* one cannot help but be struck by the similarities between the world of organized-crime families and that of sovereign states. Viewed not as a sensational piece of fiction about organized crime but rather as a critique of politics and business, *The Godfather* easily lends itself to both sociological and, for our purposes, political analysis. To promote greater interest in and understanding of the study of world politics in our time, we shall sometimes employ this analogy in this book. We must not become obsessed with or belabor the comparison, however, for this is an introductory text to the study of world politics, not to the workings of the underworld. But remember that we are dealing with a world of force and the threat of violence, the pursuit of power and spheres of influence, bribery and political assassination, the subtle and the not-so-subtle exercise of influence—competition for power in a quasi-anarchic environment.

Notes

Chapter 1

1. M. S. Gwirtzman, "Is Bribery Defensible?" *New York Times Magazine*, October 5, 1975, p. 19 ff.
2. Alexis de Tocqueville, *Democracy in America*, Vol 2 (New York: Vintage Books, n.d.), p. 284.
3. Dwight D. Eisenhower, *Peace With Justice: Selected Addresses*, edited by Grayson Kirk (New York: Columbia University Press, 1961), p. 36 (emphasis added).
4. David Easton, *A Systems Analysis of Political Life* (New York: Wiley, 1965), p. 21.
5. Hans J. Morgenthau, *Politics Among Nations: The Struggle for Power and Peace*, 5th ed. (New York: Knopf, 1973), p. 27.
6. Thucydides, *History of the Peloponnesian War*, trans. by Rex Warner (Baltimore, Md.: Penguin Books, 1954), p. 363.

7. Thomas Hobbes, *Leviathan* (New York: Collier, 1962), Part I, Chapter 13, p. 100.

8. Harold Lasswell, *Politics: Who Gets What, When, How* (New York: Meridian Books, 1958).

9. H. H. Gerth and C. Wright Mills, eds., *From Max Weber: Essays in Sociology* (New York: Oxford University Press, 1946), p. 78. The italics in the original have been deleted.

10. John H. Herz, *International Politics in the Atomic Age* (New York: Columbia University Press, 1959).

11. Richard Quinney, *The Social Reality of Crime* (Boston: Little, Brown & Co., 1970), p. 16.

12. Concerning the similar patterns of behavior demonstrated by early capitalist entrepreneurs and contemporary criminal syndicates, one authority on the underworld notes:

> Original accumulations of capital were amassed in tripartite deals among pirates, governors, and brokers. Fur fortunes were piled up alongside the drunk and dead bodies of our noble savages, the Indians. Small settlers were driven from their lands or turned into tenants by big ranchers, employing rustlers, guns, outlaws, and the law. In the great railroad and shipping wars, enterprising capitalists used extortion, blackmail, violence, bribery, armies with muskets and cannons to wreck a competitor and to become the sole boss of trade.

See Gus Tyler, ed., *Organized Crime in America: A Book of Readings* (Ann Arbor, Mich.: University of Michigan Press, 1962), pp. 44–45.

13. M. B. Clinard and R. Quinney, *Criminal Behavior Systems: A Typology* (New York: Holt, Rinehart and Winston, 1967), p. 387.

14. Joseph A. Raffaele, *System and Unsystem* (New York: Wiley, 1974), p. 118.

15. Roger D. Masters, "World Politics as a Primitive Political System," *World Politics*, 16 (July 1964): 595–619.

PART II

THE ACTOR

If everything goes right, the Corleone Family will be completely legitimate in about five years.

—Michael Corleone, in Mario Puzo's *The Godfather*

Chapter 2

The State

> Severed from its body, the black silky head of the great horse Khartoum was stuck in a thick cake of blood. . . .
>
> He had been profoundly shocked. What kind of man would destroy an animal worth six hundred thousand dollars? Without a word of warning. Without any negotiation to have the act, its order, countermanded. The ruthlessness, the sheer disregard for any values, implied a man who considered himself completely his own law, even his own God.
>
> —Mario Puzo,
> *The Godfather*

THE TERRITORIAL STATE AND INTERNATIONAL ANARCHY

The global political system is composed primarily, though not exclusively, of territorial states (see Chapter 6, Transnational Relations, for a consideration of the role of nonstate actors in the global system). At present there exist some 170 sovereign states

(147 of which are members of the United Nations), each the supreme arbiter of the fate of that portion of the human race residing within its jurisdiction, and each recognizing no higher legal authority.

Two central organizing principles govern the nature of world politics: *territoriality* and *decentralization of power*. The absence of world government means that no centralized global authority exists capable of allocating scarce values among the four billion people inhabiting this planet. No independent political entity has been entrusted with that ultimate responsibility thus far, neither has any one country been able to seize that prerogative for itself by establishing a global empire. Without world government—brought about either by a voluntary federation of the present state actors or by military conquest—the international system remains fragmented, power being distributed among numerous competing centers of authority. The concomitant principle of territoriality suggests that the process of allocating the fruits of human society takes place at two distinct levels of political interaction. On the one hand, the surface of the earth has been artificially divided into a jigsaw puzzle of independent political jurisdictions. At this level, there are 170 separate domestic political systems, each governed by an autonomous allocation mechanism and each circumscribed by generally recognized geographical limits. Each unit actor in the global system has its own territory and its own population; each arrogates to itself the task of establishing procedures for the attainment of political influence within its borders and rules to govern the competition for social benefits among the numerous groups and individuals it claims as subjects or citizens. Thus, within each country, the struggle for power is regularized, legitimized and civilized. At the second level of political interaction, the competition for influence (and, therefore, values) takes place in an anarchic environment, the inherently primitive international system. Few rules have been agreed upon to govern the perennial clash of interests among these 170 autonomous states, and fewer still are the mechanisms for ameliorating the struggle for unilateral gain.

The state is an abstraction. It is the political organization, or juridical personality, of a society. It is the organization of domination. The state is an abstraction in much the same manner that a corporation is. A corporation is an entity recognized by law as having an independent existence, and as such it is empowered to enter into binding agreements (contracts) with other legal entities such as individuals, labor unions, government and other corporations. But the essence of the corporation is its intangibility. You can touch a corporation's productive facilities, its equipment, its buildings, its employees, its managers—but you cannot put out your hand and touch the corporation itself. In short, it is a legal fiction. It is one of the great paradoxes of the modern age that the all-powerful entity called the state is also merely a set of legal relationships. You can put your hand on the state's assets—its people and its territory, its physical plant (the Capitol, the Palace of Westminster, the Kremlin) and even its "board of directors" (the government)—but the state itself remains an abstraction.

Much as a corporation must maintain its economic solvency to survive in the long run, so must the state maintain its political solvency. Most fundamentally, the state must succeed in satisfying the most basic needs of its citizens (or at least of the politically influential segment of the citizenry), as well as meeting a number of supplementary demands. This capacity has been referred to as the effectiveness of a political system.[1] Though historically the original function of the state was the provision of security (domestic order and freedom from foreign invasion), the modern state must also look after and seek to maximize the welfare of its citizens. In its international relations, a state's effectiveness will be gauged by the success of its foreign policy in pursuing the interests of its citizens abroad; that is, in providing them with security from foreign attack, in preserving the nation's cultural values against subversion by alien principles, in securing an acceptable level of international prestige (and, in some cases, glory) and in maximizing the appropriation of global economic values (i.e., wealth).

In addition to effectiveness, a stable political system seeks to attain a measure of legitimacy.[2] If a political elite is not to base its rule on coercion alone, it must instill in the masses a belief that the domestic political order is just and proper. All states, therefore, are careful to nurture the sense of legitimacy and to build a reservoir of goodwill on the part of their subjects.

The state's domination over its citizens can be legitimated in a number of ways. In his classical study of political sociology, Max Weber identified three basic techniques common to most political systems: tradition, legality and charisma.[3] In addition, we can note the crucial factors of nationalism and ideology, which we will consider at length later in this chapter. Through manipulation of various loyalty symbols—the flag, the national anthem, commemorative holidays, sacred documents—the political leadership of the territorial state constantly reinforces in its citizens feelings of devotion to the existing regime.

A word of caution is in order in our discussion of the state as the central actor on the world stage. In studies of domestic and comparative politics, the term *state* has long since been replaced by the term *political system.*[4] This latter concept has proven fruitful in the analysis of the structures, processes and subtleties involved in the allocation of values in domestic society. However, in international relations, the notion of the state actor has survived, though here too in recent years there has been a trend toward viewing politics in the global system as a world political process involving numerous nonstate participants as well as territorial entities.[5] Because the environmental constraints on freedom of action are so fundamental to an understanding of the international system and the behavior of individual national actors, it is preferable that the traditional term be preserved in our present survey (see Chapter 5 for an extensive discussion of this aspect of world politics).

Nevertheless, we must be aware of the pitfalls inherent in the oversimplified "statist" approach to the discipline. It is tempting (perhaps because of its appealing simplicity and lucidity) to identify the determinants of state behavior in the international system as being wholly outside the structure of internal politics. Often policy making is ascribed to some group in the executive branch of government—usually referred to simply as decision makers or policy makers—a group that perceives a threat to or opportunity for the domestic political system in its external environment and, reacting to this stimulus, retorts with actions of its own intended to neutralize the intrusion or transform the conflict situation in its favor. Such diverse schools of thought as realism, systems theory and environmental simulation have reinforced this distortion.[6]

All these approaches identify merely the externally determined influences on governmental behavior in the international system. In the real world, of course, states seldom respond solely to outside stimuli. The formulation of foreign policy may be viewed in much the same manner as the formulation of domestic policy (for example, agricultural programs)—as a social process involving myriad interests and opposing groups with differing notions of the general welfare. The distinction between forces affecting the making of domestic policy and those influencing the making of foreign policy has become progressively blurred with the process of modernization. The neatly divided functions of traditional societies have been transformed into the complex, overlapping jurisdictions of modern industrial and postindustrial society. Gone are the days when foreign policy in general, and war in particular, were the games of kings. With the vast growth of government authority over the affairs of its citizenry and government's rapidly expanding sphere of activity since the genesis of the modern territorial state in the seventeenth century, there is little cause for wonder that domestic group interests have projected themselves into the realm of traditionally isolated foreign policy processes.

International politics is not a grand chess tournament, with each move and countermove the result of a purely rational method of problem solving. Foreign policy is rarely the result of the machinations of a single individual, sitting alone at night in the ministry of foreign affairs (or State Department), ordering the objective interests of the state and choosing one policy out of numerous alternatives to those objectives. The state is not a unitary or monolithic actor. Neither is the national interest an objective and immutable truth which need only be discovered by the brightest and most knowledgeable individual. On the contrary, the notion of a national interest is subjective and must be defined by those governmental officials ultimately responsible for charting the state's course in foreign relations. Interest groups within the domestic polity having a stake in the political system's orientation toward its environment will seek to influence government officials to frame a policy incorporating their version of the just society. The policy prescriptions of these groups are likely to conflict. In American society, for example, the agricultural industry's goal to maximize farm income through an expansion of exports conflicts with the consumer's desire to hold down prices of agricultural products; the labor movement's demand that Congress place restrictions on the export of capital (and, therefore, jobs) runs head on against the business community's objective of gaining the greatest return on its investment; the interests of veterans' organizations and defense contractors in increasing the Pentagon's budget or building a new weapons system will not sit well with disadvantaged socioeconomic groups which prefer that additional governmental spending go for welfare services. To make matters even more confusing, each group will normally frame its argument strictly in terms of the national interest—the good of the national community as a whole. Eventually these competing claims, parochial interests and different versions of the public good must be reconciled, and a synthetic outcome agreed upon that will reflect the quiltlike nature of the societal fabric. Foreign policy is a social bargain made in light of the relative power of rival factions.

But we must not even assume that the government itself is a unified actor—a disinterested referee which merely registers the outcome of the group struggle. A state's government is, in reality, a conglomeration of agencies and departments with divergent interests, differing responsibilities and often conflicting constituencies. Inasmuch as there is no such thing as an objectively correct national interest, allocation of the government budget becomes a struggle among quasi-independent agencies and feudal departmental fiefdoms, each seeking a larger share of the budgetary pie based on arguments couched at all times in terms of the mysterious national interest. The vested interests found in vast bureaucratic empires soon develop their own momentum, and personal or agency interests inevitably become synonymous with the general interest of the nation as a whole.[7] In the end, opposing coalitions coalesce around major issues, with interest groups from the private sector, elements within the legislative branch and factions within the bureaucracy joining together in alliance.

And this is not simply a manifestation of pluralist democratic systems of the American variety.[8] When we read in daily newspapers such statements as, "Today, the United States decided . . ." or "The Soviet Union rejected . . ." or "The People's Republic of China announced . . ." we are seeing shorthand terminology used in the study of international relations. In reality, people act, not states. The government officials who speak on behalf of their polity are responding to a complex web of competing and overlapping domestic interests.

However, though domestic factors influence the formulation of foreign policy and the definition of national interest, the primitive nature of the international system elicits its own responses from its component national political systems. The general contours of the global environment set the parameters for prudent state policy; that is, the security dilemma will often dictate certain courses of action for individual national actors, or condition behavior patterns, thus severely limiting the overall influence of domestic factors. So although we must not ignore domestic inputs to foreign policy, it would be a far greater error to ignore the constraints imposed by external variables. The central fact distinguishing world politics from all other varieties of political interaction is the anarchic nature of its context. In that international relations derives its peculiar quality from its primitive environment, we are justified in emphasizing the overall global system at the expense of the specific aspects of domestic systems. Speaking of domestic political systems as state actors is the by-product of the overriding importance of that primitive environment.

SOVEREIGNTY AND THE NATIONAL INTEREST: THE COMING OF THE MORTAL GOD

The present global system is a direct descendant of the early European state system which evolved from the decay of medieval feudalism. The Europeanization of the world, which came with the spread of Western colonialism, extended this politically fragmented and primitively organized arrangement so that it eventually embraced all continents.

In the Middle Ages, Europe was hierarchically organized under the dual leadership of the Holy Roman Empire and the Roman Catholic Church. At the top of the social pyramid was the papacy, symbol of the unity of the Christian world and the supreme authority of both the spiritual and temporal domains. Exercising the secular mandate of the Holy See was the emperor, the figurative representative of the continuity of the European community which had been established by the legions of the ancient caesars. The fact that the emperor was crowned by the pope himself, and that all inferior kings received their crowns from the bishops of the Church, indicated that in theory all political authority flowed from the heir of Saint Peter in Rome. Though the pope and the emperor still held the keys to the vast kingdom of Christendom, in reality feudal society was highly decentralized and medieval life revolved around a multiplicity of more or less independent feudal lords. Despite pretentions to universality by the Church and the empire, each tiny fiefdom was really a self-contained social unit, loosely integrated into the fabric of the Christian commonwealth by means of a common religion, culture, language (Latin) and spiritual suzerain (the pope).

By the late Middle Ages, however, there were clear signs that the whole feudal structure was in rapid decline and that medieval institutions were giving way to more familiar and modern modes of organization. As the fifteenth century came to a close, the emperor was little more than *primus inter pares* (first among equals), the nominal head of a political order fast disintegrating into its component parts. While at one time the empire had included most of Europe, it now had only a remnant of its former glory, with its effective authority confined to Germany. Similarly, the political and spiritual influence of Rome was on the wane, and the papacy was the object of contending dynastic rivalries. The feudal economic system, based on land and the manor, was also being undermined by the revival of commerce and exploration following the Crusades, and the rise of towns and a middle class was leading inexorably toward larger social (and, hence, political) units. Gradually monarchs centralized power within their realms, administering justice, collecting taxes, regulating trade and expanding and eventually monopolizing military capabilities. Separate and distinct national cultures emerged in place of the previous cosmopolitanism, as the vernacular replaced Latin in literature and the burgeoning towns looked to the king for protection and promotion of their particular interests. In Spain, Portugal, France and England, the territories under dynastic rule were expanded and unifed under royal absolutism—the powers of the nobles crushed, the pope's prerogatives circumscribed or ignored.

In the sixteenth century, the facade of unity was torn asunder when the Church was confronted with the Protestant Reformation. One by one, the princes of northern Europe eagerly embraced separate Christian sects, taking advantage of the revolt against Rome to repudiate what increasingly was seen as an alien authority. Having subdued the internal threat to royal power offered by their feudal vassals, the national monarchs now divested themselves of external checks on their power. Thus, Henry VIII, upon whom the pope had bestowed the auspicious title Defender of the Faith for refuting Martin Luther's doctrines, now carried out a masterful coup and removed the pope's influence in his country, establishing himself as the supreme head of an autonomous Church of England as well as of the state of England. The hierarchy and oneness of the Europe of the Middle Ages had given way to a fragmented multiplicity of coordinate (of the same rank) territorial states. The modern age of international relations had begun.

Though the term *sovereignty* was in use during the Middle Ages, it signified simply a relationship of superordination; that is, in the hierarchical universe of feudalism, each man had a superior, each owed obedience to a suzerain. Nevertheless, interpersonal obligations were of a limited nature, every vassal having the right to appeal beyond his immediate suzerain to the next level of authority. In short, "command was never sovereign in the meaning which this word has come to have in modern times." [9] The first precise formulation of the concept of sovereignty in its modern form came in the last quarter of the sixteenth century from Jean Bodin, who sought to justify centralization of authority under the French monarchy. In regard to both internal centers of influence (the nobles) and external centers of influence (Church and empire), the territorial state, Bodin said, was sovereign, meaning that it possessed "absolute and perpetual power" over its own affairs. Hence the distinguishing mark of a sovereign power was that it "cannot be subject to the command of another." In the middle of the next century, the English philosopher Thomas Hobbes suggested that the state (or Leviathan, as he called it) was "a mortal god to which we owe, under the immortal God, our peace and defense." * The doctrine of sovereignty represented the state's declaration of independence from supranational institutions. As the Swedish king Gustavus Adolphus is reputed to have exclaimed: "I recognize no power over me but God and the conqueror's sword." By virtue of its very existence, therefore, the state refused to recognize any higher political authority and established itself as the court of last appeal within its jurisdiction. Furthermore, as a law unto itself, the territorial state jealously guards both its claim to be the sole judge of its citizens' interest and its prerogative to pursue its goals by means of its own choosing. Defense of its national interest as it perceives it (and, therefore, its autonomy) thus becomes the state's first law of motion.[10]

In point of fact, the doctrine of sovereignty is more a legal or philosophical argument on behalf of the independence of the state than a practical description of real world conditions. Though the claim to sovereignty is the basis of statehood and the international system as a whole (even the Charter of the United Nations proclaims that the organization is based upon "the sovereign equality of its Members"), even if all states are truly sovereign, some must be more sovereign than others. After all, weaker states (especially many of those in the developing world today) have had all to do to establish the supremacy of their edicts within their territory, let alone deal with intervention by the major powers.

* Compare Hobbes's statement with the quotation at the beginning of this chapter.

Certain domestic political systems are certainly more susceptible to outside interference and manipulation than others. But today, given the mounting interdependence among all countries, even the Great Powers are no longer able to insulate their economies and societies from disturbances originating outside their narrow spheres of national jurisdiction. It would seem, then, that sovereignty exists in degrees—that a particular state is more or less sovereign than its neighbors, but hardly in complete control of its destiny. But to admit this is to deny the very existence of sovereignty in any form other than the purely legal. Because sovereignty is indivisible and is an all or nothing proposition, you either have it or you do not have it. States do not really have it. Nor did they really ever possess it. To the extent that it exists, it does so as a legal myth intended to justify the rule of the territorial state over its subjects.

The doctrine of state sovereignty legitimizes international anarchy and the pursuit of naked self-interest. Politics without government comes to revolve around the dictates of power politics. Without a world sovereign to define and defend what is just, might makes right. In a primitive environment, each actor is left to look after his own interests through the exercise of his own power. According to this doctrine, those who ignore the dictum of parochial self-interest and trust in the benevolence of others will either perish or fall prey to the malevolence of the less scrupulous. As the Godfather cautioned his fellow Dons at their summit conference:

> Let us say that we must always look to our interests. We are men who have refused to be fools, who have refused to be puppets dancing on a string pulled by the men on high. . . . We will manage our world for ourselves because it is our world, *cosa nostra*. . . .

The notion of sovereignty thus leads directly to the concept of state interest. What the state defines as vital to its survival, security or welfare becomes an objective worthy of the use of force. Goals that are conducive but not necessary to the essential well-being of the nation will be promoted by means short of violence. In any event, the state—and the state alone—is the judge of what its interests are and how they may be best protected, given the capabilities at hand. The state always acts in defense of its national interest, however this may be defined.

The concomitant of the principle of sovereignty is the doctrine of *raison d'état* (reason of state). Having arrogated to itself the right of defining its national interest, the state then devised a rationalization for the pursuit of that interest by any and all expedient means. And much as Bodin and Hobbes were the fathers of the theory of sovereignty, Niccolò Machiavelli separated the affairs of government from the sphere of individual ethics. Henceforth, the standards by which we customarily measure the morality of an individual's acts would no longer apply to the acts of the state (that is, the acts of individuals acting in the name of the state). What were sins in the Christian sense—lying, cheating, stealing, killing—might now, when committed on behalf of the state, be justified (indeed, lauded) as acts of selflessness for the good of the entire nation. As one contemporary student of world politics has described this clash between humanist and nationalist ethical standards:

> Nationalistic ethics placed what are called vital national interests, and not national survival only, at the very pinnacle of the hierarchy of values. The preservation or attainment of these values—territorial integrity, colonial possessions, *lebensraum*, treaty rights, or economic interests—are assumed therefore to justify the sacrifice of almost every other value whether it be life, generosity, humane treatment of others, truthfulness, or obedience to the law.[11]

Or, as Machiavelli himself so aptly put it in the *Discourses:*

> For where the very safety of the country depends upon the resolution to be taken, no consideration of justice or injustice, humanity or cruelty, nor of glory or of shame, should be allowed to prevail. But putting all other considerations

> aside, the only question should be, "What will save the life and liberty of the country?"

So long as the territorial state is condemned to a primitive environment characterized by a perpetual "security dilemma,"[12] the impulse to power and self-preservation—national egoism—necessitates occasional reliance upon dubious means of policy. Much as "the man who makes it a rule in all circumstances to perform nothing but good actions, is bound to go under amongst so many who are evil,"[13] the state actor that refuses to engage in generally accepted practices—espionage, acquiring armaments, threats of violence, and the like—is bound to get the worst of international relations. The system ensures, in effect, that the good are at the mercy of the bad, and run the risk of becoming someone's Poland or Abyssinia. Therefore, those at the helm of the ship of state will often be (in the great Florentine's words) "constrained to act without loyalty, without mercy, without humanity, and without religion" in their dealings with foreign powers.

Despite the potential violations of human decency implied in the doctrine of *raison d'état*, most observers would agree with the point of Machiavelli's argument: We condone certain types of behavior undertaken in the name of the state while condemning similar acts committed by the individual in his private interest. In a world of competing territorial actors, it is difficult to be a moral absolutist. Though taking a human life is contrary to the Judeo-Christian tradition, only an ardent pacifist would interpret this as a total ban on killing regardless of circumstances. For example, even domestic law recognizes the individual's right of self-defense, though this right is hedged about with more restrictions than the analogous right of the state in its international relations. It is even difficult to issue a blanket condemnation of political assassination by the state in the pursuit of its policies abroad. Certainly there was an uproar in America when the secret machinations of the Central Intelligence Agency (CIA) were revealed, but it probably goes without saying that most of these critics would have welcomed the assassination of Adolf Hitler by our clandestine services, averting the carnage and genocide of the Second World War.

But if it is true, as Machiavelli suggested, that the end justifies the means, where is the line to be drawn? At what point do the means themselves become so morally reprehensible that no goal, however noble, can justify them? The moral dilemma inherent in politics was succinctly stated by Max Weber:

> No ethics in the world can dodge the fact that in numerous instances the attainment of the "good" end is bound to the fact that one must be willing to pay the price of using morally dubious means or at the least dangerous ones—and facing the possibility or even the probability of evil ramifications. From no ethics in the world can it be concluded when and to what extent the ethically good purpose "justifies" the ethically dangerous means and ramifications.[14]

In short, the moral choices involved in politics are reduced to selecting the lesser of the evils.[15] Given the overriding value of the national interest, other important values sometimes must be sacrificed on its behalf. Nevertheless, a democratic people must constantly be wary of the excesses committed in its name and weigh the harm inflicted by violating the norms of state interest against the evil resulting from the infringement of individual liberty. Thus the United States Supreme Court, in the famous Pentagon Papers Case, refused to injoin the publication of certain documents in the *New York Times* and the *Washington Post* as the Nixon administration requested. Though the President based his case for injunction on the national security, the Court concluded that the administration had not conclusively demonstrated what harm, if any, would result to the national security if the papers were indeed made public. But notice that the highest tribunal in the land did not attempt to promulgate a general rule against national security claims, and in the past the Supreme Court has usually upheld violations of civil liberties when the national security was, or seemed to be, at stake.

The inhuman acts committed in the name of truth, justice, and

God are legion indeed. Consider the strange case of Father Joseph of Paris (the original "Grey Eminence"), who in seventeenth-century France was the collaborator, confidant and foreign minister of one of history's master machiavellians, Cardinal Richelieu. Father Joseph was a dedicated mystic and Capuchin friar, a man who had forsaken worldly pleasures and comforts for the love of God. And yet the double life he led was a bizarre riddle—

> the riddle of a man concerned to know God, acquainted with the highest forms of Christian gnosis, having experienced at least the preliminary states of mystical union, and at the same time involved in court intrigue and international diplomacy, busy with political propaganda, and committed wholeheartedly to a policy whose immediate results in death, in misery, in moral degradation were plainly to be seen in every part of seventeenth-century Europe, and from whose remoter consequences the world is still suffering.[16]

To the apparently unassuming monk, God required a crusade by Christian Europe to liberate the Holy Land from the infidel Turks. Enlisted in the service of Richelieu, Father Joseph came to believe that for this glorification of God to be realized, the Christian kings of Europe must first be united under the leadership of the French monarchy. The aggrandizement of French power became his primary mission in life, convinced as he was that his native country had been chosen as the instrument of God's will. With such a noble end in sight, he was only too eager to mastermind policies that resulted in the death of countless thousands by war, starvation, mass execution, slavery, cannibalism and torture.

To catapult France to the pinnacle of power on the Continent, first domestic heretics had to be subdued. Father Joseph participated in the siege of La Rochelle, the culmination of a brutal campaign against the Protestant Huguenots. Acting as the chief of Richelieu's secret service, he did his best to subvert the fortress from within. When Richelieu wavered, he insisted that the city be taken, and while the twenty-five thousand inhabitants of La Rochelle slowly starved, he worked away at the morale of the defenders. In the end, the city fell—and with it the power of the Huguenots in France—but only after four-fifths of the population had perished. With the realm firmly united under the House of Bourbon, Father Joseph turned his attention abroad, setting his sights on the formidable power of the Hapsburgs. While France had been disunited and too weak to meet the enemy in a duel of strength, he and Richelieu had encouraged the Protestant Danes and Swedes to whittle away at the power of the Catholic Hapsburgs, therefore prolonging the Thirty Years' War, a barbarous orgy without precedent in Europe of the day. And when France's allies faltered, the French themselves entered the fray—a policy that could only increase the misery and suffering of an already prostrate Germany. And so, Father Joseph,

> [t]he child who had sobbed so bitterly because they had hurt and killed poor Jesus was father of the man who, fifty years later, did everything in his power to prolong a war which had already caused the death of hundreds of thousands of his fellow-creatures and was reducing the survivors to cannibalism.[17]

For the greater glory of God, France joined forces with the "heretical" Protestants of England, Holland, Denmark and Sweden—and even with the infidel Turks "in order that the world might be delivered from the Hapsburgs and made safe for Bourbon autocracy." [18] And for this end, one-third of the inhabitants of the lands east of the Rhine were sacrificed—dead by massacre, famine, exposure and disease. *Raison d'état* had demanded human sacrifices to the new "mortal god"—the state.

NATIONALISM: THE TRIBAL ORIENTATION OF MANKIND

Just as the territorial state developed into the highest level of legal authority and has established itself as the court of last appeal, so the nation remains the largest political entity to which men assign their allegiance. The nation serves as the repository of mankind's tribal loyalties and buttresses the compartmentalization of the human race. The state reinforces its citizens' sense of identity by manipulating loyalty symbols, and employs the herd instinct in support of the pursuit of self-interest and as an incentive for aggrandizement.

The twentieth century has been aptly described as "the age of nationalism."[19] In the modernizing societies of the Third World, national self-assertiveness has proven to be the foundation of the revolutionary drive toward political independence and economic development,[20] and in the more mature countries of the developed world, the persistent demands of national minorities for cultural autonomy (and sometimes outright separation) threaten the stability of the existing domestic orders (what Quebec is to Canada, Scotland and Wales are to Britain, the Basque country is to Spain and Brittany is to France). The sense of nationality is a universal phenomenon and molds the very nature of world politics. In an era when technological interdependence binds the human race into a community for the first time in its history, tribal sentiment remains as potent as ever, dividing the whole of mankind into competing and antagonistic segments. It is, indeed, the great and bewildering paradox of our time that

> we are fragmenting and globalizing at the same time. We spin out as from a centrifuge, flying apart socially and politically, at the same time that enormous centripetal forces press us all into more and more of a single mass every year.[21]

The rise of nationalism has been a direct result of the process of modernization itself,[22] and an outgrowth of the evolution of the sovereign territorial state. It was as if the new mortal god demanded a new cult of patriotism.

The unifying policies of the absolute monarchies of Western Europe had the effect of wielding together disparate regions, integrating diverse peoples into a single demographic unit subject to the same laws, speaking the same language, worshipping in the same church, reading the same literature and inculcating them with the same collective memory. Though the royal houses of the Continent possessed little in the way of national feeling, the ruling dynasties centralized political authority and fostered overall loyalty to the crown, teaching all those within their jurisdiction to look to one government for protection and security. Thus the monarchical state tended to shape a unified society and create a people who had a good deal more in common with one another than with those subject to a foreign sovereign.[23] In the end, a culturally homogeneous social group evolved, conscious of its unity and politically organized within a given territory.[24] With the coming of the Industrial Revolution, the technology of communication and transportation facilitated internal communication and furthered economic interdependence within the group, reinforcing the sense of social and cultural solidarity.[25] And yet the development of nationalism as a coherent doctrine hardly predates the last quarter of the eighteenth century. To be sure, its roots go much deeper into the past, and one can find elements of a nascent nationalism in ancient times (e.g., the Hebrews' conception of themselves as the Chosen People of God).[26] But modern nationalism emerged as a legitimation of the nondynastic state, and was therefore a by-product of the victory of popular sovereignty as a principle of government.[27] The French Revolution was a major turning point in the development of nationalism for now the nation was transformed into an object of worship and patriotism was embraced virtually as a religion of the state. State leaders soon became members of a secular priesthood,[28] the embodiment of the general will of the nation, and justified their rule almost as though they were leading a tribal cult. Much as their dynastic predecessors had claimed to rule by virtue of divine right, the new governing elite based their legitimacy upon the holy principle of nationality. The territorial state had come a long way since the days of a universal Church: "The power and glory passed from God's Chosen Church to God's Chosen Kings to God's Chosen People." [29]

The nation, like the state, is an abstraction. Though theorists have long attempted to define *nationhood* by isolating certain objective peculiarities of groups (linguistic, cultural, historical, religious), in reality it is a subjective affair involving the disposition of men's loyalties. All human beings have certain loyalties, that is, indispensable habit patterns through which they view the otherwise incomprehensible world, which give a satisfying sense of security and protection in a disorientating and threatening environment.[30] In modern times, the nation has become the focal point for mass loyalties, transcending those to family, class and religion. With the birth of the territorial state, man's inherent need to belong—his longing for the emotional satisfaction of association—caused his sentiments to focus on the nation. As such, the nation is but an artificial family, and it comes as small surprise that it is often founded on myths of "blood and soil." As the state became a living organism with a distinct will and interest of its own, the nation emerged as the very life and soul of that organism.[31] Above all else, the nation is a state of mind and may be defined as "a community of people who feel they belong together in the double sense that they share deeply significant elements of a common heritage and that they have a common destiny for the future." [32] This sense of a shared past (the triumphs and tragedies of which are usually commemorated by ritualistic national holidays and public shrines and monuments), as well as a commitment to a common future, forms the core of common attitudes of nationalism. For the sake of the health and survival of this mythical union, the individual becomes willing (and sometimes, fanatically eager) to sacrifice his private interests. Indeed, the essence of nationalism is willingness to sacrifice, and the nation demands that those who pledge it their allegiance be subject to the call to arms for its defense (or aggrandizement).

In terms of strict individualism, it is difficult to justify the sacrifice of private interest on behalf of the alleged interests of the whole. After all, why should I place my very life in jeopardy and bear arms for the state in military conflicts that bear little relation to my immediate self-interest? If man's basic impulse is self-preservation, then the notion of self must be redefined in terms of the collective in order for the individual to be willing to sacrifice his well-being—indeed, his life—when called upon to do so by his political superiors. Projecting his ego onto that of the nation,[33] the individual finds his interests and the national interest fused into one undifferentiated mass, as the personal self and the national self become one and the same. Whereas previous generations were willing to fight and die for the family, or for the universal Church, time and again the contemporary generation has demonstrated its love of the nation and its causes by offering to lay down its life for the greater glory of the nation-state.

The spirit of nationalism has supplanted the religious urge of an earlier age and has even assumed many of the functions and characteristics of religion: "It continues to demand devotion and scarifice, to reward believers and punish disbelievers. It has ... developed its particular rituals, ceremonies, and symbols."[34] In short, nationalism has taken over the role of older authority and institutions as the dominant object of faith and devotion in the modern world. In its extreme form, nationalism has become a state religion. In nineteenth-century Japan, the emperor was restored as a symbol of national and religious unity and an imperial decree actually prescribed service to the state as a religious duty.[35] Similarly, the European Fascist movements of this century embodied a rapacious fanaticism, totally devoid of any sense of humanity and committed to a form of organized barbarism without precedent in modern history. This "integral nationalism," hostile to liberalism and humanitarianism, relying upon force, imperialism and tyranny, carried the exaltation of the nation-state to its most frightening, though perhaps logical, conclusion. In its nineteenth-century manifestations, however, European nationalism had distinctly liberal and humanitarian qualities, and the nation was seen not as an end in itself but as the means to a better order, one based upon a prudent patriotism and devoted to the ideals of international peace, freedom from alien rule, and individual liberty. And yet the vibrant and expansionary nationalism that swept the Continent during the French Revolution and its aftermath was the harbinger of the totalitarian nationalism of the twentieth century. Spawned in the midst of foreign invasion and domestic revolutionary upheaval, Jacobin nationalism became suspicious and intolerant of domestic dissent, becoming caught up in a wave of terror and despotism and characterized by a crusading and self-righteous missionary zeal reminiscent of the age of religious wars. In the end, the nation was transformed from an agency of popular sovereignty to an instrument of jingoistic propaganda and the unbridled expansion of state power.[36]

And yet contemporary nationalism still has its integrative and constructive uses. The territorial states of the Third World today are the direct heirs of the geographical units of administration established by the former European colonial powers. As such, their present boundaries are the result of arbitrary colonial borders agreed upon by the competing imperial states of the Northern Hemisphere. State boundaries rarely coincide with national boundaries, especially in Africa; a single nation (i.e., tribe) may be divided among several territorial states, and a single state may include a number of different nationalities. Hence nation building is indeed a formidable problem. To create a unified nation out of a conglomeration of separate cultural communities, each speaking a different language and each suspicious of the others, is no mean task. But the common experience of colonialism—the collective humiliation of having been an inferior in one's own land—has been the spark igniting the urge to nationhood. If history is any guide, it is apparent that nationalism is kindled by historical wounds—a sense of collective injustice at the hands of an alien group [37]—and is, as Nehru once suggested, "essentially an anti-feeling." [38]

Nationalism, therefore, begins as a defensive reaction and is initially directed toward throwing off the foreign yoke. But it is certainly a double-edged sword, for no sooner is independence achieved and a people welded together for self-development and modernization than the urge to expand and dominate surfaces. The will to live soon becomes the will to power. Imperialism is but the reverse side of the coin of national identity. Nationalism is dangerously aggressive and destructive in its very nature. As the nineteenth-century German theoretician Heinrich von Treitschke wrote, in *Politics:* "Every people has a right to believe that certain attributes of the Divine reason are exhibited in it to their fullest perfection. No people ever attains to national consciousness without overrating itself." Mankind, like many lower forms of mammal life, has been endowed with a keen sense of territoriality and an attachment to what is near and aversion to what is foreign.[39] In the case of man, however, the herd instinct in its national form is the product of a long process of social learning and habit-pattern formation. But much as various primitive peoples (including the ancient Sumerians and some contemporary African tribes) use a single word to designate both mankind as a whole and their own particular group, and also equate "foreign" with "enemy," so the modern nation-state asserts its separate existence only in opposition to other nation-states. While providing domestic order and internal cohesion, nationalism by definition is a disintegrative force globally and an obstacle to world order. As Hans Kohn comments: "Intranationally, it leads to a lively sympathy with all fellow members within the nationality; internationally, it finds expression in indifference to or distrust and hate of fellow men outside the national orbit."[40]

IDEOLOGY AND THE QUEST FOR NATIONAL MISSION

The real world, with all its complexities and subtleties, is both confusing and disorienting for the lone individual. To make life comprehensible, to get a handle on a bewildering existence, he needs solid and protective anchors which will give him the security of a point of view. As we have just seen, national loyalty provides him with a crucial set of psychological bonds, a network of familiar ties, which give him a recognizable place in the universe and a force greater than himself in which to believe. In this sense, it may very well be true, as the great eighteenth-century conservative thinker Edmund Burke suggested, that man is by nature a religious animal, that his life of quiet desperation and meaningless inconsequentiality craves a metaphysical *raison d'être.* With the coming of modernization and its emphasis on the secular and rational, the traditional religious movements began to lose sway over men's minds, and a void threatened to develop in human existence. The void was quickly filled by the new secular religion of ideology. In general, an ideology is a structured system of beliefs intended as a guide to an otherwise confusing reality. It is a set of perceptual lenses by which events are evaluated and given significance in the grand order of things. It tells us what is a just as opposed to an unjust allocation of values, what human nature is like (whether good, bad, somewhere in between or neutral), why history unfolds as it does, who (or what) is responsible for the evil in the world, and how that evil might be conquered and the good life attained. In short, ideology claims to have discovered Truth, the ultimate interpretation of reality.

In that they represent competing claims to truth, ideologies inevitably clash with one another. And one of the distinguishing qualities of the contemporary age of world politics is the central role played by mass beliefs (the various and antagonistic *isms* of the day) in affairs of state.

In the formulation of foreign policy, ideology serves a number of functions. First it legitimizes (along with nationalism) the rule of the governing elite; those who wield power within the domestic political system justify their pivotal position in the social structure in terms of the prevailing system of beliefs. In the Soviet Union, for example, the Communist party bases its legitimacy on its claim to the mantle of Marxist-Leninist leadership, and, therefore, its inherent ability to determine and further the class interest of the international proletariat. In the United States, on the other hand, the symbol of legitimacy is the ballot box, and it is accepted that those who rule do so with the consent of the electorate (the people). Second, ideology serves as a means to motivate the masses on behalf of the objectives of the state (both foreign and domestic) as defined by the national leadership. The national interest of the state (even though the very existence of the concept may be denied, as in the U.S.S.R.) is said to be congruent with the version of truth promulgated by the national ideology. By instilling discipline in a population and priming it for the tasks of policy, ideology becomes an important element of state power in the global system. Third, ideology functions as the perceptual framework by which an elite views the world and the nation-state's place in it. Because we "see" and "hear" what we expect to—and act on that subjective view of reality—the factors that condition our analysis and understanding of events are important determinants of behavior. For example, if our ideological prism indicates that a particular actor is inherently imperialist or aggressive, we are likely to interpret his behavior as imperialist or aggressive and react accordingly. Because Marxism-Leninism teaches that the capitalist states are unalterably bent on the destruction of communism, it is second nature for Soviet leaders to distrust American gestures of goodwill or peaceful intent. By the same token, perception of the Kremlin as hostile and warlike is part and parcel of the United States' world view. In the end, each side sees its own strategy in international politics as defensive and its opponent's actions as provocative; both are locked into a relationship of mutual suspicion. Fourth, ideology may be considered merely as the rationalization of self-interest, as window dressing to mask the more mundane strategic and economic interests of the state.[41] Indeed, some suggest that ideology has little to do with setting the actual (as opposed to the declared) goals of the state, and others maintain that the ruling elite who manipulate the pseudoreligious symbols rarely believe their own rhetoric—it is purely for domestic consumption. But even if we cannot determine to what extent, if any, policy makers accept the ideological principles they spout, we still cannot discount the importance of ideology. One does not have to believe that the high priests of the secular religion of the state are the slaves of their own propaganda to recognize that their acts must bear a rough relation to their stated principles or the very foundation of their rule will be called into question. If this were not the case, government officials would not spend so much time and effort explaining their policy decisions in terms of their underlying philosophical principles. Moreover, it is inconceivable that political elites are not affected by the social belief system of which they are products as well as purveyors. Nonetheless, it would be myopic to identify vague and indeterminate ideological goals as the real springs of foreign policy. Considering the ornate rhetorical facade that embellishes the foreign relations of states, there is a refreshing honesty in the advice of *The Godfather*'s foreign minister, Hagen: "There are things that have to be done and you do them and you never talk about them. You don't try to justify them. They can't be justified. You just do them. Then you forget it."

The religious zeal characterizing certain political ideologies (especially the all-encompassing and dogmatic variety espoused by totalitarian movements such as nazism and communism) was evident in the very first manifestation of a secular cult.[42] At the height of the French Revolution, Jacobinism emerged as the first of the new state religions. Robespierre, a disciple of Jean-Jacques Rousseau whose bible was Rousseau's *Social Contract,* sought to destroy the old and corrupt order of the *l'ancien régime* and replace it with a utopian society. Like the religious zealots of the past who, well before the time of Machiavelli, were convinced that the end justifies the means, to realize a "Republic of Virtue and Justice," Robespierre was willing to employ any and all means, including mass terror, war and tyranny. Like the totalitarian ideologies of the twentieth century, the secular religion of the French Revolution demanded of its followers absolute conformity, doctrinal purity and fanatical devotion. Unable to tolerate coexistence with another pretender to the throne of absolute Truth, the new revolutionary regime persecuted the clergy, closed churches and consecrated the cathedral of Notre Dame to the "goddess of reason." Finally, armed with the moral self-righteousness typical of those who claim to be sole custodian of Truth, the revolutionaries of France asserted their right (indeed, their duty) to proselytize and bring the rest of a reluctant civilization under their enlightened tutelage.

The twentieth century totalitarians, aided by modern technologies of communication and control, instituted more refined and complete secular theocracies. In many ways, German fascism and Russian bolshevism during the Stalinist era were strikingly similar to the Christian churches of the Western world. Indeed, Lenin's blueprint for a dedicated clique of professional revolutionaries acting as the vanguard of the proletariat borrowed a good deal from the organization of the Jesuits, a Catholic order founded in 1540 as part of the Counter-Reformation. Like Christianity, the secular cults had their saviors, their prophets and saints, their sacred scriptures and apocalyptic visions. But unlike the world's great religions, the state ideologies were devoid of otherworldliness, having instead a vision of social salvation in this life, whether it be communism's classless and stateless society or the racially pure thousand-year Reich of the Nazis.

Naturally, we must not overdo the comparisons, for the fundamentally humanist and pacifist elements of early Christianity were not to be found in the crusading universalisms of Hitler or Stalin. However, while nazism became virtually the antithesis or negation of the Christian ethic, communism developed into a perversion of Christianity—a bastardized and secularized version of the doctrine of fraternity and brotherly love set forth in the New Testament. As opposed to the appealing utopia of the totalitarian Marxists, Hitler offered himself as the anti-Christ. Convinced of his own infallibility, omnipotence, and divine inspiration, the Fuehrer saw himself as the German Messiah—but quite unlike the gentle Nazarene:

> As a matter of fact, Hitler has very little admiration for Christ, the Crucified. . . . This kind of Christ he considers soft and weak and unsuitable as a German Messiah. The latter must be hard and brutal if he is to save Germany and lead it to its destiny. . . .
>
> . . . [W]hen he is addressed with the salutation, "Heil Hitler, our Savior," he bows slightly at the compliment in the phrase—and believes it. As time goes on, it becomes more and more certain that Hitler believes that he is really the "Chosen One" and that in his thinking he conceives of himself as a second Christ, who has been sent to institute in the world a new system of values based on brutality and violence. . . .[43]

Both nationalism and ideology serve to justify the expansion of state power, the first by virtue of the inherently superior culture of the group, the second by virtue of the correctness of its world view. Not surprisingly, the territorial state tends to rationalize its self-serving behavior as being for the general good of mankind as a whole, identifying its parochial national interest with that of the entire species, and claiming the right to decide what is the just distribution of global values. (Naturally, not every actor in the international system fits this generalization. In reality, we are referring to the Great Powers, which collectively determine the nature of the global order.) Of course, each competing aspirant for world power envisions a just order with the lion's share of benefits reserved for itself. In the nineteenth century, the British appropriated a vast empire upon which the sun never set, all in the name of the White Man's burden. And the French embarked upon a similar course of territorial aggrandizement under the banner of its *mission civilisatrice,* imparting to the backward races of the world the blessings of Western (meaning French) civilization. The superpowers of today's international system have been no different in their exercise of global influence. Both the United States and the Soviet Union act to maximize their national interests, but one (the Soviet Union) denies even having a national interest, while the other (the United States) speaks as if its national interest were synonymous with the extension of human freedom.

During the post–World War II era, Americans viewed the cold war as the culmination of the historical clash of good against evil, freedom against slavery, light against darkness. And all that supposedly stood between the godless and immoral tyranny of Communist totalitarianism and freedom for men everywhere was the strength of a single nation. The United States, according to this scheme, was the hope of the world, and its great power (moral as well as military) was a sacred trust granted by Providence. For Americans, the ultimate values were individual liberty and international peace; left to themselves in a world free of Soviet machinations, they would prefer to play the role of generous shopkeeper, laboring hard to attain the good life for themselves and maintaining a charitable relationship with the less fortunate and worthy. According to this view, the United States was a nation of Cincinnatuses—peaceful men periodically called from the plough to take up the sword against foreign aggressors. Like the patriot of ancient Rome, when their task was completed they would return to their farms to concentrate on the new harvest rather than on the spoils of war. In this view, America was not seen as a nation in arms but as a people in the shops, in the factories, in the schools, in the homes. But having subdued the Fascist terror in the great crusade of the early 1940s, Americans were not allowed to remain at peace for long. A new threat of subjugation was posed by the barbarous hordes of the Marxist creed, and the United States was summoned once again—this time not a transient warrior for one great decisive battle, but the sentinel for a long watch.[44] Much as Woodrow Wilson had insisted that the United States entered the First World War not to protect its security interests but "to make the world safe for democracy"—to see to it that the great conflict would be "the war to end wars"—John F. Kennedy took the oath of Presidential office echoing the traditional American theme of selflessness. Demanding sacrifices from the American people while offering them the burden and the glory of world leadership, he declared: "Let every nation know, whether it wishes us well or ill, that we shall pay any price, bear any burden, meet any hardship, support any friend, oppose any foe to ensure the survival and success of liberty."

Like America, Russia sees itself as the guardian of world freedom—not the Western tradition of individual liberty, but the Marxist notion of freedom from economic exploitation. Because all history is viewed by the Marxists as the history of class struggles, the nation-state is considered a peculiarity of that era of world history characterized by the domination of the capitalist class. Similarly, being part of the bourgeois superstructure, nationalism is considered a mere instrument of the capitalist ruling class used to keep the oppressed classes in line. The true interests of the downtrodden masses lie not with their respective states, which are no more than dictatorships of the capitalist class, but with the global proletariat. Hence, according to Marx, the workers of the world must unite and throw off the shackles of capitalist exploitation, breaking through the "false consciousness" created by the myths of national culture and national interest, and seizing control of the instruments of governmental coercion and propaganda. Marx maintained that capitalism was doomed by the same laws of social evolution that had condemned to oblivion previous economic systems (such as feudalism); the inherent contradictions in capitalism would lead to successively worsening economic crises and to a growing antagonism between the proletarian majority and the rich bourgeois minority, until the whole capitalist edifice would collapse under its own weight. The subsequent revolution would sweep away the dictatorship of the capitalist class and replace it with the dictatorship of the proletariat, and for the first time in history the masses would control both the means of production and governmental authority. The revolution, of course, had to be a worldwide phenomenon, beginning in the most advanced capitalist societies (such as Germany and England) and spreading rapidly to the fringes of the capitalist world. Eventually the new proletarian governments would carry each separate society to pure communism, liquidating the last vestiges of the capitalist class and the bourgeois mentality and instituting the classless utopia where each contributes according to his ability and receives according to his need. With the abolition of classes, the state itself (which, after all, is only an instrument of interclass warfare) would wither away, leading to a new global community based upon the principle of cooperation rather than competition.

But by accident of history, the revolution did not come in the most advanced capitalist country, but in one of the most backward. In 1917, under the double strain of world war and internal weakness, the czarist autocracy crumbled in agrarian and semifeudal Russia. Lenin, the leader of the Bolshevik party, which had proclaimed itself the vanguard of the proletariat (to the extent that a proletariat existed in Russia), had to legitimate his subsequent seizure of power from the Social Democrats. Years prior to the November Revolution, Lenin had claimed to be the legitimate heir of Marx and Engels, branding as revisionists those with different interpretations of the gospel according to Saint Marx (both within Russia and abroad). Because the Russian Revolution defied Marx's predictions, Lenin had to adapt Marxist theory to the peculiar historical circumstances of his own revolution and yet preserve his image as the only true orthodox Communist leader; he had to transform Marxism while appearing to defend its doctrinal purity against revisionist detractors. Lenin, a revisionist himself, succeeded in elevating himself to the "papacy" of the international Communist movement, all the while claiming to be the legitimate successor to the first "pope," Marx himself.

At the time of the Bolshevik coup in Russia, Lenin and his followers assumed that theirs was but the first step in a worldwide revolution and eagerly waited for the workers in Germany and other advanced industrial societies to overthrow their capitalist governments. When the heralded revolutions did not come, the Soviet Communist party was once again faced with the task of amending Marxist theory so as to justify its continued rule in Russia. In Lenin's earlier tract on imperialism, *Imperialism, the Highest Stage of Capitalism,* he explained why capitalism was not collapsing as expected, i.e., as Marx had predicted, suggesting that capitalism had entered its final stage in the form of monopoly capitalism and had staved off the day of reckoning by exploiting the developing areas of the world. Nevertheless, the ultimate collapse could be only postponed, never averted. The increasing drive for colonies and markets would lead to conflict and war among the imperialists and the resulting demise of the international capitalist order.

Further modifications made by Stalin completed the transformation of Marxism. While awaiting the final showdown among the capitalist states, all Communists would have to aid the Soviet Union in building a base for future global revolution. Stalin's doctrine of socialism in one country buried Trotsky's dream of permanent revolution, and placed the interests of the Soviet state above all other ideological considerations. The Soviet Union now became the vanguard of world revolution, a beachhead in a capitalist world which would remain, until the day of victory, menaced and encircled by hostile foreign powers. The U.S.S.R. had no national interest to protect, for that was a bourgeois invention. Rather, the Russian state came to embody the class interests of the oppressed everywhere in the life-and-death struggle against capitalism and exploitation. Henceforth, what was good for the Soviet Union was good for all humanity.

Notes
Chapter 2

1. Seymour Martin Lipset, *Political Man: The Social Bases of Politics* (Garden City, N.Y.: Doubleday, 1963), chapter 3.

2. Ibid.

3. Max Weber, *The Theory of Social and Economic Organization,* ed. by Talcott Parsons (New York: Free Press, 1964), pp. 130–132.

4. David Easton, *The Political System* (New York: Knopf, 1953); also by the same author, *A Framework for Political Analysis* (New York: Prentice-Hall, 1965), and *A Systems Analysis of Political Life* (New York: Wiley, 1965).

5. See, for example, Raymond F. Hopkins and Richard W. Mansbach, *Structure and Process in International Politics* (New York: Harper & Row, 1973).

6. See, for example: Hans J. Morgenthau, *Politics Among Nations: The Struggle for Power and Peace,* 4th ed. (New York: Knopf, 1967); Morton A. Kaplan, *System and Process in International Politics* (New York: Wiley, 1957); Thomas Schelling, *The Strategy of Conflict* (New York: Oxford University Press, 1960); Harold Guetzkow, "Simulations in the Consolidation and Utilization of Knowledge About International Relations," in D. G. Pruitt and R. C. Snyder, eds., *Theory and Research in the Causes of War* (Englewood Cliffs, N.J.: Prentice-Hall, 1969).

7. As Henry A. Kissinger remarks: "The internal requirements of the bureaucracy may come to predominate over the purposes which it was intended to serve." See his "Domestic Structure and Foreign Policy," *Daedalus,* 95 (Spring, 1966): 503–529.

8. Alexander Dallin, "Soviet Foreign Policy and Domestic Politics: A Framework for Analysis," *Journal of International Affairs* 13 (Fall, 1969): 25–64; see also Vernon V. Aspaturian, "Internal Politics and Foreign Policy in the Soviet Union," in R. B. Farrell, ed., *Approaches to Comparative and International Politics* (Northwestern University: University Press, 1966), pp. 212–287.

9. Bertrand de Jouvenel, *Sovereignty: An Inquiry into the*

Political Good, trans. by J. F. Huntington (Chicago: University of Chicago Press, 1963), p. 172.

10. Friedrich Meinecke, *Machiavellism: The Doctrine of Raison d'Etat in Modern History*, trans. by Douglas Scott (New York: Praeger, 1965).

11. Arnold Wolfers, "Statesmanship and Moral Choice," *World Politics*. (January, 1949): reprinted in his *Discord and Collaboration* (Baltimore, Md.: Johns Hopkins University Press, 1965), p. 59.

12. John H. Herz, *Political Realism and Political Idealism* (Chicago: University of Chicago Press, 1951).

13. See the discussion by Meinecke, *Machiavellism*, especially chapter 1. The quote is Meinecke's paraphrasing of Machiavelli.

14. Max Weber, "Politics as a Vocation," in *From Max Weber: Essays in Sociology*, ed. H. H. Gerth and C. W. Mills (New York: Oxford University Press, 1958), p. 121.

15. See, for example, Hans J. Morgenthau, *Scientific Man vs. Power Politics* (Chicago: University of Chicago Press, 1946).

16. Aldous Huxley, *Grey Eminence: A Study in Religion and Politics* (New York: Harper & Row, 1966), p. 15.

17. Ibid., pp. 190–191.

18. Ibid., p. 212.

19. Hans Kohn, *The Age of Nationalism* (New York: Harper & Row, 1962).

20. See Rupert Emerson, "Nationalism and Political Development," *Journal of Politics* 22 (February, 1960): 3–28; idem, *From Empire to Nation: The Rise to Self-Assertiveness of Asian and African Peoples* (Boston: Beacon, 1962).

21. Harold J. Isaacs, "Nationality: 'End of the Road'?" *Foreign Affairs* 53 (April, 1975): p. 446; idem, *Idols of the Tribe: Group Identity and Political Change* (New York: Harper & Row, 1975).

22. See Dankwart A. Rustow, *A World of Nations: Problems of Political Modernization* (Washington, D.C.: Brookings Institution, 1967).

23. See Hans Kohn, *The Idea of Nationalism: A Study in its Origins and Backgrounds* (New York: Macmillan, 1945); and Boyd C. Shafer, *Nationalism: Myth and Reality* (New York: Harcourt, Brace, 1955).

24. For further discussion, see Harry Elmer Barnes, *History and Social Intelligence* (New York: Knopf, 1926).

25. For a discussion of the process of communication as the basis of national and cultural coherence, see Karl W. Deutsch, *Nationalism and Social Communication* (Cambridge, Mass.: M.I.T. Press, 1953).

26. See Kohn, *The Idea of Nationalism* (New York: Macmillan, 1945); also, Boyd C. Shafer, *The Faces of Nationalism* (New York: Harcourt, Brace, Jovanovich, 1972).

27. See Carlton J. H. Hayes, *The Historical Evolution of Modern Nationalism* (New York: Smith, 1931); idem, *Nationalism: A Religion* (New York: Macmillan, 1960).

28. Isaiah Berlin, "The Bent Twig: A Note on Nationalism," *Foreign Affairs* 51 (October, 1972): 12.

29. Isaacs, "Nationality: 'End of the Road'?", p. 439.

30. Morton Grodzins, "The Basis of National Loyalties," *Bulletin of the Atomic Scientists* 7 (1951).

31. The characterization of the nation as a "soul" or "spiritual principle" was, of course, that of Ernest Renan, "What is a Nation?" reproduced in Alfred Zimmern, ed., *Modern Political Ideologies* (London: Oxford, 1934), pp. 186–205. See also Holland J. Rose, *Nationality in Modern History* (New York: Macmillan, 1916), p. 143.

32. Emerson, *From Empire to Nation*, p. 95; see also F. H. Hinsley, *Nationalism and the International System* (New York: Oceana, 1973).

33. Reinhold Niebuhr, *Moral Man and Immoral Society* (New York: Scribner's, 1947).

34. Boyd, *Faces of Nationalism*, p. 254.

35. J. Glen St Barclay, *Twentieth Century Nationalism* (New York: Praeger, 1971), p. 71.

36. Hayes, *Historical Evolution*.

37. Berlin, "Bent Twig."

38. Cited in Emerson, "Nationalism and Political Development," p. 16.

39. See Robert Ardrey, *The Territorial Imperative* (New York: Atheneum, 1966); idem, *African Genesis* (New York: Dell, 1967);

Konrad Lorenz, *On Aggression,* trans. Kerr Wilson (New York: Bantam, 1964).

40. Hans Kohn, *The Idea of Nationalism,* p. 17.

41. This is the "realist" perspective; see, for example, Hans J. Morgenthau, *Politics Among Nations: The Struggle for Power and Peace,* 5th ed. (New York: Knopf, 1972).

42. See William Ebenstein, *Today's Isms,* 2nd ed. (Englewood Cliffs, N.J.: Prentice-Hall, 1958); and Carl J. Friedrich and Zbigniew K. Brzezinski, *Totalitarian Dictatorship and Autocracy* (Cambridge, Mass.: Harvard University Press, 1956).

43. Walter C. Langer, *The Mind of Adolf Hitler* (New York: Basic Books, 1972), pp. 39–40. This work was originally written in 1943 as a psychological portrait for American intelligence (the OSS).

44. Richard A. Aliano, *American Defense Policy from Eisenhower to Kennedy: The Politics of Changing Military Requirements, 1957–1961* (Athens: Ohio University Press, 1975), p. 44.

Chapter 3

Power

HAGEN: Have you got all the political connections wired into you?

MICHAEL: Not all. I needed about four more months. The Don and I were working for it. But I've got all the judges, we did that first, and some of the more important people in Congress. And the big party boys here in New York were no problem, of course. The Corleone Family is a lot stronger than anybody thinks, but I hope to make it foolproof. . . . [M]y father was the only one who understood that political connections and power are worth ten regimes. . . .

—from Mario Puzo's *The Godfather*

POWER POLITICS

Power is the mainspring of the international system. If politics is a process wherein competing actors engage in conflict to allocate society's values, power is the means used to affect that distribution. Like other nebulous but popular concepts (such as *beauty* and *truth*), the term *power* evokes a host of bold images and virile poses; however, because of its many connotations (some of which are often contradictory), it seems to defy precise definition. Despite this vagueness, power is central to the political process. Indeed, politics has been defined by leading students of political science alternatively as "the shaping, distribution, and excercise of power" [1] or as "the struggle for power." [2] In the everyday parlance of foreign affairs, we find such questions posed as: Is the Soviet Union now more powerful than the United States?; and, What is the balance of power between Israel and the Arabs in the Middle East? We also find blanket statements of fact such as: Iran is the dominant power in the Persian Gulf, and Brazil is emerging as a powerful actor in world politics. Power is not something we can see or touch, or even easily describe, let alone analyze with the degree of precision and clarity we would prefer. And yet even the novice is aware of its existence and importance and can point to at least the more dramatic instances of its exercise in interstate relations. Consider the following passage from Sir Winston Churchill's history of the Second World War in which he recreates his momentous meeting with Stalin in Moscow in October 1944:

> The moment was apt for business, so I said, "Let us settle about our affairs in the Balkans. Your armies are in Rumania and Bulgaria. We have interests, missions, and agents there. Don't let us get at cross-purposes in small ways. So far as Britain and Russia are concerned, how would it do for you to have ninety per cent predominance in Rumania, for us to have ninety per cent of the say in Greece, and go fifty-fifty about Yugoslavia?" While this was being translated I wrote out on a half-sheet of paper:

Rumania	
Russia	90%
The others	10%
Greece	
Great Britain	
(in accord with the USA)	90%
Russia	10%
Yugoslavia	50–50%

Hungary	50–50%
Bulgaria	
Russia	75%
The others	25%

> I pushed this across to Stalin who had by then heard the translation. There was a slight pause. Then he took his blue pencil and made a large tick upon it, and passed it back to us. It was all settled in no more time than it takes to set down.[3]

Certainly this is power. Neither Churchill nor Stalin had consulted the governments or peoples of these Balkan states, and yet in one stroke the two heads of government determined the fate of millions. Power is an awe-inspiring phenomenon.

Power is to the study of politics what wealth is to the study of economics. Much as economists examine the production and distribution of wealth in various societies, political scientists analyze the exercise and distribution of power. To be sure, the concept of power is less susceptible to rigorous analysis and, therefore, political science tends to appear less scientific than its sister discipline. Wealth is a tangible thing, which can be measured and quantified, while power is elusive, relational and subjective. If we want to know how wealthy the United States is, we use the accepted yardsticks and so arrive at a fairly accurate answer. Because wealth lends itself to measurement in terms of national currencies, we can gauge this country's wealth in terms of its gross national product (GNP), that is, the money value of the goods and services produced by the American economy in a single year. Or we can estimate accumulated wealth rather than income (which itself is a measure of productive wealth.)[4] Thus we know that the United States has a GNP of more than one trillion dollars and a stock of wealth greater than nine trillion dollars. We can readily compare this wealth with that of other countries by translating foreign currencies into dollars. For example, in terms of GNP, the United States is nearly twice as rich as the Soviet Union, three times as rich as Japan, five times as rich as France and nearly twenty times as rich as India.

But what can we do with "power"? Power is, ultimately, a relationship in which one actor affects the behavior or predispositions of another; it is not a thing possessed. There is no index for it comparable with GNP; there is no such thing (nor can there be) as a country's gross national power. There is no generally accepted unit of measure, because there is no quantity to measure.

Power is a relationship of influence which determines the distribution of the scarce things political actors value and for which they are willing to contend. The distribution of values in any given society reflects the distribution of power in that society. Those with the lion's share of influence—the powerful—are able to appropriate a disproportionately large share of the benefits society has to offer; those with little or no influence—the powerless—must make do with considerably less. It is therefore not by coincidence that the powerful are also the haves and the powerless the have-nots. It is unfortunate, indeed, that the subject matter of politics is inherently ambiguous, but even more unfortunate is the tendency among some political analysts to assume that "since power is a difficult concept to deal with, power is not the central concept giving unity to international relations." [5] Indeed, some theorists have become so disenchanted with the concept of power that they would apparently prefer to do away with it altogether.[6] To a certain extent, political scientists' inability to agree on a standardized terminology shows how relatively primitive the discipline is; however, this also stems from the nature of politics itself, which evades rigorous scientific analysis. To avoid or even deemphasize power because of its lack of clarity is to eviscerate politics. To consider politics without examining power is like studying medicine without studying anatomy. By defining power as a relationship of influence, we make it clear that all politics is power politics. The two are inseparable.

THE DIMENSIONS OF POWER

Much of the confusion surrounding power is caused by failure to differentiate between power as influence (a relation) and power as capabilities (a quantity). Capabilities are the foundations of power, resources and assets that can be mobilized to affect the behavior and attitudes of others. But capabilities are not synonymous with power. They indicate the potential for power. When we say that an actor possesses power, we are usually referring to a potential for exercising power. We should say that the actor possesses power resources, or capabilities.[7] Power per se is a relation of influence brought about by the mobilization of power potential (capabilities). Power, then, concerns causation and may be said to exist whenever the actions or predispositions of one political actor (the subject of power) are determined by the preferences of another (the wielder of power). Power may well have a bearing on the attitudes, beliefs and expectations of the subject as well on overt behavior.[8] Moreover, the subject may be influenced by the preferences of the wielder even though the latter has made no explicit requests or demands for compliance. This is sometimes called the rule of anticipated reactions[9] or implicit influence[10] and may very well be the most prevalent and effective form of power. For example, a country may cast its vote on a particular issue in the United Nations General Assembly in a manner calculated to please the United States, though Washington may have sent no signals concerning its desires. Thus the United States exercises influence without intending to do so.

Power is of an ambiguous and subtle nature. The ambiguities of power stem from (1) difficulty of measurement; (2) subjectivity; (3) relativity; (4) contextual quality; (5) reciprocal nature. The subtleties of power revolve around the distinctions between: (1) persuasion and coercion; (2) nonviolent coercion versus force; (3) deterrence versus compellence.

The Ambiguity of Power: Measurement

When we pose the question, How much power does country A have? or How powerful is country A? we must take care to differentiate between two possible interpretations. Are we asking How much *influence* does country A wield? or are we asking How great are A's *capabilities?* When we deal with the bases or elements of power, quantification is indeed possible. But bear in mind that we are then measuring (and in a rather crude fashion at that) capabilities, or the potential for power, not the reality of influence. A country's geographical extent, population size, gross national product, self-sufficiency and military expenditures are quantifiable variables which can be measured and compared with those of other international actors. But all that they are capable of demonstrating is latent power. At most, we can only infer or predict actual influence on the basis of a state's power resources. If state A has greater capabilities than state B, all we are entitled to suggest is that, all other things being equal (which, of course, they never are), A can be more influential than B. It would be the height of folly to make a blanket statement that A has greater capabilities than B, therefore A has more influence than B. This would be the equivalent of declaring with certainty that individual A (who is six feet tall and weighs 200 pounds) will win a fight with individual B (who is five-and-a-half feet tall and weighs 150 pounds) solely on the basis of simple raw data. But what if B is in peak physical condition and A is flabby and fat? What if B holds a black belt in karate and A is spastic? What if B is twenty-five years old and A is sixty? Obviously, viewing certain attributes in isolation can be very misleading. If the only differences between A and B are height and weight (i.e., if all other variables are constant), then the prediction of A's victory seems valid. (Nor have we considered the factor of will in our example. If A is physically stronger than B but unwilling to risk injury over the object in dispute, or if he is a coward, he may very well walk away and concede victory to his "weaker" opponent. Willingness to engage in combat is an intangible capability which cannot be quantified or easily measured. But it may be the crucial determinant of influence.)

The difficulties inherent in inferring influence from capabilities are apparent in international relations. During the mid- to late-1930s, for example, American capabilities far exceeded those of Mussolini's Italy, and yet a good case can be made that Italy was a more influential actor in world affairs (or at least European affairs) than the United States during this period. Naturally, when the United States mobilized its potential, its actual influence dwarfed that of Fascist Italy. Or consider Stalin's famous remark about the power of the Holy See: "How many divisions does the Pope have?" Stalin was guilty of a somewhat different error in that he equated influence with military forces; he did not simply assume that capabilities were synonymous with power, but went further and equated influence with but one aspect of national capabilities. Certainly the influence of the Vatican cannot be deduced from its military forces (the ceremonial Swiss Guard), or its population (a thousand or so inhabitants), or its geographical size (109 acres), or even its wealth (given its art treasures, which are valued in billions of dollars, it is by far the richest sovereign state in the world in terms of per capita wealth). The power of the papacy rests largely on its spiritual leadership of the world's half-billion or so Roman Catholics. Stalin, like Mao Tse Tung, believed that "power grows out of the barrel of a gun," failing to appreciate the multifaceted nature of influence. Despite the stature of Stalin and Mao as practitioners of foreign policy, only a rash student of politics will identify influence with capabilities or predict actual power on the basis of one or two indices of potential power.

Power is what power does. If influence is defined in terms of causation (i.e., effecting a change in another actor's behavior or attitudes), then power as influence can be measured only in terms of outcomes. If it is true, as we have suggested, that the distribution of values in a society mirrors the distribution of power in that society, this is so because the allocation of benefits results from competition for power advantage. Though various theorists have devised abstract and rather complex formulas and models for the measurement of influence,[11] for our purposes it is sufficient to conclude that the relationship of influence (i.e., the power of actors in situations of conflict) can be gauged simply in terms of the final allocation of the values in dispute. The more influential get more of what there is to get; the less influential get less of what there is to get. (Or, in the words of the ancient Greek historian Thucydides: "The strong take what they can; the weak suffer what they must.")

The Ambiguity of Power: Subjectivity

Power is, ultimately, a psychological relationship. It is an affair of the mind. This is not to suggest that it is not founded upon real capabilities; however, aside from the ability physically to seize and hold onto a disputed value (for example, occupation of disputed territory), the influence relationship normally requires the acquiescence of the subject of power. If a man with a gun in his hand demands that I behave as he wishes, but I refuse to believe that he has a gun, or that it is real, or loaded, or that he will use it if necessary, the value of the weapon in gaining my compliance is nil. Of course, if he can squeeze the trigger and get what he wants without my cooperation, my initial perception matters little. The actual use, as opposed to the threat, of force can serve either as a sanction to gain compliance or as a means to seize a value without the other party's acquiescence. If my compliance is necessary for the gun wielder to attain his goal, he might shoot me in the arm to demonstrate his resolve and change my mind about disobeying his demands. In this case, force is being employed as a sanction to alter my perception of self-interest. The reverse is also possible. We are all familiar with the movie scene in which a man sticks his hand in his coat pocket and acts as though it were a gun. In this case, the real capability is lacking, but the influence may be real nonetheless (i.e., the individual threatened believes there is, or may be, a gun and behaves accordingly). A political actor's perceived capabilities may be more crucial than his actual capabilities in determining his influence.

A political actor is as powerful as others believe him to be. In the long run, of course, there must be a certain correspondence between appearance and reality. If an actor is perceived to be more powerful than objective capabilities warrant, it will be only a matter of time before these capabilities are tested and reassessed. Governments are careful to cultivate an image of state power and project it abroad; from time to time they seek to bolster the image by demonstrations of power. Prestige (the reputation for power) is also a valued resource in interstate relations, and states traditionally have jealously guarded their status at international ceremonies. The Congress of Westphalia at the conclusion of the Thirty Years' War (1618–1648) was prolonged for nearly eight years partly because of arguments over etiquette; months were consumed in haggling over who should sit at the head of the rectangular conference table, and when it was finally agreed that a round table would be used, the parties argued for several more months over who would sit nearest the door.[12] This is reminiscent of the dispute between the United States and North Vietnam over the shape of the conference table, which delayed the opening of the Paris peace negotiations for a number of weeks. Hanoi demanded a square table with each of the four participants (the other two being the government of South Vietnam and the Viet Cong) seated at a separate side; Washington, on the other hand, wanted two separated hemispherical tables with the United States and the Saigon regime at one table and the Communists at the other. To some, the haggling seemed both foolish and tragic. However, this seemingly routine matter was actually crucial. If the United States had accepted the North Vietnamese proposal, it would have conceded, even before the talks began, a pivotal point: that the Viet Cong was an international actor equal in status with the South Vietnamese government and not a mere appendage of North Vietnam, as Washington had long contended. In the end, of course, they agreed on an arrangement that allowed both Washington and Hanoi to claim victory. The struggle for prestige is therefore a substantial matter, for the status accorded a political actor is a reflection of the power attributed to that actor by others. Given the psychological basis of influence, subjective assessments of power are tantamount to the reality of power.

The Ambiguity of Power: Relativity

A state's capabilities do not exist in a political vacuum. It makes sense to speak of a country's power only in terms of the power of others. The major constraint on the expansion of an international actor's power is the power other actors can muster in opposition. For example, consider military capabilities in time of war. Today, a military establishment of forty thousand men suggests a minor power, such as Colombia, Denmark, Finland or Ethiopia. And yet Alexander the Great conquered the ancient Western world with such a force, and in the sixteenth century Charles V threatened to dominate all Europe with an army of comparable size. However, by the middle of the nineteenth century, the number of casualties at Gettysburg, one of nearly 150 major battles fought in a half-decade, was greater than all the men under arms commanded by Alexander. Napoleon was able to conquer Europe with half a million men; but a century later, Kaiser Wilhelm failed to obtain German hegemony with a military establishment nearly thirteen and a half million strong. Certainly the scale of power is anything but static.

To consider a state's capabilities in isolation is meaningless. The relationship of influence is a dynamic process between the wielder and the subject of power. The capabilities of an actor can serve as a basis for prediction of potential power only if the capabilities of potential rivals are taken into account. The wielder's power to prevail is dependent upon the subject's power to resist.

The Ambiguity of Power: Context

Power is not only relative, it is also situational. Despite the objective capabilities of the wielder and subject, the reality and degree of influence that will be exerted will depend upon the issue involved, the differing values attached to it by the contending parties and the particular circumstances. By any standard measure of national capabilities (wealth, technological know-how, military forces, population, natural resources and so forth), the United States certainly overshadowed the tiny state of North Vietnam. In 1970, North Vietnam had a population of 22 million and a GNP of $1.5 billion, and spent $300 million annually to support 450,000 men under arms. By contrast, the United States had a population of 212 million and a GNP of $1.4 trillion and spent $78 billion to maintain a military establishment of over 3 million men.[13] Washington had the sheer physical capacity to pave all Indochina and make it an eight-lane superhighway. Yet, after a decade of active intervention and the direct expenditure of well over $100 billion, in the end, David defeated Goliath. On the basis of capabilities alone, this outcome could not have been predicted. All such indicators pointed toward the United States having its way in the conflict. Then how does one account for the turn of events in Southeast Asia? Though the Pentagon was able to project more military destructive power halfway around the globe than Hanoi was able to muster in opposition, this was insufficient to make the North Vietnamese abandon their quarter-century-old struggle to reunify the two Vietnams. The stakes were worth more to Hanoi than to Washington, and consequently the Communists' commitment and staying power were superior and ultimately crucial. Successive American administrations were dissuaded from employing even more destructive force by domestic public opinion and the fear of alienating allies and provoking foes (China and the Soviet Union). Unable successfully to employ force either to seize the objective or as a sanction to make the North Vietnamese acquiesce to American demands, United States policy soon faltered and eventually collapsed.

Whatever a comparison of the relative capabilities of the wielder and subject of power might reveal, the relationship of influence has its own context, which effectively sets limits on the mobilization of power resources. As powerful as the United States may have been in terms of national capabilities, the conflict situation itself contained inherent constraints against the use of full power potential. The reality of influence may differ greatly from the reality of capabilities.

The Ambiguity of Power: Reciprocity

Influence is not a one-way street. Power is a multilateral, not a unilateral, relationship, in which the wielder and the subject of power constantly exchange roles. By its very nature, of course, power is asymmetrical, by which we mean that one party will exercise more influence than the other over the outcome of the conflict situation. If neither side exercises more influence, then both actors are equally powerful (or powerless, depending upon one's perspective). But even if one actor is more influential and its rival less influential, rarely is the latter uninfluential; that is, each party exerts a certain degree of influence over the behavior and expectations of the other. In international relations, power is exercised in a reciprocal manner. In the mid-1970s, for example, the French, convinced that Western Europe would remain dependent upon Arab oil for many years to come, were eagerly endeavoring to sell armaments to Egypt.[14] The French hoped to assure themselves a degree of leverage over Arab oil policy toward Western Europe: The two sides would be mutually dependent, the French on the Arabs for oil, the Arabs on the French for arms. In much the same manner, the United States stepped up its arms shipments to the oil-producing countries in the Persian Gulf, especially Iran and Saudi Arabia. In 1974 and 1975, more than half the United States' $20 billion–worth of arms exports was to the Middle East.[15] Thus, while the Persian Gulf states could manipulate the supply and price of petroleum as a means of influencing American policy, the military establishments of these countries were tied to the necessary flow of spare parts and technical advisors from the United States.[16] A similar pattern of reciprocal influence existed between the United States and Israel, only Jerusalem's leverage over Washington's policy was based not on oil, but on the well-organized American Israel lobby. The principle instrument of American influence over Israel was, once again, the supply of sophisticated arms, some $5 billion–worth in the three years following the war in 1973.[17]

To the extent that states possess something other states need or desire, they possess capabilities. In that most states are increasingly interdependent, they all possess potential influence. However, interdependencies, like power itself, are asymmetrical; indeed, it is the lopsided nature of mutual dependencies that creates the potential for power. The United States and Guatemala, for instance, are interdependent in a number of ways, especially economically, and therefore can be expected to possess the means to influence one another. But Guatemala is much more dependent upon the United States than vice versa; an interruption in the flow of commerce, credit and capital would be only an inconvenience or annoyance for the United States, but a matter of economic life or death for the tiny Central American republic. Gulliver and the Lilliputians might have been mutually dependent upon one another, but Gulliver did not have to fear being stepped on by a Lilliputian. The reciprocity of influence must not obscure the fundamental asymmetry of power.

The Subtlety of Power: Persuasion vs. Coercion

The Churchill-Stalin agreement referred to at the beginning of this chapter was so blatant an exercise of power that only those lacking totally in political insight could miss the element of power. But power is rarely so visible and apparent. More often than not, influence is exercised unobtrusively, quietly, with little fanfare and none of the trappings of Caesarian authority. The

Godfather was a man who understood well the subtleties of power and was heard to remark, "A lawyer with his briefcase can steal more than a hundred men with guns." He grasped that the distribution of benefits is more effectively influenced by incurring the least opposition possible, though on occasion it might be necessary or expedient to employ brute force or crude threats.

The most successful operation of power involves getting others to obey because they want to—because they believe it is in their interest to do so—not because they feel coerced into doing so. In domestic politics, we refer to the legitimacy of the political system; that is, the authority of the state is accepted by its citizens as just and proper. Through the process of socialization, we are conditioned to believe that government makes decisions in our interest, and therefore we tend to obey its decrees out of habit. Thus the state exercises increasing influence over myriad aspects of our lives without having to resort to force or the threat of force.

The absence of world government means that there is little in the way of legitimate authority in the international system. As we will discuss in greater detail in Chapter 4, power is exercised in interstate politics through either persuasion or coercion, both of which are fundamentally similar in that they revolve around the use of sanctions. Sanctions may be defined as the penalties and/or rewards offered by one actor to another in order to gain the latter's compliance. When power involves the use of positive sanctions (promises and rewards), we speak of persuasive or attractive power; when the relationship is founded upon negative sanctions (threats or the infliction of harm), we speak of coercive power. In both cases, sanctions are employed to affect the subject's behavior by transforming his calculation of self-interest.

The Subtlety of Power: Nonviolent Coercion versus Force

Some students of politics assume that power, if not identical with force, ultimately rests upon the ability to use force. Because of the anarchic nature of the international system, the instruments of force and fear play a greater role in the global political process than in the domestic sphere. If force remains the ultimate arbiter when all other means of foreign policy fail, then to this extent it is still the *ultima ratio regnum* of world politics.* Physical violence is a type of coercive sanction. Just as the police forces of the state employ this sanction internally, the military forces of the state employ it externally against other international actors. As suggested previously, force is a variety of influence when it is used to get another actor to behave in a certain fashion, that is, when it is used to affect the subject's calculation of interest. When force is threatened and not used, or when violence is applied in partial doses with the threat of more violence if the accompanying demands go unheeded, force is being used to compel changes in another actor's behavior. However, if force is used to seize an object or value without affecting the behavior of others (e.g., by a mugger who kills his victim and takes his wallet), force is being used to change the distribution of benefits but not to influence behavior. When force is employed as a means of influence, it is instrumental force; when it is employed for the purpose of seizure it is brute force. War as an instrument of foreign policy can serve either function. Wars of annihilation or conquest are instances of brute force; in every other sort of war, force is used primarily as a sanction to affect the behavior and attitudes of other states.

But as we have seen, force is neither the sole means of power nor the only example of coercive influence. Negative sanctions in general suggest the threat or infliction of harm, and harm can be done without physical violence. Coercive sanctions are intended adversely to affect the value system or well-being of the subject to such a degree that it becomes more rational for the subject to obey than disobey. Though force may be the most obvious means of causing pain, disutilities can be brought about by numerous nonviolent techniques. The nature and degree of prospective punishment necessary to compel conformity depends upon the value system of the subject of power. The more resistant an actor is to behavior modification, the greater the severity of the sanctions needed to effect the change; he must be confronted with the prospect of relatively significant harm. As force normally involves the greatest disutility, it will tend to be necessary only in matters

* This Latin phrase literally means "the last argument of kings," or the resort to arms. Louis XIV had this motto engraved on his cannon.

of prime importance. When lesser issues are at stake, either persuasion or nonviolent coercion will usually suffice. We are all familiar with such sanctions in everyday life. For example, the state threatens us with monetary fines for parking violations or the public library posts a notice in the back of the book we borrow informing us that we will be fined if we fail to abide by certain regulations. By the same token, nonviolent coercion is endemic to international relations. For example, the Arab countries coordinate a campaign to convince foreign firms with which they do business to boycott commercial relations with Israel; Libya nationalizes American-owned oil companies doing business within its borders to protest United States government policy in the Middle East; the United States places a surcharge on imports to prod other industrial countries to revalue their currencies. International politics, like all politics, is characterized by an admixture of persuasion and coercion, the carrot and the stick. And while force may not be the main instrument of power, it will remain the ultimate means of influence in an anarchic environment.

The Subtlety of Power: Deterrence vs. Compellence

Power might be said to have its positive and negative features, depending upon the nature of the behavior being modified. The wielder of power seeks either to get the subject to do something he would not otherwise do (compellence) or to prevent the subject from doing something he would ordinarily do (deterrence). In both cases, the mode of behavior modification is identical: sanctions are threatened (coercion) or promised (persuasion) in order to make the desired action (compellence) or inaction (deterrence) palatable.

Though deterrence has always been an important aspect of international influence, it has assumed a paramount position in the age of nuclear weapons. Though a detailed consideration of the mechanics of nuclear deterrence appears in Chapters 4 and 5, we can sketch the broad outlines of a successful relationship of negative power. For country A to deter country B from doing X, the following elements must be present: (1) A must convey to B its intention of punishing B in a certain manner should B in fact do X; (2) B must believe that A has the capability to do what it threatens; (3) B must believe that A is likely to do what it says it will do—the threat must be credible; (4) B must be convinced that the advantages it would gain by doing X would be nullified by the subsequent harm inflicted by A; (5) B must be rational. If all of these ingredients—communication, capability, credibility and rationality—are present, then deterrence will be operational; conversely, the greater the divergence between this ideal deterrent relationship and a real-world situation, the more likely it is that deterrence will fail. It is quite apparent that perceptions are a crucial variable in the equation. If B should miss A's signal (the threat), or fail to believe that A has the capability or the will to carry out threatened retaliation, the objective fact of A's real capability or intentions matters little.[18]

THE HIERARCHY OF WORLD POWER

Political analysts have long been aware that all social systems tend to be stratified. Much as domestic societies are stratified by income, status and power, the international system has always consisted of big powers and small powers. One student of international politics has suggested in a rather enticing manner that there exists, in effect, a global pecking order in which states may be ranked as either top-dog nations or underdog nations.[19] The authors of a popular text in international relations divide the major powers themselves into three categories of decreasing capabilities: superpowers (the United States and the Soviet Union); nuclear powers (Britain, France and China); economic powers (Japan and West Germany).[20] A. F. K. Organski has developed a ranking system based on the differing stages of power transition, as he terms it; that is, as a country industrializes, it "goes through a power transition in the course of which it passes from a stage of little power to one of greatly increased power." Organski presents a picture of a fluid interstate system with a dominant state at the apex of the power pyramid, followed by great powers, middle powers, small powers, and dependencies. The particular states placed in these categories are not forever the same, but change with the dynamic process of power transition.[21] Recently, observers of world affairs have divided contemporary states into the developed and powerful and the less-developed and weak.[22]

Moreover, theorists agree that there is a concomitant division between the satisfied and the dissatisfied. As one source notes: "Any [political] order tends to reflect the values and interests of the stronger and more influential states for it is shaped primarily by their relative power."[23] Accordingly, states that benefit from the existing distribution of global values can be expected to defend the existing international order. These are the satisfied or "status quo" powers. As might be predicted, states that feel disadvantaged by what they perceive to be an unjust allocation of benefits will challenge the international order, seeking to replace it with one based on a distribution more to their liking. These states are alternatively referred to in the literature of world politics as revisionist or revolutionary powers.[24] Naturally, the power and satisfaction variables are hardly mutually exclusive. Given the nature of politics, the more powerful will most likely also be the more satisfied, while the less powerful are apt to be less satisfied.

It is therefore common usage among both lay and professional observers of international politics to place states in various power categories or status rankings. But what does it mean to say that an actor is strong or weak, powerful or powerless? We have already seen how power is a relationship of influence, and that it is thus relative and situational. If this is so, does it make sense to refer to states as being powerful or impotent when to do so suggests that power is a stable and permanent attribute, a thing possessed? It makes sense when we remind ourselves that power is often referred to in terms of capabilities which do, indeed, represent assets or resources or other qualities attributed to actors. The international system is stratified in terms of capabilities and the share of available benefits they bring. Because there is an unequal distribution of power resources in every social system, political influence is also unevenly distributed. This holds true for domestic political systems (regardless of their ideological pretentions) and the multistate system.

The hierarchy of world power is fluid, and relative rankings are subject to change as a result of the actors' upward and downward mobility. The rise of Japan from total defeat in World War II to the status of an acknowledged major actor is an instructive example. Using but one index of capabilities, in 1947, Japan produced only three-quarters as much steel as India; within a quarter-century, Japan was annually turning out over fifteen times as much as India. And then there is the case of the other defeated Axis partner, Germany. By 1960, the West German economy was already outproducing that of the British, having reached a GNP of $183.5 billion, as compared with $116.5 billion for the United Kingdom; moreover, by 1975, the West Germans had nearly doubled their GNP (to $331.3 billion) while the British GNP had failed to increase by even half ($171.1 billion).* [25]

Though these indexes only partially reflect overall national capabilities, informed observers would concur that Japan and West Germany have been upwardly mobile powers since the Second World War, while Great Britain has been a downwardly mobile power. But take note that while we can measure certain relative capabilities with a good deal of precision, we cannot measure actual influence with equal precision. Figures are available that allow one to depict accurately the decline in British capabilities; we can only crudely and impressionistically determine the decline in Britain's world influence on the basis of her actual performance in the international system over the years.

CAPABILITIES: THE FOUNDATIONS OF NATIONAL POWER

World politics would certainly be a lot easier to comprehend if power as influence were the same as power as capabilities. If this were the case, we could measure and compare the power of states with a degree of exactitude rarely found in the social sciences. However, the real world is more complex than the casual observer might like, so much so that it sometimes appears to defy comprehension.

If capabilities are not the same as influence, then, why study capabilities? Simply because they are the only reliable criteria

* The figures given are in constant dollars; that is, they are adjusted for inflation and therefore the growth indicated is real.

available to gauge a state's power in the international system. National capabilities may not yield a very precise index of state power, but they are the only tools we have to make even rough estimates of the shifting patterns of global influence.

The power resources of a state can be divided into three categories of capabilities: (1) natural; (2) societal; and (3) governmental. To a certain extent, of course, these categories are arbitrary and by no means mutually exclusive; they are interdependent and may reinforce or counteract one another. Natural capabilities are those national attributes that are relatively stable and subject to fluctuation only in the long run; that is, they are beyond the immediate volition of policy makers. For the time being, states are either blessed or cursed with these attributes. Societal capabilities are fairly stable in the short run, but are more susceptible to manipulation by a governing elite. They include all the physical and psychological factors that contribute to the capacity of a people to cooperate for common purposes. Finally, there are liabilities or assets stemming from the type of political leadership of a country. Governmental capabilities are the least stable and least tangible of these three categories, but they may decide whether or not a state navigates successfully on the sometimes stormy seas of world politics.

Natural Capabilities: Geography

Geography is usually regarded as the most basic and enduring foundation of national power. But geography is neither the study of maps nor the recitation of capital cities. It is the study of man in his spatial context, of the reciprocal relationship between physical environment and life.[26] An examination of world politics starts with the fact that the major actors are territorial states; that is, they are defined in terms of their claim to appropriation of separate portions of the earth's surface, ranging from the Soviet Union's claim to 8.6 million square miles to the Vatican's claim to some 100 acres. Traditionally, these pretentions to sovereign control were limited to the quarter of the earth's surface that is land; however, increasingly over the last decade, political actors have laid claim to the oceans as well (see Chapter 5 for a discussion of the United Nations Law of the Sea Conference).

The three aspects of a country's geography that especially interest the student of international politics are (1) location; (2) size; and (3) terrain. The elementary observation, "everything that is, is somewhere,"[27] leads us to inquire how the location of a political entity on the earth's surface can add to or detract from its capabilities. The most obvious ramification of location is climate. The effect of climate on the evolution of the human species, its dispersion over the globe and its racial differentiation is well known.[28] But climate also affects many other attributes of a civilization, including its economy and culture.[29] A land may be rich in raw materials but unable to exploit them because of inhospitable conditions, for instance, the Amazon and Congo river basins, which are well endowed with natural resources but filled with impenetrable tropical rain forests. It is not by accident that the traditional world powers have been located in temperate zones; the polar and tropical areas tend to inhibit industrialization and full development of natural resources. However, ability to exploit resources even in marginal regions derives also from technological skill and economic wealth in general. The United States, for example, the world's wealthiest and most technologically advanced polity, initiated a massive multibillion-dollar project to tap the oil deposits on the north slope of Alaska. Constraints of climate can be surmounted if economic capabilities are present.

Location also implies the existence of natural boundaries and proximity to neighbors of varying degrees of power and hostility. If a country has powerful and hostile neighbors and lacks territorial defenses provided by nature (mountains, deserts, bodies of water, etc.), it will find itself in an intolerable and perhaps hopeless situation. The historical plight of Poland is a good illustration. If a country could choose its location, there is one place it would avoid being situated—on the great plain of Europe, sandwiched between Germany and Russia. With two such powerful and traditional antagonists as neighbors, it would find itself a constant zone of contention between the two and a convenient thoroughfare through which one might invade the other. It would soon become a client of one or the other, be divided between the two, or become a perpetual battleground for opposing armies. At the beginning of the eighteenth century, Poland was the third largest country in Europe in terms of area and the fourth largest in terms of population. Yet it was torn by internal strife, and since its extensive frontiers were not protected by natural boundaries, lay fatally exposed to attack from virtually every direction. Between 1772 and 1795, Poland was partitioned three times among Prussia, Russia and Austria until it was completely absorbed by its greedy neighbors and ceased to exist as a sovereign state. Having been reconstituted by the victorious Allies at the conclusion of the First World War, it was divided once again, this time between Stalin and Hitler at the beginning of the Second World War. At the end of this war, Poland became a satellite of the Soviet Union.

But a country is hardly home free because it borders a powerful but friendly country. Relations between the United States and Canada have been peaceful, cordial, and harmonious for nearly a century, so much so that the relationship was frequently cited as a novelty in international politics. And yet by the 1970s the Canadians were asserting their independence from the American colossus and protesting what they perceived to be their status as an economic and cultural appendage of the United States. In this instance, nearness to a powerful state has resulted in much more subtle forms of influence, but influence nonetheless. The Canadians became conscious of their distinctive identity as a people and were uneasy that Americans owned and controlled a good part of their economy and that American "cultural imperialism" had pervaded their news magazines, books, movies, television shows and educational system. The Canadians were learning an important political lesson: Being next door to a friendly superpower is like sleeping next to a friendly elephant. Not only does it go without saying who will wind up with the blanket, but if the elephant rolls over. . . .

The United States is favorably situated. Not since the early days of the Republic has the country had to contend with threatening powers on its borders. Throughout most of the nineteenth century, the United States was able to make do with a military force consisting of a few thousand men scattered along frontier outposts. In stark contrast to the Poles, the Americans faced the Canadians, the Mexicans and the Plains Indians, none of them equal in power to the continental European states. Moreover, the country was physically separated from the center of world power—Europe—by a vast ocean, which afforded the United States one of the best natural defense systems in the world. Consequently, from the War of 1812 to the development of international bombers in the 1950s, the American mainland was virtually invulnerable to attack. Great Britain has also been blessed by geography with an insular position removed from the European state system. Secure behind the English Channel (Britain has not been invaded since the time of William the Conqueror), the British were able to concentrate on naval power and expand into non-European territories, building a world power base largely on the periphery of the European balance of power.

But both the American and British examples also illustrate the impact of technology on location. Though the English Channel, at its narrowest point no more than twenty miles wide, was traditionally the crucial factor in the defense of the British Isles, thwarting the invasion schemes of Spain's Philip II and France's Napoleon, by the time of Adolf Hitler, the United Kingdom was all too vulnerable to aerial bombardment by the German *Luftwaffe* and the V-1 and V-2 rockets. Today a handful of ICBMs (intercontinental ballistic missiles) fitted with multiple warheads would effectively remove Britain from the ranks of the civilized nations of the world, as well as from the ranks of the major powers. The advantages accruing to the United States from its geographical isolation have similarly been nullified by advances in war technology. As late as World War II, not even the Japanese navy could strike at the American coast so long as the United States maintained a forward defense in the Pacific. But the value of both the Atlantic and Pacific oceans has been largely eclipsed in the nuclear age. Gone are the days when a warship would have to travel weeks or even months to reach North American shores. In a world of ICBMs and thermonuclear bombs, less than a half-hour's warning of impending attack can be expected.

Topography and territorial extent are also key factors in geographical capabilities. The internal terrain significantly affects every country's capability to deter or thwart military penetration.

Tiny but mountainous Switzerland, located in the heart of Western Europe, has preserved its neutrality in both world wars of this century. Though its location would otherwise have made it a valuable prize in the struggles for continental hegemony, ever since the late Middle Ages its treacherous mountainous terrain coupled with the mass mobilization of its citizen militia have made invasion an unattractive proposition. In contrast to Switzerland, we have the Low Countries. They are the invasion route between France and Germany and a potential staging area for an assault upon the British Isles; they have no natural barriers to invasion. These features have joined to invite, rather than deter, involvement in major European wars.

The sheer size of a country can defeat, if not prevent, attempts at subjugation. The vastness of Russia, which stretches a third of the way around the globe and consists of one-sixth of the earth's land mass, has proven too much for even the greatest of the modern would-be caesars to conquer. Napoleon's disastrous Russian campaign in 1812, which cost him virtually his entire Grand Army of 500,000 men, signaled the end of his quest for mastery of the European continent. A little over a century later, Hitler's desperate attempt to smash the Soviet state likewise led to disastrous defeat; the great expanse of Russia and its harsh winter climate stopped the Nazi onslaught at the gates of Moscow and turned the tide of military victory in the Second World War.

The size of a country can also affect its overall capabilities by denying or providing it with the natural resources which are the very sinews of a modern industrial state. Domestic sources of raw materials and energy insulate it from the inherent vulnerability of foreign dependence and buttress its self-sufficiency and freedom of action in world affairs. Naturally, mere size is no assurance of an abundance of natural resources; however, all other things held constant, the larger a state's territory, the more likely it is that it will contain a commensurate share of the earth's natural treasures, as well as the capacity to support larger populations, another attribute of state power. All considered, it appears that a state of great territorial extent has an edge in potential power over a relatively small state. (See figure 1.)

Figure 1

The Twenty-five Largest Countries in Terms of Area
(in square miles)

1	U.S.S.R.	8,649,490	14	Mexico	761,600
2	Canada	3,851,785	15	Iran	636,290
3	China	3,691,500	16	Mongolia	604,245
4	United States	3,615,198	17	Indonesia	575,893
5	Brazil	3,286,470	18	Peru	496,222
6	Australia	2,967,875	19	Chad	495,750
7	India	1,261,810	20	Niger	489,190
8	Argentina	1,072,065	21	Angola	481,350
9	Sudan	967,495	22	Mali	478,765
10	Algeria	919,590	23	South Africa	471,442
11	Zaire	905,560	24	Bolivia	424,160
12	Saudi Arabia	829,995	25	Colombia	439,735
13	Libya	679,358			

Source: Council on Foreign Relations

Natural Capabilities: Population

Throughout history, statesmen as well as political theorists have maintained that a rapidly growing population was crucial to the expansion of national power. Economists believed that population growth was essential to economic growth and prosperity. Throughout the latter part of the nineteenth century and well into the twentieth, for example, France's leaders were obsessed with the slow rate of French population growth in comparison with the German rate. During the period between the First and Second World Wars, the governments of the Axis states (Germany, Italy and Japan) initiated major programs to stimulate expansion of their population. The reasons for placing such importance upon the demographic factor are not difficult to fathom. The 1800s were the heyday of industrialization and nationalism in Europe. A vibrant and burgeoning population was necessary to run the factories and mines and expand the economic capabilities at the disposal of the state's leadership for furthering its national interests abroad. Moreover, the French Revolution had democratized warfare, replacing the small mercenary armies of the *ancien régime* with the mass citizen armies of the new age of nationalism and ideology. The transformation of the dynastic state into the truly national state greatly increased the potential power resources available to the new order for the pursuit of its foreign policy goals. The revolutionary decree of August 1793 instituted the levy en masse, and international politics would never again be the same. The decree read in part:

> . . . the French people are in permanent requisition for army service.
>
> The young men shall go to battle; married men shall forge arms and transport provisions; the women shall make tents and clothes, and shall serve in the hospitals; the children shall turn old linen into lint; the old men shall repair to the public places, to stimulate the courage of the warriors and to preach the unity of the Republic and hatred of kings.[30]

Thus began the era of total war and mobilization of entire populations for the purpose of international conflict.

It is only in recent years that students of world politics have come to realize that a large population may be a liability rather than an asset.[31] True, in the early 1800s Thomas Malthus warned that "[t]he power of population is so superior to the power of the earth to produce subsistence for man, that premature death must in some shape or other visit the human race." [32] But despite the grim forebodings of the "dismal science" of classical economics, mankind escaped overpopulation, and thus Malthus's prediction was eclipsed by boundless faith in man's technological genius to push back the natural limits imposed by a finite world. Then in the 1970s it became apparent that Malthus's day of reckoning had only been postponed. Rampant population growth was now seen as the "greatest single obstacle to the economic advancement of the majority of the peoples in the underdeveloped world." [33]

There can be little doubt that population can be a country's greatest resource. But the size of a state's population must be gauged in relation to the carrying capacity of its land and economy. Overpopulation is a relative, not an absolute, quality. Belgium and Holland are just about the most densely populated countries on earth, and yet they are quite prosperous and can by no measure be categorized as overpopulated. Similarly, the northeastern megalopolis of the United States—the great population belt stretching from Boston to Washington, D.C.—is over twice as densely populated as Holland (2,000 people per square mile), but boasts one of the world's highest standards of living.[34] A country may be said to be overpopulated in terms of national power if the size of its population detracts from its capabilities, that is, if the size of the population has crossed the threshold where additional increments in population constrain economic development. By the same token, a country may be considered underpopulated if an increase in growth would stimulate economic development and contribute to the general well-being of society.

Total population does indeed set limits on a state's power. No matter how prosperous the Belgians and Dutch may be, their influence in world affairs is severely constrained by the small size of their population, as well as by their limited territorial resource base. Canada, on the other hand, has a large territorial base (second only to that of the Soviet Union) but is constrained by a relatively small population (some 24 million); Australia is the sixth largest country in territory but has little more than half the population of Canada. At the other extreme, we have countries like India and China, where population size and growth seriously impede the process of development.

Population is a double-edged sword: Below a certain level, it can prevent realization of full power potential; but once a certain point is reached, additional people are problems, consuming more resources than they are able to produce. As the Organskis vividly suggest:

> Population is, indeed, a nation's greatest resource, though like other resources it may be squandered or misused. What greater asset can a nation have than a multitude of able bodied citizens, ready to stoke its furnaces, work its mines,

> run its machinery, harvest its crops, build its cities, raise its children, produce its art, and provide the vast array of goods and services that make a nation prosperous and content? On the other hand, what greater liability can a nation have than a mass of surplus people, living in hunger and poverty, scratching at tiny plots of land whose produce will not feed them all, swarming into the cities where there are no more jobs, living in huts or dying in the streets, sitting in apathy or smouldering with discontent, and ever begetting more children to share their misery.[35]

The Organskis believe that the size of the "effective population"—the economically productive portion of the population—is the best indicator of potential state power in the international system. Using this criterion, states may be ranked in order of the size of their effective populations. However, effectve population is, at best, but one crude indicator of demographic capabilities. One must also consider how effective the populations are. A relatively small effective population might well produce more than a larger effective population.

Obviously, there are factors in addition to population size, and even effective population size, that enter into the calculation of capabilities. It makes sense also to consider the quality of a population. A large population which is healthy, well fed, educated and skilled is the *sine qua non* of major-power status in the contemporary world. A populace with these attributes is an asset for any state. Israel is an excellent example of a small population (not much more than 3 million) which, because of the educated and skilled nature of its people, has managed to generate its military capabilities to fend off a hostile Arab world many times its size. The age distribution of a population is another important element. The effective population is drawn from the working-age population (which varies from country to country, but is usually somewhere in the 15–60 age group). A population that is either top-heavy with the very old or bottom-heavy with the very young is at a disadvantage, having a good portion of its people consuming part of the national product but unable to contribute to it. A country with an abundance of workers but a scarcity of capital may very well produce less than a country with many fewer workers, but a relatively large stock of capital.[36]

The total size of a population sets the limit for the size of its effective population, so a sizable population is necessary for major-power status. Figure 2 presents, in rank order, the largest states in terms of population and their growth rates. The quality of a people is obviously more difficult to measure. However, life expectancy, literacy and higher education, taken together, offer a reasonably useful qualitative index.

Natural Capabilities: Natural Resources

It is a fact of life that the earth's natural resources are unevenly distributed. Some countries, especially the continental-sized states, are relatively well endowed, while others, especially the smaller states, are lacking most or some key resources. It is also a fact of life that states consume these resources in uneven proportions, depending on the size of their national economies and their stages of development. Though a country may be relatively rich in natural wealth, its consumption may outstrip its domestic supply, making it dependent on foreign producers for the difference. This is the contemporary dilemma of the United States. In the early 1970s, the United States was the world's leading producer of over one-third of the most important minerals and a top producer of another third.[37] However, the huge, technologically advanced American economy has a voracious appetite and relies on imports for an increasing share of its raw materials. Of the eight most important metals, the United States is a large importer of seven; [38] it imports two-fifths of its oil and expects to import one-half by the early 1980s. Though until recently it was almost self-sufficient in the production of raw materials and energy, the United States is becoming more and more dependent on an increasingly fragile network of foreign supply.

Few countries have been so blessed with self-sufficiency. It is normal for a state to be more or less dependent on a host of other states for at least some of the necessary resources of modern industrial society. Dependence, however, implies vulnerability to

Figure 2
The Twenty Most Populous States
1975

Rank	State	Population	Annual Growth Rate %	Doubling Time (years) *
1	People's Republic of China	838,500,000	1.7	40
2	India	598,215,000	2.1	32
3	U.S.S.R.	254,390,000	1.0	68
4	United States	213,500,000	0.9	76
5	Indonesia	127,650,000	2.6	26
6	Japan	111,000,000	1.3	52
7	Brazil	107,115,000	2.8	24
8	Bangladesh	76,780,000	3.6	19
9	Pakistan	69,710,000	3.6	19
10	Nigeria	62,924,000	2.7	25
11	Federal Republic of Germany (West Germany)	62,040,000	0.7	98
12	Mexico	60,150,000	3.5	20
13	United Kingdom	56,100,000	0.3	230
14	Italy	55,810,000	0.8	86
15	France	52,900,000	0.9	76
16	Thailand	42,270,000	3.2	21
17	Philippines	41,750,000	3.0	22
18	Turkey	39,150,000	2.5	27
19	Egypt	37,240,000	2.2	31
20	Poland	34,055,000	0.9	76

SOURCE: *United Nations Demographical Yearbook, 1976.*

* Doubling Time denotes the number of years in which a population will double in size based upon present growth rates.

disruption of supply and, therefore, to political pressure from suppliers even in peacetime. And the more dependent a country is, the more vulnerable it is.

The contrast between the international positions of the Soviet Union and Japan is instructive. The U.S.S.R., with its vast territory, claims to have one-half of the world's coal reserves and is known to possess extremely large deposits of oil and natural gas and a great potential for hydroelectric power; it is the first or second leading producer of at least seventeen of the twenty-three most important minerals, and is the only major industrial power with a sizable surplus of petroleum and nonfuel minerals available for export.*[39] In comparison, Japan has long outgrown its domestic raw material and energy base. It can sustain its advanced economy only by importing the bulk of its needed resources. It imports 86 percent of its energy, 92 percent of its iron ore, 59 percent of its bituminous coal, 84 percent of its copper and 100 percent of its bauxite. Japan is the world's largest importer of food, producing only 40 percent of what it consumes and depending on overseas sources for wheat (95 percent), soybeans (96 percent), livestock feed (47 percent) and some varieties of seafood (85 percent).[40] In short, Japanese power in world affairs is severely circumscribed by its limited resource base and concomitant reliance on producing countries. This was painfully demonstrated by the Arab oil embargo of 1973 and the accompanying fourfold increase in the price of petroleum. The Japanese economy had a zero, or even negative, rate of growth in the following years, in sharp contrast to its spectacular ten percent annual growth rate for the preceding decade.

During the Arab oil embargo, the interdependence between Tokyo and the Persian Gulf producers was distinctly lopsided; the Japanese were not in a position to either retaliate or deter. Resource dependence limits a state's freedom of action in conducting its foreign policy, and it is questionable whether Japan can

* A recent study by the CIA, however, predicts that Soviet oil production will decline by the early 1980s, making the U.S.S.R. dependent on external sources of supply. (*Christian Science Monitor*, April 25, 1977, p. 1.)

evolve into a truly independent global actor. Much the same might be said of the major Western European states. West Germany, the United Kingdom and France, though major economic powers in terms of gross national product, are similarly dependent on foreign sources of raw materials and energy, and also must depend on vulnerable sea routes for transportation. Their crucial oil supply lines run from the Indian Ocean around the Cape of Good Hope and into the eastern Atlantic, or across the Mediterranean.[41] Given Europe's limited military capabilities and Russia's growing naval presence in the Mediterranean, Indian Ocean and eastern Atlantic, these countries must rely upon the United States to defend their vital transportation links. When industrial states have to base their prosperity on the goodwill of various producers and the protection of an ally, their independent action in the international arena is considerably abridged.

In former times, major powers were careful to bring into their political orbits areas of the globe that supplied them with necessary resources. During the scramble for colonies in the late nineteenth century, the European powers assured themselves access to resources by annexing the vast producing regions of the world. With the demise of imperialism following the Second World War and the rise of nationalism in the emergent nations, the former colonial powers lost control over their sources of raw materials just as they were becoming more dependent on them.

In the contemporary international system, the asymmetry of power between imperial power and colony has been replaced by a new relationship of reciprocal influence between the consumers and producers of natural resources. Technologically advanced societies need nine nonfuel minerals, which account for 85 percent of the value of all nonfuel minerals traded internationally: iron ore, bauxite, copper, manganese, lead, nickel, phosphate, zinc and tin.[42] In addition, of course, oil is a crucial ingredient in industrial economies for the forseeable future. The Arab producers alone have 60 percent of the proven world reserves of petroleum and the lion's share of probable reserves as well. Other Third World countries account for a large share of certain mineral exports: Malaysia for half of the tin and nearly two-fifths of the rubber;[43] Surinam and Guyana in Latin America for bauxite; Zambia, Zaire,

Chile and Peru for copper; India, Liberia, Mauritania and Sierra Leone for iron ore.[44] The global market shares of the four largest Third World producers are substantial in: tin (82 percent), petroleum (52 percent), copper (61 percent), rubber (60 percent) and iron ore (30 percent).[45] However, it is unlikely that producers' cartels emulating OPEC (the Organization of Petroleum Exporting Countries) will be able to exert commensurate influence in world politics, for a number of important reasons: oil is much more essential to the vitality of the developed world than the other minerals; oil is irreplaceable in the short run while other minerals can more readily be stockpiled, substituted, or recycled; nonfuel resources are more widely distributed and are found in relative abundance in a number of developed exporting countries (e.g., Australia, Canada and South Africa). It appears highly unlikely that any cartel will be in a position to strangle the rest of the world into submission.[46]

The most basic resource of all is food. Prior to World War II, every major region of the globe with the exception of western Europe was a net exporter of grain. Today, only three nations (the United States, Canada and Australia) are net exporters. The United States is becoming the world's breadbasket, controlling a proportion of the world's exportable foodstuffs greater than the Arabs' share of oil exports. Iowa alone produces more corn than the second-largest world producer—China—and Kansas and North Dakota produce more wheat than Canada and Australia combined.[47] The United States is the largest exporter of rice as well, accounting for about one-third of the volume traded internationally,[48] and also exports nearly five hundred other food products. One hundred and fifty countries—nearly every state in the international system—must import American food (principally grain), and with such a global dependence upon the United States, a number of analysts have begun to speak of *agripower.* In 1974, the Central Intelligence Agency issued a report which suggested that, "as custodian of the bulk of the world's exportable grain, the United States might regain the primacy in world affairs that it held in the immediate postwar period."[49] In the same year, President Ford made thinly veiled threats of a counterembargo against Arab countries participating in an oil embargo against the United States: agripower would confront petropower.

Just as food surpluses may be America's ace in the hole in future international conflict, chronic shortages may develop into the Soviet Union's Achilles' heel. Despite its vast territory, the U.S.S.R. is plagued by a much more unfavorable climate and environment than North America. Agriculture in the Soviet Union accounts for the labor of nearly 30 percent of the working population and absorbs about one-quarter of total Soviet investment. And yet the United States, with under 4 percent of its population and total investment devoted to the land, produces twice as much grain, potatoes and sugar beets.[50] The Soviets are unable to support their goal of higher per capita food consumption for their people without turning to massive imports from the capitalist world. Food shortages in the Soviet Union do not appear to be the result of temporary problems and can be expected to continue in the foreseeable future. Nature, of course, is not the sole determinant of food production; organizational efficiency and technological capabilities are also crucial. The remarkable amount of American productivity derives not simply from a favorable physical environment, but also from a massive investment in machines and fertilizer. Centralized planning and collectivized agriculture in the Soviet Union are major causes of inefficiency in production. As one Soviet citizen is reputed to have remarked: "If the Sahara were collectivized, they would soon be importing sand."[51] Food production is a good illustration of the important interrelationship between natural and societal capabilities.

Given societal capabilities, natural resources are not static variables in the equation of world power. They represent a potential which may be exploited and utilized in the pursuit of influence abroad. In the case of oil, for example, development of North Sea reserves may make Britain self-sufficient in energy for some time in the 1980s and somewhat relieve Middle East political pressure on all of western Europe. And the People's Republic of China, which is developing the technology for offshore drilling, may very well become a major exporter of energy, thereby gaining a positive sanction to dispense or withhold in its dealing with various states, notably Japan.[52]

Societal Capabilities: Industry and Technology

Economic capabilities are the prerequisite for major-power status in the contemporary international system. Naturally, the wealthiest state may not always be the most influential (witness the American role in world politics during the interwar years), but it can be among the most powerful if it chooses to devote a significant portion of its national product to furthering its national interest abroad.

Though the relative size of a country's gross national product is usually employed as an index of economic capabilities, GNP is a statistical measure of the "total output of goods and services produced by residents of a country and valued at market prices ultimately paid by the consumer."[53] GNP does not make provision for disparities of purchasing power, and it includes a host of entries (advertising, cosmetics, alcohol, etc.) that have little relation to the importance of a country in international relations. It does not tell us what proportion of a nation's wealth is devoted to its foreign policy or how effective that policy is. Like all capabilities, GNP merely suggests the power potential of a state—how much it would be able to devote to foreign policy if it were so inclined.

In many ways, per capita GNP is a better gauge of economic capabilities than total GNP. Though a small total GNP may set limits to potential influence abroad, a large total GNP may be canceled out by overpopulation. By the sheer size of its economy, China is a major economic power, but the bulk of its production must be used to satisfy the elementary needs of its huge population. It stands to reason that the further a national population is above the subsistence level, the greater the potential resources available for the pursuit of influence abroad.

However, this serves only as a crude index of potential power, for the amount of production that will be diverted from domestic consumption depends upon another factor. Ability to sacrifice and willingness to sacrifice are two different things. From the very beginning of its military involvement in Indochina, the United States government perceived that public opinion would never support the venture if it required a cutback in domestic consumption and so pursued a policy geared to providing both guns and butter. Therefore, though the United States (with a 1972 per capita GNP of $5,546) could easily sustain a cut in living standards, it was not willing to make the sacrifice. On the other hand, North Vietnam, one of the poorest countries in the world, accepted a full 50 percent reduction in per capita GNP during the course of the war (from $122 in 1964 to $66 in 1972).[54] A relatively high per capita GNP reflects potential for diverting domestic resources to the pursuit of international goals; whether this potential can be operationalized depends upon the ability of the government in question to mobilize this economic dividend.

Qualitative aspects of economic capabilities are also important. Even among relatively wealthy states, technological proficiency may be crucial, though it is not readily reflected in national income statistics. There is a technology gap in the international system and it affects developed as well as developing states. The United States not only is by far the largest economy in the world, but it also has an impressive lead in technology over the rest of the industrialized countries. By the mid-1970s, the United States was spending well over $20 billion dollars a year on research and development and was investing the talents of over a half-million scientists and engineers. The Soviet Union, western Europe, and Japan continue to lag behind, especially in such high-technology industries as electronics, computers and chemicals.[55] Though the U.S.S.R. holds a sizable quantitative lead in many areas of military policy, it suffers from a qualitative inferiority to Western technology, and a recent study by the National Science Foundation found the United States' lead in technology eroding, citing the relative increase in foreign inventors receiving American patents, foreign improvements in worker productivity and the recent decline in United States spending on research and development as a proportion of total GNP.[56] However, though the United States' lead may decrease in the years ahead, there is no indication that it will lose its predominance in the foreseeable future.

A ranking of states in terms of economic capabilities (as measured by GNP, Figure 3) coincides closely with the distribution of actual influence in global politics and parallels the world hierarchy of military capabilities as measured by military expenditure (see Figure 4). If we compare these two lists we discover that many of the foremost military powers are also among the top ten economic

Figure 3

The Twenty Largest States in Terms of Gross National Product (GNP) 1975

Rank	State	GNP (in US $)	Per Capita GNP (in US $)
1	United States	1,520,000,000,000	7136
2	U.S.S.R.	870,000,000,000	3421
3	Japan	507,000,000,000	4567
4	West Germany	406,000,000,000	6544
5	China	299,000,000,000	320
6	France	284,000,000,000	5358
7	United Kingdom	192,000,000,000	3660
8	Italy	158,000,000,000	2829
9	Canada	157,000,000,000	6883
10	Brazil	110,000,000,000	1028
11	India	99,700,000,000	162
12	Spain	94,400,000,000	2659
13	Poland	85,400,000,000	2511
14	Australia	78,200,000,000	5780
15	Netherlands	75,300,000,000	5513
16	Sweden	61,500,000,000	7505
17	East Germany	60,300,000,000	3571
18	Mexico	60,100,000,000	1014
19	Belgium	58,100,000,000	5933
20	Czechoslovakia	54,500,000,000	3681

SOURCE: U.S. Arms Control and Disarmament Agency.

powers. This supplies it with the wherewithal to build a modern military establishment.

The capital investment involved in today's armed forces is truly astounding. One super nuclear aircraft carrier equipped with one hundred or so aircraft costs $5 billion dollars—the equivalent of over half the entire gross national product of Bangladesh—not including the cost of operating the ship and supporting its six-thousand-man crew.[57] Only countries with huge GNPs, like the superpowers, can afford such massive investments. The major oil exporting countries of the Persian Gulf recently have opted to purchase the most advanced military hardware. Between 1972 and 1975, Iran tripled its national income and was therefore able to increase its military expenditures. But advanced industrial technology is also a potent element of military capability. Though many states may have the money to acquire sophisticated weapons systems, only a half-dozen countries are able to design and manufacture their own first-rate military equipment for every non-nuclear role. All others remain dependent upon other states for their initial supplies, spare parts and technical expertise, and thus lack fundamental military self-sufficiency.

Economic capabilities are not used for coercive sanctions only; a wealthy state can utilize its industrial productivity and technological skills as an attractive form of influence as well. Such a state is in a position to extend its defense umbrella over militarily weaker allies and can supply these clients with military material and technical expertise. In both instances, military aid is being used in a persuasive, rather than a coercive, manner. During the last decade, more than one hundred countries have had to rely upon arms imports from a few advanced states: the United States (which accounted for 51 percent of world military exports); the Soviet Union (27 percent); Britain, France and China (10 percent); Czechoslovakia, Poland, Canada and West Germany (9 percent).[58] By the middle of the 1970s, the United States alone was exporting some $10 billion-worth of arms annually. World military expenditures increased from $285 billion in 1966 to about $345 billion by 1975.[59]

But as the Middle East war of October 1973 vividly demonstrated, mere possession of sophisticated weapons is not enough to

Figure 4

The Twenty Largest States in Terms of Military Expenditures 1975

Rank	State	Mil. Expen. (in US $)	as % of GNP	Per Capita GNP	Total Armed Forces
1	U.S.S.R.	103,800,000,000	10.6	409	3,575,000
2	United States	92,800,000,000	6.0	430	2,130,000
3	China	17,000,000,000*	7.6	20	3,250,000
4	West Germany	12,669,000,000	3.6	260	495,000
5	France	10,838,000,000	3.4	233	502,000
6	Iran	10,405,000,000	9.0	314	250,000
7	United Kingdom	9,974,000,000	5.2	184	345,000
8	Saudi Arabia	6,343,000,000	15.0	712	47,000
9	Egypt	6,103,000,000	22.8	163	322,000
10	Japan	4,484,000,000	0.9	41	236,000
11	Italy	3,891,000,000	2.8	76	421,000
12	Israel	3,503,000,000	32.0	1,043	400,000**
13	Netherlands	2,936,000,000	3.4	215	112,500
14	Canada	2,665,000,000	2.0	129	77,000
15	India	2,660,000,000	2.8	4	956,000
16	Sweden	2,475,000,000	3.6	298	750,000***
17	East Germany	2,333,000,000	5.4	137	143,000
18	Australia	2,331,000,000*	3.2	179	69,100
19	Turkey	2,174,000,000	3.7	55	453,000
20	Poland	2,170,000,000	3.6	65	293,000

SOURCE: London Institute for Strategic Studies.

* 1974.
** Total mobilized within 72 hours.
*** Total mobilized strength.

confer upon states an independent role in world affairs. Quite the contrary; the amazing rate at which these weapons were consumed put the combatants at the mercy of their suppliers—the arms "pushers." Few states have the capacity to wage sustained warfare—even with conventional (nonnuclear), arms—without being critically dependent upon other actors. Dependence, it will be recalled, translates into influence for the wielder of sanctions.

Societal Capabilities: Military Forces

In a primitive political system where force remains the policy of last resort, military capabilities must assume a prominent role in the equation of world power. A discussion of military power must inevitably focus on the balance of forces between the two superpowers, because the gap between them and all other states so clearly affects the contemporary international environment. Comparison of the defense establishments of the United States and the Soviet Union shows the difficulties inherent in measuring power and also that different countries need different kinds of military capabilities.

The bases of a quantitative comparison are the data presented in Figure 4. Figure 4 presents, in rank order, the states with the largest expenditures for military forces in 1975. The U.S.S.R. spends more on its defense effort than does the United States. It has many more troops under arms and boasts a significant lead in the number of strategic delivery vehicles (see appendix) as well as in the gross throw-weight (the megatonnage that it can deliver on American targets). In addition, it has larger surface and underwater fleets, though the United States has an edge in manpower and naval aircraft. (The secondary military powers—Britain, France and China—lag far behind the superpowers in nearly all categories.)

Since the war in Vietnam, a notable decline has occurred in the American defense effort. In 1975, the United States was spending about 6 percent of its GNP for military preparedness; the equivalent figure for 1963 was nearly 9.9 percent.[60] Meanwhile, the U.S.S.R., with a national product less than three-fifths that of the United States, has been investing nearly twice as much of its GNP on military capabilities. During the 1960s, the Soviet Union expanded its armed forces in both conventional and strategic areas.[61] Soviet spending has been increasing by an annual rate of at least 3 percent while American expenditures have been decreasing. There has been an absolute decline in American capabilities in a number of quantitative areas, for example, since the early 1960s, military manpower has been reduced by over 20 percent and the number of naval vessels by a full 50 percent.[62]

These facts cannot be used to determine whether the Soviet Union is actually more powerful than the United States. The armed forces of the two superpowers are asymmetrical in composition because of the differing geopolitical positions of the two countries and the resulting divergence in military goals. Though the Soviets have more men under arms, about a half-million of these troops are deployed along the Chinese border and do not directly threaten Western security.[63] These forces, along with the KGB and MVD (border and internal security paramilitary troops), have accounted for about one-quarter of the increase in Soviet military spending over the last decade. On the U.S.S.R.'s western front, the 100,000 additional Soviet troops moved to eastern Europe have been largely offset by the expansion of the West German army by 80,000 men.[64] In regard to naval expansion, in recent years the number of new Soviet ships built has declined substantially, and if this trend continues the Soviet fleet will level off at about 435 combat and auxiliary ships instead of the present 750. The United States currently has a flotilla of about 480 ships, with naval goals of a 600-ship fleet by the mid-1980s.[65] The American navy has much greater firepower and long-range endurance than its Russian counterpart. Despite the Soviet lead in strategic launch vehicles, the United States retains a quantitative edge in the number of warheads and a qualitative lead in accuracy. Even under the worst imaginable conditions, enough of the American strategic force would survive to drop thirteen thermonuclear bombs on every Soviet city of more than 100,000 people.[66] The ability to deter nuclear attack is absolute and not relative to the numerical superiority of the opponent.

A good deal of the confusion concerning which is the superior military power stems from the variety of measures employed to gauge military spending. In making interstate comparisons of military expenditures, a common denominator must be found. Until recently, the CIA estimated that military spending absorbed 6 to 8 percent of the U.S.S.R.'s GNP, while the Pentagon's DIA (Defense Intelligence Agency) estimated that it was at least 15 percent. In 1976, the CIA doubled its previous estimate after revising its methods of determining the costs of defense programs in the Soviet Union. The new figures indicated that Soviet defense spending was growing at an annual rate of 5 percent instead of 3 percent.[67] This is a classical instance of the difficulties involved in measuring and comparing national capabilities even when quantitative factors are central to the power equation. Who is outspending whom will ultimately depend upon the yardstick used. According to CIA testimony before Congressional committees in 1976, Soviet defense spending for the previous year was about 42 percent higher than United States' expenditures if estimated in dollars, and when estimated in rubles, about 29 percent higher.[68]

The debate over whether the United States or the Soviet Union is number one is irrelevant because it addresses itself to the wrong question, a question, moreover, that cannot be answered because of the asymmetries of military capabilities and national objectives. It is more important to understand what the respective military capabilities of the two superpowers will allow them to accomplish in their mutual relations. For some years, both sides have been more than able to deter a rational adversary from initiating nuclear war or esclating any conventional conflict that might lead to a nuclear confrontation. The military forces of both sides in Europe, the area where the vital interests of the superpowers most clearly overlap, have led to a distribution of forces that makes military aggression grossly unattractive.

In other regions, however, the relative increase in Soviet capabilities has altered former patterns of superpower influence. The U.S.S.R. has emerged as a truly global military power—which was not so a decade or so ago—and is able to project its military forces into areas traditionally the preserve of the United States. The expansion of Soviet naval forces into the Mediterranean, the Indian Ocean, the Far East and even the Eastern Atlantic portends the extension of Soviet influence into the contiguous land areas. More and more in coming years, the Soviet Union will be in a position to deter American intervention by threatening counterintervention. With this newfound ability to "show the flag" throughout the contested areas in the developing world, the U.S.S.R. can be expected to increase its status as a global challenger to the United States and to reinforce its commitments to political allies. But the logic that will constrain American intervention will also check similar moves by the U.S.S.R. In the end, the absolute increase in both sides' capabilities is likely to lead to mutual restraint and deterrence—a stalemate—and thus allow greater freedom of action for the smaller states in these geographical regions. Increasing capabilities may well lead to decreasing influence for both sides.

Governmental Capabilities: Political Leadership and Organization

In addition to the tangible assets of state power deriving from an international actor's natural and social environment, there is the variable of political development. Governmental capabilities include both the level of political organization of a state and the quality of its individual leaders. These aspects of a national political system are crucial ingredients in the equation of state power. A country with a stable political structure, a dynamic ideology and an effective governing elite will be able to maximize its power potential and exploit its influence abroad. Conversely, a country plagued by chronic internal upheaval, devoid of political purpose and lacking in able leadership will founder in world politics, regardless of its other capabilities. Much as the managers of a corporation are the collective hub of the entire process of maximizing production and profits, the political core of a state can maximize its influence abroad by integrating all the other factors of national power into a coherent and effective foreign policy. Ultimately, a society's political organization determines whether the elements of national capability are to be utilized, coordinated and developed to their full potential. And it is the political leadership which must demonstrate the will to pursue the external objectives of the state in its international environment.

There can be little doubt that individual policy makers can be great assets to their national community. Though we must be careful to avoid the pitfalls of the "great man" interpretation of history, we can still identify outstanding statesmen who have done much to increase the stature and influence of their nations abroad. In many ways, it was one man, Charles de Gaulle, who brought France out of its postwar period of decay and stagnation and allowed it to reenter the ranks of the major world powers. De Gaulle restored order and discipline to a turbulent French society, liquidated the debilitating remnants of colonial empire, asserted leadership of the European Economic Community (EEC), developed a limited nuclear strike force and challenged the predominance of both superpowers on the European continent. In short, de Gaulle's vision of French glory and destiny in world affairs allowed France to exploit to the hilt its limited power potential, and even to exercise influence disproportionate to its objective capabilities.[69] (See chapter 7 for a more extensive discussion of de Gaulle's policy toward the United States.) An even greater impact on world politics was made by Nikolai Lenin, whose leadership of a small but closely knit band of revolutionaries armed with a potent and radical ideology led him to the pinnacle of power in the huge but moribund Russian empire. Under his organizational genius, Russian society was restructured and the rule of the Communist party became all-encompassing. Working with the same natural resources (both physical and human) as the czars, Lenin, and his successor Stalin, transformed backward Russia into a modern and powerful Soviet state and laid claim to the mantle of world revolutionary leadership.

The list of notable world figures who have molded the destinies of nations and consequently altered the distribution of global power can be expanded considerably. One has only to think of the great national leaders of the twentieth century (Churchill, Roosevelt, Mao, Nehru and so forth) to grasp their significance in the equation of world power. Especially in the newly emergent nations that have gained their independence since World War II, the charismatic leader has been crucial. Such states, which often lack unity, self-identity, economic viability and political infrastructure, have been largely dependent upon the organizational prowess of men of uncommon ability. Ho Chi Minh in Vietnam, Nasser in Egypt and Sukarno in Indonesia. Men such as these have not only brought a semblance of domestic stability to their lands, but they have enabled these states to attain disproportionate influence in the Third World.

Ideology, organization and individual leadership are the components of political development. Collectively, these governmental capabilities function as a power-conversion process. The role of the 1949 Communist revolution in China in modernizing the Chinese state is instructive. With its vast population (one-fifth of the human race) and potentially rich natural resources, China has always been a giant among nations—though a giant of largely untapped power potential. Prior to the consolidation of Communist rule on the mainland, China was plagued for decades by civil war, foreign invasion and economic chaos. Though it is first in population, third in area, located in a temperate zone and well endowed with natural resources, China was the victim of poverty and underdevelopment, and was thus fair game for exploitation by more powerful states. Within three years of seizing the reins of government, the Communists had restored order, checked rampant inflation and doubled industrial production. Starting with an economic base comparable to that of neighboring India, the People's Republic of China (PRC) far surpassed India within a decade in virtually all areas of economic and industrial performance, and soon emerged as the world's fifth largest economy and third largest consumer of energy.[70] By the early 1970s, some estimates suggested a prodigious economic growth rate of 10 percent annually. And while the rate of population growth has been reduced dramatically since 1949, the quality of the vast population has been greatly improved. Though China is still a poor land, widespread starvation and malnutrition have been arrested, and literacy rates have increased admirably. To be sure, the PRC is still a minor economic power when compared with the developed countries of the world, having an industrial capacity comparable to that of Belgium or the Netherlands.[71] Despite its sheer size, it can still be characterized accurately as a "second-rate power at best."[72] Nevertheless, the progress of modernization in China is certainly a proof of its new political organization and leadership. The social discipline and solidarity inspired by its rigorous collectivist ideology and the total mobilization of the masses in pursuit of common goals are a reflection of its national leadership's commitment both to economic development and the establishment of the PRC as a great power. Ideology, organization and leadership (especially that of Mao Tse-tung and Chou En-lai) have been the principle reasons for the resurgence of modern China.

THE CHANGING EQUATION OF WORLD POWER

Our survey of the foundations of national capabilities reveals that the study of international politics is characterized by inherent subtleties and ambiguities calculated to disappoint those who grasp too arrogantly at an understanding of human behavior. Power remains elusive and at times confusing. Though they are intimately related, power as influence differs from power as capability—and both, by their very nature, defy precise measurement. Even capabilities, which more readily lend themselves to quantification and comparison, can be gauged only in a tentative and crude fashion.

The study of state power gives us neither a neat index of the distribution of national capabilities nor a clear pattern of international influence. A survey of capabilities reveals potential power in the international system. But the elements of national power are not static parameters, they are dynamic variables, the relative values of which are in a constant state of flux. Not very long ago, for instance, steel production was an excellent measure of capabilities, inasmuch as steel functioned as the backbone of industrial society. Today, however, advanced technology is the prime gauge of economic capabilities. Until recently, the possession of raw materials made the developing nations natural prey to militarily superior countries. Now they can utilize these supplies to influence the behavior of their former suzerains. Military capabilities have receded in significance in the contemporary equation of world power. As former Secretary of State Henry Kissinger has stated: "Never before in history have the elements of military power been so vast, so ready, so dangerous—and so ill-suited to political objectives." [73]

Though in the past, military capabilities may have been easily translated into international influence, the world is now much more complex. The military stalemate between the superpowers has allowed other elements of national power to come to the foreground, especially economic capabilities. Western military intervention in the energy- and raw-material-producing countries is unlikely, not only because of Soviet capability to thwart such moves, but also because of the rise of nationalism in these developing countries. The days are long gone when small Western expeditionary forces could pacify and dominate vast areas of the globe, as attested to by the American experience in Indochina. Similarly, Soviet military expansion into power vacuums adjacent to the U.S.S.R. is deterred. Thus, economic and social issues have moved to the center of interstate conflict, intruding upon areas of "high foreign policy," once the exclusive preserve of military security issues.[74] Consequently, with the rise of nonsecurity issues in world politics, the nature of international influence itself has been altered. Force, though still the ultimate sanction in an anarchic environment, has become less useful, as other forms of influence (revolving around the use of coercive and persuasive economic sanctions) have become more useful in affecting the behavior of other actors.[75] As a result, the distribution of influence in the international system will be more subtle and diffuse, and intricate economic bargaining will sometimes supplant the perennial brandishing of the military big stick. It is not that power will become any less important in the global political process. Quite the contrary. Yet the nature of power is undergoing a transformation.

Notes
Chapter 3

1. Harold D. Lasswell and Abraham Kaplan, *Power and Society: A Framework for Political Inquiry* (New Haven, Conn.: Yale University Press, 1950), p. 75.

2. Hans J. Morgenthau, *Politics Among Nations: The Struggle for Power and Peace,* 5th ed. (New York: Knopf, 1973), p. 27.

3. Winston S. Churchill, *The Second World War,* vol. 6: *Triumph and Tragedy* (New York: Bantam, 1962), pp. 196–197.

4. For an interesting discussion of the differences between income and wealth, see Lester C. Thurow, "Tax Wealth, Not Income," *New York Times Magazine,* April 11, 1976.

5. Hans J. Morgenthau, *Truth and Power: Essays of a Decade, 1960–1970* (New York: Praeger, 1970), p. 243.

6. For example, see William Riker, "Some Ambiguities in the Nature of Power," *American Political Science Review* 58 (1964); 341–49; also, James G. March, "The Power of Power," in David Easton, ed., *Varieties of Political Theory* (Englewood Cliffs, N.J.: Prentice-Hall, 1966), pp. 39–70.

7. David V. J. Bell, *Power, Influence, and Authority* (New York: Oxford University Press, 1975), chapter 1.

8. Jack H. Nagel, *The Descriptive Analysis of Power* (New Haven, Conn.: Yale University Press, 1975), chapters 2 and 3.

9. Carl J. Friedrich, *Constitutional Government and Democracy* (New York: Harper and Bros., 1937); see also the discussion by Nagel, *Descriptive Analysis,* chapters 2 and 3.

10. Robert A. Dahl, *Modern Political Analysis,* 3rd ed. (Englewood Cliffs, N.J.: Prentice-Hall, 1976), pp. 30–32.

11. See the discussion by Nagel, *Descriptive Analysis,* part II.

12. Frederick L. Schuman, *International Politics: Anarchy and Order in the World Society,* 7th ed. (New York: McGraw-Hill, 1969), pp. 170–72.

13. U.S. Arms Control and Disarmament Agency, *World Military Expenditures and Arms Transfers, 1965–1974* (Washington, D.C.: GPO, 1975), pp. 50–51.

14. *New York Times,* December 11, 1975, p. 3.

15. Ibid., October 19, 1975, p. 1.

16. Ibid., August 2, 1976, p. 1; *Christian Science Monitor,* August 3, 1976, p. 1.

17. *Christian Science Monitor,* August 13, 1976, p. 2.

18. See Richard A. Aliano, *American Defense Policy from Eisenhower to Kennedy: The Politics of Changing Military Requirements, 1957–1961* (Athens: Ohio University Press, 1975).

19. Johan Galtung, "East-West Interaction Patterns," *Journal of*

Peace Research (1966): 146–77; idem, "Rank and Social Integration: A Multi-Dimensional Approach," in Joseph Berger, et al, eds., *Sociological Theories in Progress* (Boston: Houghton-Mifflin, 1966). See also, J. David Singer and Melvin Small, "The Composition and Status Ordering of the International System, 1815–1940," *World Politics* 18 (January 1966), pp. 232–53.

20. Norman J. Padelford, George A. Lincoln, and Lee D. Olvey, *The Dynamics of International Politics,* 3rd ed. (New York: Macmillan, 1976), chapter 1.

21. A. F. K. Organski, *World Politics,* 2nd ed. (New York: Knopf, 1968), chapter 14. For an early and influential discussion of the differential spread of industrialization, see W. W. Rostow, *The Stages of Economic Growth: A Non-Communist Manifesto* (New York: Cambridge University Press, 1960).

22. For example: Irving L. Horowitz, *Three Worlds of Development: The Theory and Practice of International Stratification* (New York: Oxford University Press, 1966); Charlotte Waterlow, *Superpowers and Victims: The Outlook for World Community* (Englewood Cliffs, N.J.: Prentice-Hall, 1974). Two texts which developed this theme are Richard W. Sterling, *Macropolitics: International Relations in a Global Society* (New York: Knopf, 1974); and David J. Finlay and Thomas Hovet, Jr., *7304: International Relations on thc Planet Earth* (New York: Harper & Row, 1975).

23. Padelford, et al., *Dynamics,* p. 18.

24. Hans J. Morgenthau refers to states which seek to overturn a political order as "imperialist" *(Politics Among Nations,* chapter 5). Though Morgenthau certainly uses the term in an acceptable and consistent fashion, in today's lexicon of international affairs, the term tends to create needless confusion. This is the case because of contemporary ideological polemics, which equate *imperialism* (in this instance to be read as *neocolonialism)* with the status quo. Therefore, we will avoid the use of the term in this context.

25. *New York Times,* April 11, 1975, section 4, p. 3.

26. Roderick Peattie, *Geography in Human Destiny* (New York: George W. Stewart, 1940), p. 19.

27. Ibid.

28. For example, see J. H. G. Lebon, *An Introduction to Human*

Geography (New York: Capricorn, 1966), chapters 11 and 12.

29. See, for example, William Van Royen and Nels A. Bengsten, *Fundamentals of Economic Geography* (Englewood Cliffs, N.J.: Prentice-Hall, 1964); and George F. Carter, *Man and the Land: A Cultural Geography* (New York: Holt, Rinehart & Winston, 1968).

30. Cited in Daniel B. Ralston, ed., *Soldiers and States: Civil-Military Relations in Modern Europe* (Boston: D. C. Heath, 1966), p. 66.

31. However, as early as the Chou Dynasty (c. 500 B.C.), the Chinese philosopher Han Fei-Tzu observed the relationship between fecundity and prosperity: "In ancient times, people were few but wealthy and without strife. People at present think five sons are not too many, and each son has five sons also and before the death of the grandfather there are already twenty-five descendants. Therefore, people are more and wealth is less; they work hard and receive little. The life of a nation depends upon enough food, not upon the number of people." (Quoted in Garrett Hardin, *Population, Evolution and Birth Control* [San Francisco: W.H. Freeman, 1969], p. 18.)

32. Ibid, p. 15.

33. Richard L. Clinton, *Population and Politics* (Lexington, Mass.: D. C. Heath, 1973), p. 153.

34. Jean Mayer, "Toward a Non-Malthusian Population Policy," *Columbia Forum* 12 (Summer 1969); reprinted in Daniel Callahan, ed., *The American Population Debate* (Garden City, N.Y.: Doubleday, 1971), pp. 135–53.

35. Katherin and A. F. K. Organski, *Population and World Power* (New York: Knopf, 1961), pp. 3–4.

36. See Timothy King, *Population Policies and Economic Development* (Baltimore: Johns Hopkins University Press, 1974).

37. J. P. Cole, *Geography in World Affairs,* 4th ed. (Baltimore: Penguin Books, 1974), chart p. 162.

38. Yuan-li Wu, *Raw Material Supply in a Multipolar World* (New York: Crane, Russak, 1973), p. 9.

39. Cole, *Geography,* chapter 16.

40. Saburo Okita, "Natural Resources Dependency and Japanese Foreign Policy," *Foreign Affairs* 52 (July 1974): 714–24.

41. See the discussion in Wu, *Raw Material Supply,* chapter 3.

42. Bension Varon and Kenji Takeuchi, "Developing Countries and Non-Fuel Minerals," *Foreign Affairs* 52 (April 1974): 497–510.

43. C. Fred Bergsten, "The Threat is Real," *Foreign Policy* 14 (Spring 1974): 88.

44. Wu, *Raw Material Supply,* chapter 2.

45. Stephen D. Krasner, "Oil is the Exception," *Foreign Policy* 14 (Spring 1974): 76.

46. For a discussion of the likely effectiveness of nonpetroleum producers' cartels, see Varon and Takeuchi, *Developing Countries;* Krasner, "Oil"; Bergsten, "Threat"; Zuhayr Mikdashi, "Collusion Could Work," *Foreign Policy* 14 (Spring 1974): 57–67; James E. Akins, "The Oil Crisis: The Times of the World Is Here," *Foreign Affairs 51* (April 1973): 462–90; C. Fred Bergsten, "The Threat from the Third World," *Foreign Policy* 11 (Summer 1973): 102–24.

47. *Christian Science Monitor,* May 10, 1976, p. 4.

48. Ibid., February 11, 1976, p. 6.

49. Cited in Emma Rothschild, "Food Politics," *Foreign Affairs* 54 (January 1976): p. 385. The author of this article presents a contrary interpretation.

50. Alec Nove, "Will Russia Ever Feed Itself?" *New York Times Magazine,* February 1, 1976, p. 46; *New York Times,* December 9, 1975, p. l; *Christian Science Monitor,* March 9, 1976, p. 27.

51. Nove, "*Will Russia Ever Feed Itself?*", p. 48.

52. See Selig S. Harrison, "China: The Next Oil Giant," *Foreign Policy* 20 (Fall 1975): 3–27; also Choon-ho Park and Jerome Alan Cohen, "The Politics of China's Oil Weapon," *Foreign Policy* 20 (Fall 1975): 28–49.

53. Ibid., p. 7. See also the discussion of GNP in earlier editions of this study: U.S. Arms Control and Disarmament Agency, *World Military Expenditures and Arms Trade, 1963–1973* (Washington, D.C.: GPO, 1975), pp. 10–11.

54. U.S. Arms Control and Disarmament Agency, *World Military Expenditures and Arms Trade, 1963–1973* (Washington, D.C.: GPO, 1975), pp. 61–63.

55. *New York Times,* March 14, 1976, p. 1.

56. *New York Times,* March 14, 1976, p. 23.

57. See John W. Finney, "Dreadnaught or Dinosaur?" *New York Times Magazine,* January 18, 1976.

58. U.S. Department of State, Bureau of Public Affairs, "GIST: World Arms Trade," July 1975.

59. U.S. Arms Control and Disarmament Agency, *World Military Expenditures and Arms Transfers, 1966–1975* (Washington, D.C.: ACDA, 1976), p. 1.

60. These figures are compiled from those presented by the U.S. Arms Control and Disarmament Agency, in both the 1975 and 1976 editions of its annual study.

61. Michael T. Klare, "Superpower Rivalry at Sea," *Foreign Policy* 21 (Winter 1975–76): 91. See also Norman Polmar, *Soviet Naval Power: Challenge for the 1970s*, rev. ed. (New York: Crane, Russak, 1974).

62. Barry M. Blechman and Edward R. Fried, "Controlling the Defense Budget," *Foreign Affairs* 54, (January 1976): 234.

63. *Christian Science Monitor*, April 9, 1976, p. 12.

64. Les Aspin, "How to Look at the Soviet-American Balance," *Foreign Policy* 22 (Spring 1976): 96–106.

65. *New York Times*, May 4, 1976, p. 6.

66. Aspin, "Soviet-American Balance," p. 104.

67. *New York Times*, February 23, 1976, p. 13, and May 19, 1976, p. 4.

68. *Christian Science Monitor:* October 6, 1976, p. 3.

69. See Jacques de Launay, *De Gaulle and His France: A Psychopolitical and Historical Portrait* (New York: Julian Press, 1968); François Mauriac, *De Gaulle* (New York: Doubleday, 1966); Stanley and Inge Hoffman, "The Will to Grandeur: De Gaulle as Political Artist," in Dankwart Rustow, ed., *Philosophers and Kings: Studies in Political Leadership* (New York: George Braziller, 1970).

70. See U.S. Congress, Joint Economic Committee, *An Economic Profile of Mainland China* 1 (Washington, D.C.: GPO, 1967); Alexander Eckstein, *Communist China's Economic Growth and Foreign Trade* (New York: McGraw-Hill, 1966); Yuan-li Wu, *An Economic Survey of Communist China* (New York: Bookman, 1956); Ygail Gluckstein, *Mao's China: Economic and Political Survey* (Boston: Beacon Press, 1957).

71. Ibid., p. 80.

72. Robert C. North, *The Foreign Relations of China*, 2nd ed. (Belmont, Cal.: Dickenson, 1974), p. 33.

73. Henry A. Kissinger, "Speech Before the St. Louis World Affairs Council, May 12, 1975," News Release, Department of State, p. 2.

74. Richard N. Cooper, "Trade Policy is Foreign Policy," *Foreign Policy* 9 (Winter 1972–73): 8–36; also, in the same issue, Robert E. Hunter, "Power and Peace," 37–56; see also the collection of *Foreign Affairs* articles in William P. Bundy, ed., *The World Economic Crisis* (New York: W. W. Norton, 1975).

75. Seyom Brown, "The Changing Essence of Power," *Foreign Affairs* 51 (January 1973): 286–99.

Chapter 4

The Instruments of Power

> It means all-out war with the Tattaglia Family against the Corleone Family. Most of the others will line up with the Tattaglias. The Sanitation Department will be sweeping up a lot of dead bodies this winter. . . . These things have to happen once every ten years or so. It gets rid of the bad blood. And then if we let them push us around on the little things they wanta take over everything. You gotta stop them at the beginning. Like they shoulda stopped Hitler at Munich, they never shoulda let him get away with that, they were just asking for big trouble when they let him get away with that.
>
> —Clemenza, in Mario Puzo's
> *The Godfather*

FOREIGN POLICY: MAKING AN OFFER THEY CAN'T REFUSE

War is probably the most obvious, and certainly the most tragic, manifestation of international conflict. Yet it is by no means the only, or even the most frequent, by-product of conflict among national interests in world politics. Military means are but one instrument of foreign policy. The Spanish philosopher Ortega y Gasset once wrote, "Civilization is nothing else but the attempt to reduce force to being the last resort." In this respect, international relations are generally conducted in a "civilized" manner—at least to the extent that force is rarely the first choice of policy makers. However, given the decentralized nature of the international system, the potential resort to force remains one of the most important attributes of the environment in which states must interact.

Foreign policy is a state's strategy in its international (or geopolitical) environment aimed at obtaining a favorable distribution of global values. It is the process by which the elements of national power, considered in Chapter 3, are transformed into actual influence. A state's foreign policy is thus the strategy whereby the potential for influence is converted into the reality of influence.

When we refer to foreign policy as a strategy, we are suggesting that a state's behavior in the international system is both purposeful and rational. Action is purposeful in that it is intended to attain certain goals; it is rational if it is deliberately planned to accommodate available means to desired ends. This is not to suggest that the totality of a state's behavior in the international system (that is, each and every aspect of its interaction with other actors) is always calculated to serve a particular end. There are no master plans in the world's foreign ministries for every course of action. The international system is not a chessboard, and international politics is not a chess game between single-minded masters. As we have seen in Chapter 2, governments pursue many different and often contradictory goals in their mutual relations; moreover, the national political system, composed as it is of divergent interests and views, often fails to speak with a single definite voice. Yet we are justified in referring to the rationality of foreign policy, in that the overall direction of a state's policy is comprehensible in terms of its national interests as it perceives them. Foreign policy is intended to serve the values of the state, however they are defined by decision makers. The essence of the art of conducting foreign policy lies in securing the most favorable share of benefits that available resources will allow.

As the state actors in the international system struggle among themselves over the division of global values, conflict between foreign policies is inevitable. This conflict, caused by the underlying incompatibility of national interests, may be viewed as a bargaining process—that is, as "situations in which the ability of one participant to gain his ends is dependent to an important degree on the choices or decisions that the other participant will make." [1] For a state to attain its particular goals, its rivals must acquiesce, either voluntarily or because they have been coerced into doing so. Naturally, decision makers would prefer to gain their adversaries' compliance at the least possible cost to themselves. However, if this proves ineffective and the end sought is valued highly enough, foreign-policy makers can be expected to invest more time, energy and resources in order to prevail over their opponents. In any event, to attain one's goals (in either preserving or changing a certain distribution of benefits), power must be exercised over the behavior of others and their compliance must be obtained. Securing this compliance is the task of foreign policy. Whether by sheer persuasion, offer of reward or threat or imposition of harm, the immediate aim of policy is to strike a favorable bargain by convincing others that it is in their interest to comply with the demands. The directors of policy seek to make them an offer they can't refuse.

As we discussed in the previous chapter, securing the compliance of other countries normally revolves around the threat or use of sanctions. We have differentiated between positive sanctions (persuasion) and negative sanctions (coercion). In the first case, state A seeks to convince state B that it will be in B's interest to conform with A's wishes because if B does so, A will do something to benefit B. State A's commitment may be a pledge to provide B with direct economic aid, favorable trading concessions, support for interests in disputes with third parties, votes in international organizations, military assistance in the event of attack and so forth. Alternatively, state A may threaten state B with negative or coercive sanctions; that is, A seeks to convince B that it will be in

B's interest to comply with A's demands because if B does not, A will take actions calculated to harm B. For example, A might hint that it will terminate its foreign aid, withdraw from a previous commitment to defend B in the event of attack, enter into an alliance with B's enemies or even engage in military hostilities with B. Often, of course, the use of positive and negative sanctions go hand in hand in a kind of carrot-and-stick arrangement. When the Middle East oil-producing countries promised to reward the Arab world's friends and punish Israel's allies in the October 1973 war, they engaged in just such an activity. When President Ford and Secretary of State Kissinger warned the Soviet Union in the winter of 1975–76 that the Kremlin's support for its faction in the Angolan civil war would inevitably have repercussions on Russo-American relations, they were using a two-pronged technique and conveying the simple message that the end of Moscow's involvement in the war in southern Africa would improve the atmosphere of détente and the continuation of the involvement would endanger détente and possibly lead to a renewal of the cold war.

The employment of sanctions (positive or negative) to further foreign-policy goals is expensive for the state dispensing them. As an astute immigrant worker remarked during the 1930s upon hearing that local taverns provided food at no cost when customers ordered beer, "There's no such thing as a free lunch." There was no free lunch because you first had to buy the beer. There is no free lunch in the conduct of foreign policy because resources and future options must be expended to gain compliance. Offered rewards must be paid for either in transfer of resources (as is the case with foreign aid) or in the limitation on freedom of action (for instance, in the commitment to come to the defense of another country). A price must be paid for negative sanctions as well. When a state attempts to punish an opponent for noncompliance, the opponent is not the only one who is harmed; the punishing state will normally suffer along with the punished state, though perhaps not to the same degree. Consider the case of a country that wages war against another with the intention of forcing it to desist from opposition. No matter how much more powerful the attacking state may be in terms of military might, it still must expend some blood and treasure in warfare, even if it manages to cause its enemy even greater harm. Indeed, as the Vietnam War amply demonstrated, short of the complete annihilation of one side, there is no necessary ratio between suffering inflicted and outcome of hostilities.

The United States' experience in Indochina reveals another aspect of sanctions in addition to cost—namely, risk, or the degree of probability of successfully attaining one's goals after the expenditure of resources. Despite a decade of war, hundreds of thousands of American casualties and the expenditure of over $100 billion, the United States was unable to prevail in that conflict. Naturally,. if the actual expense and the eventual outcome had been known to decision makers in the early 1960s, we can assume that American foreign policy would have been quite different. But that is just the point. The outcome and cost of policy cannot be foreseen, for there is an inherent unpredictability in international politics that defies attempts at control by even the most politically astute. Furthermore, it is difficult to measure costs, especially in advance. How does one measure the real costs of America's involvement in Vietnam? Casualty figures are cold and do not indicate the depth and extent of human suffering involved. Neither do accounting statistics adequately reflect the economic resources spent; in reality, we must consider the social opportunity costs, that is, the worthwhile social investments that could have been made with the vast sums funneled into war effort. Nearly a quarter-century ago, President Eisenhower described the burden of arms in this very manner:

> Every gun made, every warship launched, every rocket fired signals, in the final sense, a theft from those who hunger and are not fed, those who are cold and are not clothed.
>
> This world in arms is not spending money alone.
>
> It is spending the sweat of its laborers, the genius of its scientists, the hopes of its children.
>
> The cost of a modern heavy bomber is this: a modern brick school in more than thirty cities.
>
> It is two electric power plants, each servicing a town of sixty thousand population.
>
> It is two fine, fully equipped hospitals.

> It is some fifty miles of concrete highway.
>
> We pay for a single fighter with one-half million bushels of wheat.
>
> We pay for a single destroyer with new homes that could house more than eight thousand people.
>
> This is not a life at all, in any true sense. Under the cloud of threatening war, it is humanity hanging from a cross of iron.[2]

Finally, how can one measure the intangible consequences of the war: the domestic disruption, the United States' tarnished image abroad, the damage to national and world economies, and the damage to the American national psyche.

Foreign policy, then, is an expensive undertaking. The let's-make-a-deal nature of international politics involves great potential costs and risks to individual states. Values and resources are sacrificed for the sake of other values—collectively subsumed under the rubric "national interest." International conflict is the result of competition over distribution of global benefits among sovereign states, and this struggle to realize divergent versions of the just world order leads to the clash of foreign-policy strategies. There are a number of instruments at the disposal of decision makers for the implementation of policy, and states normally utilize a combination of these means to further their interests. As we shall see, they vary considerably in the degree of cost and risk they entail, and thus we can generally assume that as the stakes in a particular conflict situation mount, international actors will more readily resort to increasingly costly and perhaps riskier instruments of power. The instruments of foreign policy may be listed in four categories: (1) diplomacy; (2) economics; (3) subversion; (4) force.

Diplomacy: The Sometimes Not So Gentle Art of Persuasion

Diplomacy is the management of international relations by negotiation. It is a state's attempt by means of words to get other international actors to accept a certain distribution of values as just and proper and is the primary means of communicating desires and intentions in the international system. The diplomatic method developed soon after the evolution of contacts among separate political and social entities. The earliest recorded treaty was negotiated around 3000 B.C. between city-states in the Tigris and Euphrates Valley in the Middle East, though it is likely that exchange of envoys among these ministates had begun much earlier, perhaps as far back as 5000 B.C.[3] One authority on diplomacy suggests, quite plausibly, that the art of negotiation was probably practiced in prehistoric times among primitive tribes and that the evolution of diplomatic immunity must have occurred shortly thereafter.

> From the very first, even to our Cromagnon or Neanderthal ancestors, it must have become apparent that such negotiations would be severely hampered if the emissary from one side were killed and eaten by the other side before he had time to deliver his message. The practice must therefore have become established even in the remotest times that it would be better to grant such negotiators certain privileges and immunities which were denied to warriors.[4]

Whether we accept this tongue-in-cheek anthropological interpretation or not, it is apparent that diplomacy serves a crucial function in a quasi-anarchic environment. The ancient Greeks established a quite sophisticated network of diplomatic ties, which can be traced back in literature to the writings of Homer and indicate the regular exchange of ad hoc embassies around 800 B.C. These Hellenic city-states negotiated among themselves various types of agreements, including truces, peace treaties, alliances and commercial conventions.[5] Modern diplomatic relations date back to Renaissance Italy, when the Venetians (who borrowed much from their rivals the Byzantines) established permanent resident missions and set the tone for the rest of the city-states on the peninsula. When the French and Spanish initiated modern European international politics by vying for control over the Italian city-states in the fifteenth and sixteenth centuries, the diplomatic style adopted by Venice was soon transmitted to the rest of the continent. From their resident embassies in foreign states, Renaissance diplomats served more than the mere representational function that we associate with modern ambassadors. More important than negotiation and communication between their own capital and that to which they were accredited were their intelligence-gathering and subversive activities: "They bribed courtiers; they stimulated and financed rebellions; they encouraged opposition parties; they intervened in the most subversive ways in the internal affairs of the country to which they were accredited; they lied, they spied, they stole." [6]

To be sure, the tools of modern diplomacy no longer include the blatant duplicity and chicanery of earlier times. However, this is largely owing to the division of labor found in present political systems rather than a major transformation in international morality. Nowadays, if bribery, assassination and subversion are instruments of foreign policy, they are conducted by clandestine agencies separate from the foreign service. Still, embassies provide a good deal of information (i.e., intelligence) to their home ministries. For example, in 1965, the American ambassador to Santo Domingo sent desperate reports of an imminent Communist takeover, which caused the United States government to send American troops to the Dominican Republic. Moreover, within the U.S. State Department is a Bureau of Intelligence and Research (INR), an integral part of the foreign intelligence-gathering community (along with the Central Intelligence Agency). It has become common practice among the major powers to place intelligence officers in the ranks of military attachés assigned to overseas embassies and to provide appropriate "cover" for covert-activities operatives in associated missions (e.g., the U.S. Agency for International Development). Yet the major function of the foreign service remains representation.

The essence of diplomacy is negotiation. But diplomacy is not always synonymous with peaceful settlement of disputes. As an instrument of foreign policy, diplomacy serves the interests and goals of the state—which means that its job is to further the favorable, though not necessarily the peaceful, resolution of conflict. Ideally, of course, policy makers would prefer to have their way in the international system at the least cost and risk (that is, without having to resort to sanctions) and naturally seek to convince the other parties involved that it is in everyone's interests to accede to their demands voluntarily. But international politics is hardly a great debate in which the most articulate orators succeed in persuading others by force of logic alone. Often the logic of force is more persuasive. If the just allocation of benefits were something objective and discoverable by rational discourse, then surely negotiation would always lead to solution of conflict. Politics, however, is the struggle among different actors with divergent value systems to impose their respective and conflicting notions of justice. In the end, the resulting distribution of values reflects the balance of power among the competitors. Therefore, there can be no true solution to international conflict, if by *solution* we mean that the demands of all disputants are satisfied. This cannot be, for the demands of the parties were in conflict to begin with, and so all sides cannot be totally satisfied.

Consider the case of the Spanish Sahara. In 1975, Madrid announced it would grant independence to this sparsely populated (but resource rich) desert territory in North Africa; however, Morocco and Mauritania established conflicting claims to the area and each demanded the right of annexation. Now this problem could have been solved in a number of ways: (1) The Sahara could have become an independent sovereign state; this would have satisfied Spanish interests, but would have left Morocco and Mauritania totally dissatisfied. (2) Either Morocco or Mauritania could have been allowed to annex the entire territory; but this would have left Spain and the nonannexing neighbor totally dissatisfied. (3) Morocco and Mauritania could have been permitted to divide the Sahara between them (and this, in fact, is what was done in early 1976); but this would leave Spain totally unsatisfied and both Morocco and Mauritania only partially satisfied.* This sums up the dilemma of politics. Where conflict is present, there are only two types of outcome possible: Either one

* We have not mentioned the role of Algeria in the Saharan dispute. Initially, Algeria supported Spain's plans for an independent Sahara. When Madrid succumbed to pressure from Morocco and Mauritania and agreed to allow the two countries to divide the territory between them, Algeria vigorously objected and by early 1976 had sent troops into the area to prevent partition. As frequently happens among crime families, the division of territory between two actors is bound to incur the wrath of a third who fails to participate in the allocation of benefits.

side achieves total victory and the other total defeat; or both sides agree to live with their respective claims only partially satisfied (and thus partially dissatisfied). The first arrangement is the only true solution to conflict; the second is compromise.

Diplomacy alone can rarely achieve a true solution to a conflict unless one side values the object in dispute so little that it refuses to pay the cost of continuing the strife and simply withdraws from the game. (This was what Spain in effect did in the Sahara dispute.) Normally, compromise must be accepted by the disputants and negotiations entered into; if one or both sides refuses to compromise, and still values the prize highly enough, then diplomacy will be abandoned (at least for the time being) and other instruments of policy employed.

Even when diplomacy is not abandoned in favor of force, an intimate relationship remains between negotiation and the imposition of sanctions in the conduct of foreign policy. Some years ago, Professor Henry Kissinger wrote: "In a society of 'sovereign' states, a power can in the last resort vindicate its interpretation of justice or defend its 'vital interests' only by the willingness to employ force" and "if recourse to force has in fact become impossible, diplomacy too may lose its efficacy." [7] Diplomacy, then, does not operate in a political vacuum. To be effective, it must reflect the real capabilities of the state employing it; diplomacy without latent sanctions to reinforce it can easily become futile.

States submit to negotiation and compromise not out of respect for their opponents' oratory nor because they appreciate sweet reasonableness. Political actors choose to compromise because they become convinced that it is in their interests to do so and that in the long run there is more to be gained out of the give and take of negotiation than there is from the costly use of sanctions. When decision makers calculate the potential benefits to be derived from attaining their initial objectives, and subtract from that the likely costs and risks involved in sanctions, they often reach the conclusion that something less than the entire loaf will suffice. In a cost-benefit analysis, the price of the whole loaf may prove prohibitive, and so it is in their interest to compromise and accept less.

In diplomatic bargaining, the goal is to get the best deal possible. To compromise suggests that we must accommodate the interests of the other party and ultimately settle for less than total satisfaction. In the process of negotiaiton, we seek to exploit our potential power and outmaneuver our opponent so as to secure the largest portion of benefits possible. Ultimately, we want to discover what the other party will really settle for without himself resorting to (or escalating) sanctions. We will settle for something less than our total demands; how much less depends upon the actual process of the negotiations. If we discover that we must sacrifice more of our interests than is palatable in order to reach an agreement, then we may employ other instruments of power to attain our goals.

Negotiation may be viewed as a process in which proposals are put forward by contending parties for the purpose of reaching an agreement on the realization of a common interest.[8] If the bargaining is successful, the outcome of the interaction will be an agreement, or an exchange of conditional promises (i.e., "I will carry out my end of the bargain if you carry out yours"). This represents the final allocation of the values in contention. From the time the initial proposals are put forth until the time the accord is signed, each actor engages in a campaign of maneuver to undermine its adversary's position and reinforce its own. Proposals and counterproposals are placed on the table, allies are sought, resources are mobilized, threats and promises alluded to and warnings exchanged. In the final analysis, what happens in the negotiating room will reflect the distribution of power elsewhere. This is nowhere more apparent than when diplomatic bargaining progresses side by side with military hostilities. Here, results at the conference table are likely to parallel events on the battlefield.

Negotiation begins with the confrontation between positions that are normally far apart. Each side initially presents its maximum demands and its minimum concessions. This does not mean that the parties will not eventually settle for less or offer more, even though they have presented their claims in a totally uncompromising manner. Each will contend that it cannot budge without doing irreparable harm to its vital interests. If at the outset, or at some point later on, one or both parties presents minimum demands and maximum concessions and still cannot coax the other side into an agreement, then stalemate results and the talks break down. If the talks are resumed at a later date, it is because in the interim at least one side has reassessed its interest and power position and redefined its demands and concessions in light of this new point of view.

Let us use a simple illustration. Assume that management and labor in a certain industry are to renegotiate a union contract. Conflict concerns the distribution of values—in this case, income: profits versus wages. Both sides have a common interest in reaching an agreement that will continue the healthy operation of the factory: Neither side benefits in killing the goose that lays the golden eggs. Labor might prefer eliminating profits and running the factory, and management might prefer having its employees work for subsistence wages, but both realize that they cannot get the other to concur, so they agree to compromise. The last contract provided a base pay of $4.00 an hour, and we will assume for the sake of simplicity that salary is the only issue. Before meeting with their opposites, labor's negotiators confer and decide that, though they might prefer more, they will settle for $4.50 an hour. It is not worth going out on strike for more, but they are indeed willing to strike if they cannot get at least $4.50. In another room, management's negotiators meet and agree that the most they can offer the union and still have an acceptable profit margin is $4.75 an hour. Ostensibly, there appears to be no conflict. Labor knows it will accept $4.50 and management knows it will pay $4.75. Yet what happens when the two sides get together to present their proposals?

It would be naive indeed to believe that labor will demand $4.50 and management offer $4.75 at the outset. In all likelihood, the union will demand something in the neighborhood of $5.00 and the employer will offer, say, $4.25. But why? The answer is simple: Each side seeks the most favorable allocation of benefits possible. Not knowing what the other side will actually settle for (management not knowing labor's minimum demand and labor not knowing management's maximum concession), each party can best protect its interest by putting forth its maximum demand or (in the case of management) its minimum concession. Within the limits set by the initial proposals, each side can maneuver to maximize its gains. For instance, let us imagine that during the course of the negotiations, a temporary impasse is reached with management offering $4.40 and labor demanding $4.80 and neither side willing to budge further. At this point, each contestant might seek to strengthen its position and weaken its opponent: Labor leaders threaten a strike and begin outfitting a war chest with the help of other unions; management claims that any further concession on its part will lead to bankruptcy and threatens to close down operations. In the end, though, an agreement will probably be reached somewhere above labor's minimum demand ($4.50) and below management's maximum concession ($4.75). However, if the employer's maximum offer had been below the union's minimum demand, a real deadlock would have resulted and could have been broken only by the imposition of sanctions and the resulting reassessment of interests.

As we shall see, the principles of bargaining and negotiation are fundamentally the same for international conflict. What differences do exist result from the anarchic environment of world politics and the extreme nature of the sanctions available to state actors.

The Vietnam Negotiations. American involvement in Indochina stemmed from a Cold War conception of national interest. With the rapid breakup of the World War II coalition that allied the United States with the Soviet Union, the international system divided along lines of military and ideological bipolarity. (For further discussion, see Chapter 7.) Perceiving its security to be threatened by the spread of international communism emanating from the Kremlin, the United States adopted a policy of containing not only the direct expansion of Soviet influence but also the spread of communism itself. In a world order dominated by only two superpowers, international politics was approached in terms of a "zero-sum game"—that is, a gain for one side was, by definition, a loss for the other. By equating all Communist (and even revolutionary) movements with Soviet machinations the United States perceived itself as a global policeman preventing aggression by existing Communist states as well as the rise of local Communists to power through revolution.

With the collapse of French colonial power in Indochina in the early 1950s, the United States moved into the area. However, by the mid-sixties, the American-supported regime in South Vietnam had come under increasing pressure from indigenous Vietcong guerrillas, aided by the Communist government in Hanoi. Washington was confronted with the alternative of directly intervening in the civil war or withdrawing and allowing the fall of South Vietnam (and possibly the rest of Indochina) to the Communists. As we know, in 1965, the decision was made to accept the increase in costs and risks in order to continue the policy of containment, a massive expeditionary force was dispatched to South Vietnam and the systematic bombing of North Vietnam soon followed. The Johnson Administration's objective was to convince Hanoi that negative sanctions would continue to be imposed until it desisted from its campaign to reunify the two countries.

The Communist Tet offensive of early 1968 proved to be the turning point in the war. Politically, the United States was the loser, and Washington became convinced that the war could not be won at an acceptable cost. As Henry Kissinger later wrote, the Tet offensive "made inevitable an eventual commitment to a political solution and marked the beginning of the quest for a negotiated settlement."[9] In March 1968, President Johnson announced the end of all bombing north of the twentieth parallel, called for the beginning of negotiations and declared he would not seek reelection.

By the time the Nixon Administration took office the following year, American goals had shifted considerably: from reaching a military victory to achieving a political settlement that would allow for the withdrawal of American troops, the return of its prisoners of war and time to reinforce the Saigon regime. To be avoided was the appearance of a precipitate retreat, which would lead directly to the fall of the South Vietnamese government. The United States had to avoid the onus of defeat at the hands of the Communists.

The transformation in Washington's goal also reflected a change in its perception of the international environment in general. Nixon and Kissinger became convinced that the international system had changed dramatically and that the underlying rationale for the intervention was no longer valid. It was believed that the world was no longer politically bipolar and that the Sino-Soviet split had removed the threat of monolithic Communist menace. Thus the United States was no longer compelled to intervene everywhere Communists threatened to come to power. A Communist victory in Indochina, though not the most favorable outcome by American standards, could be tolerated, as it would exacerbate tensions between Moscow and Peking. However, the administration reasoned, the manner in which it extricated itself from Vietnam would have consequences for future dealings with the Soviet Union. There was no doubt that the war would have to be ended, but only in a way that would not cripple American credibility with both allies and adversaries. This would be the task of diplomacy.

Secret negotiations with North Vietnam began in August of 1969.[10] Henry Kissinger, representing the United States, proposed an immediate cease-fire, to be followed by withdrawal of American and North Vietnamese forces from South Vietnam and release of prisoners of war. Hanoi demanded unconditional American withdrawal and the removal of South Vietnamese President Thieu. At this point, neither side indicated any willingness to compromise. North Vietnam's goal had remained constant for decades—dismantling the Saigon regime and reunifying of Vietnam—and it had no intention of jeopardizing that objective after two and a half decades of sacrifice; moreover, Hanoi remained convinced that time was on its side and that eventually world and American domestic opinion would force the United States out of Indochina. Bargaining now shifted to the battlefield, as each side sought to persuade the other that its staying power was greater.

The diplomatic impasse remained constant for nearly two years. To quiet domestic agitation and at the same time signal to Hanoi that it would not abandon Saigon, the Nixon Administration implemented its policy of "Vietnamization"—gradual and unilateral withdrawal of American troops coupled with modernization of the South Vietnamese armed forces. In May of 1971, with its troop strength lessening, Washington made further concessions. Kissinger secretly offered to set a deadline for withdrawal of United States forces in exchange for a cease-fire and release of its prisoners of war. This was indeed a significant concession, because he made no reference to evacuation of North Vietnamese troops;

however, Hanoi remained adamant and tried to manipulate the American public's concern over its prisoners to secure removal of Thieu also. In August, Kissinger offered a revised proposal: total American withdrawal within nine months of a cease-fire, release of the prisoners of war and an overall (and unspecified) political settlement; in addition, the United States offered economic aid for reconstruction. But Hanoi rejected the new initiative, still demanding Thieu's removal, and the second phase of negotiations ended in deadlock as well.

Once again, the United States offered further concessions. In October, fearing a major Communist offensive the following spring (when there would be less than 100,000 American troops remaining), Kissinger offered to remove all United States forces within six months of an agreement, in return for a cease-fire and the prisoners' release; furthermore, he agreed to new elections in the South (supervised by a body independent of the government representing all political forces, including the Vietcong), one month previous to which Thieu would resign. Hanoi declined even to meet and discuss the new American proposal. Seeking to prod the North Vietnamese into movement on the diplomatic front and brace the American people for the possibility of a new round of escalation, the following February, just prior to his famous trip to Peking, President Nixon revealed to the public that secret negotiations had been in progress for two and a half years and outlined the latest United States offer. Washington then secretly offered to resume negotiations. Hanoi at first accepted, later to postpone them until March 31. On March 30, the North struck with a massive offensive against the South, hoping to achieve on the battlefield what the United States would not concede in Paris: the destruction of the South Vietnamese army and the fall of its government.

The United States responded on both diplomatic and military fronts. Kissinger conferred with Soviet leaders in April, trying to persuade them to make Hanoi stop the offensive. For the first time, he specifically offered to allow North Vietnamese troops to remain in the South after a cease-fire in return for the preservation of the Thieu government at least until after a political settlement had been made. Hanoi agreed to send its negotiators back to Paris, but things were going so well on the battlefield that the talks were abruptly terminated after one session. Realizing that Hanoi would not make concessions as long as the military tide was running in its favor, Nixon resumed bombing of North Vietnam and mined Haiphong. Even so, the Russians refused to cancel Nixon's planned trip to Moscow, and there Kissinger offered another concession (the carrot following the stick): The United States was now willing to accept a tripartite electoral commission which would include the Vietcong. In June, Kissinger tried to get the Chinese leadership to agree to the new American terms, and later they apparently did urge the Vietcong to accept.

As a result of these diplomatic and military developments, the peace talks began again in September, and by mid-October the broad outlines of a settlement were reached. Hanoi demanded that a final agreement be concluded before the American election, and Kissinger indicated that this deadline would be met. But President Thieu, who for the most part had been kept in the dark about American concessions, refused to go along with the peace plan, and the United States announced that signing would be postponed pending the resolution of a few details. At a press conference on October 26, Kissinger reaffirmed the American intention of concluding the agreement, though not necessarily according to Hanoi's timetable. Three weeks later, he returned to Paris to work out the final details of the accord, only to find that Hanoi's reaction was to reopen certain issues. So, to force Hanoi into final acceptance of American terms, Washington decided to launch the Christmas bombing campaign against the North. In early January, Hanoi in effect capitulated and asked for the resumption of negotiations. The secret Vietnam peace talks, which had begun in August 1969, were finally brought to a conclusion on January 13, 1973.

The long and tortuous road taken by the Vietnam negotiations illustrates well the role of diplomacy in foreign policy and its intimate relationship with other instruments of power, especially the threat and imposition of coercive sanctions. The frequent detours and roadblocks reflected the gaps between Hanoi's durable minimum demands and Washington's more flexible maximum concessions. Diplomatic bargaining began in earnest in 1969 only because American objectives had undergone a metamorphosis as a result of changing conditions in Vietnam and in the international system at large. As Kissinger and Nixon became more and more convinced of North Vietnam's tenacity and the necessity of extricating themselves from the war, the United States modified its negotiating position and its conception of the maximum concessions compatible with the objective of "peace with honor." In the final year of the war, each side sought to put pressure on the other by means of escalating its coercive sanctions. The North Vietnamese offensive of 1972 was intended to prove erroneous the American policy of Vietnamization and force the United States into abandoning the Saigon government. Washington's military response was supposed to counter this pressure and demonstrate that the North would not be allowed to win the struggle by force of arms and, therefore, must negotiate a settlement that would permit the United States to make a graceful exit. The Christmas bombing was Washington's way of informing Hanoi that its patience was wearing thin and that it had made its last concession. Diplomacy was a means of communicating demands and intentions, reflecting the transformation of objectives and registering mutual perceptions of shifting power relationships.

Economics: The International Robber Barons

Wealth and power may not be the same, but there is certainly an intimate relationship between the two. Wealth begets power; power begets wealth. As we have seen, economic and technological resources are the principal foundations of national power in the contemporary international system. On the other hand, the struggle for international influence often revolves around the distribution of global wealth.* When a state manipulates its wealth (or its control over economic resources) to affect the behavior of other international actors and further its national interest, it is using the economic instrument of its foreign policy. Potential for such influence depends upon two factors: (1) the impact of its economy on the world economy as a whole; (2) its control over access to strategic global resources. This potential for

* In Chapter 7, we will consider the contemporary struggle over the contours of the global economic order.

influence is transformed into operationalized power when economic sanctions are threatened, promised or employed.

A prime indicator of a state's impact on the international economy is the size of its own economy (as measured in terms of GNP). Currently, the American economy accounts for one-quarter of the gross world product (GWP); at the end of the Second World War, the United States (with less than six percent of the world's population) produced nearly one-half of the planetary product. Thus, though the American share of global production has been halved since 1945, the United States economy remains by far the largest and most technologically advanced economy in the world, being nearly twice the size of its nearest challenger, the Soviet Union. The inordinately large American contribution during the immediate postwar period was an aberration stemming from the physical destruction or exhaustion of the European and Japanese economies; as postwar recovery progressed, the United States economy gradually receded (in a relative sense) to a more reasonable, but nonetheless imposing, level. The decline of American economic strength coincided with a reduction of political power (especially in the post-Vietnam era), but the decline in American global influence was hardly as drastic as a comparison between today's share of the world product and that of 1945 seems to suggest. However, there have been cases of real upward as well as downward mobility in the international economic hierarchy, as the performance of the British and German economies in the last quarter-century illustrates (see Chapter 3).

For most of the post–World War II era, the United States dominated the international economy. As the war came to a close, Washington pressed for a new, liberal, global economic order based upon the principle of the free market. The new order was formulated as the Bretton Woods system, and the dollar soon became the key international currency. Later, in the postwar period, the economic hegemony of the United States receded, but America's pivotal role as world banker permitted it to avoid the painful choice between a cutback in military expenditures abroad and a reduction in foreign investments. However, by 1971 even the United States could no longer sustain this enviable position, and the Nixon administration unilaterally abandoned the Bretton

Woods system (for further discussion, see Chapter 7). Though the United States remained the world's greatest economic power, this traumatic experience "signalled a diminished international ability . . . to finance the exercise of military power abroad." [11]

In addition to a state's overall impact on the world economy, control over access to strategic resources affords a potential for international influence. The advanced countries of the developed world are highly dependent on the importation of raw materials crucial for every modern industrial economy and are therefore highly vulnerable to any interruption in supply. Certain less-developed countries account for the bulk of supply. A handful of Middle East countries, for example, accounts for more than three-fifths of the global reserves of petroleum and seven-tenths of the world's oil exports; moreover, developing countries possess about 45 percent of the world's major nonfuel mineral reserves.[12] Given these facts of supply and demand, the potential for disrupting the economies of the industrialized countries is, as the oil-producing states have demonstrated, considerable.

Potential economic power can be operationalized through the threat or use of sanctions. Wealth can also buy certain types of power (such as military power), though, strictly speaking, the economic arm of foreign policy consists of negative and positive sanctions. Negative economic sanctions include termination of direct economic aid, trade restrictions (export embargoes, import quotas, boycotts), freezing of foreign assets, manipulation of currency reserves, restrictions on foreign investments and economic blockades. Examples of positive sanctions include the provision of direct economic and technical assistance, trade liberalization, preferential tariffs and quotas and favored access to markets and resources. Though economic strength is the foundation of national capabilities in the contemporary international system, one student of world politics has concluded that "coercively wielding economic power by means of trade reprisals or special trade advantages is rarely successful." [13] Nevertheless, countries possessing a disproportionate share of influence over the structure of the international economic order (e.g., the United States in the postwar era because of its huge industrial complex, and the oil-producing states in the 1970s because of their control over the supply and price of a crucial raw material) can go a long way in imposing their conception of the just distribution of values.

OPEC and the Reallocation of Wealth. Commenting on the postwar economic order, West German Chancellor Helmut Schmidt wrote:

> Admittedly specialization, division of labor and free trade across national boundaries have increased the wealth of nations and caused an immense supply of goods in the same way as the division of labor increased production within a single nation. But the main problem then is *to define the laws which determine the distribution of this enormous output; it might be added: which determines the "fair" distribution, the "equitable" price, the "proper" value.*[14]

This distribution problem, of course, is in the domain of politics. The phenomenal growth of the economies of western Europe, Japan, and (to a smaller extent) the United States since the Second World War was greatly stimulated by the secure supply of relatively cheap energy from the petroleum-exporting countries of the developing world. From 1958 to 1973, the world consumed more energy than in all its previous history; from 1973 to 1988, it will use as much energy as it used in all its previous history. Over half this need will be supplied by oil.[15] Until the late 1950s, Europe was overwhelmingly a coal-based economy, but the availability of inexpensive petroleum steadily forced coal from the energy picture until by 1973 over 64 percent of its energy was supplied by oil, almost all of which came from the Middle East. A similar postwar development occurred in the Japanese economy. In 1950, oil contributed a mere 7 percent of Japan's energy requirement and coal 60 percent; in 1973, oil accounted for 60 percent of the total, all imported; by 1985, oil is expected to provide over three-quarters of Japan's energy needs.[16] Prior to World War II, the United States was the world's largest producer, consumer and exporter of petroleum. By the mid-1970s, the United States was still the world's largest consumer, but its production of oil was declining, making it second among the world's producers (the Soviet Union being the top producer) and first among importers. Though the United States is less dependent upon imported oil than its European and Japanese allies, this dependence is expected to increase from the present two-fifths to one-half by the early 1980s, despite Alaskan oil.

By 1946, Venezuela had become the world's most important oil exporter, a position it retained until 1970, when it was surpassed by Iran and Saudi Arabia. Throughout the postwar era, the international oil industry was dominated by seven major corporations,[17] which collectively were responsible for producing about four-fifths of all the petroleum outside North America and the Communist bloc. Beginning in the late 1950s, a world surplus of oil developed, and the companies reduced the posted prices for crude oil, which decreased the tax payments and revenues accruing to the producing countries.[18] In reaction, Venezuela (joined by Saudi Arabia and Iran) formed the Organization of Petroleum Exporting Countries (OPEC) in 1960. OPEC aimed to restore previous price levels by presenting a united front to the oil companies and preventing them from pursuing a policy of divide and conquer. In the beginning, the OPEC countries were so disunited that they failed in their attempt to restore previous price levels, though they did dissuade the oil companies from further reducing posted prices and even obtained a technical change in the method used to calculate company profits, thereby adding slightly to their revenues.

But the very organization of a producers' alliance was a harbinger of things to come. As Thomas C. Schelling, a well-known student of international conflict, suggested in a report to the National Crime Commission: "The simplest explanation of a large-scale firm *in the underworld or anywhere else,* is high costs of overhead. . . . Second is *the prospect of monopolistic price increases.*"[19] The objective of the oil-exporting countries was to rectify what they believed to be an unjust allocation of benefits and ultimately to gain control over the supply of oil so as to redistribute income, taking some away from the wealthy petroleum-importing states and their oligopolistic oil companies. To OPEC members, the industrialized economies of the West and their corporate agents were international robber barons: the oil companies reaped huge profits from the production and sale of OPEC oil, the developed nations of western Europe and Japan grew wealthier from cheap OPEC oil and they themselves made do with a pittance from the foreign exploitation of their unrenewable resources. The poor were subsidizing the rich, the strong were taking from the weak—or so it seemed to the oil exporters, and they set about changing things.

For a decade, the OPEC countries remained in the shadows,[20] unable effectively to regulate the output of oil and its price while the cost of manufactured goods they imported from the developed world increased. In December of 1970, OPEC managed effectively to mobilize for action and confronted the oil companies with the threat of closing down production if the members' revenues were not increased. The breakthrough came in February of the following year with the Teheran agreement, whereby major increases were granted immediately with a timetable for further increases over the next five years. And yet the oil producers' income was still low, and European consumers were actually paying less in real terms for petroleum than in 1958. Fresh from their first collective victory over the oil companies, the exporting countries set about gaining control over the quantity of petroleum produced and its posted price by means of demands to "participate"—to share and eventually control—in the domestic production of the international companies. By the end of 1972, the OPEC governments had successfully negotiated agreements with the companies and within a year were exercising control over the quantity of oil produced and the price per barrel charged to importing countries.

The Arab-Israeli war of October 1973 was the catalyst for the achievement of OPEC's goals. The utilization of the oil weapon for purely political (as opposed to economic) ends was initiated during the Six Day War of 1967. Prior to the outbreak of hostilities, the Arab oil producers issued a warning that, in the event of war, the flow of oil would be cut off to every state aiding Israel. When war came, production and transportation of oil ceased briefly. When production resumed, an embargo was maintained against the United States, Great Britain and West Germany, but this too was lifted within a matter of weeks. The full effects of the oil weapon had not been felt, but the outgrowth of the war was the formation of the Organization of Arab Petroleum Exporting Countries (OAPEC) and the prospect that oil might once again be used as an instrument of policy in the Middle East.

Though similar in membership, OPEC and OAPEC differed in their goals. The overriding objective of OPEC was economic: redistribution of the income produced by oil. OAPEC's objective, on the other hand, was avowedly political: redistribution of power in the Middle East to the detriment of Israel. OPEC's long-desired goals were obtained by the Arab states. When the Yom Kippur War erupted in October 1973, the Arab oil ministers seized the right unilaterally to establish the price of crude oil and its production level (thus fulfilling OPEC's objectives) and imposed sanctions against the industrialized world with the aim of isolating the Israelis (OAPEC's objective). The result was a three-pronged strategy: (1) the United States, Holland, Portugal and South Africa were embargoed (the first two as friends of Israel, the others as colonial powers); (2) western Europe and Japan were faced with cutbacks in their shipments of oil; and (3) the price of oil was increased dramatically.

The results of the oil weapon must be examined on two levels: political and economic. On the political level, the Arabs found the Europeans and Japanese responsive to their economic pressure. During the war, all the NATO allies of the United States (with the exception of Portugal) denied the American military access rights to their territory for the purpose of supplying Israel and most formally called upon Israel to withdraw from occupied territory and recognize the legitimate rights of the Palestinians. Japan endorsed Arab demands and announced that it would reexamine its policy toward Israel. Moreover, both the Europeans and Japanese scrambled to make bilateral deals with the oil producers, despite American urgings to the contrary. The use of the oil weapon may have also been the cause of Washington pressing Israel to accept a cease-fire and of Secretary of State Kissinger's urgent rounds of shuttle diplomacy. As one observer has noted: "There is little doubt that the October war would have sensitized American leaders to the dangers of the status quo and forced a new American effort to resolve the issue. ... Oil served as a lubricant, however, increasing the pace and intensity of the effort."[21]

In terms of its economic objective—monopolization of control over the petroleum resources—the oil cartel was even more successful. Within a year of the energy crisis, the price of Middle East oil had more than quadrupled, signaling an enormous and unprecedented long-term transfer of goods and services annually from the industrialized West to the petroleum-exporting countries.[22] Though initial projections of the extent of the shift in wealth and its upsetting effects on the international economy proved to be alarmist, OPEC members did increase their total GNPs by some 40 percent in 1974 alone, raising their share of the planetary product from 2.8 to 3.9 percent. Moreover, by 1980–81, the oil producers will have accumulated surplus funds (that is, oil revenues in excess of what is spent on increased imports from the industrialized economies) on the order of $100 billion,[23] a far cry from earlier calculations four and five times that amount, but nonetheless a respectable income.

The OPEC countries had struggled to overturn arrangements which they believed had been imposed on them by the rich robber-baron economies of the developed world with the aim of freezing the distribution of wealth and power. In the end, the oil cartel succeeded in establishing a new order which better approximated its version of justice. But for those in the industrialized portion of the globe who felt victimized by OPEC, it simply meant that one band of robber barons had replaced another.

Subversion: The International "Hit" Parade

If you make someone an offer they're not supposed to refuse, and they refuse, three choices remain. You can modify your initial demand to make it more palatable. You can try to coax compliance by offering rewards or threatening penalties. Or you can remove the major obstacle to having your way, that is, eliminate the opponent himself. In the parlance of international politics, this is called *subversion;* in the underworld of crime, it is called a *hit.* When the Nixon administration decided to get rid of the Marxist regime of Salvador Allende in Chile, it initiated a policy of "destabilization." When Stalin decided to install a Communist government in Czechoslovakia in 1948, he implemented a policy of "liberation." And, when the boss of an organized-crime syndicate moves to consolidate his power by eliminating recalcitrant rivals, he puts out a "contract." Subversion is the policy of undermining an opponent's regime with the ultimate intention of removing him from power and replacing him with a successor more amenable to your demands. In reality, it represents nothing less than one government putting out a "contract" on another.

Subversion may or may not include political assassination. Even in the world of organized crime, the removal of a rival Don can sometimes be accomplished by encouraging a coup d'etat within the "family." The infamous "Bananas War" in New York during the 1960s is a good illustration. Joe Bonanno, head of one of the city's "Five Families" and one of the nine members of the "Commission" (the political directorate of the underworld), had tried to arrange the murder of two other commissioners and heads of major New York crime families. In retaliation, the Commission excommunicated Bonanno, thus absolving his lieutenants of loyalty to their boss, and in the civil war within the Bonanno family which followed, the rival syndicates threw their support behind one of the dissident "capos," Gaspar De Gregorio. In the end, peace was restored to the underworld and much bloodshed avoided when a settlement was reached that stripped Bonanno of most of his power and banished him to Arizona (much as Napoleon had been exiled to Elba), allowing De Gregorio to move into a dominant position within the family.[24]

In a similar manner, the governments of major international powers often plot to topple hostile regimes in other countries, hoping to create an environment more favorable to the pursuit of their own national interests. For the most part subversion is the privilege only of states at or near the top of the hierarchy of world power, and in general they confine their subversive activities to relatively weak Third World countries.

Subversion is carried out by the intelligence establishments of the superpowers, though foreign Communist parties frequently serve as important vehicles for Soviet penetration of unstable societies. Yet we must differentiate between the intelligence function of the foreign-policy apparatus and the covert-operations function. Intelligence gathering is vital to effective policy making, and modern states devote considerable resources to the acquisition and analysis of relevant information concerning developments in the international system, especially the capabilities and intentions of their adversaries. The American intelligence establishment's annual budget is probably in the neighborhood of ten billion dollars, the bulk of which is spent on intelligence gathering as opposed to international subversion. Contrary to popular belief, the Central Intelligence Agency is far from being the principal intelligence organ of the United States government, accounting for less than 15 percent of total intelligence expenditures.[25] Most foreign intelligence is gathered by highly sophisticated and technical means (for example, reconnaissance satellites and communications interdiction) by various Defense Department agencies,[26] and the CIA itself devotes less than 10 percent of its budget to information processing. The primary purpose of the CIA is to serve as the covert instrument of American foreign policy, operating in the "underworld of international diplomacy" somewhere between the world of the diplomat and the world of the soldier.[27]

Propaganda is close kin to subversion but is usually directed at the popular base of an opponent's power with the intention of weakening support for his policies rather than overthrowing his regime. On occasion, though, propaganda (especially covert propaganda) may be employed to subvert a foreign government. The use of propaganda as an instrument of foreign policy can be dated far back in history (even to the Old Testament) and was often used by the ancient Greeks and Romans to deceive, confuse and cause panic among enemies.[28] But with the rising influence of public opinion in policy making, coupled with the central role of mass beliefs in modern societies and the technological revolution in communications, propaganda has evolved into a permanent feature of psychological warfare.

The purpose of propaganda is twofold: to create a positive image of one's own country and policies in other peoples' minds, and to foster an unfavorable image of one's adversary. The United States Informational Agency (USIA) is the official organ of the American government in this field, and pursues its ends by means of radio braodcasts (the Voice of America); information centers abroad; dissemination of films, books and reference materials in foreign countries; and staging of cultural exhibits —all of which is intended to foster a benevolent image of United States foreign policy. For its part, in the postwar era the Soviet Union has relied upon similar campaigns conducted by Agitprop, one of the principal organs of the Communist Party of the Soviet Union (CPSU). Covert propaganda is conducted by the clandestine organizations of the superpowers: the CIA and the Soviet Union's Committee of State Security (the KGB). Until 1971, the CIA secretly funded the ostensibly private stations Radio Free Europe and Radio Liberty in order to undermine the Communist governments of eastern Europe (as in Hungary in 1956, when broadcasts helped encourage the popular uprising) and the U.S.S.R. itself. The CIA has also secretly subsidized domestic and foreign publishing houses and individual authors as well as anti-Communist private foundations (for example, the Asia Foundation), and has supported dissidents within Communist countries. Both the KGB and the CIA engage in spreading "disinformation," an Orwellian word meaning false information, and the KGB even maintains a special Department of Disinformation. During the Chinese Cultural Revolution in 1967, the United States sought to exacerbate domestic turmoil and thus divert Peking's attention from the war in Vietnam by distributing leaflets on the mainland falsely attributed to Chinese sources. The use of forged documents is common practice and is intended to disrupt an adversary's internal communication network or create false impressions concerning his plans and intentions among friends and neutrals.

Covert propaganda and disinformation are examples of covert action—clandestine intervention in the affairs of another state, often with the purpose of bringing about a change in governments. There are two varieties of covert penetration: political operations and special operations. Political operations employ nonviolent manipulation of domestic actors by means of advice, subsidies, personnel training programs, covert propaganda and economic operations. Special operations denotes the use of force and paramilitary actions either to support a friendly government or overthrow an unfriendly one. In the words of a former CIA specialist: "The paramilitary operator . . . is a gangster who deals in force, in terror, in violence . . . and in the CIA, special ops types are sometimes referred to as the 'animals' of the agency." [29]

Even though it was designated an intelligence agency in its original 1947 charter, the CIA immediately got involved in covert activities as part of the American policy of containing communism in Europe. When the Communists seized power in a coup d'etat in Czechoslovakia in 1948, Washington became alarmed that Communists might also come to power in Italy, and secretly began to funnel large sums of money into the treasuries of non-Communist political parties and labor unions and into the pockets of individual politicians. By the late 1950s, covert CIA financing of the ruling Italian Christian Democrats averaged as much as $3 million a year, and the Communists' share of the electorate was stabilized at about 25 percent. When the Italian Communists picked up momentum again in the late 1960s and early 1970s, increasing their proportion of the popular vote to a full third (just two percentage points behind the Christian Democrats), the CIA resumed its subsidies, contributing $10 million to party coffers in the 1972 parliamentary elections and another $6 million directly to individual politicians in late 1975. Also in 1975, the CIA began funneling up to $10 million a month to Portugal's Socialist party in an effort to counter Soviet subsidies to the Communists, estimated at $120 million annually.[30] Thus, over thirty years after the end of the Second World War, the United States and the Soviet Union were still financing rival political factions in western Europe. In early 1977, allegations were made that the CIA had made direct cash payments to various heads of state in return for pro-American foreign policies. For twenty years dating from 1956, King Hussein of Jordan allegedly received nearly a million dollars annually to support the United States' strategy in the Middle East. Other secretly subsidized national leaders were said to include Chiang Kai-shek of Nationalist China, Syngman Rhee of South Korea, Eduardo Frei Montalva of Chile, Ngo Dinh Diem of South Vietnam, Sese Seko Mobuto of Zaire, Willy Brandt of West Germany, as well as heads of government in Cyprus, Guyana and Kenya.

In addition to direct payoffs, the superpowers regularly train foreign personnel in insurgency and counterinsurgency tactics, and the CIA has been active in instructing Latin American officials under cover of the Agency of International Development's (AID) International Police Academy. The CIA also engaged unsuccessfully in economic operations against Cuba in the early 1960s, attempting to disrupt the island's sugar trade while the Soviets were buttressing Castro's economy to the tune of several hundred million dollars annually. In short, then, the superpowers have consistently intervened in the internal affairs of other states through the use of bribery, corruption and conspiracy.[31]

But political covert actions and assorted "dirty tricks" represent a friendly game of arm wrestling when compared with special operations. Again using the Central Intelligence Agency as an example (perhaps only because its successes and failures have been much more widely publicized and studied than those of the KGB [32])we can identify four types of paramilitary involvements: (1) in civil wars; (2) in attempted coups d'etat; (3) in guerrilla attacks; and (4) in political assassination.

Considering the last category first, though there is no evidence that any foreign head of state has been killed as a result of assassination plots initiated by the CIA, United States government officials instigated plots against two foreign leaders and became embroiled in conspiracies leading to the death of three others (see Chapter 1). The CIA has been covertly involved in numerous internal wars in developing countries, including Laos, the Congo (now Zaire) and Angola. In the late 1950s, the United States invested more than $300 million to convert Laos from neutrality to a pro-Western position, and by the late 1960s, the CIA was conducting its own undeclared war at a cost of $20 to $30 million a year, complete with its own private army (35,000 mountain tribesmen supplemented by 17,000 Thai mercenaries) and air force. The agency was also deeply involved in the Congolese civil war of the early 1960s, supplying money, arms, mercenaries and its own bombers to support the pro-American faction against Soviet-supplied insurgents. In the mid-1970s, the superpowers were involved in another Angolan civil war, this time in newly independent and resource-rich Angola, with each side providing hundreds of millions of dollars in military supplies, advisors and mercenaries to rival liberation groups.[33] Throughout the post-

World War II period, the CIA also attempted to harass various Communist governments (China, North Korea, North Vietnam, countries in Eastern Europe and the Soviet Union itself) by sporadic guerrilla raids, though it failed to organize resistance movements in these countries.[34].

Special operations have had their most resounding successes, as well as their most glaring failures, in orchestrating coups d'etat in Third World countries. The Bay of Pigs fiasco of April 1961 certainly ranks at the top of the list of failures. In this ill-starred venture, the CIA secretly trained fourteen hundred Cuban exiles in Guatemala for an assault on Cuba, complete with their own B-26 bombers and naval vessels, only to have the whole affair end in complete disaster. On the other side of the ledger are the agency's "finest hours"—the overthrow of the pro-Communist Arbenz regime in Guatemala in 1954 at the bargain-basement price of seven million dollars, and the coup that saved the throne of the Shah of Iran in 1953 for a paltry nineteen million. In between the successes and failures is the abortive revolt against the Sukarno government in Indonesia in the late 1950s, which ended in failure, but caused much less embarrassment than the Bay of Pigs invasion. One of the most recent and controversial examples of special operations was the Nixon administration's campaign to bring down the Allende government in Chile in the early 1970s.

The "Destabilization" of the Allende Regime. American foreign policy toward Latin America during the 1960s used both the carrot and the stick. President Kennedy's foreign-aid program, the Alliance for Progress, was the cornerstone of the carrot aspect of Washington's policy and was intended to foster economic development and stability side by side with the evolution of Western-style liberal, capitalist political regimes. The goal was to create a viable alternative to the revolutionary Marxist movement of Cuba's Fidel Castro, which threatened United States economic interests and political influence in an area of traditional American hegemony. The stick side of the policy was amply demonstrated by the American-sponsored economic blockade against Cuba, the military intervention in the Dominican Republic in 1965 and the CIA's campaign against Ché Guevara in Bolivia in 1967. In Chile, one of the most advanced countries in Latin America, the United States contributed over a billion dollars in economic and technical assistance during the progressive administration of Eduardo Frei Montalva (1964–1970), and with Chile receiving the highest per capita American aid of any country in the hemisphere, the United States presented the country to the world as "the liberal alternative to Castro-Communism." [35]

During the 1964 elections in Chile, the CIA intervened clandestinely to make sure that Frei defeated his Marxist rival, Dr. Salvador Allende Gossens, and the Agency for International Development transferred some $20 million to the country in the election year to prop up the economy and prevent domestic discontent.[36] By 1970, the situation in Santiago had deteriorated from Washington's point of view, with Frei unable to succeed himself as president, and Chilean society becoming more and more polarized between left and right. In the presidential elections in September of that year, Allende managed to edge out his liberal and conservative opponents in a three-way race and gained a 36 percent plurality of the popular votes. Because no candidate received a majority, the final choice passed to the Chilean congress, which was expected to endorse the front-runner. At this point, International Telephone and Telegraph (ITT), which had large investments in the country, offered a million dollars to the CIA, to be used to defeat Allende in the congress. What the CIA actually did during this period is not definitely known, but it is certain that the chief of the agency's clandestine services for Latin America met several times with corporate officials from ITT and other companies with significant interests in Chile and proposed a plan to sabotage the local economy in order to force the military to intervene and block Allende.[37] While these covert economic operations were being considered, the CIA was instigating a military coup and supplied financial aid, arms and equipment to various factions in the military establishment opposed to Allende. In late October, one group of conspirators kidnapped the commander-in-chief of the army (who was considered an obstacle to a coup), only to have the plot backfire when the general was killed while resisting his abductors.[38] The United States' attempts to engineer a coup had failed, at least for the time being, and Allende was confirmed as president by the Chilean congress.

The Nixon administration now shifted its emphasis from clandestine maneuvers to a long-term strategy of economic attrition and diplomatic isolation. Though publicly advocating a wait-and-see attitude, Washington was committed to a policy of bringing Allende down and eliminating a new Communist threat to the Americas. However, Chile had too sophisticated a political system and too long a tradition of military neutrality for the use of coarse banana-republic techniques. The Nixon administration therefore embarked upon a course of action to isolate Allende diplomatically, undermine his economy, support his opponents and encourage the military to intervene.

Shortly after ascending to power, Allende moved to nationalize the remaining American ownership of the Chilean copper industry without compensation and took over the operations of ITT in his country. Confiscation of American private investments gave Washington the opportunity to threaten economic reprisals openly, though the imposition of sanctions had actually already begun. Addressing the United Nations General Assembly in 1972, Allende charged that the United States was committing aggression against Chile by means of an "invisible financial and economic blockade." In reality, the Nixon administration stopped short of a genuine economic blockade, but it had indeed brought economic pressure to bear by applying a tourniquet to the flow of credit from abroad. AID loans to Chile negotiated before Allende's election were not cut off, but no new assistance was provided to the new regime and none was requested by it. The administration directed the U.S. Export-Import Bank to suspend all loans and guarantees to Chile and, largely as a result, credit from private American banks was reduced from $219 million to $32 million between 1970 and 1972. The United States used its dominant position in the World Bank and the Inter-American Development Bank (it controls 40 percent of the votes in each institution) to thwart Chile's efforts to secure international loans. In the private sector, the expropriated copper companies increased their exports from the United States in the hope of preempting traditional Chilean markets, and the Agency for International Development funnelled money into Yugoslavia to develop its copper mines. (However, American military aid to Chile not only continued but was actually significantly increased during the Allende years.[39])

As a result of American financial pressure, coupled with the inept domestic economic policies of the Allende government, the Chilean economic situation progressively worsened: Agricultural production and industrial output dropped, inflation rose to appalling heights (323 percent between mid-1972 and mid-1973) and foreign-exchange reserves dwindled. With rampant inflation, a severe shortage of consumer goods and spare parts and government policies favoring the lower socioeconomic groups at the expense of the upper, the middle class revolted with strikes and riots. By the summer of 1973, the government was compelled to declare a state of emergency in the capital as sporadic bombings, street fighting and terrorism poised Chile on the brink of civil war.

From the time Allende came to power, the CIA funneled $8 million into this country of ten million people, distributing these funds to opposition political parties and newspapers, unions and professional organizations, paramilitary and extremist groups and even to members of Allende's governing coalition, with the hope of subverting the regime from within its ranks. The military leadership finally decided to act, and in September 1973, the regime was overthrown and Allende himself killed (either by his own hand or that of the conspirators). From the evidence available, it appears that the CIA was not directly involved in the coup itself, and yet the scenario envisaged by Washington in the early days of the Allende administration has a remarkable resemblance to events as they subsequently unfolded.

The United States government had decided to undermine the Chilean economy and covertly aid opposition groups in anticipation of a military coup. To what extent American action contributed to Allende's downfall is a matter of speculation, and it is quite possible that the regime would have fallen under its own weight. Salvador Allende was a minority president of tenuous legitimacy who had alienated Chile's large middle class and the armed forces, and his domestic policies helped bring about the country's economic dislocation and subsequent social strife. Thus, though the causal connection between United States economic pressures and clandestine operations and the overthrow of the Allende government is open to question, American intentions are not. Nearly a year to the day after the coup, President Ford publicly responded to the charges of United States complicity in Allende's ouster by declaring his support for the covert use of the CIA to "help implement foreign policy and protect national security." [40]

Force: International Extortion

There is a good deal of truth in Mao Tse-tung's oft-quoted statement, "Power grows out of the barrel of a gun." To the extent that power is normally exercised by means more subtle than blatant violence, this is an overstatement. Even in the anarchic environment of world politics, open warfare is the exception rather than the norm in relations among rival countries. However, this does not mean that force plays a peripheral role in the international system. On the contrary, the very nature of politics without government ensures a perpetual "state of war" in the Hobbesian sense that, though interstate warfare is neither constant nor pervasive, "the will to contend by battle is sufficiently known." [41] In a political system characterized by scarcity of values, lack of a common conception of justice and absence of centralized authority, it could not be otherwise. As the French theorist Raymond Aron writes:

> Relations between sovereign states may be more or less bellicose; they are never *essentially* or *ultimately* peaceful. To eliminate the possibility of war is to deprive states of the right to be ultimate judges of what the defense of their interests or their honor demands. Would it not be contradictory for states to agree to disarm if they reserved the right to take the law into their own hands? [42]

Force, or the attempt by states to affect the behavior of other states through the threat or use of armed coercion,[43] is therefore inherent in international relations.

The governments of the world devote a good deal more of their energy and wealth to providing for their armed forces than to exploring the means for their abolition; for example, the Pentagon's annual budget of over $100 billion is ten thousand times as large as the Arms Control and Disarmament Agency's. The world as a whole devotes nearly 6 percent of the planetary product (about $350 billion annually) to preparation for war. (For the sake of comparison, the annual budget of the United Nations was about $300 million in 1975.) Naturally, the lion's share of this burden is borne by the superpowers, which together account for over three-quarters of global military expenditures; moreover, the relative burden of military spending among states (as measured by its proportion to total GNP) is very unequal, ranging from over 45 percent for Israel to 0.13 percent for Panama. Nevertheless, both rich and poor spend scarce resources on military purposes. Since 1945, the United States alone has shipped over $100 billion worth of arms to 136 countries around the globe, almost all of which was given away as foreign aid until the mid-1960s. In the period between 1963 and 1973, the value of world arms exports doubled in real terms (after adjusting for inflation) and by 1975, the Third World alone was spending some $81.67 billion on the acquisition of arms every year. No matter what figures are used or what perspective is chosen, the conclusion is inescapable: states invest vast amounts of scarce resources in the instruments of military coercion.[44]

In his exhaustive study of war, Professor Quincy Wright estimated that human warfare probably began a million years ago as a form of "displacement upon an external enemy of aggressive impulses which might disrupt the group."[45] Whether we accept this explanation or not, it is apparent that military coercion is as old as human society itself, and that much of the history of modern international relations is little more than preparation for war, conduct of war, and aftermath of war. Until a few decades ago, the right of waging war was considered the unfettered privilege of state sovereignty, and despite all the progress in international law and organization (see Chapter 5), force remains the ultimate arbiter of international conflict when peaceful accommodation fails. States can, and normally do, settle disputes among themselves by less costly means. However, the resort to violence will occur at the point in a conflict at which at least one party, being frustrated in its attempt to attain its ends through nonviolent competition, feels that the potential costs, risks and benefits are such that it is rational and expedient to pursue those ends by means of acts of violence against its opponent. War is therefore a strategy of violence to persuade another state that the costs of opposition will be prohibitive. As the nineteenth-century Prussian military strategist Karl von Clausewitz so aptly put it, "War is . . . an act of violence intended to compel our opponent to fulfill our will." [46] That war is a rational means to a desired end is a concept of the utmost importance. Even in primitive societies in which war is apparently an end in itself, close examination will reveal the ultimate goal to be some intangible factor such as desire for glory or adventure or to satisfy some biological or psychological need.[47] The use of force in interstate relations is the result of a conscious decision to defend what are perceived to be vital interests. Again quoting Clausewitz: "War is a mere continuation of policy by other means." [48]

War is an instrument of foreign policy in much the same way as diplomacy, economics and subversion are, but it is usually a costly and highly risky undertaking. As is the case with all varieties of negative sanctions, the mere threat of military coercion is an important arm of policy in itself, and it is this perpetual threat of force hanging over international relations (more so than sporadic outbreaks of actual hostilities) that distinguishes international politics from domestic politics. Governments need not constantly and formally remind their opposites that force is available to compel the reallocation of regional and global values. Though during times of acute international crisis, diplomatic ultimatums and warnings may occasionally be transmitted between rival capitals, specific threats of force are not the rule. The threat of possible recourse to violence is implicit in the very circumstances of world politics, and national policy makers live and operate in an environment of endless competition punctuated by periodic journeys to the brink of war. Indeed, "brinkmanship"—the manipulation of fear of war—has become a cornerstone of the conduct of foreign policy, especially among the major powers.

War and the threat of war are the principal manifestations of force in the international system. Force is demonstrated and applied in interstate crises for either or both of the following purposes: (1) to foster or oppose redistribution of values; and (2) to demonstrate willingness to carry out threats.

Let us use an example from organized crime. In the United States today, one of the largest business enterprises is loan sharking, which, together with hijacking and sale of stolen goods, brings in (tax-free, of course) revenues of more than $100 billion annually. The loan shark sells money—"the most expensive money in the world"—at the rate of 20 percent a week, which means that the recipient of a $100 loan must pay back $20 a week in interest until the principal itself is repaid. If the borrower falls behind in his payments, two options remain open to the syndicate loaning the money: The borrower can be made to pay with "a pound of flesh" or, if he is a legitimate businessman, he might find himself with a new partner.[49] The use of force in such circumstances may prove useless, for killing or maiming the client may preclude repayment of the loan. On the other hand, the mere threat of force is more than likely enough to gain compliance. But occasionally violence must be employed if only to indicate to potential borrowers the punitive measures the loan shark has at his disposal.

This line of reasoning applies to international politics, in which statesmen continually seek to impress upon potential foes the credibility of their threats to impose military sanctions. As we have seen in our examination of the Vietnam negotiations, the Nixon Administration did not consider South Vietnam per se worth the costs involved in pursuing military victory; however, the reputation of the United States for fulfilling its commitments to allied states was deemed important enough to warrant continuation of hostilities. The credibility of the American military guarantee, not the long-run survival of the Saigon regime, was judged to be the real stake in the conflict. By the same token, when defeat in Indochina came, Washington sought to salvage a bit of its tarnished reputation by recapturing a merchant vessel seized by the new Cambodian government. Force, then, is applied in international politics to affect the distribution of values at issue at the moment or to affect the long-run allocation of values by reinforcing the credibility of future threats.

The threat of force is an effective instrument of policy when the threatening state succeeds in convincing its opponent that it has both the capability to inflict harm and the will to accept the costs involved in doing so. The prospect of punitive action is conveyed to rival governments by means of several mechanisms: (1) diplomatic threats or warnings; (2) formal commitments; (3) deployment of forces; (4) military display; and (5) reputation.[50]

There is a subtle but important distinction between a threat and a warning. A threat announces the clear-cut intention of one state to undertake coercive measures against another in the event that the latter initiates, continues or refuses to undertake a certain course of action. When in the fall of 1956 Nikita Khrushchev announced his intention of launching ballistic missiles (IRBMs) against Britain and France if they continued their invasion of Egypt, he employed just such an unambiguous threat. When the Eisenhower Administration responded with a pledge to defend the United States' allies with the American nuclear arsenal, it used the same device. A warning differs from a threat in that the communication of intention is more ambiguous. During the Bay of Pigs invasion in 1961, President Kennedy made strong representations to the Kremlin to stay out of this "domestic" Cuban matter, and yet he did not specify what action (if any) Washington would take to prevent Soviet intervention. At other times a warning may not even carry a hint of military confrontation, but may only hold out the prospect of a deterioration in relations, as in the case of Secretary of State Kissinger's warning to Moscow during the Angolan civil war in late 1975 and early 1976. A warning, then, amounts to a prediction by one state of the probable unfortunate consequences of another state's behavior.

Formal commitments are used in international relations to communicate to potential adversaries that military response will be automatic. By voluntarily accepting a legal and public obligation to come to the defense of another country, a government seeks to convince prospective aggressors that its threat of armed reprisal in the event of attack is steadfast and irrevocable. The credibility of a threat depends on rival states believing that the threatening state will indeed employ coercive military sanctions if provoked, and by solemnly committing itself in advance, the threatening state attempts to create the impression that honor will allow no way out of its obligations. The more an actor appears to have tied his hands for the future, the less likely he will be thought to be bluffing (assuming, of course, that he possesses the capability to do what he claims he will do). The United States, the principal defender of the post–World War II status quo, has made widespread use of commitments in the form of mutual security pacts, which are, in fact, the unilateral American guarantee of the territorial integrity of some forty countries around the globe.

Another way of demonstrating one's resolve is by deploying armed forces in or near an area of vital interest on a permanent basis. This has been the principal purpose of the several hundred thousand American troops stationed in central Europe since the end of the Second World War. With superiority in strategic nuclear forces vis-à-vis the Soviet Union and inferiority in conventional manpower, the Truman and Eisenhower administrations saw no need for inordinately large ground forces in Europe. Ground forces were limited to a "tripwire" contingent in western Europe, which would demonstrate politically United States determination to come to the defense of its allies with the Strategic Air Command (SAC), and which would, militarily, serve as a burglar alarm by giving early and indisputable evidence of a major Russian attack. The troops were not there to repulse a Soviet invasion or wage general war but to serve as "hostages," assuring the western Europeans and the Soviets that Washington's threat of nuclear retaliation was credible.

Troops may also be deployed on a temporary basis during international crises to signal willingness to escalate the conflict to the point of military confrontation. At several junctures during his brief tenure in office, President Kennedy dispatched American armed forces to trouble-spots in anticipation of hostilities. When Khrushchev promised to sign a separate peace treaty with East Germany, thereby threatening Western access to West Berlin, Kennedy reinforced the American military garrison in West Berlin and mobilized reserve units at home in the hope of persuading Moscow that the United States was prepared to go to war in defense of its interests. Similarly, the same administration sent troops to the Thai-Laotian border when Communist forces appeared on the verge of overrunning Laos.

Military display is similarly a means of conveying a threat of punitive action and was employed by the United States during the Cuban missile crisis of 1962, when reserve units were called into active service, an invasion force was organized in Florida and the Strategic Air Command was placed on alert. And in the wake of signs of Soviet intentions to intervene during the Middle East war of 1973, President Nixon ordered a worldwide nuclear alert of American strategic forces. Whatever means are used—diplomatic threats and warnings, commitments, military deployment, or military display—the message the initiating state seeks to convey is the same: War is an acceptable price to pay for the defense of the values in dispute.

The final instrument of the threat of force is a by-product of successful threats in the past. When judging whether a state's threats are to be taken seriously, its previous record will inevitably be taken into consideration. The successful use of the threat of force is similar to the successful use of tactics in poker, in which a player who has a reputation for bluffing is more likely to have his hand called than one who consistently bets from a position of strength. Because manipulation of the fear of war is an attempt to affect the perceptions of potential enemies, policy makers cultivate a reputation for firmness and resolution.

Nowhere is the threat of war more central to the conduct of contemporary international politics than in the superpowers' policies of nuclear deterrence. The nuclear revolution has had a fundamental effect on the relationship between the threat of violence and the use of violence in relations among rival powers. Just a generation ago, general war among hostile countries was still a viable instrument of foreign policy, as it had been since the gestation of the modern state system in the seventeenth century. Ever since the mass mobilization of the nation-in-arms during the Napoleonic Wars in the early nineteenth century, unlimited warfare increased in ferocity and destructiveness; yet, total war among the major powers could still be regarded as the rational culmination of conflict over global hegemony. Despite the unprecedented expenditure of blood and treasure that the Second World War entailed, it could still be justified as the necessary price to be paid to thwart the rise of the Nazis to supremacy.

The introduction of weapons of mass destruction in 1945 began a process that altered the role of force in foreign policy, and by the mid-1950s, when the Soviet Union acquired a significant capability to rain devastation on the United States, calculated initiation of total war lost any semblance of rationality. The policy of deterrence (for further consideration of the mechanics of deterrence, see Chapter 3), or dissuading an adversary from embarking upon a certain course of action by threatening reprisals, is nothing new in international relations. Foreign policy is and always has been a combination of deterrence and compellence. In military terms, states have always sought to deter enemy attack by affecting other states' calculations of costs and gains—that is, by convincing them that the war would bring defeat or, at the very least, would be prohibitively expensive. However, the crucial difference between deterring general war in the prenuclear era and in the atomic age is that if nuclear deterrence should fail, there is no defense against annihilation and no prospect of meaningful victory. Now, while the threat of force is central to preserving a balance of terror, actual resort to total war is no longer an option of foreign policy.

The present stability in the international system is therefore based upon the condition of mutual deterrence (for a detailed discussion of mutual deterrence, see Chapter 5), which has condemned the superpowers to an uneasy, but acceptable, coexistence. Yet even though total war is ruled out as an instrument of policy, interstate relations have not been so altered that the use of force at lower levels of confrontation has also been eliminated. As Raymond Aron aptly puts it, "If atomic war is an absurd possibility for all the belligerents, it will not take place, though this does not mean that history will be exempt from the law of violence." [51] The thermonuclear stalemate assures that general war between the United States and the Soviet Union will not occur—at least not as a rational choice by decision makers in Washington and Moscow, though the possibility of inadvertent or accidental war cannot be totally discounted. Moreover, the proliferation of nuclear weaponry among numerous small powers is expected to proceed at such a pace that a respected group of nuclear-arms experts at the Harvard-MIT Arms Control Seminar concluded that nuclear war, probably between small powers, will erupt before the end of this century.[52] But for the time being, a direct exchange between the superpowers can, for all intents and purposes, be ruled out, especially since recent studies indicate that even if the attacking state escaped nuclear retaliation (unlikely, certainly), a massive surprise attack might cause a severe ecological and economic backlash against the aggressor.[53]

The balance of terror also tends to make Washington and Moscow wary of involvement in local conflicts which might embroil them in escalating military confrontation, and, to this extent, the existence of equivalent destructive capabilities on each side tends to mitigate and civilize big-power rivalry. Recognizing their mutual interest in avoiding situations of conflict that might get out of control, President Nixon and Secretary Brezhnev signed an agreement in June of 1973 pledging their governments to remove the danger of nuclear war by avoiding encounters likely to exacerbate relations and lead to military confrontation. To be sure, there is nothing self-enforcing in this agreement, and it is merely one part of the ambiguous guidelines for détente. In fact, within four months of signing this document, the two countries were actively involved on opposite sides in the Yom Kippur War, each threatening the other with the possibility of escalation. But this is hardly surprising, for as we have seen, the threat of force is inherent in the decentralized nature of world politics; and it cannot be abolished without abolishing the anarchic character of the international system. This is not in the offing as long as each state jealously protects its sovereign right to be the ultimate guardian of its interests. Nevertheless, the dangers inherent in superpower confrontation presage a conscious policy of restraint, especially when the superpowers are engaged in the risky exercise of brinkmanship.

To sum up, it appears that war between the superpowers is no longer a viable option of foreign policy: Nuclear war can have no feasible political objective, and any conventional war between the major powers can too easily escalate into nuclear war. However, the use of force in international relations remains possible at lower levels of conflict, including: (1) conventional war between non-nuclear powers (for example, the Indians and the Pakistanis in 1965, the Arabs and the Israelis in 1967 and 1973); (2) military intervention by the superpowers in their respective spheres of influence (the Soviet Union and Czechoslovakia in 1968, the United States and the Dominican Republic in 1965); (3) indirect or paramilitary intervention by major powers in civil wars in the Third World (the Soviet Union in Angola in 1975/76); and (4) terrorism by self-styled liberation groups.[54] Wars in which the superpowers do engage will therefore tend to be of a limited nature—limited in terms of the stakes involved, the weapons employed and the theater of hostilities.

Not since before the French Revolution has the international system been dominated by limited, as opposed to total, war. But the seventeenth century was a prenationalist, preideological and preindustrial period when warfare was limited not so much by choice as by the tenuous loyalties and resources available to dynastic rulers. During the last quarter of the twentieth century, the use of force among the major powers must be limited by design, despite—indeed, because of—unprecedented potential force. As for military conflict among smaller powers, it will tend to be limited in duration because of their dependence upon the superpowers for a supply of sophisticated weaponry and because of the expensive nature of modern warfare.

For illustrative purposes, we will briefly consider two case studies: the Cuban missile crisis of 1962 and the Middle East war of 1973. The first will be used as a classical example of superpower brinkmanship and manipulation of the threat of force; the second demonstrates the use of force in international politics and its essentially political, as opposed to military, nature. By means of these two cases, we will attempt to clarify the nature of international extortion.

The Threat of Force: the Cuban Missile Crisis. The origin of the Russo-American nuclear confrontation of October 1962 [55] can be traced back to 1957, when the Soviet Union announced a successful test of the world's first intercontinental ballistic missile (ICBM) and soon followed this with the launching of the first artificial earth satellite (Sputnik). Though the Eisenhower Administration remained confident that not even a Russian quantitative superiority in ICBMs would impair the credibility of an American nuclear deterrent, opinion leaders in the United States and abroad expressed real fears of a "missile gap" which would give the Soviets a first-strike capability (that is, the capacity to disarm the United States in a massive surprise attack and escape retaliation). It was feared that, at best, having neutralized Washington at the strategic level, the Soviet Union would go on to the offensive at lower levels of conflict (for example, by using its conventional war superiority to initiate limited probes on the periphery of the "free world") and overturn the world balance of power.

Though the Soviets eventually decided against a massive investment of scarce resources in first-generation ICBMs and the dreaded missile gap did not materialize, Khrushchev embarked upon a bold policy of rocket rattling and Sputnik diplomacy so as to make the most of Western anxiety. In the wake of his space spectacular, Khrushchev claimed that his missiles rendered American bombers and overseas bases obsolete and threatened Turkey with a devastating attack. He confidently asserted that Soviet advances in rocketry would destroy the capitalist world in a war, and "socialism will live on." Well aware that power is ultimately a psychological relationship and that a state is as powerful as its opponents perceive it to be, Khrushchev struck a bellicose pose, brandishing his illusory military might at every turn, pursuing a policy of bluff to undermine the postwar international status quo protected by the United States.

When John F. Kennedy became President in 1961, Washington sought to blunt the Soviet diplomatic offensive, and the new administration (which had exploited domestic fears of a missile gap during the preceding election campaign) immediately announced that the United States still had overwhelming strategic superiority and would increase its lead in the years ahead, thereby creating a "missile-gap-in-reverse." Kennedy's first year in office was full of recurring crises with the Soviet Union (in Cuba, Laos, Vietnam, the Congo and Berlin), and in response to Khrushchev's continuing aggressive rhetoric (this time in reference to "wars of national liberation"), the United States began the largest and swiftest military buildup in its peacetime history.

It is in this context that we must try to understand Khrushchev's risky decision to secretly install some seventy medium- and intermediate-range ballistic missiles (MRBMs and IRBMs) in Cuba. If he succeeded in pulling off the gamble and presenting Washington with a *fait accompli*, in one stroke the Soviet Union would have doubled its first-strike capability against the American heartland and done so at a cost commensurate with Russian economic capacity. Though his new missile force in Cuba would still leave America with an overall two-to-one edge in strategic power, he probably reasoned that "the shift in the military balance of power would be less crucial than that in the political balance."[56] That is, if he could outflank Kennedy ninety miles from American territory, he would demonstrate for all to see that the tide of the cold war was turning in Moscow's favor. In particular, Krushchev hoped to demoralize the NATO allies and force them to reassess the credibility of the United States' commitment to go to war on their behalf. If the United States balked at removing some 150 nuclear-tipped Soviet missiles from Cuba, would it commit suicide in order to defend its foreign allies? If the American guarantee of the global status quo could be shaken, the Soviets could make diplomatic inroads into western Europe, the Middle East, south Asia and even Latin America.

Throughout the summer of 1962, President Kennedy received reports of a massive influx of Soviet military personnel and materiel into Cuba. In mid-September, the President issued a public warning at a press conference:

> If at any time the Communist buildup in Cuba were to endanger or interfere with our security in any way . . . or if Cuba should ever . . . become an offensive military base of

> significant capacity for the Soviet Union, then this country will do whatever must be done to protect its own security and that of its allies.[57]

In response, Kennedy received public and private assurances from Moscow that its purposes in Cuba were strictly defensive. Within a month, aerial surveillance revealed the extent of the Soviet deception, and on October 16, the President was informed that offensive missile installations were indeed nearing completion and would soon be operational. Kennedy immediately appreciated the consequences of Soviet duplicity as "the supreme . . . probe of American intentions."[58] and concluded that the missiles must go. The question now was how to get Soviet compliance and yet not enter a military confrontation that might end in mutually destructive war. Diplomatic warning had failed to deter Khrushchev from installing the missiles. To have them removed, the prospect of force would have to be conveyed to the Kremlin.

The President assembled an ad hoc Executive Committee (Ex Comm) of the National Security Council to present him with an analysis of the means available. On October 18, Kennedy went ahead with a prearranged conference with Soviet Foreign Minister Gromyko and, while giving no indication that he knew about the Cuban installations, he reiterated his warning of the previous month. Meanwhile, Ex Comm had narrowed the responses to two: an air attack and a naval blockade. An air attack would be quicker, more forceful and more efficient, but a limited attack was not feasible and a massive one would have to be followed by invasion. An air attack would kill Soviet personnel and might precipitate a Soviet military response in another theater (probably Europe). This was too great a price to be paid—at least for the time being—so Ex Comm decided to rely for the moment on what would be termed a quarantine (a blockade is a formal act of war under international law). Since the superpowers' nuclear arsenals precluded recourse to general war, the confrontation would be kept at a conventional level of intensity. Given the proximity of America's vast air, naval and ground forces, the Soviets would have no alternative but to capitulate or initiate another crisis somewhere else, where the ratio of conventional military power might be more in their favor. But in the latter case, the onus of escalation would be placed on Khrushchev.

On October 22, President Kennedy presented Khrushchev with what amounted to an ultimatum. Before a nationwide television audience, he declared that the deception perpetrated by the Soviet Union was "a deliberately provocative and unjustified change in the status quo which cannot be accepted by this country, if our courage and our commitments are ever to be trusted again by friend and foe." In order to secure removal of the missiles, he announced his willingness to go to war if need be: "We will not prematurely or unnecessarily risk the costs of worldwide nuclear war . . . but neither will we shrink from that risk at any time it must be faced." Kennedy then presented his initial plan of action, reinforcing the credibility of this threat: a quarantine of all offensive weapons en route to Cuba to be enforced by the armed forces. He emphasized that this was only a first step, and if construction of the installations was continued, "further action will be justified. . . . I have directed the Armed Forces," he said, "to prepare for any eventuality." [59] The next day United States strategic forces were placed on maximum alert and an invasion force of 200,000 troops began assembling in Florida. The message conveyed to Moscow was clear: Either withdraw the missiles or force will be employed against Cuba.

For several days, this confrontation between the superpowers remained unsettled. Khrushchev, caught off balance, struggled to get out of the corner into which he had been maneuvered. He called the blockade piracy, refused to acquiesce to it and accelerated construction of the missile complexes. At the end of the second week of the crisis, the President received word that the missiles would be in place and ready to fire in a matter of days. The blockade could not prevent this and, as an implicit threat of force, it had thus far failed to achieve its objective. On October 27, a note was sent to Khrushchev demanding notification by the next day of his intention to withdraw the missiles or "the consequences would be extremely grave for the Soviet Union." [60] Finally convinced of the American resolve to use force, the Soviet premier agreed to remove the missiles and refrain from reintroducing them, in return for Washington's pledge not to invade.

So both sides backed away from war. For the United States, the missiles were a symbol of Soviet doubt of the credibility of American resolve in defense of its interests. By means of the threat of violence, the missiles, and that doubt, were removed. The credibility of Washington's threat to use force had been re-established.

The Use of Force: the Yom Kippur War. In recent decades, no region of the globe has been more susceptible to interstate violence than the Middle East. Since the end of the Second World War, there have been no less than four wars between Israel and its Arab neighbors (1948, 1956, 1967, 1973), and violence continues to haunt that area in the late 1970s.

The phenomenon of recurring war in the Middle East signifies the inability of either side to impose its will upon the other and allocate the values in dispute—for the most part, territory and security—on a permanent basis. Moreover, superimposed upon the local configuration of power (that is, the balance between Israel and the Arabs) is the global competition for influence between the United States and the Soviet Union. Because both superpowers have defined their vital national interests in terms of the area the conflict cannot be resolved solely by local distribution of power. Any long-term settlement of outstanding issues must satisfy the minimum demands of all the participants, and distributing values to the liking of the various (and often antagonistic) Arab countries and Israel, as well as the contending global powers, is certainly a tall order. Thus far, a settlement has not been possible because the minimum demands of all the parties have proven incompatible.

The war of October 1973 was a continuation of the politically inconclusive Six Day War of 1967. Militarily, the Israelis had registered a quick and decisive victory over their opponents in 1967 and had occupied not only the Gaza Strip and the Arab sector of Jerusalem, but also the whole of the Sinai Peninsula, the west bank of the Jordan River and the Golan Heights portion of Syria. For the Israelis, these occupied territories provided a security buffer shielding their geographically vulnerable country from the surrounding hostile Arab states. The new boundaries gave Israel a margin of safety that it had not known since its creation some twenty years before. Given the long history of Arab animosity, guerrilla raids, artillery barrages and sporadic large-scale fighting, Israel preferred these boundaries to the precarious pre-1967 borders.

For the Arab states, on the other hand, the results of their defeat in the Six Day War were totally unacceptable. If a Jewish state in Palestine was perceived to be an affront to Arab nationalism prior to 1967, the loss of additional lands and the memory of the Arab legions' military humiliation at the hands of their hated enemy would prove to be more than they could bear. Yet, the Arab world, with a population of 130 million, could not match Israel, with a population of 3 million, on the field of battle, and this knowledge could serve only to compound their wounded pride and increasing frustration. The distribution of values decreed by the Israeli victory in 1967 had to be overturned, but even the great influx of sophisticated military equipment and advisors from the Soviet Union in the years following the war could not redress the military balance.

By 1973, the Israelis had slipped into dangerous complacency and were firmly convinced that the Arabs knew that Israel was invincible and would not attack in the forseeable future. If their enemies were so foolhardy as to try their hands at hostilities again, the Israelis believed there would simply be a replay of the lightning victory of 1967. But Jerusalem failed to appreciate the intensity of Arab frustration with the stalemate of the past several years.

War is a political act. Its object is to further the ends of policy. If war were a purely military exercise, it would degenerate into conflict without quarter, mass annihilation without purpose, a blood feud among nations. It is for this reason that civilians, not soldiers, are responsible for the conduct of foreign policy. As Georges Clemenceau remarked: "War is too important a matter to be left to the generals." While a general thinks of military victory and vanquishing the enemy on the battlefield, a statesman must utilize force, not for the sake of force itself, but in the interests of the state as he perceives them. As the Israelis would soon discover, military victory and political victory are not always synonymous.

Discontented groups were extremely volatile in Egypt, the key Arab country. After years of diplomatic struggle to eradicate the consequences of past defeat, the stalemate continued, the Egyptian economy stagnated and society as a whole remained demoralized. President Anwar Sadat, lacking the legitimacy and charisma of his predecessor Gamal Nasser, realized that his tenure of office would depend largely on gaining ground on the Israeli front. Under strong pressure from his military chiefs and elements in the governmental bureaucracy, Sadat concluded that "any war short of one that was certain to end in quick and total disaster would be preferable to staying still." [61] The Egyptian goal, therefore, was to break the stalemate politically, not to win the war militarily. At most, the Arabs felt they might be able to seize and hold a strip of territory along the east bank of the Suez Canal; at the very least, perhaps they could prevent a repetition of the 1967 disaster long enough to involve the United States and the Soviet Union in bargaining for the recovery of occupied lands. As one Middle East observer notes:

> One important lesson the Israelis began to learn is that even a militarily inferior opponent might find it advantageous to go to war if he is left with no better options. Israelis deemed war "impossible" because they thought Sadat could not possibly hope to win. They did not realize that it might pay for him to go to war if he had reasonable chances of not suffering a crushing defeat very quickly.[62]

In October, with careful preparation and coordination, the Arab countries struck in a surprise attack. On the Sinai front, the Egyptians poured across the Suez Canal, overran the Israeli defense lines and established a major bridgehead on the east bank; on the Syrian front, the Israelis were forced back by the onslaught of enemy troops spearheaded by nearly a thousand tanks. Having seized the initiative, the Arabs fought well, denying the Israelis air supremacy and inflicting high casualties.

However, by the second week of the battle, the Israelis were everywhere on the offensive, advancing beyond the Golan Heights into Syria and crossing the canal and establishing their own bridgehead in Egypt. In the interim, first the Soviet Union and then the United States launched massive resupply operations to the belligerents as the ferocity of the fighting consumed enormous quantities of matériel. (Estimates of the cost of the war to Israel alone run as high as seven and a half billion dollars—equivalent to the Israeli gross national product for the entire year.)[63] The tide of battle had turned decisively against the Arabs.

When the Israelis were on the verge of surrounding the Egyptian army in the Sinai and within twenty miles of Damascus, the Soviets and the Egyptians joined the United States in calling for an immediate cease-fire in place. Despite two United Nations Security Council resolutions to that effect, the fighting continued. Fearing that their Arab allies would soon suffer resounding defeat, the Soviets threatened to intervene unilaterally and enforce the cease-fire. Apparently they believed the United States indeed desired a cessation to hostilities, but feared that Washington had lost control over the Israelis. The United States countered with a threat of its own, placing its worldwide strategic forces on alert, and simultaneously increased its pressure on the Israelis to halt their advance.* Finally, the superpowers agreed on a UN emergency force free of major-power participation to supervise the cease-fire.

Despite détente, both powers employed the threat of force: the Soviets to demonstrate their support to their Arab friends and prevent a decisive Israeli victory; the United States to neutralize the Soviet threat.

By any standards of military strategy, the Israelis had won the war, though they had been deprived of total victory. But, politically, the Arabs were the victors. Though they gained no territory (in fact, they lost some), their performance during the war vindicated their past humiliation. More important, the Arabs had demonstrated a newfound unity, successfully employed the

* In his 1977 interview with David Frost, former President Nixon characterized his attempt to bring the Israelis under control in the following way: "We reasoned with them. . . . To paraphrase the Godfather, we made them an offer they could not refuse."

weapon of oil against the West, inflicted real harm on the Israelis and destroyed the myth of Israeli invincibility and involved the major powers in a search for a settlement. In short, they had broken the stalemate of the past six years. This had been their goal to begin with.[64]

War, then, is the ultimate strategy when all other means of foreign policy prove futile. But whether or not the threat of force is explicitly involved in the conduct of foreign relations, it is always implicit in the very nature of the international system. Whether by persuasion (friendly or otherwise), manipulation of wealth, subversion or extortion, states mean to carve out for themselves as large a portion of the global pie as their resources will allow. This is the essence of politics without government.

Notes
Chapter 4

1. Thomas C. Schelling, *The Strategy of Conflict* (New York: Oxford University Press, 1963), p. 5.
2. Dwight D. Eisenhower, *Peace With Justice: Selected Addresses,* ed. Grayson Kirk (New York: Columbia University Press, 1961), pp. 37–38.
3. Frederick L. Schuman, *International Politics: Anarchy and Order in the World Society* (New York: McGraw-Hill, 1969), pp. 33–34.
4. Harold Nicolson, *Diplomacy,* 3rd ed. (New York: Oxford University Press, 1964), p. 6.
5. Harold Nicolson, *The Evolution of Diplomacy* (New York: Collier, 1962), chapter 1.
6. Nicolson, *Diplomacy,* p. 20; also Garrett Mattingly, *Renaissance Diplomacy* (Baltimore, Md.: Penguin, 1964).
7. Henry Kissinger, *Nuclear Weapons and Foreign Policy* (New York: Harper, 1957), pp. 4–6.
8. Adapted from Fred C. Ikle, *How Nations Negotiate* (New York: Praeger, 1967), pp. 3–4.

9. Quoted in Stephen R. Graubard, *Kissinger: Portrait of a Mind* (New York: Norton, 1974), p. 264.

10. The discussion here concerning the progress of diplomatic negotiations between Washington and Hanoi is adapted largely from Tad Szulc, "How Kissinger Did It: Behind the Vietnam Cease-Fire Agreement," *Foreign Policy* 15 (Summer 1974): 21–69.

11. Klaus Knorr, *The Power of Nations: The Political Economy of International Relations* (New York: Basic Books, 1975), p. 89.

12. Bension Varon and Kenji Takeuchi, "Developing Countries and Non-Fuel Minerals," *Foreign Affairs* 52 (April, 1974): 508.

13. Knorr, p. 165.

14. Helmut Schmidt, "The Struggle for the World Product: Politics Between Power and Morals," *Foreign Affairs* 52 (April, 1974): 442. (Emphasis added.)

15. Jahangir Amuzegar, "The Oil Story: Facts, Fiction and Fair Play," *Foreign Affairs* 51 (July, 1973): 676.

16. Peter R. Odell, *Oil and World Power: Background of the Oil Crisis,* 3rd ed. (Baltimore, Md.: Penguin, 1974), chapters 5 and 6.

17. Of the seven major oil companies, five are American-based (Exxon, Mobil, Gulf, So-Cal, and Texaco) and two are European (Royal Dutch Shell and British Petroleum).

18. The discussion presented here concerning the formation of OPEC is drawn from James E. Akins, "The Oil Crisis: The Time of the Wolf is Here," *Foreign Affairs* 51 (April, 1973): 462–90; and Odell, *Oil and World Power,* chapters 1 and 4.

19. Thomas C. Schelling, "Economic Analysis and Organized Crime," in *Task Force Report: Organized Crime* (Washington, D.C.: President's Commission on Law Enforcement and Administration of Justice, 1967); quoted in Thomas Plate, *Crime Pays!* (New York: Simon and Schuster, 1975), note p. 211. (Emphasis added.)

20. OPEC presently consists of thirteen states: Saudi Arabia, Iran, Qatar, United Arab Emirates, Iraq, Libya, Algeria, Kuwait, Venezuela, Ecuador, Gabon, Indonesia and Nigeria.

21. Joseph S. Szyliowicz, "The Embargo and U.S. Foreign Policy," in Joseph S. Szyliowicz and Bard E. O'Neill, eds., *The Energy Crisis and U.S. Foreign Policy* (New York: Praeger, 1975), p. 210.

22. Thomas O. Enders, "OPEC and the Industrialized Countries: The Next Ten Years," *Foreign Affairs* 53 (July 1975): 625–37.

23. *Christian Science Monitor,* January 16, 1976, p. 13.

24. Clark R. Mollenhoff, *Strike Force: Organized Crime and the Government* (Englewood Cliffs, N.J.: Prentice-Hall, 1972), chapter 2.

25. Victor Marchetti and John D. Marks, *The CIA and the Cult of Intelligence* (New York: Dell, 1974), pp. 94–96.

26. Air Force Intelligence, the National Security Agency, Army Intelligence, Naval Intelligence, and the Defense Intelligence Agency (DIA).

27. Leslie H. Gelb, "Should We Play Dirty Tricks in the World?" *New York Times Magazine,* December 21, 1975, p. 15.

28. Urban G. Whitakers, ed., *Propaganda and International Relations* (San Francisco: Chandler, 1962), pp. 3–4.

29. Marchetti and Marks, *The CIA,* p. 123. (Emphasis added.)

30. *New York Times,* January 6, 1976, p. 1.

31. Marchetti and Marks, *The CIA,* pp. 71–72, 113. See also the *New York Times,* February 19, 1977, pp. 1, 9.

32. The KGB maintains a strong capability in covert operations which date back to the 1930s. Recently it has been involved in insurgencies in Portugal's former African colonies, as well as in Cambodia, Thailand, Laos and the Dhofar region of Oman on the Arabian peninsula. See the *New York Times,* June 2, 1975, p. 16.

33. David Wise and Thomas B. Ross, *The Invisible Government* (New York: Bantam, 1965), chapters 9 and 10; Marchetti and Marks, *The CIA,* pp. 53–54, 132, 245; *Christian Science Monitor,* January 2, 1976, p. 1, and January 9, 1976, p. 1.

34. Marchetti and Marks, *The CIA,* pp. 126–28; Wise and Ross, *Invisible Government,* pp. 112–16.

35. James F. Petras and Robert LaPorte, Jr., "Can We Do Business With Radical Nationalists? Chile: No," *Foreign Policy* 7 (Summer, 1972): 135.

36. Marchetti and Marks, *The CIA,* p. 39; Elizabeth Farnsworth, "Chile: What Was the U. S. Role? More Than Admitted," *Foreign Policy* 16 (Fall, 1974): 132; Anthony Sampson, *The Sovereign State of ITT* (Greenwich, Conn.: Fawcett, 1974), chapter 2. For the definitive study of American involvement in Chile, see U.S. Senate,

Select Committee to Study Governmental Operations With Respect to Intelligence Activities, *Covert Action in Chile, 1963–1973: Staff Report,* 94 Cong., 1st Sess. (Washington, D.C.: Government Printing Office, 1975).

37. Sampson, *ITT,* Marchetti and Marks, *The CIA,* pp. 41–42.

38. *New York Times,* November 21, 1975, pp. 50–53.

39. Petras and LaPorte, "Can We Do Business"; Farnsworth, "Chile"; Paul E. Sigmund, "The 'Invisible Blockade' and the Overthrow of Allende," *Foreign Affairs* 52 (January, 1974): 322–40; Paul E. Sigmund, "Chile: What was the U.S. Role? Less Than Charged," *Foreign Policy* 16 (Fall, 1974): 142–56.

40. *New York Times,* September 16, 1974, p. 1.

41. See the discussion in Chapter 1.

42. Raymond Aron, *On War,* trans. Terrence Kilmartin (New York: Norton, 1968), p. 8.

43. Adapted from Robert E. Osgood and Robert W. Tucker, *Force, Order and Justice* (Baltimore, Md.: Johns Hopkins University Press, 1967), p. 3.

44. *New York Times,* October 19, 1975, p. 18; *Christian Science Monitor,* October 16, 1975, p. 10, and November 3, 1975, p. 4; U.S. Arms Control and Disarmament Agency, *World Military Expenditures and Arms Trade, 1963–1973,* and *World Military Expenditures and Arms Transfers, 1966–1975.*

45. Quincy Wright, *A Study of War,* 2nd ed. (Chicago: University of Chicago Press, 1965), p. 373.

46. Karl von Clausewitz, *On War,* ed. R. A. Leonard (New York: Putnam's, 1967), p. 41.

47. Wright, *A Study of War,* p. 523.

48. Clausewitz, *On War,* p. 57.

49. Plate, pp. 146–60.

50. James L. Payne, *The American Threat: The Fear of War as an Instrument of Foreign Policy* (Chicago: Markham, 1970).

51. Aron, *On War,* p. 2.

52. *Christian Science Monitor,* November 13, 1975, p. 13.

53. U.S. Arms Control and Disarmament Agency, *Worldwide Effects of Nuclear War: Some Perspectives* (Washington, D.C.: Arms Control and Disarmament Agency, 1975); *New York Times,* October 5, 1975, p. 8. In a National Academy of Science study for

the ACDA, it was suggested that many large-scale nuclear detonations would cause "widespread and long-lasting environmental damage" to the aggressor country. The principal effect would not be caused by radioactive fallout, but by "the depletion of the ozone layer in the stratosphere that shields the earth from the lethal effects of the sun's ultraviolet radiation."

54. Louis J. Halle, "Does War Have a Future?" *Foreign Affairs* 52 (October, 1973): 20–34.

55. Some of the better discussions of the missile crisis include Eli Abel, *The Missile Crisis* (New York: Bantam, 1966); Arthur M. Schlesinger, Jr., *A Thousand Days* (Boston: Houghton-Mifflin, 1965); Theodore Sorensen, *Kennedy* (New York: Harper & Row, 1965); Robert F. Kennedy, *Thirteen Days* (New York: Norton, 1969); Henry M. Pachter, *Collision Course* (New York: Praeger, 1963).

56. Roberta Wohlstetter, "Cuba and Pearl Harbor," *Foreign Affairs* 43 (July, 1965): 706.

57. U.S. Department of State, *Bulletin* 47 (October 1, 1962): 482.

58. Schlesinger, *A Thousand Days,* p. 796.

59. John F. Kennedy, *Public Papers of the Presidents, 1961–1963* (Washington, D.C.: Government Printing Office, 1962–64), vol. 2 (1962), pp. 806–09.

60. Graham T. Allison, *The Essence of Decision: Explaining the Cuban Missile Crisis* (Boston: Little, Brown, 1971), chapter 2.

61. Nadav Safran, "The War and the Future of the Arab-Israeli Conflict," *Foreign Affairs* 52 (January, 1974) 216.

62. Ibid., p. 230.

63. Don Peretz, "Energy: Israelis, Arabs, and Iranians," in Szyliowicz and O'Neill, *Energy Crisis,* p. 99.

64. John C. Campbell, "The Energy Crisis and U.S. Policy in the Middle East," *ibid.,* pp. 110–124.

PART III

THE SYSTEM

My father . . . refuses to live by the rules set up by others, rules which condemn him to a defeated life. But his ultimate aim is to enter that society with a certain power since society doesn't really protect its members who do not have their own individual power. In the meantime he operates on a code of ethics he considers far superior to the legal structure of society.

—Michael Corleone, in Mario Puzo's
The Godfather

Chapter 5

The Management of Power

> Don Corleone carried his message through the United States. He conferred with compatriots in Los Angeles, San Francisco, Cleveland, Chicago, Philadelphia, Miami, and Boston. He was the underworld apostle of peace . . . and he had achieved a working agreement amongst most powerful underworld organizations in the country. Like the Constitution . . . this agreement respected fully the internal authority of each member in his state or city. The agreement covered only spheres of influence and an agreement to enforce the peace in the underworld.
>
> —MARIO PUZO, *The Godfather*

POLITICS AND THE RESOLUTION OF CONFLICT

Without conflict, there would be no exercise of power. Without power, there would be no politics. Conflict of wills, then, is central to political relationships, bringing about competition for power among political actors seeking to allocate societal values.

That conflict of interest among contending parties is central to all political systems was acutely appreciated by the founders of the American Republic. Writing in the tenth essay of *The Federalist Papers,* James Madison suggested that "the regulation of these various and interfering interests forms the principal task of modern legislation." [1] Madison recognized that conflicting interests (or factions, as he called them) can be eliminated only by the eclipse of liberty and imposition of an absolutist state. Barring such an extreme solution (which in international politics would entail establishing a totalitarian world government), alternative means must be devised to ameliorate the struggle for power in a pluralist environment. To paraphrase the father of the United States Constitution, pluralism is to conflict what air is to fire.

This is not to suggest that politics is undiluted conflict. If this were the case, political relations would be little more than wars of mutual annihilation. Pure conflict is rarely evident even in the most violent and intense confrontations, though it may be approached in ideological crusades which allow no quarter. Far more often, however, even the bitterest foes recognize that some element of common interest and mutual dependence exists alongside strife and contention. As one student of international relations puts it:

> "Winning" in a conflict does not have a strictly competitive meaning; it is not winning relative to one's adversary. It means gaining relative to one's own value system; this may be done by bargaining, by mutual accommodation, and by the avoidance of mutually damaging behavior. If war to the finish has become inevitable, there is nothing left but pure conflict; but if there is any possibility of avoiding a mutually damaging war, of conducting warfare in a way that minimizes damage, or by coercing an adversary by threatening war rather than waging it, the possibility of mutual accommodation is as important and dramatic as the element of conflict.[2]

Politics is certainly not fundamentally harmonious, yet neither is it totally conflictual. As a variety of social interaction, it is best viewed as sliding along a continuum ranging from pure conflict at one extreme to pure cooperation at the other. Political relationships between allies are characterized more by agreement than disagreement over the distribution of values: Cooperation tends to predominate over conflict. Relationships between adversaries revolve around quite different perceptions of distributive justice: Conflict normally takes precedence over cooperation. Yet in neither conflict-dominant nor cooperation-dominant relationships is the opposite impulse lacking. For example, though relations between the United States and its western European allies have been relatively harmonious for the last third of a century (largely because of a perceived common threat—the Soviet Union), there have always existed certain incongruities stemming from differing notions of what constitutes a fair distribution of burdens and benefits. (As will be examined in Chapter 7, recently the Western alliance has been subjected to increasing stress and friction over economic issues, as the importance of military security matters has subsided.) On the other side of the spectrum are Soviet-American relations. Though the two superpowers have been locked into a contest for global hegemony since the end of the Second World War, even at the height of cold war confrontation there always existed at the very least a mutual interest in avoiding nuclear war. In recent years, mirroring developments in the Atlantic Alliance, relations between Moscow and Washington have moved, at first imperceptibly and then gradually, toward the center of the continuum.

All political systems—primitive and sophisticated, domestic and international, centralized and decentralized—must come to terms with the potentially disruptive effects of competition for power inherent in the conflict over division of society's benefits. To use Madison's phrase, they must seek to control the "mischiefs of faction." [3] An environment lacking any mode of conflict resolution save sheer force would be nothing less than a Hobbesian state of nature—war by every man against every man, and "the life of man: solitary, poor, nasty, brutish and short." [4] Such a state of affairs would be truly anarchic, totally devoid of any order or structure and riven by constant confusion and chaos. Unabated and unregulated conflict leads inexorably to turmoil and turbulence. Given this intolerable unpredictability and perennial lack of security, it is not surprising that pure anarchy is rare in human relations. Even the simplest political systems known to man—that of the Eskimos and of certain primitive hunting and food-gathering bands in Africa—hardly qualify as truly anarchic. Though such systems may have few, if any, differentiated political roles or specialized political structures, they nonetheless provide procedures for the regulation of strife and the preservation of order. For example, when two Eskimo men quarrel over a woman, the dispute is adjudicated by means of a butting duel fought according to predetermined rules before the entire community.[5] Such rudimentary processes for the management of rivalry are analogous to those found in the similarly primitive international system.

Though not totally anarchic in the purest sense of the term, the international system is plagued by the absence of legitimate authority to manage power and conflict by means of legislation, enforcement and adjudication of rules of conduct. In a primitive system, the management of power will remain primitive and, therefore, largely inadequate in terms of the magnitude of conflicts generated in an increasingly interdependent and technologically advanced world. Yet even in the quasi-anarchic environment of present international relations, certain truncated structures and processes exist to ameliorate the struggle for power among legally sovereign entities.

THE BALANCE OF POWER: THEORY AND PRACTICE

The Logic of Competition

The momentum of a primitive political system favors competition over cooperation, and this tends to be the case quite aside from the benevolence or malevolence of its component actors. In a quasi-anarchic environment, there is no help but self-help. Lacking even a rudimentary governmental structure to determine and implement allocation of benefits, each participant is confronted with the alternative of providing for its own security and welfare or placing itself at the mercy of its neighbors. Without external guarantees of its safety, each state is compelled to view all other states as potential opponents and to respond accordingly. The logic of competition in a stateless environment requires acquisition of power (and especially coercive power) sufficient to give at least a modicum of protection. The insecurity inherent in politics without government is behind the inscription which the Venetians displayed in their armory: "Happy is the city which in time of peace thinks of war."

This undesirable state of affairs is inevitable given the existence of many states, each claiming to be sovereign and yet all forced into precarious coexistence. The dilemma posed by environmental constraints has long been appreciated by students of international relations. The eighteenth-century French philosopher Jean Jacques Rousseau recognized that hostility was natural to interstate behavior. Regardless of the internal nature of a political system (whether a state is inherently militaristic or not), he maintained that "its security and preservation demand that it make itself more powerful than its neighbors." [6]

According to Rousseau, the logic of competitive advantage and the quest for self-interest overshadows the urge to cooperate in furthering the common interest of all participants. His parable of the stag hunt aptly illustrates the tension between the short-run interest of the individual actor and the long-run interest of the community. Assume that five hungry men agree to cooperate to kill a stag, each aware that the needs of all can thus be satisfied. However, each separately can have his hunger satisfied by trapping a hare. When a hare crosses the path of one of the stag hunters, he abandons the common project, grabs the hare and allows the deer to escape. All, therefore, learn that they cannot depend upon others to provide for their needs, and self-interest will thenceforth take precedence over the common interest.[7] (See Figure 5, which illustrates the calculations involved between two of the participants.)

Some contemporary political theorists have drawn ideas from a branch of mathematics called game theory. Transposed to politics, game theory is a description and analysis of strategic decision making between competitors seeking to minimize the harm the other might cause. The resulting "prisoner's dilemma" story is the modern version of Rousseau's stag hunt.[8] In this story, two men are arrested for a crime. The district attorney, lacking sufficient evidence to convict the suspects, separates them and makes each the same offer: (1) If both refuse to confess, he will see to it that they are each convicted of a lesser charge and serve a year in jail; (2) if both confess, each will be sentenced to five years in prison; (3) if one confesses and the other does not, the one who turns state's evidence will receive a three-month sentence while the one who holds out will be prosecuted to the full extent of the law and spend ten years in prison. Obviously, the ideal outcome for the two prisoners would be for both to remain silent. Yet clearly the

Figure 5

Rousseau's Stag Hunt

HUNTER B

HUNTER A	continues stag hunt	grabs hare
continues stag hunt	(1) both satisfied	(2) A: hungry B: satisfied
grabs hare	(3) A: satisfied B: hungry	(4) both hungry

best outcome for both—1

most rational outcome—4

rational strategy is for each to abandon the other and confess. Each must reason that if he refuses to confess but his partner confesses then he will receive the worst possible penalty. Thus, self-interest dictates that the two players betray one another; each confesses and both end up worse off than they would have been if they had maintained their faith in one another (see Figure 6).

The lessons of the "prisoner's dilemma" and Rousseau's parable are identical: Competition leads to mutual harm. This is also the dilemma of nation-states. If one state arms, its opponent may arm also, thus leaving each no better off in terms of security and each a lot poorer in terms of resources; yet if a state fails to arm, its rival may arm anyway and then threaten from a position of military strength. Each would surely be better off if neither armed, but neither can safely base its survival on the good intentions of its neighbor. In short, the most rational strategy for each actor in a quasi-anarchic environment ensures mutually disadvantageous behavior. Yet even this appears more attractive to states than being duped by their adversaries.

The Balance of Power in History

Throughout history, there is evidence that the quest for competitive advantage in a system characterized by diffusion of capabilities and security dilemmas produces a peculiar set of relationships known as the *balance of power.* This concept has a distinguished lineage and has been identified and analyzed by political thinkers both ancient and modern, occidental and oriental. The philosopher Kautilya described its operation in ancient India; Thucydides studied its dynamics in the struggle between Athens and Sparta in ancient Greece; Machiavelli, though not dealing with it by name, identified its underlying rationale in Renaissance Italy; Montesquieu, Bolingbroke, Hume, Burke, Rousseau and Voltaire examined its functioning in eighteenth-century Europe; a modern theorist infers its existence in ancient China.[9] Given the popularity and longevity of the concept among observers from different ages, various cultures and diverse regions, it is probably only a slight exaggeration to say that the balance of power is "as nearly a fundamental law of politics as it is possible to find." [10] Or, as Hans J. Morgenthau has stated, the balance of power seems to be a "necessary outgrowth" of power politics, a "particular manifestation of a general social principle ... inevitable ... essential ... [and] universal." [11]

The study of modern Western diplomatic history substantiates the thesis that the balance of power is a recurrent feature of international relations. It is imperative that the student of world politics be acquainted with at least the essential aspects of man's field record. This is not to embrace a deterministic view that history occurs in cycles or that history is bound to repeat itself or even that historical analogies are invariably accurate or useful. We must take care to temper our approach to history with a healthy

Figure 6

The Prisoner's Dilemma

SUSPECT B

SUSPECT A	confesses	does not confess
confesses	(1) A: 5 years B: 5 years	(2) A: 3 months B: 10 years
does not confess	(3) A: 10 years B: 3 months	(4) A: 1 year B: 1 year

best outcome for both—4

most rational outcome—1

dose of skepticism, especially in regard to prediction. In the words of one recent observer of and participant in world politics:

> Prediction is dangerous because the large number of forces at work in historical situations permit many outcomes consistent with their existence; and the role of accident, including magical (or satanic) accident of individual personality adds a dimension calculated to humble those who grasp too arrogantly at the future. Nonetheless, *history unfolds within limits which give a rough shape and continuity. . . .*[12]

In short, then, while steering clear of the excesses of historical determinism, we will briefly examine the contours of the past, sifting it for its political content and patterns.

European diplomatic history from the Renaissance to Waterloo can be characterized as the "era of coalitions." Although alliances in time of war were hardly new to interstate relations, alliances in times of peace grew along with modern territorial states out of the breakdown of medieval Christendom and feudalism.

No sooner had the monarchs of postmedieval western Europe consolidated their domestic power than they embarked upon policies of external rivalry and expansion, vying with one another to extend their influence and prestige abroad. Renaissance Italy, which first broke the bonds of the Middle Ages, developed into a sophisticated microcosm of future international affairs. By the fifteenth century, the waning influence of pope and emperor had led to diffusion of power among a number of independent city-states and principalities. By constant warfare and expansion, the strong gradually absorbed the weak until the peninsula was dominated by a half-dozen or so political actors with assorted vassals and buffers relegated to the periphery.

As none of the major powers was strong enough to subdue the rest and unify the peninsula, a political system developed founded on fear, vigilance and constant maneuvering. In a state of perennial and internecine conflict, the city-states constantly formed shifting and temporary alliances and counteralliances, with the intent of balancing the power of rival princes and coalitions. The power of potential adversaries (and everyone was a potential adversary) became the sole criterion for forming opposing alignments. For example, when Florence and Venice felt threatened by the imposing capabilities of Milan, they joined in an alliance and waged war against Milan; however, as the power of Milan was whittled away, Venice's relative power position was augmented. Gauging Venice to be the new threat to her security, Florence defected from the alliance and joined forces with her former enemy to thwart the aggrandizement of her former partner.

As the Northern European monarchs obtained domestic stability and foreign affairs moved into the foreground, the practices of a divided Italy became those of a divided Europe. It was the ambitions of France's Charles VIII that precipitated the age of coalitions. When French armies invaded Italy in 1494 and seized Naples, an alliance of Italian states was organized, soon to be supplemented by the Holy League consisting of Spain, Austria and England. It soon became Henry VIII's policy (backed by his astute minister Wolsey) to secure the independence of his relatively weak island kingdom by pursuing a policy of divide and conquer. His goal was to protect English interests against those of France and Spain by constant maneuvering between the two stronger neighbors. "Instead of definitely committing himself to either side," writes one historian, "Wolsey schemed and intrigued, craftily playing one power off against the other in order to preserve a certain equilibrium between the two without involving England in a war." [13] (Acting opportunistically to achieve the position of "chief arbiter of Europe" would become a cardinal principle of Britain's foreign policy and endure well into the twentieth century.)

When the crowns of the Spanish and Austrian Hapsburgs were united in the person of Charles V, Spain replaced France as the object of international anxieties. After France was defeated by a coalition of European states in 1526, the fear soon became widespread that Charles was growing too powerful and, therefore, menacing. Accordingly, successive coalitions were formed against him until Spain's numerous foes were organized into an elaborate system of alliances linking most of the major powers of Christian Europe with the infidel Turks. Soon internal and external pressure on Charles's empire proved too great, and the tide of affairs turned against him. By the end of the reign of his successor, Philip II, Spain's power was rapidly declining, in large measure because of the almost constant warfare waged in a futile attempt to maintain its supremacy. The death blow to Hapsburg primacy was dealt by France's Richelieu (and later Mazarin), who succeeded in engaging the Hapsburgs in a debilitating and prolonged war of attrition, the Thirty Years War (1618–48).

The rise of French power and the decline of Spain brought a commensurate shift in alignments. Speaking of the situation in Europe when he ascended the throne, Louis XIV later remarked: "Everything was quiet everywhere. . . . Peace was established with my neighbors probably for as long a time as I should desire." [14] Things were not to remain quiet for long. For nearly his entire seventy-two-year reign, France was pitted against one coalition after another in its attempt to dominate the continent. After his occupation of the Spanish Netherlands in 1667, Louis was confronted with the Triple Alliance of Holland, England and Sweden; when, five years later, his armies invaded Holland, a coalition consisting of Austria, Spain, Brandenburg (Prussia) and Denmark was organized; the League of Augsburg (Spain, Holland, Savoy, Austria, the lesser German states and later England) formed to curb France's ambition to annex Alsace and Strasbourg (1681); still another coalition was necessary to thwart Louis's attempt to unite the crowns of Spain and France (the War of the Spanish Succession). Thus the powers of Europe waged war after war against the Sun King to stabilize the international system and check France's dreams of continental hegemony. Though Louis XIV's extravagances literally bankrupted the French monarchy, by the end of the eighteenth century France was once again at war with nearly all Europe.

The French Revolution of 1789 threatened the legitimacy of all the monarchies in Europe, and the great increase in French capabilities which it entailed threatened the precarious international balance of power. The revolutionary government was soon at war with Austria and Prussia, and the unexpected success of its zealous armies and the spread of its revolutionary ideology ushered in the Coalition of 1793 (England, Spain and smaller states) against it. But by 1797, all but England had been forced to sue for peace. Now the power of the new France fed on its victories. Napoleon led an expedition to Egypt, and a ring of satellite states was created on France's borders, thus bringing about the Second Coalition (1799), which included Russia and Turkey as well as England. Yet this alliance broke up like the one before it, and, in 1802 even England opted for peace. When Napoleon tipped the balance even more in his favor by declaring himself president of the Italian Republic (which he created), annexing Piedmont, reorganizing the Swiss cantons, reviving colonial ambition and virtually excluding British goods from the Continent, war and coalition were inevitably resumed. Napoleon's struggle with the Third Coalition dragged on for nearly a decade, with England at times totally isolated diplomatically, until the disastrous Iberian and Russian campaigns turned the tide against the French, and Napoleon's hold on Europe was broken once and for all.

After a quarter-century of internecine warfare, European statesmen reexamined coalition as a means of regulating competition for power. True, Napoleon's dream of universal dominion had been thwarted, as had the expansionist urges of Louis XIV before him. Yet coalition diplomacy had proven to be a precarious and costly vehicle for managing international politics. Not only had the wartime alliances been difficult to hold together, but also they had failed for the most part to deter aggression. Those launched against Napoleon demonstrated this well, being held together by little more than British tenacity. In the end, Napoleon was defeated more by overextension than by the miracle of coalition. By the time of France's defeat in 1814/15 it was apparent that coalitions were effective only after the fact—that is, only in war. The attempt was now to be made to replace the wartime coalition with the peacetime concert of Great Powers in order to provide interstate relations with a modicum of stability.

The so-called Metternich system, which resulted from the Congress of Vienna, "secured for a full century the preservation, if not of peace, at least of an era without major war." [15] This was due less to the genius of the statesmen of the time than to their success in securing a settlement conforming to existing international conditions. As Henry Kissinger has written:

> The major problem of an international settlement, then, is to so relate the claims of legitimacy to the requirements of security that no power will express its dissatisfaction in a revolutionary policy, and so to arrange the balance of forces as to deter aggression produced by causes other than the conditions of the settlement.[16]

The first task was accomplished by extending a rather generous peace to defeated France and allowing her to reenter the system on equal terms with the victorious states; the second was achieved by the concert system. The Concert of Europe (see Figure 7) following the Napoleonic Wars, was a joining of the Great Powers preoccupied with the preservation of the balance of power[17]—

Figure 7
The Concert of Europe

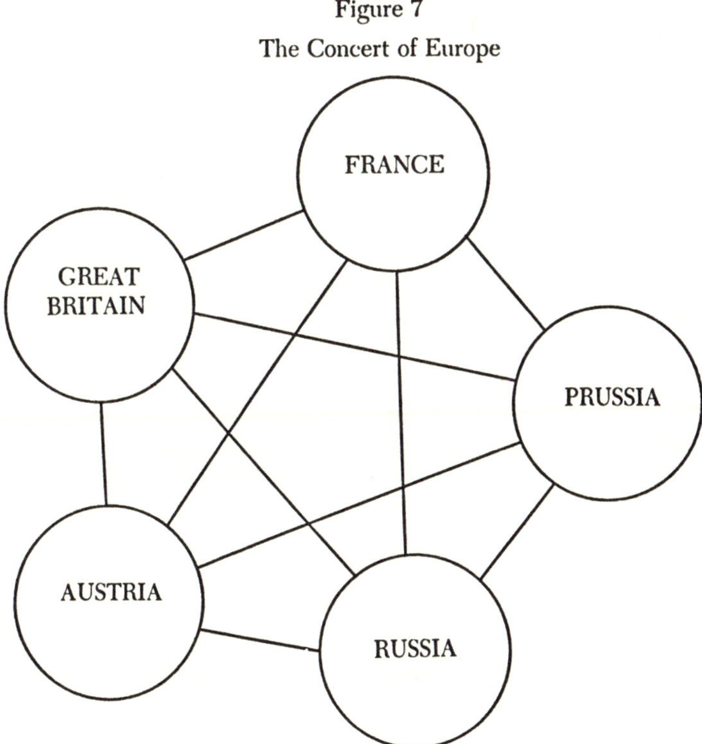

"not a mere physical equation of forces, but a mutual understanding about, and acceptance of, the relation between national aspirations and the capacity to realize them in view of other nations' capacity and will to resist." [18]

It was generally accepted in the major capitals of Europe that all changes in the international arena that might affect the balance of power among the Great Powers were subject to periodic review and collective approval by the powers concerned. Thus the primary international actors modified the coalition-based balance-of-power system and established themselves as a European board of directors. Their representatives met periodically to ratify all important changes in the territorial status quo established at the Congress of Vienna: the independence of Greece in 1832, and Belgium in 1839; the affairs of Turkey and the Straits in 1840/41; control over Schleswig and Holstein in 1852; and the dispute involved in the Crimean War in the Treaty of Paris in 1856.[19]

The concert system, then, sought to manage power by precluding shifts in the balance of power which might otherwise precipitate mutually destructive war. After several centuries of coalition diplomacy, the leading European states briefly awoke to the realization that they might have their cake and eat it too; that is, they could have peace *and* a balance of power—the two were not necessarily mutually exclusive. (The concert principle seems to be a logical development in the evolution of a primitive political system. Even the lords of the underworld of crime reached the conclusion, after decades of wars of coalition, that their interests would be better served by regulating competition. Accordingly, the "Commission"—a concert of the most powerful families—was established to oversee internal affairs and ensure that families whose territories overlapped would respect each others' sphere of influence.) [20]

It was not until a major shift in the distribution of power occurred, owing to the rise of new states (Germany and Italy) and the decline of the anachronistic polyglot Austrian empire that the concert system found itself in deep trouble. By the end of the nineteenth century, the system had deteriorated into a division of Europe into two competing camps, the Triple Entente and the Triple Alliance. This reversion to coalition diplomacy ushered in the twentieth century's version of the Thirty Years' War, for in many ways the two world wars (1914–19 and 1939–45) were actually one great struggle for global supremacy on the part of Germany. In both wars, grand coalitions reminiscent of the era prior to the concert system were organized to contain and defeat this threat to the balance of power. (Later in this chapter, we will focus more closely upon the struggle for power in the interwar and post–World War II periods and examine the mechanisms of international organization devised to manage international conflict.)

The Meaning of the Balance of Power

Now that we have briefly surveyed the operation of the balance-of-power principle in modern diplomatic history, we can turn to the content of this much used (and much abused) concept. Though the balance-of-power concept has been referred to in numerous scholarly studies of world politics and even by practitioners of foreign policy, its very popularity has led to a fundamental ambiguity concerning its substance. Its nature is rarely carefully defined, and often the reader must infer from the context the exact meaning the author is ascribing to it.

To make matters worse, an author may use the term in a number of different (and often contradictory) senses in the same study, often without bothering to differentiate among them. For example, Inis L. Claude, Jr., notes that Hans J. Morgenthau attaches at least five meanings to *the balance of power.*[21] Claude finds that the concept has been used by various thinkers in at least four different ways: to describe an objective situation (either a situation of equilibrium *or* disequilibrium *or* any distribution of power); to describe a policy (either to promote equilibrium *or* disequilibrium *or* any struggle for power); to describe a system (whether self-regulating *or* semiautomatic *or* the result of conscious human contrivance); and to describe the use of prudence in the conduct of foreign policy.[22] Still another student of the term *the balance of power* concludes from his survey of its meanings that there are four categories of possible application and eight more or less distinct connotations.[23]

Similarly, there is a profound difference of opinion concerning whether a balance of power leads to peace or war. On the one hand, there are those who maintain that a balance of power is identical with peace and security in the international system;[24] others hold that "[t]he claim that a balance of power is conducive to peace does not stand up [and indeed] is not even logical";[25] still others suggest that the balance of power "is, on the whole, a situation favorable to the maintenance of peace."[26]

Obviously such clouding of the issue will not do. Yet we must bear in mind that the theory of the balance of power is not in the least disproven by nuances and the ambiguities of meaning. "If the theory is stated with care, its logic holds up and its meaning is clear."[27] We have seen how the decentralized nature of the international system and the correlative security dilemma lead to competition for power among the component actors. We have also concluded that this is the case regardless of the predisposition of individual states. The balance of power, then, is:

> a theory about the results produced by the uncoordinated action of individual states. It is not a theory of state policy, but rather a theory of environmental constraints. The environment is produced by the actions and interactions of states, but that environment then appears, like a market in a competitive economy, as a force that no state acting alone can control.[28]

As long as independent states exist and seek to survive and prosper in a primitive system based on self-help, they will inevitably endeavor to increase their capabilities, either internally or by means of alignment with other states. And much as desire for profit on the part of business enterprises leads to a certain equilibrium in a free market, the quest for power among states tends to result in a balance of power, regardless of the motivations of those states or coalitions that seek to overturn the balance and of those that seek to preserve it. Thus, "balances of power tend to form whether some or all states consciously aim to establish and maintain a balance, or whether some or all states aim for universal dominion."[29]

The Mechanisms of the Balance of Power

The balance of power is the net result of the independent decisions of a multiplicity of states, each acting selfishly to further its own national interest. Though none may consciously work for the ends of the system as a whole, the intersection of the ambitions and goals of all leads to the preservation of the balance. The equilibrium is almost automatically ensured by the logic of competition, which propels each actor to thwart the hegemonic designs of potential adversaries. The balance of power is therefore a dynamic, not a static, equilibrium. It is inherently precarious, constantly subject to disturbances and readjustments. In the words of one historian:

> To the degree that stability is achieved, it is not the static stability of a pyramid, but the dynamic stability of a Gothic cathedral, in which the vaults, arches, and flying buttresses, thrusting against each other, thereby hold each other in a single equilibrated structure. Abruptly remove one vault or one buttress, with its thrust, and the balance is destroyed, the whole structure collapses. It may be a delicate matter to build a Gothic cathedral; once built, however, to take it down is even more delicate.[30]

The dynamics of the balancing process revolve around the dictates of national egoism: Acting out of self-interest, states undertake policies which have the effect of preserving global equilibrium. Morton A. Kaplan refers to the "essential rules" of the balance-of-power system. According to these rules, states will:

1. Act to increase capabilities but negotiate rather than fight.
2. Fight rather than pass up an opportunity to increase capabilities.
3. Stop fighting rather than eliminate an essential actor.
4. Act to oppose any coalition or single actor which tends to assume a position of predominance with respect to the rest of the system.

5. Act to constrain actors who subscribe to supranational organizing principles.

6. Permit defeated or constrained national actors to reenter the system as acceptable role partners . . . Treat all essential actors as acceptable role partners.[31]

The pursuit of narrow self-interest causes states to undertake a number of actions which in the end prevent domination by any state or group of states. Collectively, these acts may be referred to as the mechanisms of the balance of power. They are (1) eternal vigilance, (2) alliances, (3) armaments, (4) intervention, (5) holding the balance, (6) flexibility, (7) reciprocal compensation, (8) moderation, and (9) coalitions and war.[32]

Vigilance. This is, obviously, the most basic instrument of the balancing process. The preservation of security requires continuous attention to developments in the international system and in the domestic systems of particular states, which may alter the distribution of capabilities and adversely affect one's relative power position. Accordingly, virtually all states, especially the major powers, devote considerable effort to gathering and analyzing information about the capabilities and intentions of potential adversaries.

Because the actual capabilities (especially the military capabilities) of a country are easier and more accurately gauged and subject to less fluctuation than the intentions of policy makers, those responsible for assessing the potential threat posed by rival states are apt to emphasize capabilities over intentions. Not surprisingly, framers of foreign policy are likely to gear their own defense preparations to the worst possible contingency, believing it more prudent to err on the safe side. The result is a process of continual readjustment of relative capabilities among rivals: however, as the "prisoners' dilemma" discussed earlier suggests, it may also lead to the investment of more resources in military preparedness than objective circumstances warrant and an invitation to opponents to do likewise. For example, consider former Secretary of Defense Robert McNamara's explanation of the

United States' vast buildup of strategic weapons in the early 1960s:

> In 1961 when I became Secretary of Defense, the Soviet Union had a very small operational arsenal of intercontinental missiles. However, it did possess the technological and industrial *capacity* to enlarge that arsenal very substantially over the succeeding years. We had *no evidence* that the Soviets did plan, in fact, to use that capacity. But . . . a strategic planner must be conservative in his calculations; that is, *he must prepare for the worst possible case* and not be content to hope and prepare for the most probable.
>
> Since *we could not be certain of Soviet intentions*, since we could not be sure that they would not undertake a massive build-up, we had to insure against such an eventuality by undertaking a major build-up of our own.
>
> . . . Thus, in the course of hedging against what was then only a theoretically possible Soviet build-up, we took decisions which have resulted in our current superiority . . . But the blunt fact remains that *if we had more accurate information* about planned Soviet strategic forces, we simply would not have needed to build as large a nuclear arsenal as we have today.
>
> . . . Whatever their intentions or our intentions, actions—or even realistically potential actions—on either side relating to the build-up of nuclear forces *necessarily* trigger reactions on the other side. It is precisely this action-reaction phenomenon that fuels an arms race.[33]

Similarly, the subsequent Soviet missile buildup of the late 1960s may be viewed as a reaction to the American advantage caused by our buildup in the early 1960s.[34] In short, then, eternal vigilance is a twin-edged sword and is both the child and parent of fear.

Alliances and Armaments. There are two fundamental ways in which a state may increase its capabilities. It can join in an alliance with other actors perceiving a common threat, thereby supplementing its own capabilities with those of its allies. Alternatively, or in conjunction with a policy of alignment, it can also undertake internal efforts to increase its own capabilities. This second course of action may be accomplished by accelerating economic growth or by allocating a greater portion of present production to military expenditures. In a multipolar balance-of-power system (characterized by the distribution of capabilities among a number of comparable, if not equal, actors), shifting alignments are the central mechanism in the preservation of equilibrium; in a bipolar system (in which effective capabilities are possessed by only two dominant actors), competition in armaments is the central instrument in the balancing process, because changing alliance patterns cannot crucially affect the balance between the two superpowers. Both peacetime alliances and arms races function to deter expansion or attack by rivals; should deterrence fail, wartime coalitions and violence attempt to prevent domination by the enemy.

Intervention. A state may perceive its security to be threatened by changes within the international system (e.g., formation of menacing alliances) or by changes within the domestic system of a specific country. As we have seen, the transformation of the domestic structure of France from 1789 to 1792 precipitated intervention by Prussia and Austria in a vain attempt to prevent the contagion of revolutionary upheaval from spreading and French capabilities from expanding. Similarly, the Allied powers (including the United States) sent expeditionary forces to fight the Bolsheviks in the Russian civil war of 1917–20, with the aim of ousting Lenin's revolutionary government and bringing Russia back into the First World War against Germany; moreover, as was the case with Austria and Prussia a century and a quarter before, the Western democracies perceived the victory of communism in Russia as a threat to the legitimacy of their own domestic social orders.

In a bipolar balance-of-power system, the superpowers will intervene in their own spheres of influence to prevent the defection of a client state; the Soviet invasion of Hungary in 1956 and

Czechoslovakia in 1968, and the American intervention in Guatemala in 1954 and the Dominican Republic in 1965, illustrate the operation of this principle.

Holding the Balance. From our brief survey of the history of the balance of power, it is clear that each time the European state system was challenged with the prospect of conquest or domination by any state, a peripheral power would swing into the balance against it and the scales would once more return to a position of equilibrium. A German historian suggests that the dreams of all would-be caesars (Charles V, Philip II, Louis XIV, Napoleon, Kaiser Wilhelm and Hitler) have been thwarted by insular powers, the isolated positions of which enabled them to tip the balance in defeating successive drives for world domination.[35] The role of the balancer is traditionally ascribed to Great Britain. Perceiving it to be in her interest to prevent any state or group of states from achieving hegemony on the Continent, and relatively secure because of her geographical separation from the European mainland, England pursued a balancing policy from the time of Henry VIII. Indeed, Henry is reputed to have stated: "*Cui adhaereo, prae-est*" ("Whomever I support will prevail"). In the words of a more recent British diplomat, Britain contrived to maintain the balance of power "by throwing her weight now on this scale and now on that, but ever on the side opposed to the political dictatorship of the strongest single State or group at a given time." [36] However, in the twentieth century, Britain could no longer fulfill its function as holder of the balance and it abdicated its role to another peripheral power, the United States, which threw its weight on the side of the status quo in both world wars. With the defeat of the Axis powers and the exhaustion of the western European countries in 1945, no power was capable of playing the balancer in the struggle between the United States and the Soviet Union. The postwar system would then be a bipolar one, lacking the mechanism of holding the balance.

Flexibility. Ideally, the sole criterion by which states judge prospective alliance partners is power. In the traditional multipolar system, and especially prior to the age of ideology and democracy, this ideal was approached if not attained. The greater the flexibility of alignment, the smoother the balance-of-power principle functioned. Eighteenth-century Europe provides numerous examples of diplomatic alignments and realignments. For example, in the War of the Austrian Succession (1740–48), England allied itself with Austria against the combined forces of France, Prussia and a number of other states, hoping to prevent the dismemberment of the Austrian empire. Soon after the conclusion of these hostilities, England allied itself with Prussia against Austria and France in the Seven Years' War (1756–63).

A similar diplomatic revolution occurred during the transition from World War II to the cold war. The Grand Coalition, linking the United States and the Soviet Union in an anti-Axis pact, dissolved and a new set of alignments was formed. The United States became allied with West Germany, Italy and Japan (all former Axis powers) and the U.S.S.R. with East Germany and Hungary (also former Axis states). However, the lines of cold-war confrontation soon solidified, and flexibility of alignment was lost to a dual-bloc, or two-camp, division in the international system.

This loss of flexibility was not due only to bipolarity. Some of the damage was done by the ideological intensity of the postwar era, for ideological affinity complicated the policy of alignment in accordance with strict power considerations. As it happened, the subsequent ideological decontamination of world politics coincided with the waning of bipolarity, and thus a certain flexibility has been reintroduced to interstate relations in the post–cold war era.

Compensation and Moderation. The long period of general peace in Europe following the Congress of Vienna (1814–15) suggests that several lessons can be drawn from the operation of the concert system. The amelioration of the struggle for power inherent in the balance of power can be brought about by the major powers' recognizing the legitimacy of their mutal desire for security and accepting the principles of reciprocal compensation and moderation. In his study of the Congress of Vienna settlement, Henry Kissinger noted:

> The logic of war is power, and power has no inherent limit. The logic of peace is proportion, and proportion implies limitation. The success of war is victory; the success of peace is stability. The conditions of victory are commitment, the condition of stability is self-restraint. The motivation of war is extrinsic: the fear of an enemy. The motivation of peace is intrinsic: the balance of forces and the acceptance of legitimacy.[37]

Stability in the balance of power rests on mutual self-restraint and self-limitation. In his pursuit of a policy of détente with the Soviet Union (which, in effect, was a bipolar system's version of the Great Power concert), Kissinger placed a great deal of emphasis on reciprocity and moderation in the superpowers' relations. What he termed a "stable structure of peace" required "a serious effort to ease tensions on a reliable and *reciprocal* basis" [38] and an agreement between the superpowers "to bring about *restraint* . . . in their international relations." [39] No doubt Professor Kissinger drew a good deal of inspiration from the territorial settlement of 1815. At Vienna, the participants, through compensation, managed to avoid disproportionate aggrandizement of any of the victors. While czarist Russia received the lion's share of Poland, Prussia was given the Rhineland and Austria was assured compensation in northern Italy and predominance in all of Italy.[40] In much the same manner, according to the protocol agreement of the Moscow summit conference of 1972, both the United States and the U.S.S.R. pledged not to seek "unilateral advantage" at the expense of the other.

War. As we have seen, warfare was an instrument of the balance of power throughout four centuries of the European state system. It has always been the ultimate mechanism for the preservation of equilibrium in the primitive interstate system. However, general and total war among the major world powers can no longer serve as a means of achieving stability. While peace was formerly a fortunate, if haphazard, by-product of equilibrium during certain historical periods, it is now the *sine qua non* for continuation of the present global order and, indeed, for the continued survival of the human race. The total destructiveness of modern nuclear warfare has rendered it useless as an instrument of the balancing process. Nevertheless, weapons of mass annihilation serve a vital function in the modified balance-of-power system which exists in the thermonuclear age.

THE BALANCE OF TERROR: THE *MAD* WORLD OF SUPERPOWER POLITICS

As long as international relations remain a situation of politics without government, one is entitled to assume that the logic of competition and the resulting balance of power will continue to serve as the basis for the management of conflict. However, the contemporary approach to global equilibrium is not simply a replay of Europe's classical balance-of-power system. Additional management techniques have evolved to supplement the perennial balance of power and promote international security. (For our purposes, international security may be defined as "a state of affairs in which the inhibitions and disincentives to waging war are stronger than the incentives . . . [and] in which the alternatives to a forceful solution are . . . numerous." [41]) In this section we will consider the extent to which the revolutionary destructiveness of modern weaponry contributes to restraint in interstate conflict.

Addressing the House of Commons in 1955, Winston Churchill said: "Then it may well be that we shall, by a process of sublime irony, have reached a stage in this story where safety will be the sturdy child of terror, and survival the twin brother of annihilation."

Sir Winston was referring to the recent development of the hydrogen bomb and the Soviet Union's newly acquired capability of launching an attack upon the United States by means of long-range bombers.

Prior to the mid 1950s, North America had been virtually invulnerable to aerial devastation. Though the U.S.S.R. had broken the American atomic monopoly as early as 1949, for some years after it possessed neither the overseas bases nor the intercontinental-delivery vehicles necessary to respond in kind to a nuclear strike by the United States. For a decade after World War II, then, there was an imbalance of terror; the two sides had distinctly asymmetrical military capabilities, with Washington able to launch a nuclear attack against the Soviet heartland, but Moscow able to overrun western Europe with its huge but conventional military establishment.

By 1955, the development of thermonuclear weapons and long-range delivery systems had fundamentally altered the secure position of the United States. A single 15-megaton H-bomb was more than enough to destroy all New York City and make radioactive an area the size of New Jersey. Moreover, though atomic bombs could not lead to the extinction of the human species, thermonuclear weapons could. When the Soviets came into possession of the "ultimate weapon," it became possible for them to level the major American population centers with relatively few aircraft. The "balance of terror" had arrived.

The cold war rivals were forced by technology to co-exist like two scorpions in a bottle. Each was capable of striking a mortal blow at the other, but only if it were willing to accept a similarly deadly wound in return.

The logic underlying the balance of terror (see also the discussion of deterrence in chapter 3) can be examined by once again borrowing some tools from mathematical game theory. (see pp. 191-92). The use of strategy assumes rationality, and this is crucial in understanding the different plays in the game of nuclear deterrence. If one or both players is irrational, all bets are off, and mutual deterrence fails. Churchill himself, in the speech quoted from earlier, acknowledged this formidable qualification: "The deterrent does not cover the case of lunatics or dictators in the mood of Hitler when he found himself in his final dugout."[42]

The nuclear weapons that count for deterrent purposes are those that can be expected to remain intact and able to penetrate opposing defenses after an enemy first-strike. Simply having nuclear weapons is not sufficient to prevent attack; indeed, the possession of a primitive strategic force susceptible to destruction by a surprise salvo may very well invite, rather than inhibit, attack. What ensures that a rational enemy will be dissuaded from attacking one's homeland is an invulnerable retaliatory capability. When the strategic arsenals of both players have this capability, mutual deterrence—or a balance of terror—is said to exist. When this state of affairs is unlikely to be upset by a technological breakthrough (either in offense or defense), the situation is said to be stable. If however, the situation of mutual deterrence is unstable—if one or both opponents is on the verge of acquiring an effective first-strike capability—the result is likely to be war. On one hand, the state anticipating its own vulnerability to a disarming surprise attack may strike first, thereby hoping to settle affairs before it is in an intolerable position. Alternatively, the rival state, upon gaining the ability to launch a surprise attack with impunity, may opt to do so while having a temporary advantage. It is important to bear in mind that any first-strike which is less than 100 percent effective will leave the aggressor open to some sort of nuclear retaliation. Only if the aggressor calculates in advance that likely retaliation may wreak too much damage will that state be deterred from initiating hostilities.

The vast and technologically advanced military establishments of the United States and the Soviet Union (which together account for over seventy-five percent of global military expenditures) set them apart from all other states. This factor, in addition to the eclipse of the former power of European and Asian countries in World War II, signified a shift in the postwar international system, from multipolarity to bipolarity (see Figures 8 and 9). But in addition to this crucial gap between the superpowers and their former international peers, the United States and the U.S.S.R. were themselves at different stages of strategic development for most of the cold war, since until the late 1960s, the American Strategic Air Command (SAC) retained a significant quantitative and qualitative lead over its Soviet counterpart.

The process of international equilibrium, however, has never implied or required strict equality in capabilities among the principal actors—only a rough comparability in overall power. Moreover, nuclear weapons have become the "great equalizers" in interstate disputes (much as the Colt .45 revolver did on the

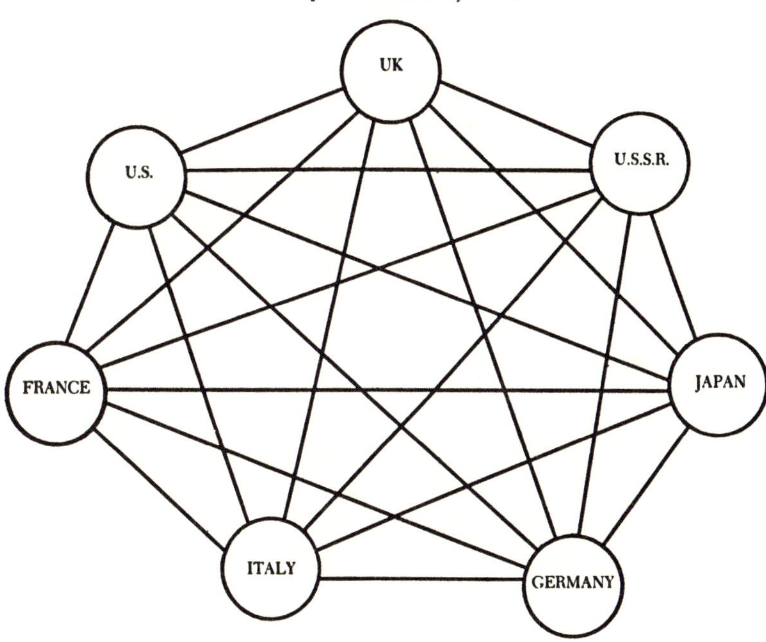

Figure 8
The Multipolar International System, 1939

American frontier). Even a state with markedly fewer deliverable nuclear warheads at its disposal can confront a superior challenger with a "Mexican standoff." Although in the past the relative number of weapons (tanks, planes, ships, men etc.) in the arsenals of enemies would have been the crucial determinant of victory, to

Figure 9
The Bipolar International System, 1945

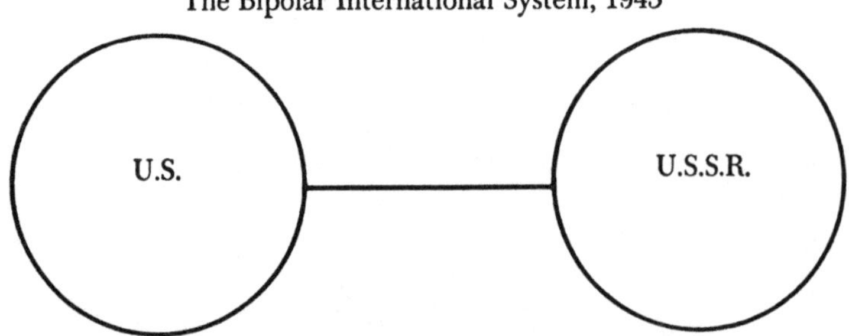

prevail in a spasmodic nuclear exchange is to live perhaps only to envy the dead. It can be said, therefore, that mutual deterrence is operational even between nuclear powers of differing magnitudes. Below the threshold of first-strike capability, the size of a deterrent force is absolute and not relative to that of a potential aggressor.

Much as the overall international balance of power tends toward equilibrium regardless of the commitments of individual states, the balance of terror has gravitated toward *strategic parity*. Parity does not mean a perfect symmetrical equality between the superpowers' nuclear arsenals, but rather a state of "essential equivalence" or approximate equality in the overall strategic capabilities of the two sides.[43] Both the United States and the Soviet Union aim for at least an assured destruction capability—a nuclear strike force able to ride out an attack with enough left over to guarantee unacceptable losses to the aggressor. Because both sides have this capability, we speak of *mutual assured destruction* (MAD).[44] This does not mean, however, that the two rivals have agreed on equipoise. At various periods during the postwar era, one or both has consciously sought a margin of superiority. Despite the desire of either or both for overall superiority in capabilities, though, neither will permit the other to reach such a goal and each will respond accordingly to counteract possible disturbance in the equilibrium. The tendency is thus toward a dynamic balance of terror, but at progressively higher levels of capability.

Again, a key element in the balance of terror is the notion of unacceptable losses. For a MAD world to persist, both sides must be able to inflict unacceptable losses on an aggressor; however, judging what is unacceptable damage to the other side is subjective and not objective. Decision makers in Washington and Moscow must ask themselves: "How much second-strike destruction will it take to deter my opponent?" Both have reached a very conservative answer to this question. It has been estimated that the two superpowers have in their arsenals the equivalent of fifteen tons of TNT for every man, woman and child on the face of the earth. The balance of terror rests on the MAD principles of overkill and megadeaths, and the statistics of potential destruction on both sides are so overwhelming that it is inconceivable that a rational policy maker would even contemplate a first-strike.

At present levels of overkill, the balance of terror appears to be quite stable, and any attempt to attain superiority seems not only futile but meaningless. After all, how many times must a superpower be able to destroy its adversary for deterrence to be assured? If this is the case, then why do the United States and the Soviet Union place so much emphasis on avoiding strategic inferiority?

Any "superiority" that falls short of a first-strike capability (which in itself is highly improbable given the astronomical levels of nuclear arms) has no appreciable effect on mutual deterrence.

Some analysts suggest that the Soviets do indeed believe it possible for a nuclear war to be "won" and are actively seeking the ability to prevail.[45] In the spring of 1977, a debate began within United States governmental circles over whether the Soviet Union is developing and testing a directed energy-beam weapon that could destroy American missiles in flight. Such a development might seriously undermine the present balance of terror. It is sometimes argued that even if a nuclear–war winning capability is unattainable, benefits will nonetheless accrue to the side possessing superiority (whether measured by number of launch vehicles or sheer megatonnage). One benefit suggested is that during crises, policy makers may be something less than totally rational and will base their decisions on crude indicators of relative nuclear strength rather than on sophisticated analyses of deterrence;[46] another, that because relative power is ultimately psychological, third parties (allies or neutrals) will be impressed with indexes of superiority and react accordingly (those who subscribe to this view hold out the prospect of the "Finlandization" of western Europe, should the U.S.S.R. appear to be the dominant nuclear power). In short, then, the illusion of superiority is deemed important not so much because it changes objective capabilities for mutual annihilation, but because it is the essentially subjective nature of power and deterrence that counts. A state is as powerful as others consider it to be, and therefore diplomatic leverage may be the by-product of an otherwise pointless superiority. The detached observer of contemporary world politics may consider this reasoning insane; however, it does indeed underlie the behavior of the superpowers, and as analysts, we must accept it as part of the operational environment of international rivalry.

We must also differentiate between what the balance of terror can and cannot do in restraining international conflict. General war between the superpowers, at least as a rational instrument of foreign policy, has been more or less ruled out. However, we cannot ignore the frightening possibility of war by accident, miscalculation, or sheer insanity, or the possibility of limited military engagements between the superpowers—hostilities that are limited in terms of geographical theater, war aims and weapons employed. Indeed, at the beginning of the era of mutal deterrence, most strategic thinkers in the United States emphasized the concomitant necessity of preparing for a series of limited military probes and encounters along the periphery of Soviet-dominated Eurasia. The balance of terror had not made all warfare irrational, it was suggested, only general nuclear war; nuclear stalemate might well encourage military action on a nonnuclear level, for the side with an advantage in conventional war capabilities could employ that power and prevail while deterring its adversary from resorting to thermonuclear war. (Some theorists even argued that limited nuclear war between the superpowers was conceivable, either with so-called tactical nuclear weapons in Europe or with strategic weapons in the enemy's own territory.[47])

In reality, though, subsequent developments in our MAD age

indicate that the balance of terror acts as a powerful constraint on all types of military confrontations between Moscow and Washington. Both sides have avoided even limited military clashes and in addition have exercised remarkable caution in the many crises that might easily have escalated out of control. Though many types of military conflict may, in strict game theory, be consonant with the balance of terror, thus far political decision makers have behaved more responsibly than expected and have appreciated that, in reality, mutual deterrence lowers the threshold of permissible violence in superpower disputes. As Bismarck is reputed to have said: "I don't like war; you can't control it."

The balance of terror has given both superpowers a stake in avoiding conflicts that might escalate out of control. At the same time, however, mutual deterrence has granted other states greater freedom of action in their own foreign relations. States in regions outside the spheres of influence of the United States and the Soviet Union can often count on the rival interest of the two superpowers to provide them with a certain degree of diplomatic flexibility. Although in the past, third parties might have feared direct intervention by Moscow or Washington, now they can confidently predict that the global powers will keep one another in check. The Middle East is a good example of such a no-man's-land where the vital interests of the superpowers overlap. Though the regional actors are all dependent upon one superpower or the other for arms and economic support, they still avoid becoming client-states and retain for themselves the ultimate decisions on war and peace. Thus, the United States and the U.S.S.R. find themselves on the horns of a dilemma: They cannot totally control the behavior of third parties, and yet these third parties can precipitate superpower confrontations. The logic of survival in a MAD world demands that the superpowers avoid collision courses. Therefore, the balance of terror is supplemented by attempts to reduce tensions and institutionalize conflict.

DETENTE: THE CONCERT OF THE SUPERPOWERS?

As we have seen, the underlying assumption of the Concert of Europe was that perennial warfare was too precarious and costly as a central mechanism of the balance of power, and so to maintain systemic equilibrium, the Great Powers tried to regulate international conflict by means of periodic consultations. By the same token, relations between the United States and the Soviet Union in the contemporary international system have changed from being almost totally conflictual to a mixture of conflict and cooperation.

Literally, *détente* means "the relaxation of tensions," though the term is normally used to signify more, that is, a complex process of readjustment in the superpowers' mutual relations. It is not synonymous with *entente,* which is a fundamental reconciliation between the two rivals as a prelude to formal or de facto alliance. (This relationship, exemplified by the Triple Entente among Britain, France and Russia prior to the First World War, is primarily a cooperation-dominant form of competition.) As Henry Kissinger has said, "the very concept of 'détente' has always been applicable only to an adversary relationship."[48] Détente, then, may be viewed as an attempt to supplement both the balance of power and the balance of terror with a more stable pattern for the management of superpower conflict. To quote its chief American architect, former Secretary Kissinger, again:

> Our generation has been traumatized by World War II, because we remember that war broke out as a result of an imbalance of power. But neither must we forget the lesson of World War I, when war broke out despite an equilibrium of power. An international structure held together only by a balance of forces will sooner or later collapse in catastrophe. In our time this could spell the end of civilized life. We must therefore conduct a diplomacy that deters challenges if possible and that contains them at tolerable levels if they

> prove unavoidable; a diplomacy that resolves issues, nurtures restraint and builds cooperation based on mutual interest.[49]

Détente represents the need "to seek a world based on something more stable and hopeful than a balance of terror constantly contested." [50] It is a supplement to, and not a substitute for, global equilibrium resting upon mutual deterrence.

Détente, as a stage in the evolution of superpower competition, means more than a relaxation of tensions. At various times in the past half-century, there have been periods in which the intensity of rivalry between the United States and the Soviet Union has subsided and the threat of hostilities has diminished.[51] Each occasion, however, proved to be only a temporary convenience for one side or the other, and none brought about lasting changes in the mutual perceptions of the powers or a real recognition of the need at least partially to accommodate the security interests of the other side. These brief interludes in what was otherwise a long interaction based on fear, suspicion, and enmity failed to achieve permanence because they were perceived as being purely tactical retreats on a path to ultimate victory over an implacable foe. (This is reminiscent of Lenin's famous dictum about the need to improvise during emergencies: "One step backward, two steps forward.") If the present détente is to be a significant addition to the traditional tools for managing global conflict, then it must demonstrate real progress in strengthening incentives for long-term moderation and self-restraint by expanding the areas of superpower cooperation.

The present period of détente dates back to the waning years of the cold war. The Cuban missile crisis of 1962 is often considered a watershed in superpower rivalry for global hegemony. Khrushchev's adventurist gamble and subsequent humiliation taught the Soviet leadership to fear nuclear escalation and the debilitating effects of marked strategic inferiority. Therefore, they simultaneously embarked upon a massive buildup of nuclear forces and moved to reduce the likelihood of those forces ever being used. The United States, in effect, chose to allow them to attain nuclear parity. During the years 1966–68, a thaw began in the cold war, and modest bilateral agreements were reached in such fields as direct airline communications, consular representation and cultural exchanges; more important, discussions began on the limitation of strategic arms. However, further progress was stifled by the Soviet invasion of Czechoslovakia in 1968 and the growing American involvement in Vietnam.[52]

Though progress toward détente faltered, it was not reversed. The Kremlin was prodded onward by the stagnation of the Soviet economy and the growing threat posed by the People's Republic of China. The Soviet leadership came to see the West as a source of both advanced capital and technological know-how, by which they could modernize the Communist economic system without a painful reexamination of its basic premises and partially satisfy the rising expectations of Russian consumers who had been long neglected in favor of heavy industry and armaments. At the same time, the rise of a hostile and potentially powerful (and nuclear-armed) China on their eastern borders, made the Russians hark back to the traditional formula of avoiding intense conflict on both their eastern and western fronts (recall that the Soviet Union concluded a nonaggression pact with Japan in World War II). They moved to consolidate their hold over eastern Europe, secure the status quo in western Europe and prevent any collusion between Peking and Washington. For its part, the Nixon Administration was eager to solicit the good offices of the U.S.S.R. in extricating itself gracefully from Indochina and, more generally, sought a cold-war truce because the post–World War II domestic consensus on containment was disintegrating. Each superpower, in its own interest, was being drawn toward a policy of détente. Of course, both stood in awe of the balance of terror hanging like the sword of Damocles over their constant global frictions.

Post–World War II Russo-American rivalry began over the division of Europe; it was here that the process of reconciliation would also have to begin. The chief bone of contention in the cold war was Germany and the status of the Western enclave in Berlin. In 1970, after West German chancellor Willy Brandt's *Ostpolitik* normalized relations between Bonn and Communist Eastern Europe (including the U.S.S.R.), West Germany formally acknowledged the division of Germany (and in effect Soviet predominance in eastern Europe), and Moscow agreed to recognize the rights of the Western powers in West Berlin. The issue of access to the defenseless city, a recurrent source of friction, was removed. With the groundwork laid for *rapprochement*, the Moscow and Washington summit conferences of 1972 and 1973 ushered in the heyday of superpower détente. Indeed, the momentum for détente was such that despite American bombing of North Vietnam and mining of Haiphong harbor on the eve of the scheduled 1972 summit (both of which resulted in the loss of Russian lives), the Soviets refused to cancel the Moscow conference.

The beginning of détente inaugurated a flurry of diplomatic negotiation and agreements in numerous fields as well as cooperative endeavors in areas such as space, the peaceful uses of atomic energy, science and technology, health and medicine, environment, transportation, agriculture and oceanography. The rapid expansion of contacts and communication was unprecedented. In the two years after the 1972 summit conference, the Soviet Union and the United States signed forty-one treaties and other internationl agreements.[53]

Three issues came to be the supporting pillars of détente: (1) the strategic arms limitations talks (SALT); (2) the management of international crises; (3) the expansion of trade. It is in these crucial areas that a meaningful détente is made or unmade. The success or failure (it would be better to say, the reality or illusion) of a superpower concert will hinge on progress in them. Arms control and crisis management are by far the most important, and constructive movement regarding them will be the gauge of progress toward amelioration of the struggle for power. (Although SALT is central to détente, we will examine it in the next section of this chapter, which deals with arms control as a mechanism for the management of power and conflict.)

The essence of the concert system is recognition of the desirability of international stability and acceptance of self-restraint and self-limitation. Accordingly, the United States and the Soviet Union formally agreed at the 1972 Moscow summit to a statement of "Basic Principles of Relations." Pledging to conduct their foreign policies "on a basis of peaceful coexistence," they proclaimed their intentions to "always exercise restraint in their mutual relations" and "do their utmost to avoid military confrontations and to prevent the outbreak of nuclear war." They agreed in advance to renounce "efforts to obtain unilateral advantage at the expense of the other" and prevent "the development of situations capable of causing a dangerous exacerbation of their relations." The following year, at the summit meeting in Washington, Nixon and Brezhnev restated their desire to "refrain from the threat or use of force against the other Party" so as to "avoid military confrontations, and as to exclude the outbreak of nuclear war between them." They agreed that should conflict between them "involve the risk of a nuclear conflict," they would "immediately enter into urgent consultations with each other and make every effort to avert this risk."

These two diplomatic communiqués of the superpowers would be, if the spirit and letter of the accords were lived up to, a viable concert system. However, the record of performance is spotty at best. The rhetoric of self-restraint does not ensure self-restrained behavior. (One is unfortunately reminded of the ill-fated Kellogg-Briand Pact of 1928, which resulted in a general renunciation of war as an instrument of policy. Without compulsory machinery to enforce the prohibition, "it was rather like declaring oneself against sin." [54]) The Middle East War of October 1973 is often cited as proof of the lack of substance to détente.[55] As was discussed in Chapter 4, the Soviets knew the Egyptians planned to attack Israel but did nothing to restrain them; in fact, they resupplied the Arab combatants and threatened to intervene unilaterally to forestall total Israeli victory. In response, the United States put its strategic forces on worldwide alert.[56] On the surface, it appears that the crisis was resolved more by traditional cold-war confrontation than by concert methods.

Nonetheless, one can still discern the operation of the restraint and consultation indicative of détente. The Soviet resupply effort and alert of airborne divisions were for the most part an attempt to save face and prevent the humiliation of client states. It is evident that Moscow desired a quick end to the fighting and (unsuccessfully) urged a cease-fire on Egyptain President Sadat. Brezhnev did indeed consult with Kissinger in Moscow, and the two agreed to a United Nations cease-fire resolution. Only when the Israelis refused to halt, and with rout of the Egyptians imminent, did the Soviets threaten to enforce the cease-fire, if need be alone—and they probably resorted to this stratagem more to deter the Israelis than the Americans.

There can be little doubt that the concert system worked very imperfectly. It did not prevent the outbreak of the war. It did not prevent the superpowers from reinforcing their clients. It did not preclude power plays by both sides. Yet détente may have been indispensable in keeping the channels of communication open between the Kremlin and the White House. What might have happened otherwise is subject to conjecture, but one is entitled to conclude that even a limited concert system is better than none at all. As one observer notes: "Détente, to the United States, no less than to the Soviet Union, has been a very limited proposition, in no sense eliminating their adversay relationship. Based entirely on self-interest, it has been merely a step in the right direction." [57]

Another cardinal principle of détente between the United States and the Soviet Union was to be expansion of economic relations between the two countries, the underlying assumption being that a web of interdependence would be an incentive to avoid deterioration of relations and thus more or less lock them into détente. (One must be careful to bear in mind, however, that Britain and Germany were each other's best customer on the eve of World War I.) Therefore, an important aspect of the 1972 summit was a commercial agreement, which was to lead to a United States grant of "most-favored-nation" (MFN) status to the Soviets in return for settlement of the lend-lease debts still unresolved from the Second World War (under most-favored-nation status, the U.S.S.R. receives the same treatment accorded the United States' other trading partners). As negotiations proceeded, so did the expansion of trade, and within four years trade between the Soviet bloc and the developed capitalist world increased nearly fourfold. A U.S.–U.S.S.R. Trade and Economic Council was established to facilitate economic transfers, and before long there was talk of multibillion-dollar ventures and joint projects. Yet Soviet-American trade still amounted to only one-half of one percent of total United States trade by 1975, and in the same year, a major snag developed. Through the Jackson-Vanik amendment to the adminstration's Trade Act of 1974, Congress linked granting of credits and MFN status with Soviet emigration practices, and the Soviets promptly rejected what they considered a discriminatory trading relationship and interference in their internal affairs. Though trade continues to expand, the failure of the 1972 agreement seemed to suggest a loss of momentum in this area of détente.[58]

The balance sheet on détente is ambiguous. Certainly the initial, unwarranted euphoria is past, and events in crisis management and economic relations suggest that as a concert system, détente is incomplete. But what about attempts to slow down the nuclear arms race? Together with crisis management, stabilization of mutual deterrence at parity would be the backbone of meaningful détente. Before reaching even a tentative conclusion on the utility of superpower détente as a mechanism for the management of power, we must examine SALT and the issue of arms control.

ARMS CONTROL AND DISARMAMENT: SALTING DETENTE

Armaments are but the symptoms, not the cause, of international conflict. As Hans Morgenthau puts it: "Men do not fight because they have arms. They have arms because they deem it necessary to fight."[59] And, therefore, in the words of John G. Stoessinger, "disarmament seems to be not so much a means for the attainment of political order as a product of its achievement."[60] This is not to suggest that arms races do not exacerbate international tensions. What we have in world politics is a vicious circle in which the security dilemma causes competition in arms, which in turn compounds the security dilemma and leads to a further quest for arms. Tensions produce arms; arms bring about more tension.

Arms control includes disarmament (actual reduction in number and types of weapons) as well as various methods of limiting the accumulation of weapons and their being used. Arms control has a long history in interstate relations, though in ancient times it amounted to little more than disarming states that had been defeated in war. During the Middle Ages, the Church placed many limitations on time, location and modes of combat.[61] From the inception of the modern state system until the mid-nineteenth century, the issue of arms control lay dormant, the destructiveness of warfare checked by the prenationalist and preindustrialist nature of European societies. With the progress of industrialization and the growth of nationalism, the ferocity of war intensified and the European states occasionally considered restrictions on the conduct of hostilities: for example, the first Geneva Convention of 1864 established rules concerning the treatment of the sick, wounded and prisoners of war. Such accords were obviously intended to "civilize" war, though no real attempt was made prior to this century to reach a comprehensive agreement on arms control.[62] (The Rush-Bagot Convention of 1817 was an exception, in that it resulted in the complete demilitarization of the entire American-Canadian border.) The Hague conferences of 1899 and 1907 resulted in the most comprehensive codification of the laws of war yet attempted and some limitation on the use of weapons, but no disarmament.[63] Nevertheless, ever since the Hague conferences, disarmament has been a permanent feature of international negotiation.

Both the League of Nations, which was established after the First World War, and the United Nations, established after the Second, were committed by their respective charters to furthering the cause of world peace through disarmament. Indeed, the disarming of Germany in 1919 was hailed by the victorious Allies as the first step toward general limitation on arms for all states. Not surprisingly, this noble goal never materialized. When the World Disarmament Conference of 1931–33 convened, each of the major powers sought to place limitations on the particular weapons in which its adversaries enjoyed an advantage until, finally, the Soviet Union suggested complete and total disarmament. In response to this Russian proposal, Salvador Madariaga of Spain replied with the following fable:

> When the animals had gathered, the lion looked at the eagle and said gravely, "We must abolish talons." The tiger looked at the elephant and said, "We must abolish tusks." The elephant looked back at the tiger and said, "We must abolish claws and jaws."
>
> Thus each animal in turn proposed the abolition of the weapons it did not have, until at last the bear rose up and said in tones of sweet reasonableness:
>
> "Comrades, let us abolish everything—everything but the great universal embrace." [64]

With this fable, Madariaga aptly portrayed the difficulty of arms control. All arms-control arrangements (especially those involving a degree of genuine disarmament) freeze some distribution of capabilities among the participants. Because power is a relative phenomenon, the ratio of military capabilities resulting from an arms-control agreement is all-important. As Inis Claude notes, "a scheme for the regulation of armaments must involve either freezing the configuration of power, at or below existing quantitative levels, or its alteration through the prescription of differential levels of disarmament." [65] In any event, some distribution of power will be stabilized, and states will maneuver to secure an agreement that enhances their power positions.

It is thus a difficult task to reach a meaningful ceiling on arms as long as states remain in a fundamentally hostile relation based on mutual fear and suspicion. Accords concluded in such an environment will deal with peripheral issues involving an obvious common interest. An example is the Geneva Protocol of 1925 (see Figure 10) which banned poisonous gases and bacteriological warfare, modes of combat which had already been proved unreliable in World War I. During a period of relaxation of tensions and settlement of outstanding political disputes, more meaningful arms control can be accomplished; however, if the political climate turns sour, competition in arms will be renewed. The Washington Naval Conference of 1922, one of the few cases of true big-power arms control prior to the nuclear age, illustrates this well. Following the First World War, the former allies agreed to establish a

Figure 10

Major Arms-Control Accords

Agreement	Date Signed	Contents	Signatories
Geneva Protocol	1925	prohibits use of poisonous, asphyxiating and other gases and bacteriological weapons	104 countries
Antarctic Treaty	1959	internationalizes and demilitarizes Antarctic continent	18 countries
"Hot Line" Agreement	1963	establishes teletype communications link	U.S.-U.S.S.R.
Nuclear Test-Ban Treaty	1963	prohibits nuclear testing in the atmosphere, underwater and in space	107 countries
Outer Space Treaty	1967	prohibits weapons of mass destruction in earth orbit, on the moon or any celestial body	73 countries
Latin America Nuclear-Free Zone	1967	prohibits introduction of nuclear weapons into the region	22 countries
Nuclear Nonproliferation Treaty (NPT)	1969	prohibits spread of nuclear weapons	109 countries
Seabed Treaty	1971	prohibits emplacement of nuclear weapons on seabed or ocean floor beyond 12-mile coastal limit	63 countries
Accidents Agreement	1971	safeguards against accidental or unauthorized use of nuclear weapons	U.S-U.S.S.R.
"Hot Line" Agreement II	1971	improvement in direct communications link	U.S.-U.S.S.R.
Biological Weapons Convention	1972	prohibits development, stockpiling or acquisition of biological agents	112 countries
ABM Treaty	1972	limited each party to 2 antiballistic-missile sites	U.S.-US.S.R.

Interim Agreement	1972	sets 5-year limit on number of ICBM and SLBM launchers	U.S.–U.S.S.R.
ABM Protocol	1974	reduces number of ABM sites to one for each party	U.S.–U.S.S.R
Threshold Test-Ban Treaty	1974	prohibits underground nuclear weapons tests in excess of 150 kilotons	U.S.–U.S.S.R.
Peaceful Nuclear Explosion (PNE) Treaty	1976	prohibits any individual nuclear explosion over 150 kilotons; provides for on-site inspection under certain circumstances	U.S.–U.S.S.R.

SOURCE: U.S. Arms Control and Disarmament Agency.

future ratio for tonnage in capital ships which awarded the United States and Britain parity with one another and made the other allies inferior to them. As relations among the powers deteriorated in the interwar period, the freeze became intolerable for the states challenging the global status quo and, in 1934, Japan withdrew from the treaty and began to expand its naval capabilities.

It is apparent, then, that progress toward arms control will parallel developments in the political sphere, that the regulation of armaments does not occur in a political vacuum. Relaxation of tensions decreases weapons competition and affords an opportunity for stabilization of existing ratios of military capabilities. Pronounced political conflict promotes the quest for arms, and arms races during periods of confrontation exacerbate tensions and heighten perceptions of insecurity.

The evolution of the post–World War II era from cold war to détente bears out what we have said. A realistic approach to arms control was not possible for nearly a quarter of a century after the war because of the intensity of superpower rivalry and the mutal perception of the superpowers that the conflict was a zero-sum game. The United States refused to relinquish its superiority in nuclear weaponry and sought an agreement to freeze the status quo. The Soviet Union was unwilling to accede to any arrangement dooming it to permanent inferiority, and struggled to attain equality. This deadlock began with the American-sponsored Baruch Plan in 1946 (which the Soviets rejected as a gimmick to keep them militarily weak forever) and continued until SALT I in

1972. Like the animals in Madariaga's fable, each superpower sought to use arms control to gain an advantage over the other, and soon disarmament negotiations degenerated into propaganda sessions. Finally, in tones of sweet reasonableness, Nikita Khrushchev rose up before the United Nations General Assembly in 1959 and proposed general and complete disarmament. Cold-war efforts at disarmament had reached an impasse.

Even during periods of confrontation, peripheral arms-control agreements are possible and also may contribute somewhat to lessening international tensions. At the end of the 1950s, two measures broke the ground in arms control. The United States, Britain and the U.S.S.R. tacitly agreed to a "moratorium" on further atmospheric nuclear testing in an informal understanding that was terminated by the Soviets in 1961.[66] In 1959, the superpowers signed the first postwar arms-limitation agreement, the Antarctic Treaty, which internationalized and demilitarized the Antarctic. This accord was a first step in establishing a modicum of mutual trust and later served as the model for a number of other "nonarmament" treaties which excluded nuclear weapons from outer space (1967), Latin America (1967) and the seabed (1971).

Following the Cuban missile crisis of October 1962 the United States and the Soviet Union began a serious inventory of their adversary relationship, appreciating the dangers of misunderstanding during nuclear confrontations. Accordingly, the following year they agreed to assure quick and reliable communication by means of a teletype link (the "hot line") between their capitals. Also in 1963, the superpowers signed a limited test-ban treaty, outlawing nuclear testing in the atmosphere, in space and underwater.

By the late 1960s, a thaw had begun in Soviet-American relations, and the Russians had virtually achieved equality with the United States in strategic weaponry. With a respectable record in arms control behind them, the two countries could now grapple with the two crucial problems of proliferation and deterrence stabilization.

Proliferation. Two decades after Hiroshima, any state with access to sufficient fissionable material could put together at least a crude nuclear device, and so in 1968 the United States and the Soviet Union submitted to the United Nations a treaty to prevent the spread of nuclear weapons. The Nonproliferation Treaty (NPT), which came into force in 1970, provides that: (1) no nuclear state will transfer nuclear weapons to any other state; (2) nonnuclear states will neither acquire nuclear weapons from any other state nor manufacture the devices themselves; (3) nonnuclear states will accept inspection by the International Atomic Energy Agency (IAEA). To counter the nonnuclear states' fear of potential blackmail by states in possession of the bomb, the superpowers offered vague assurances that nuclear aggression, or the threat of such aggression, would require immediate action by the United Nations Security Council.

Unfortunately, no sooner had the ink dried on the document than it became apparent that the greatest threat of proliferation came not from the transfer of nuclear weapons but from the inexorable diffusion of nuclear technology in the form of power reactors to produce energy. While nuclear power reactors cannot produce weapons, reprocessing plants can separate plutonium from the reactors' spent uranium rods and then reprocess the plutonium to produce weapons-grade material for nuclear explosives. It is estimated that by the late 1980s, at least forty countries will have a "nuclear option"—the means to manufacture a bomb on short notice. At present, India and Israel already have joined the once-exclusive nuclear club, eight states more have the option to join and a dozen others will soon have it.[67]

The new danger of proliferation has been caused by competition among the major nuclear suppliers to capture profitable markets in the less-developed world. Prior to 1975, the nuclear "have" nations refused to export plutonium-reprocessing plants to the "have-nots." West Germany broke with this policy in that year by contracting with Brazil (which did not sign the NPT agreement) for the sale of a complete nuclear industry (including the reprocessing cycle) for four billion dollars. Soon France was offering reprocessing plants to Pakistan and South Korea. In 1975, responding to these moves, the United States convened a conference among major supplier states for the purpose of setting stringent conditions for the export of reprocessing facilities. The results of this secret meeting were disappointing. Though it was agreed that IAEA safeguards would be applied to all future exports, this amounted to no more than "a paper umbrella of unenforceable guarantees." [68]

The United States and the Soviet Union collaborated to stem the tide of proliferation for an obvious reason: A world of many nuclear powers is bound to be more unstable than one in which there is a nuclear oligopoly of the major powers. But the true test of superpower desire for stability rests on the strength of their mutual commitment to the maintenance of mutual deterrence. Discussions on the limitation of strategic arms between the United States and Russia began in the fall of 1969; the first phase (SALT I) concluded in the summer of 1972 with the Antiballistic Missile (ABM) Treaty and a five-year Interim Agreement placing ceilings on offensive weapons; the second phase of the negotiations (SALT II) began the following autumn and led to the Vladivostok agreement two years later.

Deterrence Stabilization. SALT, along with joint management of international crises, is the cornerstone and chief gauge of the progress of détente. If these negotiations reflect the commitment of both sides to stabilization of mutual deterrence, then détente rests on solid foundations. However, if arms control becomes merely an instrument to secure unilateral advantage, then SALT will be a harbinger of stormy times in future superpower relations.

Each superpower developed its own rationale for agreeing to the limitation of strategic arms. Washington sought to preserve strategic stability by slowing down the massive Soviet buildup. Without a limitation on Soviet expansion, projections pointed to a two-to-one Soviet superiority in land- and sea-based missiles by 1977, a ratio which might have posed a threat to the American Minuteman force or, at any rate, given Moscow a diplomatic advantage.[69] For the Soviets, the Interim Agreement of SALT I preserved their numerical superiority in missile launchers (2,359 *vs.* 1,710) and ratified their strategic and political equality with the United States, a goal they had consistently worked for since

World War II. Moreover, by forgoing the development of an extensive missile-defense system (the ABM Treaty), each side in effect permitted the other to hold its population hostage, thus accepting the principle of mutual deterrence. Though the superpower arsenals remained asymmetrical (the Soviet Union having a lead in the number of missile and in "throw weight," and the United States retaining the edge in the number and accuracy of deliverable warheads), the balance of terror remained fundamentally stable.* That is, neither side would be in a position to acquire a first-strike capability.

At the Washington summit of 1973, Nixon and Brezhnev agreed to seek a permanent treaty on offensive arms by the end of the following year. However, that same year the Soviets tested their first MIRV. Fearing that American qualitative balance to Soviet quantitative superiority would be eroded, American negotiators pressed for equality in the strike forces of the two sides. The Soviet Union was preoccupied with the United States' qualitative edge and sought to retain its numerical advantage as insurance. The discussions deadlocked until Ford and Brezhnev reached an accord at Vladivostok in 1974. It was agreed that the basis of discussion for SALT II would be equality in total number of launchers (2,400) with each side free to apportion them as it saw fit among bombers, ICBMs and SLBMs; however, no more than 1,320 missiles on either side could be fitted with multiple warheads. This agreement did not produce any genuine arms control;[70] it merely placed new ceilings on strategic weapons far above those already reached. Then, negotiations on a new treaty bogged down. Arms control was in trouble.

An area of arms control in which virtually no progress has been made is the mutual reduction of forces in Europe. At the Moscow

* The Soviet "throw weight" advantage means that they possess more and larger missiles capable of carrying larger payloads. The United States lead in MIRV (multiple independently targeted reentry vehicles) technology and in strategic bombers (nearly 4:1) assures it a significant numerical edge in warheads. American missiles are also more accurate than their Russian counterparts, thus partially compensating for the throw-weight differential.

summit of 1972, Nixon and Brezhnev agreed to two separate negotiations: a Conference on Security and Cooperation in Europe (CSCE) and talks between NATO and Warsaw Pact–countries on reciprocal reduction of armed forces in central Europe (termed "mutual and balanced force reductions," or MBFR, by the United States).

The MBFR negotiations began in October 1973. The chief obstacle derives from the asymmetrical nature of the opposing forces, especially the Soviet bloc's superiority in manpower and tanks. The NATO powers have proposed parity between the two sides in the form of a common ground-forces ceiling of 700,000, thus requiring a disproportionately large cut in Soviet-bloc forces. The Warsaw Pact seeks a mutual reduction based upon equal percentages, meaning that the pact's existing margin of superiority would be enhanced. The crux of the matter (as is the case with all disarmament issues) is the ratio of military power that will exist after mutual reduction in forces is effected. Thus far, the Soviet Union has rejected parity, and the United States and its allies have refused to ratify the existing ratio of forces at a lower level. The result has been a deadlock in negotiations.[71]

In the summer of 1975, the European security conference was held in Helsinki, Finland. With thirty-five states participating, this was the most impressive gathering of heads of government since the Congress of Vienna. Unfortunately, the results of the CSCE were not nearly as impressive as those produced in 1815. The Helsinki accord was not a treaty, nor was it legally binding on any of the participants. It involved merely "political and moral commitments aimed at lessening tensions and opening further the lines of communication."[72] The document contained a package on security to please the U.S.S.R. and another on human rights to satisfy the West. In short, in return for Western acceptance of the postwar territorial status quo (in particular, the division of Germany), the Soviets gave vague verbal assurances about freer movement of peoples and ideas, and increased cultural and educational exchanges between the two blocs. In addition, both sides renounced the use of force and promised to notify one another in advance of large-scale military maneuvers. Though the Helsinki conference may have contributed to a temporary relaxation of tensions in Europe, without any movement on MBFR, its effects will be mainly cosmetic.

The indexes of détente (arms control, crisis management and economic relations) suggest that progress has slowed down considerably, if it has not already halted. Since 1975, détente has been on the defensive in the United States, with domestic criticism of détente as a one-way street so severe that early in 1976 President Ford dropped the word from the administration's lexicon in favor of the ominous phrase "peace through strength." Moreover, the Carter Administration, which took office the following year, immediately began a verbal assault on the Soviet Union's treatment of its dissidents, a policy that the Ford Administration had consciously shunned for fear of antagonizing the Kremlin leadership. All considered, the balance sheet on détente remains ambiguous. It is not altogether clear whether the relaxation of tensions initiated by the Moscow summit of 1972 will develop into a true relationship of self-restraint and self-limitation—that is, a concert of the superpowers. One thing, however, is certain: Détente is not irreversible. If détente does not regain its momentum, the superpower relationship may very well regress to cold war and confrontation.

INTERNATIONAL ORGANIZATION: MODIFYING THE BALANCE OF POWER

A third of a century after the founding of the United Nations, it is quite apparent that international organization is neither a panacea for world conflict nor a harbinger of world government. it remains (along with the balance of terror, détente, arms control and international law) a structure for management of conflict and modification of the underlying balance of power system. International organization has evolved not to abolish or supplant the multi-state system, but to perpetuate it by restraining the use of violence. In discouraging warfare, it serves to contain instability and thus to enable the decentralized international system to survive, if not prosper. Much as Franklin Roosevelt's New Deal sought to cure the ills of unregulated American capitalism so as to preserve its essence, the United Nations (and its predecessor, the League of Nations) was framed by the representatives of national governments, not to legislate independent states out of existence but to correct the excesses of anarchic competition. (Recall our reference earlier in this chapter to the Madisonian scheme of government: Factions are not to be eliminated, but their mischievous effects must be controlled.)

The creation of intergovernmental associations to regulate conflict is not a revolution or even an innovation in world affairs. In the seventeenth century, the Peace of Westphalia, inaugurating the modern state system based on diffusion of power, established the fundamental rules of the balance-of-power system and established certain provisions for pacific settlement and collective sanctions. In setting up elaborate rules for peaceful settlement of international conflict and providing machinery for the application of sanctions against violators of these rules, the league and the United Nations merely continued in the tradition of the Peace of Westphalia. Twentieth-century international organization "would seem to have left essentially unchanged the framework of the state system and of international law resulting from the Peace of Westphalia." [73]

The origin of both the League of Nations and the United Nations is found in the desire of the victorious states in the world wars to institutionalize the concert system—to refine, enlarge and elaborate upon the principle of big-power collaboration established at the beginning of the nineteenth century. There was no attempt to do away with the balance-of-power sytem (as if that were possible without doing away with independent states), only to create a board of directors responsible for seeing that the system operated more effectively. War could not be abolished; however, it was hoped that peace could be made more attractive.

The new global-concert system revolved around two mechanisms: (1) the peaceful settlement of disputes; and (2) a "collective security" arrangement. The Covenant of the League of Nations was the first substantive attempt under international law to limit the right of a sovereign state to wage war. Under traditional international law, the state legitimately had recourse to war as an instrument of policy, though custom and convention sought to place limitations on its conduct so as to make it more humane. Under the provisions of the Covenant of the League of Nations (Article 12), all members of the league pledged themselves to resolve disputes by means of diplomacy, arbitration or judicial settlement by the Permanent Court of International Justice. If the disputing states could not agree to arbitration or judicial settlement, they were obligated (Article 15) to bring their conflict before the council, which was the heart of the concert system. The council (the predecessor of the United Nations Security Council) consisted of permanent members (the major powers belonging to the league) as well as other states elected by the assembly for a temporary term of office. The council was empowered to investigate disputes and recommend specific settlements.

If these procedures for peaceful settlement failed, the members of the league were prepared to constitute a universal alliance against aggression, to offer any would-be conqueror the prospect of being confronted with overwhelming opposition from the rest of the international community. It was hoped that the threat of collective sanctions would deter aggressors, and that collective security would serve as "a halfway house between the terminal points of international anarchy and world government."[74] Though war was in no way prohibited, the covenant did in effect outlaw illicit force (i.e., resort to war in disregard of covenant obligations). Though all members agreed to "respect and preserve as against external aggression the territorial integrity and existing political independence" of all other members (Article 10), and further declared "any war or threat of war" a "matter of concern to the whole League" (Article 11), they also made a careful distinction between permissible and impermissible violence. For example, if states were deadlocked in a dispute and the council was unable to reach a unanimous recommendation for a settlement, then all that was required legitimately to wage war was a three-month cooling-off period. Only if a member of the league resorted to force immediately would it "*ipso facto* be deemed to have committed an act of war against all other Members of the League" and be subject to automatic economic sanctions and eventual military sanctions, if recommended by the council (Article 16). Thus, there were significant loopholes in the league's collective security arrangements. Moreover, the power of the council was incomplete. Unless all council members (permanent as well as nonpermanent) agreed, no settlement of a conflict could be imposed on disputants. And in regard to military sanctions against a transgressor, the council could only recommend (and only then if it were unanimous) what measures the league's members might individually take. Obviously, the League of Nations' version of collective security was fatally flawed. And as the interwar period proved, a little collective security is no collective security at all.

Though collective security seems to be an ideal instrument for maintaining international peace and security, its implicit underlying assumptions fail to hold up in reality. For collective security to work, all states (or at least the major powers) must be committed to the international status quo—that is, to the general distribution of global values as they exist at a particular time. Unfortunately, this is often not the case; and if it were, general war among the major powers would be unlikely in any event, with or without provisions for collective security. (During the 1930s, no less than three major powers—Germany, Japan, and Italy—were dissatisfied with the status quo and intent on overturning the existing international order.) For collective security to work, states must truly believe that "peace is indivisible" and that their security is threatened by events that may seem remote. Rarely is such farsightedness found in international politics, as the history of interwar appeasement of the Axis powers demonstrates. Finally, states must be willing to apply sanctions indiscriminately against every state designated an international outlaw, which is not likely given the normal division of the world into competing alliances and spheres of influence. In short, the theory of collective security, while valid in the abstract, is irrelevant in terms of political reality.[75]

The United Nations was originally envisaged as a reconstructed League of Nations, which would profit from its predecessor's mistakes. In legal terms, the United Nations Charter corrects a number of the covenant's most glaring deficiencies, but the inherent difficulties in applying a collective security system eventually led to abandonment of collective security.

While the league equivocated on the legitimacy of war, the United Nations Charter provides a sweeping ban not only on war, but on "the threat or use of force" in general (Article 2). Though nowhere in the charter is the word *war* to be found, for all practical purposes "war in the legal sense is outlawed under the United Nations system."[76] War, of course, cannot be abolished simply by avoiding use of the term; even in strictly legal terms, prohibition of war must be followed by a mechanism whereby the international community can enforce its will.[77] The Security Council is entrusted with primary responsibility for "maintenance of international peace and security" and is given extremely wide latitude to carry out this function. At least on paper, the powers of the Security Council are very impressive and, provided that the Big Five (the United States, the Soviet Union, Britain, France and China) are united, it can serve as a concert of powers with supranational authority, a position that the Great Powers of nineteenth-century Europe would have envied. While the league's council could only recommend measures to enforce peace, the Security Council can decide what sanctions are to be applied, including the use of armed forces, and all members of the United Nations are obligated (Article 25) to "accept and carry out the decisions of the Security Council." In effect, the Security Council is granted what amounts to international police power.

The charter of the United Nations is therefore an institutionalized concert system, and the Big Five were granted an international mandate to oversee the functioning of the state system. Though the organization is supposedly based upon the "sovereign equality" of all its members (Article 2), this is not the case in reality. The unanimity rule (Article 27) provides that all substantive matters are governed by the affirmative vote of nine of the Security Council's fifteen members, "including the concurring votes of the permanent members." In contrast to the League of Nations, there is no universal veto; nonpermanent members do not have veto power. A hierarchy of global power was acknowledged and legitimized by giving the major powers permanent Security Council status and veto prerogative. The charter in effect provides that no collective sanctions can be applied against a permanent member of the Security Council, and therefore the system of collective security was never intended to apply to all states indiscriminately, but only to all states other than the Big Five. Thus, true sovereignty (the ability to acknowledge no higher legal authority) is reserved to the Big Five alone.

But the prerogatives of the major powers was a double-edged sword. With unity of purpose, a true concert system would result. With disunity, the Security Council would be moribund and enforcement machinery paralyzed. The charter was written in 1945, before the cold war and before the nuclear age. By the time the United Nations went into operation at the beginning of the following year, the world situation had changed dramatically. The Grand Coalition of the Big Five was rapidly disintegrating and being replaced by a new alignment that pitted one superpower against another. Nuclear weapons and the debilitating effects of the war were causing a bipolarization of power, making a fiction of the major power status accorded Britain and France. (The inclusion of China in the Security Council was a fiction to begin with and was done only at the insistence of President Roosevelt.)

These postcharter developments tore asunder the collective-security rationale of the United Nations, which immediately became a pawn in the Soviet-American struggle for global supremacy. Because most of the fifty-one original members of the United Nations came from western Europe and North and South America, Washington was able to muster a virtually automatic two-thirds majority in the General Assembly (which is based upon the principle of "one state, one vote"). The United States dominated the Security Council by means of its hidden veto: Without casting a single veto until 1970, it was able to obtain a majority of votes against resolutions it opposed.[78] The U.S.S.R., permanently in a minority, was forced to rely on its veto to prevent UN action inimical to its interests, and by 1969 it had used its veto 105 times while the United States had yet to cast its first. Thus, in the early years of its existence, the United Nations functioned more or less as an instrument of American foreign policy.

The climax of this phase in the evolution of the United Nations came in 1950, with the Korean War. Seizing upon the Soviet Union's absence from Security Council deliberations, the United States got the council to endorse and legitimize its intervention on behalf of the South Korean government. The Security Council recommended (but did not order) that all members "furnish such assistance to the Republic of Korea as may be necessary to repel the armed attack and restore international peace and security in the area." This action came only after President Truman had ordered American air and sea forces into combat, and later all UN troops were placed under a unified military command responsible to Washington. Upon returning to its seat on the council, the Soviet Union denounced the decisions taken in its absence as illegal and blocked further enforcement action. In a parliamentary coup, the United States had future responsibility for the Korean action transferred to the General Assembly. What the United States failed to foresee was that someday it would lose its control over the General Assembly, a body in which neither it nor any other state possessed a veto.

Following the Korean War, the mechanism of "peacekeeping" replaced that of collective security. The objective of the United Nations was now not to fight or to deter aggression, but to serve as a neutral buffer between the rival superpower blocs, to contain international violence in the gray areas separating the Soviet and American spheres of influence. The United Nations soon developed a whole panoply of devices to further this end, including field missions, observation teams, cease-fires, truce supervisions, mediation and modest international forces (borrowed from smaller powers) to separate opposing armies. Under Secretary-General Dag Hammarskjold, the organization sought, through "preventive diplomacy," to insulate military crises on the periphery of the superpower spheres of influence by interposing the presence of the United Nations. The two most ambitious attempts at peacekeeping were the United Nations Emergency Force (UNEF) sent to the Middle East following the 1956 Suez war, and the United Nations

Operation in the Congo (ONUC), which intervened in the Congolese civil war in the early 1960s with the intention of establishing order in that war-torn country.

Though, by the early 1960s, collective security had long been abandoned for peacekeeping, the primary function of the United Nations remained conservative: "Maintenance of international peace and security" translated as preservation of the status quo. For the first decade of its existence, the United Nations had a fairly stable membership as each superpower blocked the entry of the other's clients. Only nine new states were allowed to join the organization.[79] However, the floodgates were opened in 1955, when a package deal made possible the immediate admission of sixteen applicants and, with the rapid process of decolonization, by the early 1960s, the United Nations's membership had doubled. With the changing complexion of the General Assembly, both the function and instruments of the organization underwent a metamorphosis. As the less-developed countries of the Third World gained control of the General Assembly, they began to call into question the legitimacy of the entire global order, substituted "peaceful change" for "peacekeeping" and transformed the aim of the United Nations from security to welfare. The Third World's initial goal was completion of the process of decolonization, and this soon became the cause of the United Nations as a whole. The charter gave no direct jurisdiction to the United Nations over the colonial affairs of its members. The imperial powers agreed only to a nonbinding "Declaration Regarding Non-Self-Governing Territories," in which they accepted their colonies as "a sacred trust" and pledged to promote the well-being and "self-government" of the inhabitants. They did not promise independence, nor would they allow United Nations supervision over their colonies.

In 1960, the General Assembly passed by an overwhelming margin the Declaration on Colonialism, calling for "immediate steps" for the transfer of power to indigenous populations. The following year the assembly established a Special Committee on Colonialism to implement the resolution, and this committee came to function as a potent pressure group for the eradication of the remnants of European imperialism. By the end of the decade, the developing countries had succeeded in forging an international consensus against colonialism, making the continuation of imperial rule illegitimate and burdensome. Three decades after the founding of the United Nations, there were only two remaining colonial questions of consequence: Rhodesia and Namibia.

Now that the United Nations was operating as the midwife of colonial emancipation, the developing countries could make the organization focus on economic development. In 1963, their domination of the General Assembly (in which they exercised a virtually automatic two-thirds majority) brought about a revision of the UN Charter to enlarge the Economic and Social Council (ECOSOC) from eighteen to twenty-four members, thus assuring them a solid majority in that body as well. The following year, the ECOSOC-sponsored Conference on Trade and Development (UNCTAD) convened in Geneva and soon became a permanent adjunct to the United Nations, complete with its own secretariat and periodic conferences to focus on the needs of the developing world (for detailed consideration of UNCTAD and the North-South confrontation, see Chapter 7). In 1969, the General Assembly declared the 1970s the Second Development Decade, and in 1974, it passed the Declaration on the Establishment of a New International Economic Order, calling for an end to "the remaining vestiges of alien and colonial domination" and declaring the right of all colonially dominated states "to restitution and full compensation for the exploitation and depletion of . . . the[ir] natural resources." In the same year, over the objections of most of the developed countries, the assembly ratified a Charter of Economic Rights and Duties of States, incorporating the poor nations' most contentious proposals into a declaration intended to serve as the basis of a new global order.

The United Nations has gone through a number of evolutionary stages. Founded on the twin principles of peaceful settlement of disputes and collective security, it soon became a mechanism for peacekeeping and then peaceful change. Though it was conceived as an instrument of the entire international community, it became first an instrument of American foreign policy in the cold war and then an instrument of the developing countries in their confrontations with the richer ones. Throughout its history, it has been the mirror of the international system, reflecting the parliamentary balance of power in the international community. Yet today influence in the United Nations (and especially in the General Assembly) is inversely related to military and economic power status in the world as a whole. Because of this fundamental incongruity, the United Nations will best serve as a mechanism for the management of conflict by providing a forum for dialogue between rich and poor countries. Though this may seem a paltry alternative to the grandiose scheme of collective security, we must bear in mind what the real alternative to that dialogue is—not collective security, but collective insecurity.

INTERNATIONAL LAW: THE "ETIQUETTE" OF NATIONS

The concept of international law is inherently paradoxical. State sovereignty means that no state is subject to the will of another; it acknowledges no higher authority and is thus a law unto itself. The notion of a law that sovereigns must obey is a contradiction. As far back as the thirteenth century, Marsilius of Padua set forth the principle that law could be defined only in terms of its enforceability by a higher power. This line of reasoning was later adopted and elaborated by the nineteenth-century English legal theorist John Austin, one of the foremost representatives of the positivist school of jurisprudence. According to the Austinian view, a law is "a rule laid down for the guidance of an intelligent being by an intelligent being having power over him," and therefore "every positive law, or every law simply and strictly called, is set by a sovereign person, or a body of sovereign persons, to a member of the independent political society wherein that person or body of persons is sovereign or supreme." Austin found that "international law" was not law at all, but simply one of "those objects improperly but by close analogy termed laws"; in fact, the so-called law of nations was no more than "positive international morality."[80] Many other students of law have concurred with the positivist theory. The English philosopher John Stuart Mill, for example, termed international law the "customs of nations," [81] and Professor Woodrow Wilson wrote in 1890 that international law is "not law at all" since "it is law without forceful sanction." [82] It seems, then, that "international law" is law only by analogy.[83]

As the Axis powers brutally dismantled the legal order between the world wars, even enthusiasts for the League of Nations system became disillusioned with international law. The events leading to the Second World War demonstrated, in the words of one contemporary, "to what extent the sense of law has ceased to be an effective factor in the decisions of statesmen. They show that . . . a formal observance of legal technicalities, an empty shell without any substance in it, is all that is really left of international order." [84] Of course, others maintain that the proliferation of international organizations, the precedent of the Nuremberg trials and the numerous multilateral conventions signed since World War II are proof of both the reality and the vitality of international law in the twentieth-century.[85] Marshaling evidence to prove its existence, defenders of international law are quick to point out that despite the few dramatic violations, most interstate rules are observed and complied with. As one student comments, "It is probably the case that almost all nations observe almost all principles of international law and almost all of their obligations almost all of the time." [86] And another maintains that "there are, in fact, fewer violations of international law than of municipal laws." [87]

Whether international law is a reality or an illusion seems to depend on the definition of *law*. If we assume that true *law* requires the existence of a central authority compelling compliance and punishing deviation, then no international law can be said to exist. The international system has no such central authority. However, if we are somewhat less demanding and define *law*, as Max Weber did, as "directives in a community, deviations from which are met usually by means to compel conformity or by punishment," [88] then international law is probably *law*. (As we shall see, sanctions are usually applied not by a central authority, but by other states acting individually or collectively.) If we require only that law consists of a body of rules of behavior which are commonly observed,[89] then international law definitely qualifies. But more important than the definition of *law* employed is the domain of conduct affected by regulation.

It is important to distinguish between two types of international law: constitutional and reciprocal. *Constitutional* international law is used here to denote the body of interstate agreements pertaining to the overall structure of political competition. This includes all significant arrangements in the realm of high politics that affect the struggle for power: treaties of alliance, arms-control accords and the various mechanisms of international organization such as collective sanctions, procedures for the peaceful settlement of disputes and the institutional means available for peaceful change.

The law of *reciprocity* applies to matters that are normally little related to the pursuit of power. In broad areas such as commercial intercourse, diplomatic privileges and immunities, protection of foreign nationals, and usually (though not always) recognition of borders and domestic jurisdiction, states regularly cooperate out of a common desire to preserve at least a minimum of order and stability in their mutual relations.

The most developed and sophisticated variety of law is found in this second, more technical, category. There is a paucity of law in the constitutional field, and the little that exists either reinforces the decentralized nature of the international system or tends to be vague and ambiguous. The further one gets from issues affecting distribution of capabilities among political actors, the more likely are binding commitments of a legal nature; the closer one gets to issues affecting the state's freedom of action to pursue its vital interests, the less likely are infringements on sovereignty. Thus, when it is claimed that most international law is strictly adhered to, or even that it is breached less frequently than domestic law, the claim ought to be coupled with the admission that there is much less international law to be violated in the first place. More often than not the most crucial areas of state behavior are beyond its purview. We can no more laud the accomplishments of the international law of reciprocity while constitutional law remains stunted than we can admire a domestic society in which citizens agree to obey traffic regulations but refuse to relinquish the right to use violence against one another. The authority of law, therefore, is relegated to the periphery of international relations. Its domain is exceedingly circumscribed.

The primitive development of international law mirrors the primitive state of international politics. Historically, the modern law of nations may be traced back to the formal initiation of the balance-of-power system at the Congress of Westphalia in 1648. In fact, "the existence of a political equilibrium has frequently been regarded as a necessary condition for the existence of the Law of Nations."[90] The starting point of international law was the doctrine of state sovereignty; hence its essential characteristic is that it is based on common consent. It is therefore a law of coordination rather than a law of subordination, as is the case in domestic society. The ultimate impetus for this self-limitation is self-interest. States by and large obey the laws they create because it is in their interest to do so and they are deterred from whimsically departing from convention by the knowledge that they are not alone in the world and can expect retaliation in kind. The laws of war, for example, are—as is all international law—rules of expedience. In World War II, Nazi Germany chose not to execute prisoners of war not because its leaders felt morally bound by the Geneva Conventions, but because it made sense not to execute prisoners of war. When we examine the sanctions of these rules,

> we find that it lies in the fact that such observance is in the interest of all concerned. Any temporary or incidental advantage to be gained by a disregard of these rules, it is recognized, would be overweighed by the deterioration of the conflict into pure savagery. In other words, the laws of war are observed because ... they help to protect the interests of both parties.[91]

The sanction of law in a primitive environment, therefore, is the prospect of mutually damaging behavior.[92]

This abbreviated version of law lacks most of what we associate with a well-ordered domestic legal system. There is no central legislature to make rules, no executive authority to enforce them and no judiciary to adjudicate disputes arising under them. Though ad hoc multilateral conferences may address themselves to certain problems or issues, under normal circumstances only the states ratifying the instruments resulting from conferences are bound to observe them. States have to depend on themselves for redress of legal grievances: Mandatory collective sanctions have been extremely rare, the first instance under the United Nations being those levied by the Security Council against Rhodesia in 1966. (An effective collective security system, which, as we have noted, is incompatible with the state system as presently constituted, would of course rectify the decentralization of executive authority.) Though a World Court exists (the International Court of Justice), its jurisdiction in interstate conflict is not compulsory, it may hear only those cases in which both disputants agree to submit to judicial settlement. Even if both disputants should agree (which is unheard of in matters of high politics), there is no international police power to enforce the judgment of the tribunal. In sum, the legal infrastructure of world politics is severely handicapped by its haphazard processes and truncated structures.

This attenuated body of law has resulted from centuries of accumulated customs and usages and, more recently, from international conferences. Since the Hague Peace Conferences of 1889 and 1907, there have been periodic attempts to codify the regulations thus evolved and to bring new areas of dispute under the rule of law. The process of building a universal edifice of legal norms has been painfully slow and cumbersome, and as the countries of the world become more interdependent through technology and industrialization, new types of potential conflict are generated and additional regulations must be devised. Whenever new rules of conduct are added, newer areas of friction develop; moreover, many of the principles of international law that have evolved over the years are often challenged by new participants in the global political process. Law in general, and international law in particular, serves a conservative function and is an instrument of the status quo. Legal order tends to reflect the distribution of power in the political system. As one observer concludes: "Law is that system of manipulable symbols that functions as a representation, a model, of social structure."[93] In this sense, all law is ultimately political and is thus a product of the dominant interests in a society. The Hague Conventions, for example, with their emphasis on the wartime protection of private property, civilians, cultural monuments and art museums, were a product of the nineteenth-century European liberal mind. Indeed, the whole system of international law until that time was greatly influenced by the values of the world's dominant states. After the Bolshevik Revolution in Russia, the new leaders of the Soviet Union at first rejected certain obligations under the reigning law of nations as part of the bourgeois superstructure of the capitalist world. In much the same way, after the Second World War, the newly emergent nations of Africa and Asia viewed the international order as a tool used by their former European overlords to continue neocolonial relationships. Though both the Soviet Union and the less-developed countries eventually found it in their short-run interests to work within the existing legal framework of international relations, they have endeavored to replace that framework in the long run with a new order more to their liking.

The enormous difficulty in building a legitimate and universally accepted structure of law in a world of over 150 independent states with differing value systems, interests and cultures and at different stages of economic development is exemplified by the attempt to negotiate a new legal regime to manage conflict over use of the seas. This is urgently needed because of the growing number of coastal states and the rise of new techniques for projecting state power far beyond the traditional three-mile limit of territorial domain (the range of eighteenth-century canon). The United Nations International Law Commission, charged with responsibility for codifying and further developing international law, labored for nearly a decade preparing for the First UN Conference on the Law of the Sea in 1958. This conference failed to reach agreement on the breadth of territorial sea, the extent of fishing jurisdiction or the limits of coastal states' exclusive rights over continental-shelf resources. Neither was any progress made at a second conference held two years later.

Almost immediately, these unresolved traditional problems were compounded by new issues, which promised to intensify international conflict. Overfishing was leading to serious depletion of some stocks; ocean ecology was threatened with disruption from industrial pollution. Even more ominous was the new technology developed by private corporations in advanced nations to exploit the mineral resources of the ocean floor. At the third sea-law conference in 1973, the Third World countries demanded strict international control of deep-sea mining by an international authority, with revenues to be shared so as to benefit the developing states. Industrial states wished to legitimate their access to the ocean's mineral wealth and proposed instead an international agency to supervise private ventures, but not to exploit the seabed itself. Crosscutting this cleavage was the division between coastal and inland states. States with little or no access to the ocean (a fifty-two-member group of developing and developed countries) threatened to block any treaty that failed to recognize their rights to share in the fisheries and offshore mineral wealth of the maritime nations. After numerous sessions during a three-year period, the third conference failed to reach a comprehensive treaty. Negotiations foundered over fundamental conflicts of interest, and numerous states were unilaterally establishing conflicting national claims to the sea.[94]

International law is a law without government, without force and of limited authority. Though many aspects of "low politics" are effectively regulated by the etiquette of nations, crucial areas of global interaction remain outside the legal order. Where there is no law to break, no violations are possible. The law that does exist contributes to the management of power by providing means for channeling conflict in nonviolent directions. It can be effective only to the extent that it is employed by the members of the multistate system. Throughout diplomatic history, however, states have framed their foreign policies according to *raison d'ètat* and only afterward have appealed to law and morality. When Frederick the Great of Prussia decided to seize Silesia in the second half of the eighteenth-century, he conferred with his generals first and his legal scholars second, directing the scholars to devise a legal basis for his claim. In 1962, when President Kennedy decided upon a selective blockade of Cuba to force the Soviet Union to remove its offensive missiles, only after the decision were the State Department legal theorists instructed to prepare a legal brief on the United States' behalf.

Until the legal order is expanded into the area of constitutional regulation—that is, until states agree to relinquish more of their sovereign prerogatives—international law will remain a marginal mechanism for the management of interstate conflict.

Notes
Chapter 5

1. Alexander Hamilton, James Madison, John Jay, *The Federalist Papers*, ed. R. P. Fairfield (Garden City: Doubleday, 1961), Number 10, p. 18.
2. Thomas C. Schelling, *The Strategy of Conflict* (New York: Oxford University Press, 1963), pp. 4–5.
3. Hamilton, et al., *Federalist Papers*, p. 20.
4. Thomas Hobbes, *Leviathan* (New York: Collier, 1962), part I, chapter 13, p. 101.
5. Gabriel A. Almond and G. Bingham Powell, Jr., *Comparative Politics: A Developmental Approach* (Boston: Little, Brown, 1966), pp. 41–44.
6. Quoted in F. H. Hinsley, *Power and the Pursuit of Peace: Theory and Practice in the History of Relations Between States* (London: Cambridge University Press, 1967), p. 50.
7. Cited in Kenneth N. Waltz, *Man, the State and War: A Theoretical Analysis* (New York: Columbia University Press, 1965), pp. 167–8; also see the discussion by Stanley Hoffmann, *The State of War: Essays in the Theory and Practice of International Politics* (New York: Praeger, 1965), chapter 3.
8. Robert D. Luce and Howard Raiffa, *Games and Decisions* (New York: Wiley, 1967), p. 95.
9. K. J. Holsti, *International Politics: A Framework for Analysis,*

2nd ed. (Englewood Cliffs, N.J.: Prenctice-Hall, 1972), pp. 31–52.

10. Martin Wright, *Power Politics* (London: Royal Institution of International Affairs, 1946), p. 45.

11. Hans J. Morgenthau, *Politics Among Nations: The Struggle for Power and Peace,* 5th ed. (New York: Knopf, 1972), p. 167.

12. W. W. Rostow, *The United States in the World Arena* (New York: Harper & Row, 1960), p. 286. (Emphasis added.)

13. Robert Ergang, *Europe from the Renaissance to Waterloo,* 3rd ed. (Boston: D. C. Heath, 1967), p. 225.

14. Ibid., p. 473.

15. Robert A. Kann, "Metternich: A Reappraisal of His Impact on International Relations," *Journal of Modern History* 32 (December 1960): 338.

16. Henry A. Kissinger, "The Congress of Vienna: A Reappraisal," *World Politics* 8 (January 1956): 268; idem, *A World Restored: The Politics of Conservatism in a Revolutionary Age* (New York: Universal Library, 1964); also, by Harold Nicolson, *The Congress of Vienna: A Study in Allied Unity, 1812–1822* (New York: Harcourt Brace Jovanovich, n. d.).

17. Inis L. Claude, Jr., *Swords into Ploughshares: The Problems and Progress of International Organization,* 3rd ed. rev. (New York: Random, 1964), p. 21.

18. Gerhart Niemeyer, "The Balance Sheet of the League Experiment," *International Organization* 14 (September 1960): 540.

19. David Thomson, *Europe Since Napoleon,* 2nd ed. rev. (New York: Knopf, 1965), p. 221.

20. Clark R. Mollenhoff, *Strike Force: Organized Crime and the Government* (Englewood Cliffs, N.J.: Prentice-Hall, 1972), chapter 2; also see Martin A. Gosch and Richard Hammer, *The Last Testament of Lucky Luciano* (Boston: Little, Brown, 1975).

21. Inis L. Claude, Jr., *Power and International Relations* (New York: Random, 1962), pp. 25–37.

22. Ibid., chapter 2.

23. Ernst B. Haas, "The Balance of Power: Prescription, Concept or Propaganda," *World Politics* 5 (July 1953): 446–77. The four categories of possible application are description, propaganda, analytical concept, prescription. The eight distinct meanings are

equilibrium, distribution, hegemony, stability, instability, power politics, universal law, guide to policy making. See also Martin Wight, "The Balance of Power," in H. Butterfield and Martin Wight, eds., *Diplomatic Investigations: Essays in the Theory of International Politics* (London: Allen and Unwin, 1966).

24. Ibid., pp. 450–51.

25. A. F. K. Organski, *World Politics*, 2nd ed. (New York: Knopf, 1968), p. 294.

26. Claude, *Power and International Relations*, p. 66.

27. Kenneth N. Waltz, "Theory of International Politics," in Fred I. Greenstein and Nelson W. Polsby, eds., *International Politics*, vol. 8 of the *Handbook of Political Science* (Reading, Mass.: Addison-Wesley, 1975), p. 41.

28. Ibid.

29. Ibid., p. 38.

30. Louis J. Halle, *The Cold War as History* (New York: Harper & Row, 1967), pp. 319–20.

31. Morton A. Kaplan, *System and Process in International Politics* (New York: Wiley, 1957), p. 23.

32. Adapted with modifications from Edward Vose Gulick, *Europe's Classical Balance of Power* (New York: W. W. Norton, 1967), chapter 3.

33. Robert S. McNamara, *The Essence of Security: Reflections in Office* (New York: Harper & Row, 1968), pp. 57–59. (Emphasis added.)

34. The four-to-one ratio of American strategic missile strength to that of the Soviets progressively decreased from 1964 to virtual equality in 1970. See London Institute for Strategic Studies, *The Military Balance, 1969–1970* (1969), p. 55.

35. Ludwig Dehio, *The Precarious Balance: Four Centuries of the European Power Struggle*, trans. Charles Fullman (New York: Vintage, 1965).

36. Sir Eyre Crowe, quoted in Robert Pfaltzgraff, Jr., ed., *Politics and the International System* (New York: Lippincott, 1969), p. 385.

37. Kissinger, *A World Restored*, p. 138.

38. Henry A. Kissinger, Speech before the Southern Council on

International and Public Affairs and the Atlanta Chamber of Commerce, News Release, Bureau of Public Affairs, Department of State, June 23, 1975, p. 4. (Emphasis added.)

39. News Conference, June 22, 1973, Department of State Publication 8733, p. 33. (Emphasis added.)

40. See Kissinger, *A World Restored,* chapter 9.

41. Alastair Buchan, "The Age of Insecurity," *Encounter* 20 (June 1963): 3. Quoted in John Garnett, ed., *Theories of Peace and Security: A Reader in Contemporary Strategic Thought* (London: St. Martin's, 1970), p. 34.

42. Quoted in Fred C. Ikle, "Can Nuclear Deterrence Last Out the Century?" *Foreign Affairs* 51 (January 1973): 269.

43. U.S. Arms Control and Disarmament Agency, *SALT Lexicon,* rev. ed., ACDA Publication Number 71 (July 1975), p. 9.

44. The acronym "MAD" was coined by Donald G. Brennan, "The Case for Missile Defense," *Foreign Affairs* 47 (April 1969): 468–87.

45. For example, Paul H. Nitze, "Assessing Strategic Stability in an Era of Détente," *Foreign Affairs* 54 (January 1976): 207–32.

46. For example, as Senator Edward M. Kennedy has put it: "To be sure, a major difference in numbers of nuclear weapons can have political significance. It can shape the way we and the Russians would behave in a crisis." See his "Beyond Deterrence," *Foreign Policy* 16 (Fall 1974): 11.

47. For a discussion of the strategic debate in the United States in the late 1950s and early 1960s, see Richard A. Aliano, *American Defense Policy from Eisenhower to Kennedy: The Politics of Changing Military Requirements, 1957–1961* (Athens: Ohio University Press, 1975).

48. Henry A. Kissinger, Speech before the London Institute of Strategic Studies, June 25, 1976 (as presented in the *New York Times,* June 26, 1976, p. 7). See also *The Meaning of Détente,* Department of State Publication 8766 (Washington, D.C.: GPO, 1974).

49. *New York Times,* June 26, 1976, p. 7.

50. Ibid.

51. One critic of détente notes at least six such cycles in Soviet-

American relations: Lenin's détente (1920); Stalin's détente (1935); the Devil's détente (1941); Khrushchev's détente (1954); Brezhnev's détente, phase I (1968); Brezhnev's détente, phase II (1972). See Gerald L. Steibel, *Détente: Promises and Pitfalls* (New York: Crane, Russak, 1975), chapter 1.

52. George F. Kennan, "The United States and the Soviet Union, 1917–1976," *Foreign Affairs* 54 (July 1976): 670–90.

53. *The Meaning of Détente,* p. 10.

54. H. Stuart Hughes, *Contemporary Europe: A History,* 2nd ed. (Englewood Cliffs, N.J.: Prentice-Hall, 1966), p. 156.

55. See, for example, Walter Laqueur, "Détente: What's Left of It?" *New York Times Magazine,* December 16, 1973; also, Steibel, *Détente,* chapter 3.

56. For an excellent and concise account of the activities of the superpowers during the Middle East war, see Marvin and Bernard Kalb, "Twenty Days in October," *New York Times Magazine,* June 23, 1974.

57. Vladimir Petrov, *U.S.–Soviet Détente: Past and Future* (Washington, D.C.: American Enterprise Institute for Public Policy Research, 1975), p. 51.

58. See Steibel, *Détente,* chapter 4; also Theodore C. Sorensen, "Most-Favored-Nation and Less Favorite Nations," *Foreign Affairs* 52 (January 1974): 273–86.

59. Morgenthau, *Politics Among Nations,* p. 400.

60. John G. Stoessinger, *The Might of Nations: World Politics in Our Time,* 3rd ed. (New York: Random House, 1969), p. 347.

61. See J. D. Tooke, *The Just War in Aquinas and Grotious* (London: William Clowes, 1965), chapter 1.

62. See Morris Greenspan, *The Modern Law of Land Warfare* (Los Angeles: University of California Press, 1959); also L. Oppenheim, *International Law,* vol. 2, *Disputes, War and Neutrality,* 7th ed., by H. Lauterpacht (London: Longman, Green, 1951).

63. A. P. Higgins, *The Hague Peace Conferences and Other International Conferences Concerning the Laws and Usages of War* (Cambridge, Eng.: Cambridge University Press, 1909); James B. Scott, ed., *The Hague Peace Conventions and Declarations of 1899 and 1907,* 3rd ed. (New York: Oxford University Press, 1918).

64. Cited in Aliano, *American Defense Policy,* note p. 140.

65. Claude, *Swords into Ploughshares,* pp. 268–69.

66. For the text of and background on the major arms control agreements reached since World War II, see U.S. Arms Control and Disarmament Agency, *Arms Control and Disarmament Agreements: Text and History of Negotiations* (Washington, D.C.: ACDA, 1975).

67. The states with nuclear options are Argentina, Belgium, Canada, Italy, South Africa, Spain and West Germany; Australia, Austria, Brazil, Czechoslovakia, East Germany, Iran, Japan, Norway, Pakistan, Sweden, Switzerland and Taiwan will soon have the technological means. See Adlai E. Stevenson III, "Nuclear Reactors: America Must Act," *Foreign Affairs* 53 (October 1974): 64–76.

68. Norman Gall, "Atoms for Brazil, Danger for All," *Foreign Policy* 23 (Summer 1976): 193; see also Steven J. Baker, "Monopoly or Cartel?" *Foreign Policy* 23 (Summer 1976): 202–20.

69. See Alton H. Quanbeck and Barry M. Bleechman, *Strategic Forces: Issues for the Mid-Seventies* (Washington, D.C.: Brookings Institution, 1973). For an in-depth consideration of the issues involved in contemporary arms-control negotiations, see the following: William R. Kintner and Robert Pfaltzgraff, *SALT: Implications for Arms Control* (Pittsburgh, Pa.: University of Pittsburgh Press, 1973); Mason Willrich and John B. Rhinelander, eds., *SALT: The Moscow Agreements and Beyond* (New York: Free Press, 1974); Walter C. Clemens, *The Superpowers and Arms Control* (Lexington, Mass.: Lexington Books, 1972); James E. Dougherty, *How to Think About Arms Control and Disarmament* (New York: Crane, Russak, 1973); Michael Howard, "The Relevance of Traditional Strategy," *Foreign Affairs* 51 (January 1973): 253–66; Jan M. Lodal, "Assessing Strategic Stability: An Alternative View," *Foreign Affairs* 54 (April 1976): 462–81; Colin S. Gray, "Rethinking Nuclear Stratgey," *Orbis* 17 (Winter 1974): 1145–60; Paul H. Nitze, "The Strategic Balance Between Hope and Skepticism," *Foreign Policy* 17 (Winter 1974–75): 136–56; Wolfgang K. H. Panofsky, "The Mutual-Hostage Relationship between America and Russia," *Foreign Affairs* 52 (October 1973): 109–18; Herbert S.

Scoville, Jr., "Flexible Madness?" *Foreign Policy* 14 (Spring 1974): 164–77; James Dougherty, "The Soviet Union and Arms Control, *Orbis* 17 (Fall 1973): 737–77.

70. For further discussion, see Gerard C. Smith, "SALT After Vladivostok," *Journal of International Affairs* 29 (Spring 1975): 7–18; Herbert Scoville, Jr., "An 'Iffy' Arms Control Agreement," *The New Republic*, January 18, 1975, 19–20; Jack Ruina, "SALT in a MAD World," *New York Times Magazine*, January 30, 1974; F. A. Long, "Should We Buy the Vladivostok Agreement?" *Bulletin of the Atomic Scientists*, February 1975, 5–6; Colin S. Gray, "A Problem Guide to SALT II," *Survival* 17 (September–October 1975): 230–34.

71. See the following: U.S. Department of State, "Europe: Mutual and Balanced Force Reduction," *Foreign Policy Outlines*, May 1974 and January 1975; J. I. Coffey, "Arms Control and the Military Balance in Europe," *Orbis* 17 (Spring 1973): 132–54, John Yochelson, "MBFR: The Search for an American Approach," *Orbis* 17 (Spring 1973): 155–75.

72. Gerald R. Ford, Statement Prior to his Departure for the Helsinki Conference on Security and Cooperation in Europe, Department of State News Release, July 25, 1975.

73. Leo Gross, "The Peace of Westphalia, 1648–1948," *American Journal of International Law* 42 (1948): 21.

74. Claude, *Swords into Ploughshares*, p. 224.

75. For a more in-depth critique of collective security, see Claude, *Power and International Relations*, chapter 5.

76. William L. Tung, *International Law in an Organizing World* (New York: Thomas Y. Crowell, 1968), p. 427.

77. Hans Kelsen, *Principles of International Law* (New York: Rinehart, 1952), p. 43.

78. For an excellent discussion of Soviet-American conflict at the United Nations, see John G. Stoessinger, *The United Nations and the Superpowers*, 2nd ed. (New York: Random House, 1970).

79. Ibid., p. 4.

80. John Austin, *Lectures on Jurisprudence, or the Philosophy of Positive Law*, vol. 1 (New York: James Crockcraft, 1875), pp. 3–5; also W. Jethro Brown, ed., *The Austinian Theory of Law* (London: John Murray, 1906), pp. 5–6, 96.

81. John Stuart Mill, *Dissertations and Discourses: Political, Philosophical, and Historical,* vol. II (London: Parker & Son, 1867), pp. 173–77.

82. As quoted in Frederick L. Schuman, *International Politics: Anarchy and Order in the World Society,* 7th ed. (New York: McGraw-Hill, 1969), p. 144.

83. Interestingly enough, this was the view of a past president of the respected *Institute de Droit International;* cited in Nagendra Singh, *Nuclear Weapons and International Law* (New York: Praeger, 1959), pp. 3–5.

84. Gerhard Niemeyer, *Law Without Force* (Princeton, N.J.: Princeton University Press, 1941), p. 11.

85. For example, Tung, *International Law,* chapter 1; also Julius Stone, *Legal Controls of International Conflict,* rev. ed. (London: Stevens, 1959).

86. Louis Henkin, *How Nations Behave: Law and Foreign Policy* (New York: Praeger, 1968), p. 42.

87. Tung, *International Law,* p. 24.

88. H. H. Gerth and C. Wright Mills, eds., *From Max Weber: Essays in Sociology* (New York: Oxford University Press, 1958), p. 180.

89. Tung, *International Law,* p. 1.

90. Gross, *Peace of Westphalia,* p. 27.

91. E. C. Stowell, "The Laws of War and the Atom Bomb," *American Journal of International Law* 39 (October 1945): 786.

92. See, for example, Michael Barkun, *Law Without Sanctions: Order in Primitive Society and the World Community* (New Haven: Yale University Press, 1968).

93. Ibid., p. 92.

94. John Temple Swing, "Who Will Own the Oceans?" *Foreign Affairs* 54 (April 1976): 531.

Chapter 6

Transnational Relations

Don Corleone nodded. "Revenge is a dish that tastes best when it is served cold."

—Mario Puzo, *The Godfather*

THE INTERNATIONAL CONNECTION: GLOBAL INTERDEPENDENCE

Primitive, lawless and fragmented though the international environment is, nations are now joined together as never before, by a variety of connections. The current political framework, was established by the Treaty of Westphalia—a multitude of separate political entities, each claiming sovereignty over its destiny and all competing for power, resources and allegiance. However, in all other respects, the contemporary world bears little resemblance to that of the seventeenth-century. In the past, decentralization of power was accompanied by limited technology and minimal interstate economic relations. Prior to industrialization, countries could insulate themselves from neighboring states by military means and successfully maintained economic and social self-sufficiency.

In the eighteenth-century however, human knowledge started to expand at an exponential rate, with the total body of scientific knowledge doubling every fifteen years.[1] With greater control being exercised over both the physical environment and social organization, the nation-states of western Europe had rapid increases in both population and national income. The population of Europe more than doubled during the nineteenth-century, and the combined national products of the industrialized European economies expanded at a rate even higher than that of population. The result of this demographic and economic explosion (both rooted in technological growth) was an increasing demand for resources—a demand which outgrew domestic supply—and so the extension of economic activities beyond national boundaries soon followed. Colonialism and the concomitant collision of expanding national interests around the world were the most obvious effects of this technologically-generated lateral pressure.[2] However, international trade and investment were also important by-products. Measured in constant dollars, the value of the United Kingdom's total foreign trade nearly tripled between 1870 and 1913, and Germany's nearly quadrupled.[3] Investment also flowed across national boundaries, with most developed economies exporting capital to North America to the less-advanced countries of Europe (especially Russia), to the Turkish empire and to their colonial territories and spheres of influence. By the beginning of this century, then, the process of modernization in Europe had led to the eclipse of self-sufficiency and the creation of a broad web of interdependence.

The continued expansion of technology and the progress of modernization after World War II has brought interdependence to an unprecedented level. The transfer of goods and services across national boundaries has proceeded at an amazing rate. Between 1950 and 1970, the value of interstate commerce increased by 600 percent and the total value of world exports grew to 10 percent of the gross world product (GWP). Measured as a proportion of gross national product (GNP), the value of exports became more and more important to the prosperity of the vast majority of countries. The Western world is especially dependent upon international transactions for its economic well-being. The twenty-four countries of the Organization of Economic Cooperation and Development (OECD)—the advanced capitalist economies of North America, western Europe, Japan and Oceania—now account for three-quarters of the world's trade, though they account for only two-thirds of the world's annual production.[4]

The story is much the same for international investment. Long-term American investments overseas (the United States accounts for over half of all foreign investment) rose between 1960 and 1974 from $31.8 billion to $120 billion; during the same period, foreign direct investment in the United States rose from $6.9 billion to $21.7 billion.[5] (Contrary to popular thinking, over three-quarters of the developed countries' investments go to other developed countries and not to the less-developed countries.[6]) Moreover, foreign investment must be considered in terms of the production it generates abroad. For the most part, foreign direct investment (as opposed to portfolio investment—ownership of foreign stocks and bonds) creates foreign subsidiaries of domestically based private corporations. These foreign affiliates produce commodities in their own right. By 1975, the value of international production (total sales of the foreign subsidiaries of all multinational corporations *) reached $570 billion—more than the individual GNP's of every country in the world with the exception of the two superpowers.‡

The significance of the internationalization of production is made clear every day. The worldwide automobile industry is an

* Note that international production does not include the value of the production of corporations in their home countries. If this is included, the gross sales of the world's 50 largest industrial corporations in 1975 was $540 billion. There are three hundred major multinational corporations in the world.

‡ In reality, the gross sales of a corporation are not exactly equivalent to a country's GNP. Gross national product is a value-added figure, while corporate sales include not only the value added in production, but also the company's purchase of raw materials, parts and services. However, the two measures (GNP and gross corporate sales) are often used for comparison. Moreover, even if the value-added statistic is employed, the wealth of corporations is truly impressive. A UN study estimated that the value added of all multinational corporations—including home-country production—was some $500 billion in 1971. This was equivalent to one-fifth of the non-Communist world's GNP. (*Christian Science Monitor,* November 4, 1975, pp. 14–15.)

excellent example of the new globalization of production.[7] The distinction between "foreign" and "domestic" cars, for instance, is becoming progressively blurred. Your new Volvo (produced by a Swedish-based company) or Volkswagen (German-based) will more than likely have been manufactured in the United States by American subsidiaries of these firms; in the near future, your Japanese automobile (Toyota, Datsun, or Honda) or Italian car (Fiat) will also be made in this country. If you want to purchase a car manufactured overseas, bear in mind that the British and German Fords are made by a subsidiary of Ford Motors of Detroit, that Opel is owned by General Motors and that Simca of France is a subsidiary of Chrysler. On the other hand, if you decide to "buy American" and select a domestic model, do not be surprised to find out that its major components were manufactured abroad: Ford's Pinto has a German transmission, a British motor and a Canadian body.

In addition to the newly acquired mobility of commodities and productive capital, financial institutions have also been following multinational corporations into foreign markets in order to service the needs that go with expanded economic transactions. American banks have been in the forefront of this movement and since 1960 they have increased the assets of their foreign branches at an annual rate of nearly thirty percent.[8] People as well as money have been pouring across state frontiers in increasing numbers. To be sure, mass migration, a hallmark of the nineteenth- and early twentieth-centuries, has not been repeated. Unlike the European nations, developing countries have been unable to blunt the debilitating effects of their population explosions because of the emigration restrictions long since established by Western societies. Nonetheless, there has occurred a socially significant migration of educated professionals—the so-called brain drain—from the poor to the rich countries. Labor also has been mobile, especially in Europe, where during the 1960s and early 1970s workers from Spain, southern Italy, Greece and Turkey filled industrial jobs in the countries further north. International travel for business and pleasure has shown a marked upswing, the total number of world travelers has doubled every decade since World War II. By the early 1970s, there were over 200 million people annually crisscrossing national boundaries, including well over 100 million tourists.[9]

Not so long ago it was said, "When Wall Street sneezes, Europe catches cold," the health and vitality of the American economy being essential to the well-being of the rest of the world. Today, the contagions of inflation and unemployment no longer follow a one-way path. The developed world's economy is now so integrated that industrialized states experience prosperity or recession together. In late 1976, a group of economists from government and industry indicated that the slowdown in the United States' economic recovery was tied to a general trend in the non-Communist world.[10] Another observer, commenting on the economic troubles of the western European economies, suggests that there is an economic version of the domino theory: no one country can insulate itself from the economic contraction of its partners.[11] In short, in an interdependent world, no country is master of its economic destiny—not even the United States. With national economies so intertwined, governmental leaders are losing the ability to lead; they are rapidly losing control over their environment. The net result of states seeking to do more in the way of domestic welfare, but succeeding in providing less, must be a heightened sense of frustration. In economics, as in many other areas, control over the outcome of events is fast eluding traditional power centers.

Global interdependence has been accentuated and complicated in recent years by the increasing reliance of the developed countries upon the less developed ones for their necessary supplies of energy and nonfuel resources, together with the Third World countries' need to obtain from the industrial countries investment capital, technology, concessional aid and a larger share of world exports. The new unity, and militant stance of the world's poor countries will henceforth ensure that the twin crises of underdevelopment and overpopulation will no longer be confined to their countries of origin.

Neither will an irreversible upset in the balance of our ecological system be stopped by national frontiers. Modern technological marvels have brought us, at the very least, into an age of increasing scarcity. Exponential population growth, coupled with unchecked economic expansion, offers the prospect of the depletion of natural resources, mass hunger, and the deterioration of our physical environment. The world, as it is presently organized, may be approaching the limits of growth. A primitive global political system burdened with mounting scarcity is bound to be plagued by intensification of conflict and likelihood of increasing violence.

Our daily newspapers are filled with the telltale signs of progressive global interdependence in diverse spheres of interaction: Multinational corporations can precipitate an international financial crisis by speculating in national currencies; the Soviet Union makes massive purchases of grain from the United States, and world food prices soar, causing further deterioration in the poorest countries' food supplies; Libya's Colonel Qaddafi gives terrorists and separatist groups financial support and sanctuary, and transnational violence intensifies; the People's Republic of China detonates a nuclear bomb and radioactivity increases in the atmosphere over Long Island; the Organization of Petroleum Exporting Countries (OPEC) hikes the price of oil, and developing countries suffer from skyrocketing fertilizer costs and rising balance-of-payments deficits; American consumers prefer cosmetics in spray cans, and the earth's ozone layer, shielding life from the sun's ultraviolet rays, is depleted. The evolution of modernization has multiplied and intensified interaction between states in recent years, integrating distant corners of the world as never before into a truly global community. Events occurring in any part of the international system, or within domestic political systems, will increasingly affect other parts of the system.[12] More and more, national frontiers (which have never been truly impermeable) are becoming porous, and national societies are becoming increasingly sensitive and vulnerable to decisions and behavior which take place beyond the narrow jurisdiction of the territorial state.[13]

There is a continuously widening gap between the reality of global interdependence and the anachronistic organizational base of the multistate system. Indeed, since the Second World War, political fragmentation has been aggravated by the emergence of some eighty-five new states and the waning of superpower hegemony. As a consequence of these two trends, power has been further decentralized in the international political system. The primitive nature of world politics, premised on the interrelated principles of national sovereignty and self-help, places inherent limits on the potential for global cooperation to meet the new global challenges.

TRANSNATIONAL RELATIONS AND THE COMPETITION FOR GLOBAL VALUES

Until recently, students of world politics viewed their field of inquiry from a strictly *state-centric* vantage point. They recognized only one type of actor—the territorial state—in the competition for power to allocate global values. If other participants in the world's political process were considered, they were treated as peripheral elements. Traditional texts concentrated on military-strategic issues, relegating economic, demographic and social factors to the sphere of "low politics." With the rapid progress of interdependence and the rise of important nonstate actors, however, the dominant state-centric view of world politics has been modified to accommodate the increasing role of transnational relations. Unlike interstate relations, which consist only of the interactions among national governments, transnational relations consist of activities across national boundaries involving actors which are not agents of governments or intergovernmental organizations.[14]

Though states are still the dominant actors, contemporary world politics now includes a host of nonstate (or transnational) actors of varying degrees of influence and importance. A global political actor is any participant in the world pattern of conflict and cooperation that tries to affect the distribution of global benefits. As such, a political actor must: (1) be relatively autonomous (i.e., pursue an independent policy in defense of its interests as it defines them); (2) possess substantial capabilities (i.e., power resources); (3) be able to influence the behavior or predispositions of other actors.[15] Because of their continuing ability to manipulate the loyalties of their populations, as well as their near-monopoly of instruments of physical coercion and force, territorial states remain the primary (if no longer the sole) actors in world politics. Yet control of their environment by governmental elites has been dwindling because of the pressures of interdependence. Transnational actors are both a result and a cause of this transformation in the political status of the nation-state. Some possess capabilities dwarfing those of many territorial actors, and others can outinfluence even major states on certain important issues. Those who herald the imminent demise of the territorial state are certainly premature,[16] but those who ignore transnational forces are losing sight of the dynamic and evolutionary nature of global politics. We are in a transitional phase in world history. Given the meshing of national societies into a net of interdependencies, the international system cannot remain primitive forever.

TRANSNATIONAL ACTORS

Nonstate actors have always had a role to play in modern international relations. Americans are familiar with the transnational revolutionary activities of individuals like Lafayette, Kosciuszko, and Tom Paine; students of European history will remember the role of groups like the Zionists and the Garibaldians. There were international movements that championed the rights of women or the cause of temperance, or crusaded against gross injustices like the slave trade; there were Christian missionaries who journeyed to the far corners of the globe in search of souls to save, minds to teach and bodies to heal.[17] Let us not forget the private entrepreneurs who contracted with sovereign states to settle and develop the New World (e.g., the Plymouth Company and the Virginia Company), or the great commercial monopolies (the Dutch East India Company, the British East India Company, the Hudson Bay Company) which preceded their home-country governments as agents of imperialism and change across the vast non-European world. For example, one precursor of the modern global corporation, the British East India Company, conquered and ruled a quarter of a billion people on the Indian subcontinent, and raised and supported the largest standing army in the world of its day.[18]

The contemporary international environment is populated by a plethora of such groups. Though their individual impact on the global pattern of political interaction may not be quite as dramatic as that of the great commercial enterprises of the seventeenth century, they are much more numerous and are involved in many more fields of endeavor; and their total effect is probably a good deal more significant for the future course of world affairs. Obviously, some transnational actors are more germane to the global political process than others. But all global actors (states as well as nonstates, the strong as well as the weak) are similar in that they seek to mobilize their resources to further their own interests in the world political arena. Where they differ, of course, is in their ability to influence the distribution of global benefits. Nongovernmental actors have an impact on the international political process: (1) to the extent that they directly influence the allocation of values; or, (2) to the degree that they indirectly do so by affecting the distribution of power among states; or, (3) by collectively rechanneling power away from territorial states and contributing to the loss of control of national governments over their environments. For the sake of convenience and clarity, we can divide transnational actors into three categories: (1) traditional transnational actors; (2) revolutionary transnational actors; and (3) multinational corporations.

Traditional Transnational Actors: NGOs

On occasion, the activities of certain organizations (like Amnesty International, the International Red Cross and the International Olympic Committee) are brought to our attention by the news media. These are but examples of a variety of global actors which rarely basks in the limelight of publicity—international nongovernmental organizations (NGOS). International NGOs differ from international governmental organizations (IGOs) in that their members are nationals of a number of states, but not representatives of those states. NGOs are unofficial organizations made up of private citizens from various countries who band together to further their common interests. They are far more numerous than IGOs. There are over two hundred IGOs composed of members from three or more states, and probably an equal number consisting of only two states. However, it has been estimated that there are about three thousand nonprofit NGOs in the world.[19] These private transnational associations have been growing at a faster rate than official international organizations. In recent years, NGOs have proliferated at an annual rate of 6.2 percent, and during the 1960s alone, their number increased by a full 73 percent.[20]

Such transnational organizations are found in a variety of fields, including commerce and industry, science and technology, health and education, agriculture and transportation. Yet those concerned with the economic sector tend to be dominant and are growing in number at a much higher rate than other types of NGOs.[21] This is hardly a surprising development, given the amazing increase in global economic activity during the postwar era. Nor should it come as a surprise to discover that NGO membership is concentrated in the developed capitalist regions of the globe. Only one-quarter of all NGOs draw their membership from all five continents; another quarter is confined exclusively to Europe; all in all, citizens of the First World make up over half the worldwide membership of all nongovernmental organizations.[22]

The same pattern is evident when the resources and effectiveness of NGOs are compared. The vast majority of NGOs are small, 84 percent having fewer than one hundred individual members and only a handful being in a position to claim more than ten thousand adherents. Those that can boast a sizable membership are for the most part confined to the developed countries. The financial resources of most NGOs are meager, to say the least. The paid staff of the average NGO numbers but nine people, and the mean budget is a little over $600,000. Only a few transnational associations drawing their membership from the rich countries of the developed capitalist world are able to muster a considerable treasury and a staff of over one hundred.[23]

The strong representation of the developed countries of western Europe, North America, Japan and Oceania stems from their advanced economic and social development, and the pluralist nature of democratic political systems, which facilitates free movement of ideas and people across political frontiers. Citizens of authoritarian countries (especially the Communist nations of Europe) are inhibited from engaging in independent transnational activity by their governments and, consequently, these states are not well represented in NGOs. To this extent, transnational activities parallel the divisions brought about by intergovernmental competition. Rather than transcending the interstate system, these transnational networks tend to reflect and reinforce fundamental political and economic schisms.

There has been a marked increase in the number of NGOs that have been granted consultative status with various IGOs. Indeed, between 1959 and 1971, the number of NGOs accorded consultative status by intergovernmental organizations (especially the United Nations and its specialized agencies) has grown from 677 to 1,290.[24] Ostensibly, the remarkable growth in the number of nongovernmental organizations and the rapid increase in the number of them given privileged access to IGOs indicates an important transformaiton in the international environment. But we must be careful not to overemphasize the importance of NGOs. As global interest groups with ties to decision makers in IGOs, they can be no more influential than these IGOs themselves—and thus far, international organizations as a whole have hardly dented the sovereign shells of territorial states. Though NGOs have no doubt brought about changes in the international system, "their impact is undramatic, diffuse, slow and does not suggest any single direction." [25] The growing role of NGOs—though still peripheral—is but one aspect of the new transnationalism.

Traditional Transnational Actors: The Church

The first international nongovernmental organization came into being in the mid-nineteenth century. Prior to that time, the principal nonstate actor in international affairs (other than joint-stock trading companies) was the Roman Catholic Church. During the late Middle Ages, the Church successfully claimed both spiritual and temporal supremacy over the rulers of Europe. Until the middle of the fifteenth century, by which time the papacy had lost much of its effective influence throughout the Christian world, the pope was at the center of political and religious life. He exercised total control over ecclesiastical matters, and his powers of excommunication and interdiction made him the arbiter of secular affairs. A recalcitrant ruler could be brought literally to his knees by the threat of personal exclusion form the rites of the faithful (excommunication) or by the threat of suspending administration of the sacraments in his territorial realm (interdiction)—both of which would destroy the legitimacy of the prince's rule and absolve his subjects from their allegiance to him. The Protestant Reformation of the sixteenth century effectively broke the monopoly of spiritual power wielded by the papacy and ended the ideological unity and centralization of authority that characterized the medieval world. Ideological and political loyalties came to center on the sovereign nation-state, and the stage was set for the emergence of the fragmented multistate system.

Nevertheless, to this day, the Holy See retains spiritual dominion over some 560 million Roman Catholics spread over the whole world but concentrated in Europe and the Americas. Though it has long since abandoned its claim to political sovereignty (at least outside Vatican City), the Church remains a transnational actor, and the pope is still the most influential religious leader in the contemporary world. Naturally, the Church's present political objectives seem banal compared with the caesarian authority wielded in earlier times. But the Vatican maintains an extensive global network of diplomatic channels and conducts a "foreign policy" geared to furthering access to its religious followers residing under a multitude of national jurisdictions and to preserving the autonomy of the many branches of the Church hierarchy that are subject to the whims of state sovereignty. In some countries (such as Colombia) the Church is granted total freedom of action and official state protection; in other countries (such as the People's Republic of China), it is altogether denied access to citizens. Between these two extremes, there are various categories of national policy.[26]

The Roman Catholic Church's relationship with the eastern European Communist governments since World War II is an excellent illustration of an attempt by a transnational actor to influence the domestic policies of a state actor. When the Soviet Union established Stalinist governments in its eastern European satellites after the war, there was a head-on collision between the Catholic hierarchy and the new political elites. On the ideological plane, neither party could accept the other's pretensions to absolute truth; on the political level, the new totalitarian societies would tolerate neither the propagation of the Church's subversive doctrines nor an independent locus of power within their borders. Accordingly, the governments persecuted the clergy, incarcerated their leaders (such as Jozsef Cardinal Mindszenty, the primate of Hungary, and Stefan Cardinal Wyszynski, leader of Poland's thirty million Catholics), closed down religious presses and schools, and intimidated believers.

In the early 1960s, though, both sides realized that a policy of confrontation was not working for them. The Communists were failing to win over the Church's following and were merely alienating large portions of the domestic population, and the Vatican was unable to gain access to its flock. Consequently, in 1963, Pope John XXIII initiated his own policy of détente and sent emissaries to the Eastern European governments to bargain over the fate of sixty million Roman Catholics. Switching to a policy of containment instead of confrontation, a number of countries (especially Poland) began to allow greater religious freedom and autonomy for Church operations; in return, the Vatican had to make concessions of its own, such as appointing progovernment priests and retiring enemies of the Communist regimes from prominent positions in national Church hierarchies. Finally, Pope Paul VI joined thirty-five other heads of state in signing the Helsinki agreements on security and cooperation in Europe, after securing a reference to religious freedom in the final document.[27]

While the Vatican's relations with Communist Eastern Europe have entered a phase of détente and co-existence, the Church's traditionally cordial arrangements with Latin American governments have degenerated into a cold war type of confrontation. Once closely allied with the ruling elites of the Catholic countries of the Southern Hemisphere, the Church hierarchy is now increasingly at odds with a number of governments. While the leadership of these countries is conservative or authoritarian, religious leaders have taken an increasingly militant and liberal stance against political repression and torture. Churchmen have been arrested and deported for alleged subversive plots in Ecuador and Argentina; Chilean bishops were the target of government-inspired demonstrations in Santiago after they spoke out against the oppressive policies of the rightest military junta (the Church retaliated by excommunicating a government official); clerics in Uruguay, Paraguay and Brazil have been harassed by the dictatorships of those countries for protesting against their police-state tactics.[28] This social activism on the part of the Catholic Church seriously threatens to undermine the stability of the existing political order in Latin America and to foster domestic opposition to the status quo.

The Church's opposition to the oppressive policies of South American dictatorships is one example of its objective of furthering certain values in the international system. In this regard, it is joined by other religious movements which also engage in transnational activities. A number of religious organizations have criticized the developed countries for allowing abject poverty and human suffering to exist in the Third World, and the issue of global hunger has emerged as a top priority of the Catholic Church.

The Roman Catholic Church is far from the only religious organization that engages in transnational activities. There are more than sixty religiously oriented NGOs, but none possesses anything like the capabilities or influence of the Catholic Church. No church-related NGO can claim comparable following, geographical scope, or financial resources. The only other religious actor of any political significance is the World Council of Churches, which has representatives from numerous Christian churches in some seventy-nine countries, as well as official observers from the Vatican (which has not formally joined it).[29] Though the council has in the past taken an activist role on behalf of the United Nations and disarmament and against American policy in Vietnam, it lacks the Catholic Church's hierarchical organization. As an amalgam of independent churches from many countries, it must work by consensus and avoid alienating national factions. For example, in its recent criticism of the Soviet government for refusing to allow the free exercise of religion, the council had to mute the language of its resolution and avoid specifically mentioning the U.S.S.R. in order to keep the Russian Orthodox representatives from withdrawing.[30] In many ways, then, the Roman

Catholic Church is in a category by itself in terms of its transnational activities.

Traditional Transnational Actors: Political Parties

At least since Karl Marx founded the First International in 1864, certain political movements have demonstrated a proclivity for collaboration across national boundaries. We can identify four political parties that engage in transnational relations and that have demonstrated a significant degree of ideological congruity; Socialists (or Democratic Socialists), Christian Democrats, and Liberals—all democratic, or parliamentary, parties—and Communists, whose party at one time was a potent international actor, but which has since fragmented into a number of national constituencies and coalesced around a number of ideological poles.

The Democratic Socialists (who embrace Marxist economic policies but are committed to political liberty and Western-style pluralist democracy) are affiliated through the Socialist International, and are the oldest and most cohesive of the democratic transnational parties. The Socialist International is composed of national parties from forty-nine countries throughout the world, all of which taken together, claim a total membership of fifteen million and have attracted some seventy million votes in recent elections. Though its membership is concentrated in Europe (the British Labour Party accounts for forty percent of the total following), individual socialist parties play a prominent role in the political processes in thirty-four countries; moreover, the Socialist International is the parent body of several other groups, such as the International Union of Socialist Youth, which has subsidiary organizations in seventy-four countries.[31] To the right of the Social Democrats, one finds the conservative Christian Democrats, who banded together in 1961 to form the Christian Democratic World Union. These parties are of much more recent origin than the Socialists, display less ideological affinity and cohesiveness and are found for the most part only in western Europe and Latin America. A centrist group, the World Liberal Union (or Liberal International) is composed of Liberal parties mainly from Europe and the English-speaking world outside the United States.

These three political parties are in the process of forging transnational alliances in western Europe, and cooperation among like-minded political groups and leaders in different countries is evolving toward the formation of truly multinational parties. The European Community's Parliament in Strasbourg—which has as of yet no real authority—is composed of representatives presently selected by the various national legislatures. Nevertheless, members of the parliament are seated not by nationality but by political allegiance. The three parties have developed the practice of caucusing and organizing along transnational lines. Moreover, party cooperation is expected to increase significantly, as is the power of the parliament itself, when direct elections for the European Parliament are held in 1979.* In anticipation of this arrangement, the national leaders of the parties have held conferences to coordinate policies and develop joint programs. Increasingly, the parties are serving as catalysts for the interpenetration of European politics and are acting as if national frontiers no longer exist.

One must remember that even the so-called national political parties in the United States are little more than conglomerations of independent state and local organizations that find it expedient to cooperate quadrennially during Presidential election campaigns. In much the same manner, national European parties are allied in the development of common strategies for continent-wide programs: The West German Social Democrats have funneled funds into Portugal to aid that country's Socialist party; French conservatives have been actively, if quietly, supporting the Christian

* In that year, the people of the nine countries of the Common Market (or, more precisely, the European Community) will vote for members of a legislative body which will owe allegiance to no single national government. The reconstituted parliament will consist of 410 members, apportioned in the following manner: 81 each from the United Kingdom, France, West Germany and Italy; 25 from the Netherlands; 24 from Belgium; 16 from Denmark; 15 from Ireland and 6 from Luxembourg. As an indication of the new European Parliament's expected prestige and authority, some of western Europe's senior political figures have already announced their candidacy (former German Chancellor Willy Brandt and French Socialist leader François Mitterrand). (*Christian Science Monitor*, July 14, 1976, p. 1.)

Democrats in Italy; the Italian Christian Democrats, in turn, have advised their German counterparts to avoid policies that would give all Christian Democrats a right-wing tinge; Socialist leaders have conferred on the advisability of allowing Communists to participate in European governments; the heads of the Socialist parties in Germany, Sweden and Austria have written a book setting forth their common vision for European society; Liberal party members have discussed the possibility of their weaker third party holding the balance of power between right and left in a supranational legislature.[32] Increasingly, then, the political parties of western Europe are losing their parochial national identities.

In years past, it was not only fashionable but also more or less accurate to speak of "international communism." In 1919, Lenin founded the Communist International (or Comintern), a collection of left-wing splinter groups of the European Marxist movement dedicated to worldwide revolution against capitalism and "bourgeois democracy." At the time, the only state in the international system ruled by a Communist party was the Soviet Union, and early ideologues saw it as the vanguard of a global revolt of the proletariat. Within a decade or so, however, the original relationship between the Comintern and the U.S.S.R. was reversed: Stalin saw to it that the Comintern (and thus all foreign Communist parties) became an appendage of Soviet foreign policy. At its dissolution in 1943, the Comintern was more a collection of Soviet-dominated fifth-column organizations than a truly independent transnational movement.[33]

Immediately after World War II, national Communist parties came to power in Yugoslavia and China without the aid of the Soviet army. Unlike the puppet governments of Eastern Europe, neither Tito nor Mao owed their tenure in office to Moscow, and each sought to adapt Marxist-Leninist doctrine to his country's social environment rather than blindly follow the Kremlin's model for constructing a Communist society. By the late 1940s, Stalin had excommunicated Tito from the Cominform, and when in the late 1950s the Chinese denounced the Russians for their alleged perversion of their common secular religion, a major schism developed in the once-monolithic world Communist movement (for a detailed discussion of the Sino-Soviet split, See Chapter 7).

In much the same way that early Christianity divided into Eastern Orthodox and western churches, there now existed two competing ideological centers for the Communist movement—Peking and Moscow. In the late 1960s, still another variation appeared on the horizon: The Italian Communist party led a reformation against both the Russian and Chinese variants of Marxism. With each ideological pole avidly seeking to spread its dogma beyond its national sphere, the formerly unified international Communist movement split into three antagonistic transnational actors.

The Italian Communist party, the largest in western Europe, has been at the forefront in forging a distinctly Western version of Communism. The founder of Italy's party, Antonio Gramsci, had shunned both "the dictatorship of the proletariat" and violent revolution. Working through the parliamentary system, the Italian Communists established themselves firmly in labor unions and local government, and by 1976 they governed nearly half the population and garnered a full third of the popular vote, coming within a couple of percentage points of the reigning Christian Democrats. Claiming to be committed to the democratic order, the Communist party under its present leader, Enrico Berlinguer, has called for "historic compromise"—a coalition government with the non-Communist parties.

If we take them at face value, the Italian Communists seem little different from the Social Democrats. They have proclaimed their dedication to pluralist politics, the parliamentary and multiparty systems, free elections, free speech and freedom of religion, individual liberties, and even to the necessity of Italy remaining in the North Atlantic Treaty Organization (NATO) and the European Community. They have also been vociferous critics of Moscow's policies, especially the Warsaw Pact–invasion of Czechoslovakia in 1968, the Soviet Union's persecution of dissidents and the Kremlin's backing of a Communist coup d'etat in Portugal. There can be little doubt that the Italian Communists are, as one observer has suggested, a strange breed.[34]

But in addition to proffering their eclectic philosophy of government to the Italian people, the Communists have been actively pursuing transnational relations with other important European Communist parties. Italian communism has had an obvious impact on the Spanish Communists, who now go even further than their neighbors in espousing Western-style democracy and opposing Moscow. Western Eruope's second largest Communist party, the French party, led by Georges Marchais, has been gradually prodded by the Italians toward a more liberal position. Though lagging behind Berlinguer (it did not condemn the Soviet-sponsored invasion of Czechoslovakia), the French Communist party has been demonstrating more and more independence from the Soviet Union in recent years. Following the Italian lead, they decided in 1975 to drop from their statement of party goals the principle of "the dictatorship of the proletariat," and have publicly denounced Moscow for the imprisonment and mistreatment of certain dissidents. In the end, the Italian Communists hope to weave a web of common ideological purpose among the national parties of western Europe, and bring forth a new transnational actor—Eurocommunism.

REVOLUTIONARY TRANSNATIONAL ACTORS: LIBERATION MOVEMENTS AND THE TERRORIST INTERNATIONAL

The present international system is having a crisis of legitimacy. The global order is increasingly under fire from state actors (especially the developing countries of the Third World) and from nonstate actors. Several revolutionary movements, based in different countries and operating across national boundaries, have proclaimed universal world revolution as their goal. The name Ché Guevarra conjures up the mysterious image of a truly cosmopolitan revolutionary, leading international brigades of followers into various countries in Latin America and Africa in search of weak links in the global status quo. By and large, however, despite the bold rhetoric of supranational revolution, the majority of contemporary revolutionary organizations is concerned with the "liberation" of particular countries and the establishment of counterstates.[35] In a world of primitive allegiance to blood and soil, the Ché Guevarras have always been something of a curiosity, an aberration within the dominant tribal orientation of mankind. Nevertheless, national revolutionary groups are increasingly involved in transnational links with territorial states, intergovernmental organizations and other nonstate actors. For example, the several liberation movements of southern Africa dedicated to ousting the white minority governments in Rhodesia, South Africa and Namibia (and formerly in the Portuguese colonies of Angola and Mozambique) are nominally coordinated by the Organization of Africa Unity (OAU), an international organization of sovereign states intent on abolishing European colonialism in Africa. The Palestine Liberation Movement (PLO) was originally founded by the League of Arab States, though by 1969 it had fallen under the independent leadership of Al-Fatah's Yasir Arafat. Like the black African liberation movements, it is more a government-in-exile than an instrument of regional revolution.

Though violence has always been endemic to international politics, the network of transnational revolutionary movements has spawned a new type of international violence: transnational terrorism. As we have seen in Chapters 3 and 4, force and the threat of force are instrumental sanctions in the competition for political values. Terrorism is a particular variation of political violence and is an attractive weapon to the weak. It has been described as the strategy of "those who are prepared to use violence but who believe that they would lose any contest of sheer strength." [36] Though indiscriminate violence by terrorists may appear senseless and purposeless, an irrational outburst of crazed fanaticism, it is intended to serve a political objective, much as is the case with interstate warfare and crisis confrontation. As opposed to brute force, which seeks physically to overcome an opponent's resistance, instrumental force is used as a psychological tool of policy—that is, to change the behavior of other actors by altering their interpretation of self-interest. Terrorist campaigns were crucial to the Irish Republic's obtaining independence from the United Kingdom and to the Jews' forcing the British to relinquish their mandate over Palestine. In both cases, mounting violence convinced the colonial power that continuation of imperial rule could no longer be justified in terms of a cost-benefit ratio. Similarly, in the 1950s, Algerian nationalists employed terrorism to force France out of Algeria. Though terrorism may appear barbaric, it is no less rational than war itself, and has the same objective: the utilization of force to influence the behavior of governmental actors.

Terrorism is thus "violence for effect: not only and sometimes not at all, for the effect on the actual victims of the terrorists. . . . Terrorism is violence aimed at the people watching."[37] In the last decade, there has been a marked increase in acts of terrorism committed by nonstate actors, so much so that a study sponsored by the Central Intelligence Agency has suggested that "we may be entering a veritable age of terrorism."[38] Since 1968, the number of transnational terrorist groups has increased substantially, a trend has developed toward cooperation among these organizations, the geographical scope of terrorist activities has widened and the terrorist acts have become more and more harrowing and bizarre. Between 1968 and 1975, there were over nine hundred kidnappings, bombings, armed assaults and ambushes, hijackings, incendiary attacks, assassinations, barricade and hostage episodes and other incidents of international terrorism committed by some 140 terrorist organizations based in nearly fifty countries. The human toll has been 800 killed and 1700 wounded, and this does not include the casualties of domestic terrorism. (The turmoil in Northern Ireland claimed a greater number of human lives in the same period, and in Argentina alone in 1975, there were an estimated 1100 political killings.[39])

This upsurge in transnational terrorism is the result of the changing nature of the international environment. Technological advances in weaponry have provided would-be terrorists with the means and mobility to strike swiftly and effectively. In an age of letter bombs, one-man surface-to-air missiles and automatic weapons, the purveyors of political violence can inflict maximum harm with minimum resources. The communications revolution enables publicity-seeking groups to reach worldwide audiences and bring their cause literally and instantly into our living rooms. Modern societies are in a position of unprecedented vulnerability, as symbolized by jumbo-jet airliners, which are virtually defenseless against sabotage or seizure. Finally, the political schism in the contemporary global system assure terrorist groups ideological allies and helpful national governments. The world's states are unable to agree to outlaw revolutionary violence, regardless of how distasteful it may be. The legitimacy or illegitimacy of a particular variety of violence is judged by governments not so much by its means as by its objectives. A United Nations convention against abduction and assassination of diplomats signed in 1973, for instance, had been ratified by only nine member states a full three years later. The weak and dissatisfied countries, which actively oppose the international status quo, have shown little inclination to deprive frustrated groups of the means of striking back against the powers that be while the perceived injustices (the root causes of terrorism) continue to exist. It makes little sense for the weak voluntarily to surrender a weapon reserved solely for the weak, and thus buttress the present global order dominated by the privileged. As an Egyptian spokesman warns, "the world will not move collectively to crack down on terrorism until it stamps out racism, colonialism, and other factors fueling the violence."[40] While most countries have remained passive in the face of mounting terrorist activities, several countries actively provide aid and encouragement. The Soviet Union provides the Palestinians with funds and weapons; the Cuban government maintains contacts with members of the "Carlos" group; Algeria has been willing to provide a safe haven for terrorists without punishment or extradition; a number of other Arab countries have given sanctuary and other forms of support; Libya's Colonel Qaddafi has granted financial, logistical and technical aid to a host of such groups, ranging from the Irish Republican Army (IRA) and separatist organizations in western Europe to the Palestinians to revolutionary factions in the Philippines, Ethiopia, Somalia, Yemen, Chad, Morocco, Tunisia, Thailand and Panama.

Terrorist groups, in turn, exchange aid and comfort. The reciprocity and increasing collaboration found among these transnational actors compels us to recognize them collectively as a kind of "Terrorist International" (or Terrortern). Latin American terrorists from Argentina, Bolivia, Chile, Paraguay and Uruguay have gone so far as to create an umbrella organization—the Revolutionary Coordination Junta (JCR) to coordinate their assaults upon the existing political and economic order. Far more common than conspiratorial conferences, however, is the "growing network of overlapping *ad hoc* alliances and mutual assistance arrangements."[41] The Baader-Meinhof gang, a band of West German anarchists, prepared the way for the Palestinian Black September Organization's attack on the Israeli Olympic team in Munich in 1972, and is believed to have helped the Japanese Red Army carry out the massacre at Lod Airport in Tel Aviv in 1972; the Irish Republican Army has held discussions with Basque separatists from Spain, French separatists, the Tupamaros and the Palestinians; the Basques, in turn, have collaborated with the Tupamaros and the Baader-Meinhof gang.[42] Terrorist groups thus collaborate in the execution of their individual and joint ventures in international violence, granting one another arms, men, sanctuary and safe passage. In this, as in their reliance upon fear, the transnational terrorist conspiracy resembles the underworld of organized crime in the United States, whose umbrella organization (the Commission) facilitates the exchange of favors, "hit men" and police protection among the two dozen or so criminal syndicates in the country. Moreover, a recent international conference on world terrorism warned of the appearance and increasing visibility of terrorists for hire—a version of Murder, Inc.[43]

Effective violence by terrorist groups has led to more and more disgruntled peripheral political factions getting into the act. In December 1975, some South Moluccan nationalists seized and held a Dutch train for twelve days, while others took hostages and barricaded themselves in the Indonesian consulate in Amsterdam. In one dramatic stroke, an obscure, forgotten and frustrated people succeeded in communicating their existence and their grievances to a busy world.

The global Terrortern, of course, has invented neither political violence nor terrorism itself. As long as human beings have been organized into tribal communities, they have employed force in their mutual relations. The most obvious instance of organized violence is international warfare.

Nationalist and revolutionary groups within states have used terrorism in the past as a response to perceived oppression and injustice. Yet today we are entering an age of transnational violence, in which frustrated political formations strike across national boundaries against an increasingly vulnerable global order. Interdependence has created a global society of pronounced sensitivity to disruption, which thus becomes an inviting target for all those who feel left out, bypassed and powerless to affect the distribution of benefits in the world by nonviolent means.

The Palestinians are a case in point. Until their terrorist actions forced the world to stop and listen, their very existence as a nation was denied by Israel, ignored by the West and manipulated by their Arab brothers. While the Fadayeen engaged in terrorist raids against Israel in the 1950s they were controlled by Arab states from which they operated. Since the late 1960s, however, the Palestinians have assumed the role of an independent counterstate actor engaging in transnational terrorism to impress the rest of the world that if their diaspora is not ended, no country will henceforth live in security. Their terrorism has brought them recognition and new stature in the world community. While United Nations Security Council resolution 242 of November 1967 simply recommended "a just settlement of the refugee problem," making no mention of the national aspirations of the refugees, seven years and a good deal of international terrorism later, the General Assembly invited Yasir Arafat, head of the Palestinian Liberation Organization, to address it, accorded him the status of a head of state, formally recognized the sovereign rights of the Palestinian people and granted the PLO permanent-observer status in the assembly. Some fifty countries have allowed the PLO to open what amount to diplomatic embassies in their capitals, and subsidiary UN organizations (for example, UNESCO) have admitted the Palestinians. The impressive successes of Palestinian terrorist groups may very well serve as a beacon to other frustrated peoples.

THE MULTINATIONAL CORPORATIONS: THE TRANSNATIONAL TITANS

Political violence is hardly the only means available to influence the distribution of global values. Indeed, force is ill adapted to some circumstances and thus not likely to translate itself into political power. As the Godfather was fond of saying, "A lawyer with his briefcase can steal more than a hundred men with guns."

The industrial and financial magnates of late nineteenth- and early twentieth-century America appropriated a disproportionately large share of the economy's expanding wealth and power with little resort to force. Similarly, the modern transnational business enterprise, like the pope, has no legions at its disposal, yet within the last few decades, the multinational corporation has emerged from relative obscurity to challenge the authority of even the most powerful territorial actors. As two students of international enterprise suggest, its power comes "not from the barrel of a gun but from control of the means of creating wealth." [44]

Before considering the contemporary role of corporate transnationalism, let us first define what we mean by a multinational corporation. Unfortunately, there is no agreed-upon definition in the literature. The terms *multinational corporation, international corporation, transnational corporation,* and *global corporation* are sometimes used with specific connotations, but here, all these terms will be used interchangeably to refer to a cluster of affiliated companies functioning simultaneously in a number of different countries and joined together and to a parent company by ties of common ownership or control, a common management strategy and a common pool of financial and human resources.[45] In our terminology, then, *parent company* will refer to the corporate headquarters of a worldwide enterprise, which is based in a *parent country; affiliates,* or *subsidiaries,* are various branches of the firm located in other *(host)* countries. The popular term *multinational,* therefore, should not be taken to suggest that the typical firm is either owned or managed by the nationals of several countries. On the contrary, the representative firm draws its owners and directors largely from the parent country. It is a cosmopolitan enterprise, "a company without a country," which views the world economy as a single unit devoid of significant boundaries; it is dedicated to the development of a world market through centralized planning. Its branches based in foreign countries are not seen as mere adjuncts to home operations, as they were in the past, but are considered, along with domestic activities, integral parts of a business enterprise of truly global scope and dimensions.[46] As Charles Kindleberger has written: "The international corporation has no country to which it owes more loyalty than any other, nor any country where it feels completely at home."[47] In this crucial sense, the multinational corporation endeavors to be an independent actor in the world, master of its own destiny and beholden to no political authority, and is thus an entity with primary interests that correspond to those of no specific territorial actor. For the global managers, corporate interest has replaced national interest as the principal frame of reference. Much as governmental leaders strive to obtain security, growth and autonomy for the nation-state, the directorates of transnational business enterprises struggle to maximize profits and expand their share of the market while preserving a stable international environment conducive to their survival, prosperity and freedom of action. To the extent that it seeks to operate as if political boundaries did not exist, and to the degree that it fights to escape the restrictive authority of national governments, the international global firm is bound to view the territorial state as an anachronism and a threat to its further development. Nevertheless, as an actor lacking instruments of physical coercion, it must co-exist with the very states it seeks to transcend.

Independent economic actors are not new in the international system. Even before the Industrial Revolution, the merchants of the Renaissance city-states of Venice, Florence, Genoa and Pisa developed lucrative commercial arrangements with Constantinople and the Moslem cities of the Middle East and North Africa. To facilitate trading relationships, international banking firms established branches throughout the commercial centers of the Mediterranean world, and soon the Italians (and especially the Florentines) became the bankers for all Europe. Following in the footsteps of the great Italian banking families, the Fugger family of Germany established its ascendance in northern Europe in the sixteenth century and became the financier of princes and emperors. Earlier in this chapter, we mentioned the transnational role of the joint-stock trading companies which evolved in the seventeenth century in the maritime nations of England and Holland; these predecessors of contemporary multinational business enterprise extended the scope of European economic activity throughout the world and paved the way for the formal annexation of vast stretches of the earth's surface by parent-country governments. By the turn of the last century, the pioneers of modern transnational production had established a firm foothold on foreign soil, and well-known American companies (like Heinz and Singer) and European firms (Nestlé and Unilever) were already engaged in direct foreign investment. Soon afterward, British and American oil companies sought drilling concessions in the Middle East, Latin America and Indonesia. Until the Second World War, however, the international activities of private corporations were largely confined to investments in extractive industries—petroleum, mining and agriculture.

The modern transnational corporation is a creature of the post-1945 period, which saw not only a massive growth in the volume of direct foreign investment (the creation of foreign-based subsidiaries), but a change in its direction, nature and importance. While all direct foreign investment has increased immensely since World War II, by far the largest proportion has been devoted to manufacturing, service and financial sectors in the developed countries. Most of the expansion in American foreign investment has taken place in Western Europe. In a single decade (1959–69), American investments in the Common Market countries increased by 500 percent.[48] While Latin America was the primary recipient of United States investment at the beginning of the 1950s, within twenty years, it became a poor third behind Europe and Canada.[49] Measured in terms of both trade and capital movements, the less-developed countries are of declining importance to the advanced countries.[50] Though total direct foreign investment in the Third World quadrupled between 1950 and 1971, total direct foreign investment in the developed countries increased tenfold.

The growth in the size and number of global corporations, as well as the proliferation of foreign subsidiaries,[51] is certainly one of the more dramatic of the new facts of international life. There are some ten thousand transnational business enterprises, though about three hundred dominate the field. International investment has moved at a rapid pace since 1945—the average growth of the large, successful multinational firm has been two or three times as great as that for the most advanced national economies of the developed world.[52] Howard Perlmutter has estimated that by 1985, two or three hundred of these economic titans will control

80 percent of all the productive assets of the non-Communist world;[53] Richard Barber has estimated that by 1980, three hundred multinationals will account for 75 percent of all the world's manufacturing assets.[54] Whether or not one accepts these predictions, there can be little doubt that these nonterritorial entities have amassed economic capabilities that dwarf those of many sovereign states (see Figure 11). By the mid-1970s, Exxon, the largest industrial corporation in the world, had annual gross sales greater than the GNP of some 140 countries. Of the one hundred largest economic units in the world in 1975, nearly half were multinational corporations, and the two leading oil companies (Exxon and Royal Dutch Shell) had sales greater than the GNPs of every petroleum-exporting country with the exception of Iran.

Figure 11

Countries vs. Corporations:
The 100 Largest Economic Units in the World, 1975

Rank	Unit	GNP/Sales ($000)
1	United States	1,520,000,000
2	U.S.S.R.	870,000,000
3	Japan	507,000,000
4	West Germany	406,000,000
5	China	299,000,000
6	France	284,000,000
7	United Kingdom	205,000,000
8	Italy	158,000,000
9	Canada	157,000,000
10	Brazil	110,000,000
11	India	99,700,000
12	Spain	94,400,000
13	Poland	85,400,000
14	Australia	78,200,000
15	Netherlands	75,800,000
16	Sweden	61,500,000

Rank	Unit	GNP/Sales ($000)
17	East Germany	60,300,000
18	Mexico	60,100,000
19	Belgium	58,100,000
20	Czechoslovakia	54,500,000
21	Iran	52,100,000
22	Romania	46,800,000
23	*Exxon* (U.S.*)	44,864,824
24	*General Motors* (U.S.)	35,724,911
25	South Africa	35,600,000
26	Austria	35,400,000
27	Denmark	32,700,000
28	Turkey	35,700,000
29	Yugoslavia	35,300,000
30	*Royal-Dutch Shell* (U.K.-Neth.)	32,105,096
31	Venezuela	29,800,000
32	Saudi Arabia	27,400,000
33	Norway	25,900,000
34	Hungary	25,500,000
35	Nigeria	25,300,000
36	Indonesia	25,100,000
37	*Texaco* (U.S.)	24,507,454
38	*Ford Motor* (U.S.)	24,009,100
39	Finland	23,900,000
40	Greece	22,700,000
41	*Mobil* (U.S.)	20,620,392
42	South Korea	19,600,000
43	*National Iranian Oil* (Iran)	18,854,547
44	Philippines	17,400,000
45	*British Petroleum* (U.K.)	17,285,854
46	*Standard Oil of Cal.* (U.S.)	16,822,077
47	Taiwan	15,500,000
48	Thailand	15,300,000
49	*Unilever* (U.K.)	15,015,944

*NOTE: the parent-company countries for MNCs are in parentheses.

Rank	Unit	GNP/Sales ($000)
50	*International Business Machines* (U.S.)	14,436,541
51	New Zealand	14,400,000
52	*Gulf Oil* (U.S.)	14,268,000
53	Colombia	13,500,000
54	*General Electric* (U.S.)	13,399,000
55	Portugal	13,200,000
56	Peru	12,900,000
57	Iraq	12,400,000
58	*Chrysler* (U.S.)	11,699,805
59	Israel	11,500,000
	Egypt	11,500,000
60	*International Tel & Tel.* (U.S.)	11,367,647
61	Kuwait	11,000,000
62	*Philip's Gloeilampenfabrieken* (Neth.)	10,746,485
63	Libya	10,600,000
64	*Standard Oil Ind.* (U.S.)	9,955,248
65	Pakistan	9,900,000
66	Malaysia	9,400,000
67	*Cie Français dès Pétroles* (France)	9,145,778
68	*Nippon Steel* (Japan)	8,796,902
69	*August-Thyssen-Hutte* (West Germany)	8,764,899
70	*Hoechst* (West Germany)	8,462,322
71	*ENI* (Italy)	8,334,432
72	United Arab Emirates	8,200,000
73	*Daimler-Benz* (West Germany)	8,194,271
74	*U.S. Steel* (U.S.)	8,167,269
75	*BASF* (West Germany)	8,152,318
76	*Shell Oil* (U.S.)	8,143,445
77	Morocco	8,040,000
78	*Renault* (France)	7,831,330
79	*Siemens* (West Germany)	7,759,909

Rank	Unit	GNP/Sales ($000)
80	*Volkswagenwerk* (West Germany)	7,680,786
81	Chile	7,650,000
82	Ireland	7,410,000
83	*Atlantic-Richfield* (U.S.)	7,253,801
84	*Continental Oil* (U.S.)	7,253,801
85	*Bayer* (West Germany)	7,223,302
86	*E.I. du Pont de Nemours* (U.S.)	7,221,500
87	*Toyota Motors* (Japan)	7,194,139
88	*ELF-Aquitaine* (France)	7,154,390
89	*Nestlé* (Switzerland)	7,080,160
90	North Korea	7,000,000
91	*Imperial Chemical Industries* (U.K.)	6,884,219
92	*Petrobras* (Brazil)	6,625,516
93	*Western Electric* (U.S.)	6,590,116
94	Cuba	6,400,000
95	*British-American Tobacco* (U.K.)	6,145,979
96	*Procter & Gamble* (U.S.)	6,081,675
97	*Hitachi* (Japan)	5,916,135
98	*Westinghouse Electric* (U.S).	5,862,994
99	Singapore	5,760,000
100	*Mitsubishi Industries* (Japan)	5,693,994

SOURCES: 1975 GNP data is from the U.S. Arms Control and Disarmament Agency; the figures on gross sales of industrial corporations are from *Fortune* magazine, August 1976.

Nationalism being the potent force it is, many people tend to view the multinational corporation as a mere appendage of the home country's government and its policies. Nearly all these firms are based in a handful of developed countries with the highest proportion in the United States. Indeed, a number of Europeans fear that their countries will soon suffer the fate of Canada (where two-thirds of industry is American-owned). In the late sixties, J. J. Servan-Schreiber warned that European industry would soon be consigned "to a subsidiary role, and Europe herself to the position of a satellite." [55] Despite these anxieties about American multinationals, global corporations based in Europe and Japan have been gradually whittling down the gap in recent years, and the supremacy of transnational enterprises with headquarters in the United States is being successfully challenged.[56]

But global enterprise is not important in the contemporary international system solely bacause of its sheer size and control over productive wealth. The novel and overriding significance of the international corporation is its autonomy.

Because its operations transcend state boundaries, multinational enterprise "is not accountable to any public authority that matches it in geographical scope." [57] To be sure, individual affiliates are subject to the laws of the host countries in which they operate, and the parent company is responsible to the home country's regulations. But the planetary dimensions of the transnational firm as a whole allow it to escape the jurisdiction of governments—either the host or the parent or both. For example, Mobil Oil Corporation fashioned an elaborate set of bogus companies to disguise the flow of petroleum to Rhodesia over the last decade, circumventing both United States and United Nations sanctions against the Rhodesian government.[58] During the cold war, several American-based companies avoided Washington's restrictions on the sale of strategic goods to Communist countries by working through their foreign affiliates. In 1973, the Philippine subsidiary of Exxon refused to sell oil to the American navy at Subic Bay, proclaiming its observance of the Arab oil embargo against the United States.[59] In each of these cases, multinationals managed to defend their corporate interests at the expense of the national interest of the parent country.

Besides playing parent government against host government, the international corporation can pit one host against another to maximize its freedom of action. When the French government kept certain American-based firms from establishing affiliates in France, the parent companies simply set up shop in neighboring Common Market countries and, through free trade within the

European Community, invaded the French market through the back door. Developing countries are especially vulnerable to transnational business because they have little countervailing power. Barnet and Müller have identified three major institutional weaknesses in less-developed states which make them even more open to corporate influence: (1) antiquated governmental structures; (2) lack of a strong labor movement; (3) absence of competition from local businessmen.[60] What the multinationals have to offer—capital, technology and managerial skills—are the essential ingredients of economic development and the primary goal of Third World governments: but except in the extractive industries, the international business organization is by no means locked into any particular country and can easily shift its facilities to other eager hosts if the political climate turns sour. By its flexibility and mobility, a corporate giant can effectively deter government policies that may benefit the host country but prove detrimental to corporate interests. Developing countries are more susceptible than developed countries to direct political intervention by global corporations. The larger firms have the equivalent of foreign offices, complete with facilities for diplomatic negotiation, propaganda and subversion. A host of transnational companies have regularly employed various techniques for political penetration including bribery of government officials, campaign contributions to political parties and candidates, extensive lobbying in legislatures and bureaucracies, financial support for friendly elements in the communications media and general propaganda efforts to influence the values and attitudes of the host country's population.[61]

In addition, corporate leaders can forge transnational coalitions in pursuit of their private foreign policies. If we bear in mind that national societies (as well as governments) are not monolithic actors in world politics, but rather consist of competing groups and divergent interests, it becomes easy to imagine a multilateral alliance of various parties from different countries joining together to attain common objectives. Thus, when ITT concluded that the Chilean government must be deposed, it found willing accomplices within the United States Government, within Chilean society (labor, business, opposition political parties and newspapers, the military), within the transnational business community (other international firms with an economic stake in Chile) and even within the Allende governing coalition itself.

The multinational corporations (like all counterelites who grasp at social power) aspire to legitimacy. As we have seen in regard to the leadership of territorial states (see the discussion in Chapter 2), political groups justify their acquisition of power in ideological terms. Much as big business rationalized its right to rule in late nineteenth- and early twentieth-century America by a mixture of social Darwinism (progress results from the survival of the fittest) and laissez-faire economics (the free interaction of economic forces leads inexorably to the greatest good for the greatest number), modern global corporations claim that their unfettered operation can lead only to international peace and worldwide prosperity.[62] As corporate executives see it, transnational enterprise has been and will continue to be a distinctly beneficial development for all mankind, transcending petty nationalist rivalries and organizing the global economy to foster maximum economic efficiency. As Henry Ford II said: "In my mind, no better mechanism exists for stimulating, producing, and distributing the economic benefits of industrialization and commerce among nations" [63] Reginald Jones, chief executive officer of General Electric, believes that the multinational corporation is "a peaceful force mediating between disparate social and political systems in a world that necessarily requires interdependence." [64]

Nor do corporate leaders believe that the international firm has escaped governmental jurisdictions. On the contrary, they see only a vast array of national restrictions on products, prices, wages, investments, plant locations, employment policies and virtually every other aspect of business operations, all of which, they feel, have the effect of interfering with economic efficiency. In a world of sovereign states, the global corporation stands naked before the imposing authority of numerous governmental decision centers.

As the corporate hierarchies see their role in the world, transnational business is at the forefront of a new interdependence which will supplant a fundamentally divisive parochialism with an inherently harmonious order based upon the ascendance of corporate economics. Echoing these sentiments are the views of respected economists and students of world politics who see the eventual submergence of political conflict in a world organized according to the logic of the new business internationalism. Charles Kindleberger has stated emphatically: "The nation-state is just about through as an economic unit."[65] George Ball, former undersecretary of state, believes that the global corporation is in the vanguard of organizational change and that the territorial state is an anachronism in a complex world of mounting interdependence.

Corporate ideology, then, seeks to legitimate the international corporation in terms of its appropriateness as a means of organizing human effort in the modern age. The multinational firm is presented as the successor to the nation-state. The partisans of transnational enterprise tell us that the territorial state has outlived its usefulness, that in an era of interdependence, no state is really in control of its own destiny. Just as, in the past, primitive social structures (e.g., the city-state or the feudal manor) were cast aside in favor of more rational patterns of organization, the nation-state is said to be merely a lingering relic of a simpler age. At present, it co-exists with the new sovereign—the multinational corporation.

Yet the global corporation is not simply an international horn of plenty. Worldwide business enterprise is no doubt a force for economic growth and industrialization: but it is a private economic entity. By its very nature, it is a money-making, not a humanitarian, institution. Its management is not accountable to any constituency able to harness its vast productive power to socially responsible ends. On the contrary, a number of commentators have compared the directorships of multinationals with the political structures of authoritarian states.[66] The new managerial elite (what John Kenneth Galbraith has termed the *technostructure*[67]) exercises power without responsibility, but claims to be acting in accordance with the general welfare of mankind. In this respect, corporate leadership is like the Soviet Politburo, where decisions about the distribution of benefits are supposedly made on behalf of the masses by the high priests of communism. Indeed, one is hard pressed to think of a governing elite which has not proclaimed both the legitimacy of its rule and the beneficial nature of its stewardship of power.

Ideally, direct foreign investment ought to be a boon for host countries, transfering technology, capital and managerial expertise from countries where there is a surplus to areas where they are scarce. The creation of subsidiary plants tied to a worldwide marketing and supply network should bring more and better jobs to people plagued by unemployment, create additional tax revenues for governments lacking sufficient finances and increase the productivity of sluggish economies. Because transnational business tends to be export oriented and leads to import substitution, some suggest that the balance of payments for foreign-exchange-starved countries is bound to improve. Direct foreign investment does in fact increase the global product; but the difficulties lie in how the increment is allocated among competing actors and social groups. Parent-country governments urge repatriation of profits. Host countries want the multinationals to maximize domestic productivity and economic growth. In between these two territorial actors is the global corporation itself, anxious to preserve itself from the interference of both host and parent, and ever eager to expand the scope of its operations abroad.

Multinational corporations are viewed as both a threat and an opportunity. Since virtually all governments (including those of the Communist world) allow international business firms to operate in their territories, clearly these firms are perceived as potentially valuable partners in development. If they were seen only as interlopers, states could easily deny them access to their domestic economies. The difficulty confronting a state is to negotiate terms that will yield maximum benefit to the national polity. Host governments (especially those of the Third World) fear that multinational firms will circumvent national policies, bring undue influence to bear on domestic decision-making processes, and dominate key sectors of—or the entire—economy. In regard to the transfer of technology (the crucial ingredient of modernization), host countries argue that the actual transfer is minimal, that the technology received is inferior, outdated and overpriced and that the corporations use capital-intensive techniques of production which aggravate unemployment in labor-abundant economies. As for the inflow of capital, this is said to be more than offset by the repatriation of profits to the parent company. (In fact, the amount of capital the multinationals bring into a host country is negligible because the subsidiaries tend to absorb local capital that might otherwise be available to small national entrepreneurs.[68]) Some host countries maintain that the multinationals' profits are excessively high and that too little is reinvested in the host country. On balance, then, they believe that they are being decapitalized by the transnational giants. As to foreign investment improving the host country's balance of payments, hosts claim that most of a subsidiary's foreign transactions are with the other tentacles of the corporate octopus located abroad, and the company's bookkeeping too often overprices imports and undervalues exports, with an adverse effect on the host country's balance of payments. An accompanying accusation is that these companies dodge taxes. While host-government revenues are based on the subsidiaries' taxable incomes, an international corporation can cause its profits to appear on the books of affiliates in countries that are tax havens.

Perhaps the most serious indictment leveled against multinational business is that it reinforces the inequitable distribution of wealth in the contemporary world. Students of the international corporation are divided over whether the net effect of transnational investment is to transfer income from the rich countries to the poor countries or vice versa. It is true that a number of developing states are unable to deal effectively with the corporate goliaths and therefore lose benefits they would otherwise gain, but not that the multinationals are the cause of poverty in these states or that they make them poorer. The grievance of Third World countries is that while benefits may be mutual, they are not equal; the host does not get as much out of the relationship as it feels it should. Accordingly, in recent years, host governments have endeavored to get the best possible deals from the multinationals and have adopted a variety of techniques to maximize their return on foreign investment.[69] Host governments have compelled subsidiaries to tap external sources for financing investment and required them to export a significant portion of their product. Job quotas have been instituted to increase the number of nationals in managerial positions, and standards have been set for training local workers. Hosts often require that parent companies carry out research-and-development programs within the country. A number of states insist on local majority ownership of the subsidiary, and others have declared their intention to assume control of subsidiaries after a specified period from the time of initial investment. Some developed countries have contracted for specific services from the multinationals (e.g., technological know-how) thereby keeping out foreign-based affiliates, and it is probable that developing countries will someday follow suit. All in all, host governments now have a greater say in the local operations of the global corporations and have tilted the distribution of benefits somewhat more in favor of the territorial state. Consequently, one commentator has been moved to say that, "sovereignty is no longer at bay in host countries."[70]

The definitive balance sheet on the effects of the global corporation has yet to be compiled. There are those who see the multinational as the emerging sovereign and benefactor, creating and distributing the fruits of industrialization and modernization, utilizing the earth's scarce resources with the utmost efficiency and rationality. There are those who see it as just another robber baron and foreign investment as neoimperialism reinforcing patterns of inequality and injustice in the world. In between these two extremes is the view that the international corporation spurs economic growth but does not guarantee that affluence will be equally shared among, and within, nations; that the new economic titans are independent global actors of some significance, but not omnipotent world powers threatening to eclipse the territorial state.

In the decentralized international system, the distribution of benefits parallels the overall pattern of global influence. If the developing countries do not fare as well as they might like in their dealings with multinationals, this is because at present they lack the capabilities to tilt the balance of benefits more in their favor. As an autonomous actor seeking to maximize its gains, the world corporation cannot be expected to place vague abstractions such as global justice above self-interest. After all, how many territorial actors have a selfless urge to sacrifice national interests to the good of the species as a whole? Like the governing elites of nation-states, company managers have devised their own ideological rationalization of self-interest, identifying their economic gains with the well-being of the entire world. In many respects, then, the multinational corporation is little different—no better and probably no worse—than territorial actors.

TRANSNATIONAL FORCES: THE LIMITS OF MAN'S POLITICAL ENVIRONMENT

The proliferation and growing significance of nongovernmental actors are producing a gradual transformation of the international landscape. Of equal if not greater importance for the future of the global political system are transnational forces—trends originating within or among national societies and transcending governmental jurisdiction and control. These are the signs of mounting global interdependence. More and more areas of human activity beyond the nation-state's boundaries are impinging upon the welfare of its citizens, and yet territorially based governments are incapable of controlling these forces by their necessarily parochial and individualistic policies. Nor have governments demonstrated any willingness to surrender their traditional sovereign prerogatives and cooperate in the solution of common problems. Though the fundamental operating principle of the primitive international system—self-help—is being progressively undermined by the process of modernization, territorial actors have shown little inclination to abandon the decentralized multistate system. A gap is developing between technological progress, with the network of interdependence it entails, and the present political organization of the human species. The gap is rapidly widening and the resulting tensions are bound to bring about a substantial alteration in the nature of the global political process.

Much as compound interest leads to an exponential increase in the principal in a savings account, the exponential growth in man's knowledge places increasing strains on the delicate balance of ecology which sustains life on this planet. The concept of exponential growth is central to the understanding of man's increasingly adverse impact on his physical environment. Exponential (as opposed to arithmetic or linear) growth means that fixed-percentage increases in a quantity lead to successive doublings in the size of that quantity. (For example, if I place one hundred dollars in a bank account which offers a 5 percent annual interest rate, in fourteen years my balance will be two hundred dollars.*) This may seem innocuous enough, but consider the implications for resource consumption and population growth. The world's use of energy is growing at 5 percent a year, which means that total energy consumption will double in fourteen years. With an annual increase of just under 2 percent, the present world population of 4 billion will grow to 8 billion within 35 years. The exponential growth in human knowledge has produced exponential growth for a host of interrelated quantities. Rapid strides in modernization (the application of expanding knowledge to the organization of human effort) has led to the planetary product doubling every decade and a half. But all the ingredients of industrialization—raw materials, energy resources, clean air and water, space and so forth—are being consumed at a similar rate. Since our physical environment is finite, eventually the limits of growth will be reached. Moreover, exponential growth ensures that these limits (which are unknown to us) will be reached abruptly, and that we are approaching a collision with the laws of nature at an accelerating pace. Students of ecology use the lily-pond analogy to bring home this point. A farmer has a pond on which a lily plant is growing and doubling in size each day. The farmer has a maximum of thirty days to trim the plant, for by the thirtieth day the lily will cover the entire surface and choke all life in the pond. As he walks by the pond at the beginning of this period, he notices that the lily is small and decides to trim it when it covers half the pond. On the twenty-fifth day, the lily still covers only 1/32 of the surface. But on the twenty-ninth day, the farmer discovers it covers half the pond and that only one day remains to prevent disaster.

For most of his half-million years of existence, man was a hunter of other animals and a gatherer of food. Men were few in number and scattered across the face of the earth.[76] A relatively high fertility (birth) rate was matched by a high mortality (death) rate,

* Doubling is time calculated by dividing 70 by the growth rate.

resulting in population equilibrium. About ten thousand years ago, men began to cultivate the soil and domesticate animals and as this agricultural revolution gradually spread throughout the world, the larger and more dependable supply of food enabled a modest expansion in population; however, recurrent peaks in the death rate were precipitated by famines and epidemics (the Black Death killed 75 million people in Europe between 1347 and 1351). World population was probably somewhere between 5 and 10 million on the eve of the Agricultural Revolution; by the beginning of the Industrial Revolution (1750), it had increased to about 750 million. The development of science and technology that accompanied the Industrial Revolution drastically altered the demographic picture by significantly reducing the death rate. The introduction of basic medicine and sanitation, coupled with better communication and transportation, checked high mortality rates

Figure 12
The Global Population Explosion

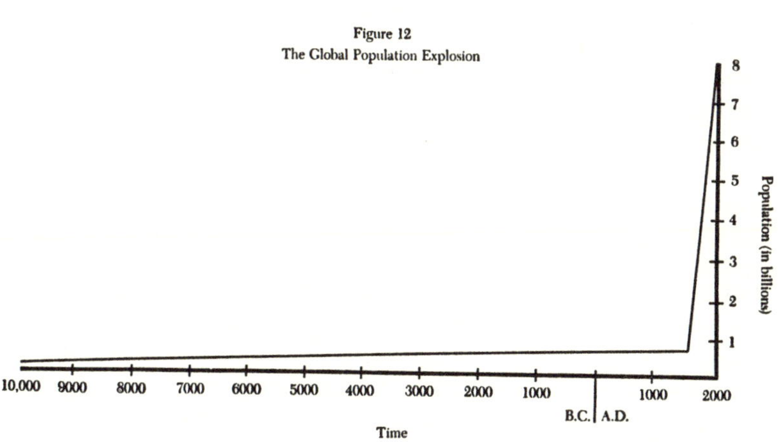

(especially among infants and children) and lengthened the average life span. A demographic explosion followed (see Figure 12). The demographic evolution of modernizing societies indicates that the fertility rate also tends to decrease in time. With urbanization and the extension of governmental welfare services (social security, child labor laws, compulsory education, etc.), children are transformed from producers to consumers and parents eventually limit themselves to two or three offspring. The population explosion is, therefore, a result of "demographic transition"—the time lag between the initial depression of the death rate and the subsequent fall in the birth rate, both brought about by industrialization. The worldwide population explosion began in Europe at the turn of the eighteenth century and has since subsided in the developed world, with the restoration of a new equilibrium (low fertility and low mortality). Population growth today stems from a 2 to 3 percent growth rate in the less developed countries (which also account for the bulk of the human race*), which is a result of the introduction of the low mortality rates characteristic of industrial society into basically agricultural societies, which retain high fertility. The death rates in the LDCs (though still higher than those in the developed countries) have been artificially depressed by the adoption of Western technology and advances in medicine, sanitation, disease and pest control and nutrition. Consequently, the largely preindustrial Third World has been the beneficiary of two centuries of accumulated knowledge from the industrial world, resulting in a prolonged demographic explosion which will continue until the birth rate slows down to match the decline in mortality.

The LDCs cannot afford the luxury of waiting for the birth rate to be brought down by the natural results of industrialization and the concomitant improvement in living standards. They are already suffering from an overabundance of people in relation to other resources, and this overpopulation is directly hindering the process of economic development. They are caught in a vicious circle of underdevelopment and overpopulation: population pres-

* According to United Nations projections, 90 percent of world population growth in the last quarter of this century will take place in the LDCs.

sures stifle industrialization. Failure to industrialize encourages population pressures.

The exponential expansion of world population means that the consumption of resources necessary to sustain life also increases exponentially. The most basic resource of all, of course, is food. Despite the so-called Green Revolution (the development of high-yield varieties of grain), and though the LDCs have increased food production by a full third since the early 1960s, food output is barely keeping abreast of population growth (see Figure 13). Even Norman Borlaug, the "father" of the Green Revolution, has warned that the day of reckoning has been merely postponed, not averted.[77] Just to maintain the inadequate diet of the mass of humanity subsisting in the poor countries, world food production will have to double by the year 2000.[78] The shortage of food is now endemic to international relations: At least half of mankind (including some 60 percent of the population of the Third World) is undernourished;[79] nearly a half-billion people are starving or suffering from chronic hunger;[80] ten to twenty million deaths a year (no one knows the exact number) are directly or indirectly attributable to inadequate nutrition.[81] In 1972, for the first time in two decades, world output of food actually declined; in the two years following, a half-million people starved to death in Ethiopia and neighboring countries, and 100,000 in the Sahel region of the southern Sahara;[82] in India, food shortages claimed one million lives.[83] The growth of population is simply outstripping the capacity of the world, as presently organized, to produce and distribute food. While the price of grain has tripled in recent years and global reserves have fallen sharply, there are 200,000 more mouths to feed every day in the developing world, and India alone must contend with 13 million additional people each year. In Latin American, which has a population growth rate of some 3 percent a year, the number of people has gone from 126 million in 1940 to 276 million in 1970 and will reach an estimated 645 million by the end of the century.[85] The dilemma reminds one of Lewis Carroll's *Through the Looking Glass:* "Now, here, you see, it takes all the running you can do to keep in the same place. If you want to get somewhere else, you must run at least twice as fast as that!"

The debate concerning the limits of growth in our finite world

Figure 13

Food vs. People
In the Developing Countries

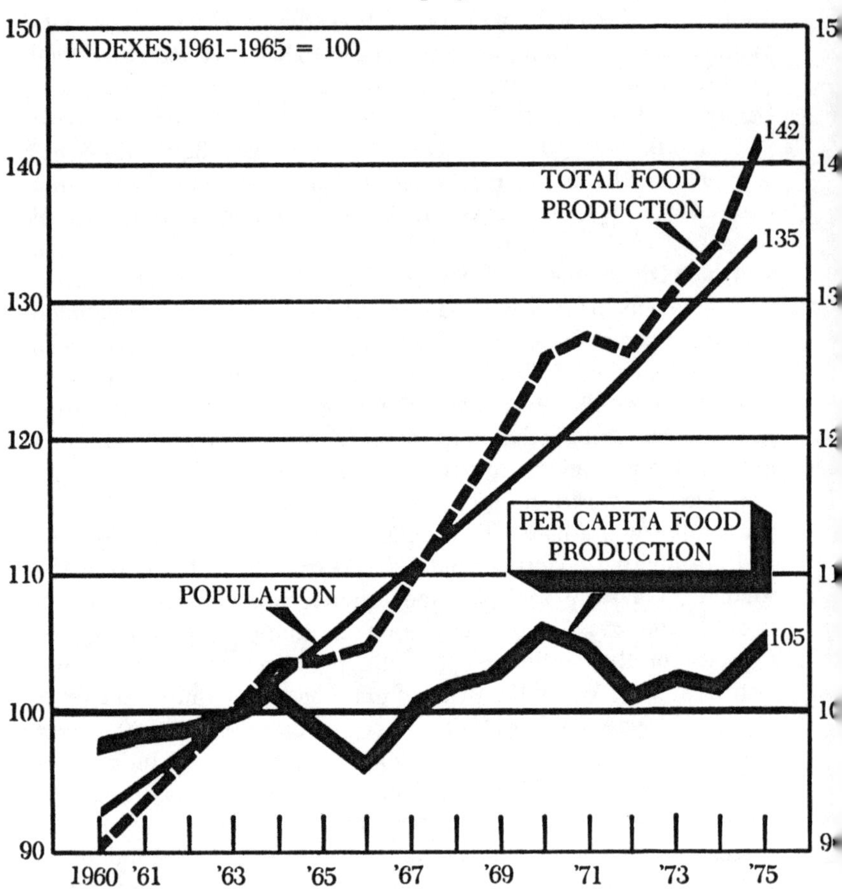

Total food production in the developing countries has increased over the years, but population growth has nearly canceled out the gains.

SOURCE: U.S. Department of Agriculture.

NOTE: Data for non-Communist countries only.

has been going on for some years. In the now-famous study by the Club of Rome,[86] first published in 1972, a group of researchers used a mathematical model and computerized techniques of analysis to consider the interaction of a host of factors, and concluded that the limits of growth on this planet would be reached within a century. Recently, however, a group of Hudson Institute futurologists led by Herman Kahn has suggested that we are presently in a period of transition from mass poverty and scarcity to global affluence, when man will control the forces of nature fully.[87] These optimists conclude that technology will save the human race by replacing fossil fuels with solar and geothermal energy sources, by devising unconventional food sources and advanced methods of securing raw materials and by solving the problem of pollution. They believe that in a century, there will be some 15 billion people on earth enjoying a per capital income of $20,000 (in 1972 values), as opposed to the present 4 billion people with $1400 per person. Though even the Club of Rome has revised its initial forecast somewhat,[88] most scholars are a good deal less sanguine than Kahn about the human prospect and are convinced that growth must be curtailed and that the conspicuous consumption of the rich few must yield to a more equitable distribution of a necessarily finite product.[89] In a massive computerized three-year study for the United Nations completed in 1976, economist Wassily Leontief has concluded that the income gap between rich and poor countries can be cut in half by the turn of the century without running out of food or natural resources and without excessive damage to the environment—if, however, the developed countries accept a slightly lower rate of economic growth in order to give the less-developed countries a far greater rate of growth.[90] It would seem, then, that the limits to growth are less physical than political.

However one looks at the challenges of man's future, it is apparent that the ultimate problem is to be found in the political organization of the species. The dilemmas of exponential growth transcend national boundaries but are exacerbated by the dominant herd mentality of the human race. The progress of modernization has created an increasingly interdependent world. The expansion of economic activity has resulted in the proliferation of independent and influential nongovernmental actors and created an interwoven global economy from which no territorial actor can escape. The welfare of nations is tied together as never before. All nations are vulnerable to disruptions originating far beyond their state frontiers; none can opt out of the new web of mutual dependence. The political foundations of the international system—national self-help and self-sufficiency—are increasingly at odds with the dynamics of modernization, which logically call for global solutions to problems. It is becoming clear that if the dilemmas of modernization are to be solved, a more equitable distribution of world benefits will have to be devised and governments must cooperate to an unprecedented degree, even to the extent of yielding their sovereign prerogatives. The dominant assumption of the multistate system has been irrevocably undermined: The territorial state can no longer guarantee the security and welfare of its citizens by means of particularistic policies and independent actions. Politics without government is anachronistic.

Chapter 6
Notes

1. Harold and Margaret Sprout, *Toward a Politics of the Planet Earth* (New York: Van Nostrand, Reinhold, 1971), p. 212.
2. For an interesting discussion of the theory of lateral pressure and the causes of the First World War, see Nazli Choucri and Robert C. North, *Nations in Conflict: International Growth and International Violence* (San Francisco: Freeman, 1975), pp. 30–34.
3. Ibid., p. 35.
4. *New York Times,* May 26, 1976, p. 1.
5. *Christian Science Monitor,* November 4, 1975, p. 14.
6. Ibid., February 18, 1976, pp. 10-11.
7. Ibid., October 15, 1976, p. 38.
8. Gregory Schmid, "Interdependence Has Its Limits," *Foreign Policy* 21 (Winter 1975–76): 188–96.
9. Edward L. Morse, "Transnational Economic Processes," in Robert O. Keohane and Joseph S. Nye, Jr., eds., *Transnational*

Relations in World Politics (Cambridge, Mass.: Harvard University Press, 1972), p. 35; Lester R. Brown, *World Without Borders* (New York: Vintage, 1972), chapter 14.

10. Brown, *World Without Borders,* p. 194.

11. Oran Young, "Interdependence and World Politics," *International Journal* 24 (Autumn 1969): 726.

12. Ibid.

13. Joseph S. Nye, Jr., "Independence vs. Interdependence," *Foreign Policy* 22 (Spring 1976): 135.

14. Joseph S. Nye, Jr., and Robert O. Keohane, "Transnational Relations and World Politics: An Introduction," in Keohane and Nye, *Transnational Relations,* p. xl.

15. Adapted from Nye and Keohane, ibid.

16. In the late 1950s, John H. Herz prematurely predicted the passing of the state as the dominant form of political organization in the world as a result of the impact of nuclear weapons on its continuing ability to function as the guardian of its citizens' security—the historical *raison d'être* in the evolution of the territorial state. A decade or so later, he recanted and admitted that the state had not only persevered, but had even received a new lease on life. See "The Rise and Demise of the Territorial State," *World Politics* 9 (July 1957): 473–93; *International Politics in the Atomic Age* (New York: Columbia University Press, 1959); "The Territorial State Revisited," *Polity* 1 (Fall 1968): 11–34. The two articles are included in Herz's *The Nation-State and the Crisis in International Politics in the Twentieth Century* (New York: David McKay, 1976).

17. James A. Field, Jr., "Transnationalism and the New Tribe," in Keohane and Nye, *Transnational Relations,* pp. 3–22.

18. Richard J. Barnet and Ronald E. Müller, *Global Reach: The Power of Multinational Corporations* (New York: Simon & Schuster, 1974), chapter 4.

19. Kjell Skjelsbaek, "The Growth of International Non-governmental Organizations in the Twentieth Century," in Keohane and Nye, *Transnational Relations,* pp. 70–92.

20. Ibid.; Werner L. Feld, *Nongovernmental Forces and World Politics: A Study of Business, Labor and Political Groups* (New York: Praeger, 1972), chapter 6.

21. Feld, *Transnationalism*, p. 178.

22. Skjellsbaek, *Growth*.

23. Feld, *Transnationalism*, pp. 183–87.

24. Ibid., pp. 194–95.

25. Ibid., pp. 208–9.

26. See the discussion by Ivan Vallier, "The Roman Catholic Church: A Transnational Actor," in Keohane and Nye, *Transnational Relations*, pp. 129–52.

27. Alvin Shuster, "The Vatican's Version of Détente," *New York Times*, October 10, 1976, section 4, p. 2; also ibid., August 1, 1976, p. 8.

28. *Christian Science Monitor*, September 8, 1976, pp. 1 and 9.

29. Feld, *Transnationalism*, pp. 235–37.

30. *New York Times*, December 10, 1975, p. 16.

31. The discussion of transnational parties presented in this paragraph parallels closely that by Feld, *Transnationalism*, pp. 214–30.

31. *New York Times*, February 9, 1976, p. 1.

33. See Feld, *Transnationalism*, pp. 221–22; also Vernon V. Aspturian, "The Soviet Union and International Communism," in Roy C. Macridis, ed., *Foreign Policy in World Politics*, 3rd ed. (Englewood Cliffs, N.J.: Prentice-Hall, 1967), pp. 216–45.

34. Alvin Shuster, "Communism, Italian Style," *New York Times Magazine*, May 9, 1976, p. 13.

35. J. Bowyer Bell, "Contemporary Revolutionary Organizations," in Keohane and Nye, eds., *Transnational Relations*, pp. 153–68.

36. David Fromkin, "The Strategy of Terrorism," *Foreign Affairs* 53 (July 1975): 692.

37. Brian Jenkins, *International Terrorism: A New Mode of Conflict*, Research Paper No. 48, California Seminar on Arms Control and Foreign Policy (Los Angeles: Crescent Publications, 1975), p. 1. Quoted in David L. Milbank, *International and Transnational Terrorism: Diagnosis and Prognosis*, Research Study for the Central Intelligence Agency (April, 1976), p. 8.

38. Milbank, *Terrorism*; also see the *Christian Science Monitor*, June 23, 1976, p. 13. (The discussion of transnational terrorism presented in this paragraph is drawn largely from the data and analysis provided in this CIA-sponsored study.)

39. *New York Times,* January 11, 1976, p. 11
40. *Christian Science Monitor,* October 14, 1975, p. 34.
41. Milbank, *Terrorism,* p. 14
42. *New York Times.* August 17, 1975, section 4, p. 3.
43. *Christian Science Monitor,* May 3, 1976, p. 34.
44. Barnet and Müller, *Global Reach,* p. 15.
45. Adapted from Raymond Vernon, "Multinational Business Transnationalism, and National Economic Goals," in Keohane and Nye, *Transnational Relations,* p. 344; Feld, p. 23.
46. Barnet and Müller, *Global Reach,* p. 16.
47. Charles P. Kindleberger, *American Business Abroad* (New Haven, Conn: Yale University Press, 1969), p. 179.
48. Gus Tyler, "Labor's Multinational Pains," *Foreign Policy,* 12 (Fall 1973): 124.
49. David P. Calleo and Benjamin M. Rowlands, *America and the World Political Economy: Atlantic Dreams and National Realities* (Bloomington: Indiana Univ. Press, 1973), chapter 7.
50. In 1948, a full third of the total exports of the developed world went to the Third World; within twenty years, the proportion was down to one quarter. See Abdul A. Said and Luiz R. Simmons, eds., *The New Sovereigns; Multinational Corporations as World Powers* (Englewood Cliffs, N.J.: Prentice-Hall, 1975), p. 6.
51. In one study of major United States–based companies, it was found that since the beginning of this century, the number of corporations engaged in transnational operations has increased by 800 percent and the number of foreign subsidiaries has increased sixty fold. See Feld, *Transnationalism,* pp. 24–26.
52. Barnet and Müller, *Global Reach,* p. 15.
53. Ibid., p. 15.
54. Richard J. Barber, *The American Corporation: Its Power, Its Money, Its Politics* (New York: E. P. Dutton, 1970), p. 264. For a critical view of this type of projection, see Raymond Vernon, "The Future of the Multinational Enterprise," in Charles P. Kindleberger, ed., *The International Corporation* (Cambridge, Mass.: M.I.T., 1970), pp. 373–400.
55. J. J. Servan-Schreiber, *The American Challenge* (New York: Avon, 1969), p. 52.
56. While in 1968, eighteen of the largest twenty multinationals were based in the United States, in 1970, only fifteen were (see

Feld, *Transnationalism* p. 33). The same slippage is evident if we examine the world's top twelve industrial firms: ten of these were American in 1973, but only eight were a year later. See *Fortune World Business Directory*. 1975, p. 9.

57. Raymond Vernon, *Sovereignty at Bay* (New York: Basic Books, 1971), p. 249.

58. *New York Times*, August 2, 1976, pp. 1 and 36.

59. Barnet and Müller, *Global Reach*, chapter 4.

60. Ibid., chapter 6.

61. See Joseph S. Nye, Jr., "Multinational Corporations in World Politics," *Foreign Affairs* 53 (October 1974): 153–75.

62. See the discussion of what is called the new gospel of peace and plenty in Barnet and Müller, *Global Reach*, chapter 1.

63. *Christian Science Monitor*, March 3, 1976, p. 10. This statement is taken from a report entitled *Corporate Citizenship in the Global Community* (Washington, D.C.: International Management and Development Institute, 1976).

64. Ibid., February 18, 1976, p. 10.

65. Kindleberger, *American Business Abroad*, p. 207.

66. For example, see Anthony Sampson, *The Sovereign State of ITT* (Gr enwich, Conn.: Fawcett, 1974).

67. John Kenneth Galbraith, *The New Industrial State* (Boston: Houghton Mifflin, 1967).

68. Servan-Schreiber maintains that nine-tenths of American investment in Europe is financed from European sources—or, as he puts it, "we pay them to buy us" *(American Challenge)*, p. 43). Barnet and Müller *Global Reach*, p. 153) find that between 1957 and 1965, American-based multinationals financed 83 percent of their Latin American investments locally.

69. This discussion of host-country strategies is drawn from C. Fred Bergsten, "Coming Investment Wars?," *Foreign Affairs* 53, (October 1974): 135–52.

70. Ibid., p. 138.

71. See the discussion of international vs. national equity in Robert O. Keohane and Van Doorn Ooms, "The Multinational Firm and International Regulation," in C. Fred Bergsten and Laurence B. Krause, eds., *World Politics and International Economics* (Washington, D.C.: The Brookings Institution, 1975), 169–209.

72. Perhaps the best argument of this type is put forth by Barnet and Müller, *Global Reach*, especially chapter 7. See also Ronald Müller, "Poverty is the Product," *Foreign Policy* 13 (Winter 1973–74): 71–102; Richard J. Barnet, "Comment," ibid: 118–122; Raymond Vernon, et al., "An Exchange on Multinationals," ibid., 15 (Summer 1974): 83–92. The version of this thesis discussed in this section is drawn from Barnet and Müller.

73. See Irving Louis Horowitz, "Capitalism, Communism and 'Multinationalism," in Said and Simmons, *New Sovereigns*, 120–38.

74. T.S. Ashton, "The Standard of Life of the Workers in England, 1790–1830," in F.A. Hayek, ed., *Capitalism and the Historians* (Chicago: University of Chicago Press, 1954). p. 41.

75. See the discussion in Herman Kahn, et al., *The Next Two Hundred Years: A Scenario for America and the World* (New York: Morrow, 1976).

76. The following discussion relies heavily upon that by Carlo M. Cipolla, *The Economic History of World Population*, 6th ed. (Baltimore, Md.: Penguin, 1974).

77. Cited in Paul R. Erlich, et al., *Human Ecology: Problems and Solutions* (San Francisco: Freeman, 1973), p. 96.

78. See Lester R. Brown, "Rich Countries and Poor in a Finite, Interdependent World," in Mancur Olson and Hans H. Landsburg, eds., *The No-Growth Society* (New York: Norton, 1973), pp. 153–64.

79. *Christian Science Monitor*, September 24, 1975, p. 27.

80. Ibid., October 20, 1975, p. 13.

81. Donella H. Meadows, et al., *The Limits to Growth: A Report for the Club of Rome's Project on the Predicament of Mankind*, 2nd ed. (New York: New American Library, 1975), p. 61.

82. *New York Times*, January 11, 1976, p. 6. (The estimates were made by the Carnegie Endowment for International Peace.)

83. *Christian Science Monitor*, October 28, 1976, p. 1.

84. *New York Times*, February 29, 1976, section 4, p. 7, and March 5, 1976, p. 5.

85. *Christian Science Monitor*, October 22, 1975, p. 9.

86. Meadows, et al., *Limits*.

87. Herman Kahn, et al., *Next Two Hundred Years*.

88. Mihajle Mesarovic and Eduard Pestel, *Mankind at the*

Turning Point: The Second Report of the Club of Rome (New York: New American Library, 1974).

89. *Christian Science Monitor,* November 3, 1976, pp. 16–17.

90. Ibid., November 8, 1976, p. 10: *New York Times,* October 14, 1976, p. 1.

Chapter 7

The Axes of World Conflict

"... The fact is that Sollozzo and the Tattaglias could not go into their new business without the assistance of Don Corleone. In fact, his disapproval injured them. That's not his fault of course. The fact remains that judges and politicians who would accept favors from Don Corleone even on drugs, would not allow themselves to be influenced by anybody else when it came to narcotics. Sollozzo couldn't operate if he didn't have some assurance of his people being treated kindly. We all know that. We would all be poor otherwise.... Don Corleone controls all that apparatus. His refusal to let us use it is not the act of a friend. He takes the bread out of the mouths of our families. Times have changed, it's not the old days when everyone can go his own way. If Corleone had all the judges in New York, then he must share them or let others use them. Certainly he can present us with a bill for such services, we're not communists after all. But he has to let us draw water from the well. It's that simple."

—Don Barzini, in Mario Puzo's
The Godfather

PATTERNS OF GLOBAL COMPETITION

A primitive political system inexorably leads to conflict rather than cooperation, the pursuit of parochial goals at the expense of the common interest. Given the scarcity of values and the uneven distribution of power, collision of political wills is inevitable. Thus far in our study of world politics, we have analyzed the nature, manifestation and management of the struggle for power. At this juncture, we will consider the dynamics of global competition and the patterns of international conflict.

During each historical period, world politics is characterized by certain major axes of conflict. An *axis of conflict* may be defined as a dominant pattern of competition between states, or a coalition of states, which assumes priority on the world agenda and preoccupies the major powers. To be sure, inter-state politics normally consists of multiple sets of conflictual relations, and the interests of even the closest allies frequently diverge. National actors are in a more-or-less constant state of tension with one another, though the intensity of their conflict situations varies considerably. In the vast majority of cases, persuasive sanctions or nonviolent coercion will be the dominant mode of interaction. For some pairs of actors, however, the severity of competition is such that it is likely that one or both will resort to the ultimate sanction: violence. The atmosphere of world politics will be determined, not by the myriad low-level conflictual relations among governments, but by the overriding schisms which align some states in opposition to others. Of the thousands of issues that propel the 150-odd sovereign entities in the contemporary international system to contend for power over one another, only a handful are of the first magnitude. These axes of conflict pertain to the fundamental nature of the international order.

The number of dominant axes of global conflict ultimately depends upon the distribution of world power. A bipolar international system will result in one central axis. The conflict for primacy between two rival actors (as individual states or coalitions of states) serves as the fundamental division in the international system, all other issues among all other actors being relegated to the periphery and being dependent on the outcome of this paramount struggle for power. In this century, there have been three such periods where capabilities have been polarized between two antagonistic camps. During both world wars and the cold war that followed, world power was effectively monopolized by two blocs, which clashed in great duels for global hegemony. While the major powers were thus engaged, latent conflict within each coalition was overshadowed by the task of defeating the common foe. Moreover, relations between the major powers and all other states (those which were neither allies nor enemies) were determined by the exigencies of the preponderant dispute.

On the other hand, in historical periods during which there is diffusion of capabilities (multipolar systems), numerous other issues and overlapping patterns of competition surface. The nature of international relations prior to both world wars bears out this relationship between the distribution of power and the number of dominant axes of conflict. During the age of imperialism preceding the First World War, colonial expansion by the various European powers led to a number of collisions of interest wherever spheres of influence overlapped or imperial frontiers were ill-defined. In North Africa, France clashed with Britain in Egypt and the Sudan and with Germany in Morocco; in South Africa, British expansion northward intersected Germany's lateral pressure in an east-west direction; in Central Asia, Britain and Russia were involved in an imperial dispute over the fate of Persia; in the Far East, Russia and Japan went to war over the definition of their spheres of influence in Manchuria and Korea, and all the European powers and Japan scrambled over the division of China; in eastern Europe and the Balkans, the expansionist ambitions of Germany and Russia clashed head-on, and friction here would eventually precipitate global war among all the powers.The international system was crisscrossed by multilateral competition, the salience of a number of issues and overlapping patterns of conflict. A similar, if less pronounced, pattern developed during the post–World War I era. Following the defeat of the Central Powers, the Allies found their national interests diverging: The United States lapsed into its traditional isolationist stance, leaving European equilibrium in the hands of its former coalition partners, Britain and France. These two countries failed to evolve a common policy to deal with defeated Germany. England, from its insular perspective, took a more conciliatory position convinced that a revitalized Germany was crucial to Britain's economic vitality. The French, having been twice invaded by their expansionist neighbor in the recent past, were preoccupied with the overriding necessity of keeping German power in check. This fissure between the United Kingdom and France would prevent an early formation of a united front against Hitler's Germany. Moreover, the Western democracies were now in a strange twilight relationship with their natural ally to the east of Germany: Russia. Traditionally wary of Russian expansionist pressures all along her extensive Eurasian borders and now uneasy about Russian Communism's messianic urge, Britain and France were more than usually suspicious of Moscow's ambitions. Thus, both Germany and Russia were perceived as potential threats to the European balance of power.

Relations between the future Axis partners were also in a state of flux during most of the interwar period. Though they had a common ideology, Germany's and Italy's political spheres of influence overlapped, and as late as 1934, Mussolini seemed ready to wage war rather than permit the Nazis to stage a coup d'etat in Austria and absorb it into the Third Reich. Thus, until Europe coalesced into two antagonistic camps in the late 1930s it was the scene of constant maneuver and shifting alignments over a host of outstanding issues.

The pattern of global competition can be examined in terms of the number and variety of actors involved and the nature of the stakes in contention. A bipolar system revolves around a conflict between two dominant rivals for hegemony, one defending and one challenging the distribution of global benefits (the status quo and revisionist powers, respectively). The values at stake involve questions of security, ideology, and welfare. The ultimate issue is the right to function as the chief arbiter of global values. A multipolar system, on the other hand, produces a number of axes of conflict, each involving different combinations of participants and different sets of issues; that is, different status quo powers and different revisionist powers.

The international system that evolved from the outcome of the Second World War has contained elements of both a bipolar and a multipolar distribution of power. Until the 1960s, contemporary world politics was molded by the cold war between the United States and the Soviet Union. During this era of superpower duopoly, the United States endeavored to pursue its version of the just international order against the challenge presented by the U.S.S.R., and eventually all geographical regions of the globe were woven into an integrated policy of containment. With the waning of bipolarity and the rise of new centers of power in Europe, Japan, China and the Third World, the superpowers' struggle for primacy receded and was soon supplemented by new and largely autonomous axes of conflict, which brought new actors and new issues to the forefront of international politics. While the question of international security was still largely monopolized by Washington and Moscow (given the remaining bipolarity in military capabilities), confrontation was gradually transformed into détente, and the fear of a thermonuclear gladiatorial duel was substantially reduced. However, other issues previously reserved for the arena of superpower competition now devolved toward the emergent centers of influence: The primary ideological struggle, which had been part and parcel of the East-West cold war, now tore the Communist bloc asunder and recast the Soviet Union (the erstwhile challenger of the United States) in the role of defender of the status quo against a revolutionary and revisionist China; in terms of the distribution of the global economic product (the welfare issue), a new found unity among the countries of the developing world ranged them against the advanced industrial societies in a struggle for a new global economic order; finally, as the cold war lessened in intensity, competing national interests placed increasing stress on the once-unified Western Alliance. Thus, the dominant East-West axis of world conflict has been supplemented by an East-East axis, a North-South axis, and even a West-West axis.

THE POST-WAR ERA: NEITHER PEACE NOR WAR

The search for villains and heroes in analysis of the origins of the cold war, which has long been popular in contemporary historiography, excludes the possibility of objectivity. The analysis of history (and especially recent history) can never be completely value free. The analyst, much as he might try not to, cannot but color his interpretation of reality with the biases inherent in his psychological makeup and social vantage point. Nevertheless, a demonological approach to international conflict (one that seeks to indict one participant for its intentions and policies) causes the observer to ignore the limits imposed by environmental constraints and to attribute to decision makers greater freedom of action than is warranted by real world conditions. As we have seen, the primitive nature of the international system virtually dictates certain courses of action to actors by severely limiting the alternatives and options available. The dilemma of world politics is that competing actors are constrained by the very nature of the anarchic system to undertake "defensive" measures which can be perceived by potential opponents only as indications of hostile intent. Threat perceptions are endemic to interstate relations and are mutually reinforcing. Conflict is the norm, not a pathological condition caused by quirks of personality or domestic aberrations. This is the stuff out of which cold wars spring. As Arthur Schlesinger, Jr., sums up the genesis of the Soviet-American rivalry for preeminence:

> [The cold war] was the product not of a decision but of a dilemma. Each side felt compelled to adopt policies which the other could not but regard as a threat to the principles of peace. Each then felt compelled to undertake defensive measures. Thus the Russians saw no choice but to consolidate their security in Eastern Europe. The Americans, regarding Eastern Europe as the first-step toward Western Europe, responded by asserting their interest in the zone the Russians deemed vital to their security. The Russians concluded that the West was resuming its old course of capitalist encirclement; that it was purposefully laying the foundation for anti-Soviet regimes in the area defined by the blood of centuries as crucial to Russian survival. Each side believed with passion that future international stability depended on the success of its own conception of world order. Each side, in pursuing its own clearly indicated and deeply cherished principles, was only confirming the fear of the other that it was bent on aggression.[1]

Or as Hans J. Morgenthau suggests:

> Two factors distinguish the Cold War between the Soviet Union and the West from the many hostile confrontations history records and, hence, justify its name. The first factor was the impossibility for all concerned, given the interests at stake and the position taken, to pursue conciliatory policies through compromise, which might have led to a settlement of the outstanding issues. The second was the necessity, following from this impossibility, for both sides to protect and promote their interests through unilateral direct pressure on the opponent's will by all available means ... short of the actual use of force. Thus we have a "war" because the purpose was not to accommodate the other side in return for reciprocal accommodations, but rather to compel the other side to yield.... And the war has been a "cold" one because the use of force upon a major opponent was excluded from the instruments of unilateral action.[2]

That this irreconcilability of national interests did not degenerate into a new world war, as such conflicts had in the past, hinged upon the novel existence of weapons of mass destruction, which made recourse to open hostilities distinctly unattractive as well as irrational. Thus the cold war began when Soviet and American leaders became aware of "the impossibility of peace and the improbability of war." [3]

The Genesis of the Cold War: The East-West Axis of Conflict

Ever since the end of the Second World War and the initiation of the global superpower rivalry that followed, two Western schools of thought have evolved diametrically opposed explanations to account for the existence of the cold war. The orthodox, or *traditional,* historians place the onus of responsibility on the Soviet Union and laud the postwar American policy of containment as a necessary and proper response to the Kremlin's aggressive designs.[4] By the 1960s, a growing impatience with the cold war and general disillusionment with the war in Vietnam reinforced the intellectual movement of *historical revisionism,* a school which boasts descent from the Henry Wallace revolt of the late

1940s. The revisionist historians have sought to recast the Soviet Union's hostility as a defensive reaction amenable to détente and accommodation.[5] Placing the foreign policy of the United States in a much less favorable light, the revisionists place the origins of the cold war in the American attempt to deny the Russians a defensive ring of buffer states in eastern Europe at the end of World War II.

Implicit in both theories is the underlying assumption that the cold war was avoidable, that a different, more enlightened set of policies by one side or the other would have obviated the necessity of confrontation. Both schools see the tragedy of the cold war as a Christian tragedy ("the tragedy of possibility") rather than as a Greek tragedy ("the tragedy of necessity").[6] Herein lies the error of both approaches. The groundwork for the cold war was not laid by specific decisions made in Washington or Moscow in the closing days of World War II or even in the months that followed; the broad contours of the conflict were an inevitable result of the war itself. In a brilliantly prophetic but forgotten treatise on American foreign policy published in 1943,[7] Walter Lippmann (who was to baptize the Russo-American struggle for power the "cold war" some four years later [8]) succinctly projected the dilemma of world politics for the postwar period. Recognizing that the core defense area of the United States was the Western Hemisphere, Lippmann suggested that isolationism, a passive defense, was no longer a viable foreign-policy option. Both world wars demonstrated that "the American regions cannot be defended by waiting to repel an attack by a formidable enemy," and that consequently "the strategic defenses of the United States are not at the three-mile limit in American waters, but extend across both oceans to all trans-oceanic lands from which an attack by sea or air can be launched."[9] The United States would be strategically vulnerable against "the combined forces of the Old World," [10] should they be united under a hostile state of coalition of states. From its base in the Western Hemisphere, the United States would have to maintain a secure chain of overseas bases in order to project its military power onto the Eurasian landmass. In Lippmann's analysis, "a nation has security when it does not have to sacrifice its legitimate interests to avoid war and is able, if challenged, to maintain them by war." [11] The security of the United States was inseparable from the continued independence of western European states, and it was in the vital interest of the North American power to preserve the integrity of these nations against potential aggression.

Writing in the midst of the second global war of the twentieth century, Lippmann predicted not only that the Axis Powers would be defeated, but also that "as a result of the defeat Germany will never again be able to make a bid for the mastery of Europe and the transatlantic region of American security" and that "Japan will never again be able to seek to make an empire over China and the Indies." [12] However, with the elimination of both Germany and Japan as major powers and potential disturbers of international equilibrium:

> Russia will . . . be the greatest power in the rear of our indispensable friends—the British, Scandinavian, Dutch, Belgian, and Latin members of the Atlantic Community. In Asia, Russia will be our nearest neighbor across the Northern Pacific and by air over the polar regions; Russia will be the nearest neighbor of China.[13]

The precarious nature of postwar Soviet-American relations would stem, therefore, directly from the transformation in the global distribution of power made inevitable by the defeat of the Axis states. The only hope for avoiding a new war, Lippmann believed, was a European settlement that would satisfy the legitimate security interests of both powers. Specifically, the testing ground for whether there would be peace or war would be "the borderland between Russia and the Atlantic states": eastern Europe. As Lippmann accurately warned:

> If in this region the effort to settle territorial boundaries and to decide what governments shall be recognized discloses deep and insoluble conflicts between Russia's conception of her vital interests and that of the Western Allies, then every nation will know that it must get ready and must choose sides in the eventual but unavoidable next war.[14]

Only one solution to this dilemma of conflicting security interests existed: the neutralization of eastern Europe. Only this could assure the Soviets a secure frontier by eliminating the possibility that the countries of central and eastern Europe might become the spearhead of future aggression of the Western allies. At the same time, such a ring of buffer states would insulate western Europe from the prospect of Russian aggression. If eastern Europe were to lose its independence and become a mere satellite of the U.S.S.R., however, then the nations of the West would lie exposed and defenseless. Neutralization was the only alternative to the cold war. And yet it was not a viable alternative. Hence, the cold war became inevitable.

The neutralization of eastern Europe was incompatible with the Soviet Union's conceptions of security. At the very least, Stalin wanted a defensive rim of friendly (i.e., Russian-dominated) states on his western borders following the end of hostilities with Germany. The revisionist school maintains that the U.S.S.R.'s paramount objective was not expansion but security, and that the United States' rejection of this objective represents the "cardinal, outstanding fact which explains the Cold War." [15] In reality, the United States did not oppose legitimate Soviet security interests in the area. What it did oppose was Stalin's exaggerated notion of Russian security needs—the creation of satellite states—which was deemed incompatible with the legitimate security needs of western Europe and, thus, the United States.

While the United States, long relatively safe in its position far from the center of international politics, could espouse grand schemes for big-power cooperation and international organization, the Russian historical experience dictated the opposite approach. Two all-important factors have dominated the long and brutal history of the Russian state: invasion and economic backwardness. As one early revisionist thinker accurately relates:

> While America, protected by the Atlantic Ocean from superior European land Powers, expanded westward over an empty continent in relative security against external attack, the Russian community, expanding eastward over an empty continent, was at all times exposed to, and relatively defenseless against, external attack by major land Powers of Europe.

> Once freed from the Mongol yoke, Russia was obligated to repeatedly fight for national survival against formidable foes to the north, to the west, to the south. Disunity and weakness in the heart of Muscovy have usually led to invasion or intervention from abroad—by Swedes, Germans, Lithuanians, and Poles in the Mongol period . . . ; by Turkey, Poland and Sweden in the late 16th, 17th, and early 18th centuries; by France in the early 19th century; by Germany in World War I; by Poland, France, Britain, Japan and America after World War I; by Germany, Italy and their allies in World War II.[16]

For a millennium, going back at least to the ninth century, Russia has existed in mortal fear, stranded on the great plain of Europe, devoid of any defensive frontiers and subjected to wave after wave of invasion and devastation. Not surprisingly, then, "the prime driving force in Russia has been fear."[17] In addition to this understandable obsession with physical security, the Russians have long been preoccupied with the gap in economic development between their country and the nations of the Western world. At least since the time of Peter the Great, Russian leaders have been aware of the relationship between economic backwardness and military weakness and have striven to catch up with the West in technology and industrialization. The Russian situation in 1945 had a fundamental continuity with the past: Human losses at the hands of the German army were staggering (some 20 million); the economy lay in ruins, the western region of the country (the industrial heartland) having been virtually leveled. While British and American officials looked at Soviet Russia and saw only an invincible Red Army hanging over a prostrate Europe, Stalin could see only the new economic colossus of capitalism—the United States—as the preponderant power in the world. The outcome of the war had done little to alleviate the Soviet Union's nervous uncertainty.[18]

There has been remarkable continuity also in the traditional Russian response to invasion and backwardness: dictatorship, suspicion of foreigners, territorial expansion and messianic universalism.[19] The history of Russia is one long chronicle of territorial aggrandizement; tiny fifteenth-century Muscovy has expanded to comprise one-sixth of the world's land area and stretch a third of the way around the globe. Nevertheless, this phenomenal geographical growth was in the main a defensive expansion—"an expansion prompted by the lack of natural defensive frontiers in a world of mortal dangers on all sides." [20] The traditional Russian perception of its environment as being populated with hostile and aggressive neighbors bent on destruction of Russia has created both a siege mentality and a pretension to universal mission. Indeed, the early czars (the Russian word for *caesar*) conceived of their imperial domain as the Third Rome—the rightful heir to the glorious mantle of the Roman and Byzantine empires—and their successors kept these aspirations alive by means of the ideological mechanisms of the Orthodox Church, the Pan-Slav movement and the Communist International (Comintern). In short, the Bolshevik Revolution precipitated less of a break with the Russian past than is often believed. Marxist-Leninist ideology reinforced and accentuated the Russians' sense of insecurity and mission. Their Communist dogma provided the new leaders of the U.S.S.R. with a vision of a world of hostile forces bent upon the destruction of the vanguard of global revolution. The capitalist states were enemies by definition, and though short-term alliances might be necessary (as in World War II), the inexorable progress of historical conflict denied the possibility of permanent accommodation with the bourgeois democracies. Viewing the postwar world through these historical and ideological lenses, Stalin expected an early resumption of confrontation with the capitalist West and was intent upon shoring up Soviet defenses as rapidly as possible. From such a vantage point, eastern Europe had to be communized, not for the sake of some distant world revolution but to ensure the immediate security of the Soviet state.

The dual personality of Russia—as both the dominant national power on the European continent and the self-proclaimed mecca of a subversive and expansionist ideology—confronted Western leaders with a dilemma. Even a non-Communist Russia, thrust into the center of Europe, surrounded by power vacuums and dominating satellite states on its periphery, would have been an inherent threat to the balance of power. If the Soviets were really the fountainhead of international communism, driven by the dynamic imperative of limitless expansion, then containment was all the more necessary, and the policy of confrontation would assume the proportions of a crusade. Whatever Stalin's long-range objectives, his immediate demand for control of eastern Europe threatened international equilibrium and, hence, the security of the West. Conversely, the West's opposition to this domination was seen as a threat to the security of the Soviet Union. Thus, the East-West conflict was, in essence, a Greek tragedy of necessity.

A World Divides: The Struggle for European and Global Supremacy

As we have seen in the balance-of-power discussed in Chapter 5, the quest for power and advantage in a fragmented and anarchic environment tends to result in a balance of power regardless of the motivations of individual actors. The power vacuums caused by the demise of German and Japanese influence in Europe and the Far East necessitated a new waltz among the remaining Great Powers in the search for a new global equilibrium. As Walter Lippmann had been quick to grasp in 1943, a diplomatic revolution (realignment of states) was bound to involve overtures by the victors to the vanquished.[21] With Moscow and Washington deadlocked over a mutually acceptable disposition of the eastern Europe question, each proceeded to consolidate its sphere of influence, shoring up its first line of defense against the potentially aggressive designs of the other.

The irreconcilability of the former allies' diverging national interests was registered in their inability to compromise their differences through diplomatic negotiation. A Council of Foreign Ministers of the Big Three had been established to arrange peace treaties with the defeated enemy states, but by the end of 1945, no settlement was in sight. Deadlock resulted from differing interpretations of the agreements concluded by Churchill, Roosevelt and Stalin at the Yalta Conference in February of that same year.* Within a few months of the Yalta summit, however, it had

* In regard to eastern Europe, it was agreed that a new government (including Communist and non-Communist elements; would be established in Poland pledged to the "holding of free and unfettered elections as soon as possible on the basis of universal suffrage and secret ballot." In the other east European countries which had been Axis satellite states, the Big Three promised to establish interim governments "broadly representative

become apparent that the Soviet conceptions of security encompassed nothing less than totally subservient governments on its borders.

Gradually, but unmistakably, the lines were being drawn for intense conflict between the western and eastern centers of the former Grand Alliance. In February of 1946, Stalin reverted to ideological rhetoric against the Western allies, and Soviet propaganda returned once again to the familiar theme of capitalist hostility. The following month, Winston Churchill delivered his famous "Iron Curtain" speech in Fulton, Missouri:

> . . . From Stettin in the Baltic to Trieste in the Adriatic, an iron curtain has descended across the Continent. . . . This is certainly not the Liberated Europe we fought to build. Nor is it the one which contains the essentials for a permanent peace.
>
> . . . From what I have seen of our Russian friends and allies during the war, I am convinced that there is nothing they admire so much as strength, and there is nothing for which they have less respect than weakness, especially military weakness. . . .

The opening salvos of the cold war had been fired.

By the beginning of 1946, Stalin was intent upon "expand[ing] Soviet power and influence without setting into motion a sequence of events that would lead to a confrontation with the greatest power in the world": the United States.[22] Believing that the capitalist world would soon be consumed by and preoccupied with one of its periodic economic depressions, he began exerting pressure at a number of points outside eastern Europe, testing how far he could extend the Russian sphere without precipitating a hostile American response.

The Soviets continued their wartime occupation of Iran beyond a previously agreed upon deadline and created a puppet regime in Azerbaidzhan. When the Western allies supported the Iranians'

---

of all democratic elements"; subsequently, there was to be "the establishment through free elections of Governments responsive to the will of the people."

complaint to the United Nations, Russia demanded, in return for withdrawal of its troops, oil concessions in the northern part of the country and posts for Communists in the Iranian governemnt. In the face of harsh Western warnings, Stalin agreed to withdraw his troops, pulling the rug out from his satellite regime, which collapsed immediately.[23] Throughout 1945 and 1946, the Soviets intensified pressure on Turkey for control over the Bosporus and Dardanelles straits and the dissociation of the Ankara government from Great Britain. The United States, buttressing the British, responded to Russian troop movements on the Turkish border with the dispatch of a naval task force to the eastern Mediterranean. Again, Stalin was compelled to retreat.

By the beginning of 1947, the fluidity of the immediate postwar period was subsiding and limits to the Soviet sphere of influence were being set by the Western powers. Negotiations on the future of Germany, divided by the victors into what were supposed to be temporary zones of military occupation, had reached an impasse, and now the Americans and British merged their zones into the nucleus of a separate German state. Western Europe as a whole was on the verge of economic collapse. The leading nations of the region had not recovered from the devastation of the war, and there was little likelihood that any would do so without massive outside aid. Communists were already participating in the governments of France and Italy, holding out the frightening prospect of economic and social upheaval and a prostrate western Europe falling behind the Iron Curtain.

The alarm was sounded in Washington by the British, whose desperate economic situation poised them on the brink of bankruptcy and compelled them to abdicate their role as a world power. In late February of 1947, London notified Washington of its intention to abandon its traditional role of counterweight to the Russians in the eastern Mediterranean and pull back from Greece and Turkey. For the Truman Administration, a crucial juncture in the postwar period had been reached. The British decision to withdraw support from Turkey and Greece, where they were backing the royal government against Communist insurrection, meant that unless the United States took up the slack, the southern flank of Europe would probably succumb to Soviet pressure. With western Europe already tottering on the brink of economic disaster, it was conceivable that America's entire continental defense perimeter would crumble and fall into the Russian sphere. Abandoning its long-cherished policy of nonentanglement, the United States directly intervened in the affairs of the Old World, first with the Truman Doctrine in March 1947 and then with the Marshall plan, or European Recovery Program, in July 1947.

In order to sell the American people on a policy of military and economic aid to Greece and Turkey, the administration and congressional leaders believed it necessary to present the strategy of containment "in terms of free governments everywhere that needed our aid to strengthen and defend themselves against Communist aggression and subversion."[24] The Truman Doctrine thus cast the struggle with the Soviet Union in ideological and global terms, and the United States was portrayed as the last bastion of freedom and democracy in a world threatened by Communist totalitarianism. This blank check given the President, this open-ended commitment on behalf of dubious ideological distinctions, helped transform the cold war from a classical struggle for power between two territorial states into a worldwide crusade by the "Free World" against "International Communism." Indeed, American involvement in the war in Indochina was the logical culmination of the universal and ideological mission assigned the United States by the Truman Doctrine.

The final division of Europe came with the Marshall plan and the Soviet response to it. Three months after President Truman enunciated the doctrine that bears his name, Secretary of State George C. Marshall invited all European nations to take the initiative in drafting a program of recovery to be financed by American aid. Not surprisingly, Moscow refused to participate and instructed its eastern European satellites to do likewise. Moreover, the U.S.S.R. responded with the creation of Comecon (Council for Mutual Economic Assistance) to orient the economies of the eastern European countries more closely to its own and insulate its bloc from contamination by a unified West. With the Marshall plan and the Soviet sponsorship of Comecon, Europe was divided formally between East and West. And yet, despite occasional saber rattling by both sides, the cold war had not yet been defined in military terms.

Two momentous events would lead to the militarization and globalization of the Soviet-American struggle for power: the Berlin blockade of 1948–49 and the Korean War of 1950–53. In June 1948, in retaliation against Western moves leading to the political unification of their zones of occupation in Germany, the Soviet Union cut off all land access to Berlin, located deep within its zone. The city of Berlin, like the rest of Germany, had been divided among the wartime allies, but in the absence of a peace treaty with defeated Germany, the rights of the Western powers were precarious indeed and largely dependent upon Russian goodwill. Stalin obviously reasoned that the untenable position of the Western powers in the blockaded enclave would compel them to abandon unilateral policies for Germany and follow the Soviet lead. Stalin had seriously miscalculated. Far from being intimidated, the United States saw the blockade as an integral part of Russian strategy to dominate all Germany and all Europe. Its response was the famous airlift to Berlin, which lasted until the spring of 1949. In May of that year, Stalin ordered the blockade lifted, but not before he had precipitated the first major crisis and war scare of the cold war. By brandishing the big stick over Berlin, he reinforced the West's impression that Russia intended to expand its sphere of influence by force. As a direct result, in April 1949, the North Atlantic Treaty was signed, linking eleven states in an anti-Soviet military alliance.

Another error in judgment on Stalin's part, the invasion of South Korea, caused the cold war to become a worldwide confrontation. The year that produced the Atlantic Alliance also witnessed the victory of Mao Tse-tung's Communist forces in the Chinese civil war. Though the pro-Western forces of Chiang Kai-shek had retreated to the island of Taiwan, the Truman Administration had decided to accept the outcome of the struggle in China and leave the Nationalists to their fate; in effect, then, Washington was not yet prepared to allow the cold war to embrace Asia as well as Europe and the Middle East. However, the Soviet-sponsored North Korean invasion of South Korea in June 1950 entirely altered the United States' Far Eastern policy. To the Americans, the Korean attack, coming on the heels of Mao's victory and the signing of the Sino-Soviet military alliance, proved both the monolithic nature of world communism and its goal of conquest by force. In consequence, the American attitude toward Chinese and Vietnamese Communist movements underwent a change. Truman ordered the United States' Seventh Fleet to prevent the expected Communist assault on Taiwan, thus perpetuating the division of China and further alienating the Peking regime. The United States no longer doubted that the war being waged by the French against Ho Chi Minh was part of the Free World's battle against the Communist menace; henceforth, it supported France and gradually took over its role in Indochina. Meanwhile, in Europe, the Atlantic Alliance was expanded into the North Atlantic Treaty Organization (NATO), an elaborate network of integrated commands and logistical support, and the decision was made in Washington to permit West German rearmament as a check to Russian military preponderance on the Continent.

In retrospect, it is obvious that the tempo and direction of Soviet foreign policy shifted significantly as early as 1952, with Stalins's conciliatory proposal for a neutralized and unified Germany.[25] Despite a number of conciliatory gestures by the post-Stalin Russian leadership (including a reversal of policy toward Turkey, Greece and Iran), the United States could not be persuaded that the character of Soviet Russia and its supposedly unified Communist movement had changed. The intensely anti-Communist commitment of the American public and its leadership, molded at the height of the cold war, ensured American rigidity. If anything, United States foreign policy became even more "cold warrior" during the 1950s and grew all but impervious to important developments abroad like the Sino-Soviet rift, which undermined the original rationale for containment. The United States erected a wall of pacts around the rim of Soviet-dominated Eurasia. In the Far East, Washington concluded bilateral defense agreements with Japan, South Korea and Taiwan; in the South Pacific, there was the ANZUS pact, joining the United States with Australia and New Zealand; in southeast Asia, there was the Southeast Asia Treaty Organization (SEATO); in the northern tier of the Middle East, there was the Central Treaty Organization (CENTO). In the end, the United States was linked militarily to over forty countries around the globe.

The world was divided between the two superpowers, and relations between Moscow and Washington were doomed, for the time being, to a twilight zone of neither peace nor war. The prophecy of Alexis de Tocqueville, written in the 1830s, had been fulfilled:

> There are at the present time two great nations in the world, started from differing points but seem to tend toward the same end. I allude to the Russians and the Americans. . . .
>
> Their starting point is different and their courses are not the same; yet each seems marked out by the will of heaven to sway the destinies of half the globe.[26]

THE POST-POSTWAR ERA: BETWEEN BIPOLARITY AND MULTIPOLARITY

For two decades following the Second World War, the atmosphere of world politics was dominated by the inability of the superpowers to reach an accommodation concerning the global order to be built on the rubble of the Axis defeat. The postwar period was characterized by continual maneuvering as each side searched for positions of strength vis-à-vis its rival. Periodically their mutual relations were punctuated by major international crises in which one party would challenge, and the other defend, the territorial status quo, or they both collided in the no-man's-land separating their spheres of influence.

By the early 1960s, however, the distribution of capabilities in the world was undergoing a profound change. First, the nuclear duopoly of the superpowers proved to be short-lived: In 1957, Britain tested its first hydrogen bomb; in 1960, France exploded an atomic bomb; in 1964, China also joined the nuclear elite. By the end of the 1970s, there were a half-dozen nuclear powers and some twenty additional countries with the technical competence and fissile material to "go nuclear" on short notice.[27] Second, by the late 1950s, the Japanese and west European economies were expanding rapidly as a result of postwar reconstruction and would soon be challenging the economic preeminence of the United States and the Soviet Union. Third, the postwar era witnessed a proliferation of new states resulting from the demise of European colonialism, and increasing collaboration among these new nations for the twin objectives of speeding up the liquidation of imperial rule and restructuring the world economy. Fourth, fissures in the Communist bloc, foreshadowed by the defection of Tito in Yugoslavia in 1948 and the domestic unrest in eastern Europe in the 1950s, erupted into a clash of military forces along the long and disputed border between Russia and China.

Three decades after the Second World War, the East-West struggle was but one of four major axes of global conflict.

The Third Rome vs. the Middle Kingdom: The East-East Axis of Conflict

In the spring of 1969, three hundred years after the armed forces of the two nations first clashed at the mouth of the Ussuri River, first the Chinese and then the Russians launched military assaults against one another's positions, both vying for control over disputed islands in that same Ussuri River.[28] These two battles symbolize the continuity of the Russo-Chinese struggle for power, a conflict only briefly interrupted by an "unnatural alliance" concluded in 1950.[29] The sole basis for accommodation between the two powers was the common threat posed by the United States after World War II. Aside from this mutual interest, there was no broad commonality of interests between Russia and China. That the two countries shared an ideology seemed to matter little. If anything, their competing claims to the mantle of worldwide Communist leadership exacerbated their historical rivalry.

Despite the facade of unity displayed during most of the 1950s, the People's Republic of China and the U.S.S.R. had widely divergent interests. In addition to a long history of Russian imperialism (both Czarist and Soviet) against China and different interpretations of Marxism, China and Russia were in different stages of economic development; the Soviet Union was an advanced industrialization power in pursuit of higher material living standards for its already relatively prosperous population, while China, overpopulated and underdeveloped, was intent upon breaking out of the circle of economic backwardness and political impotence it was in. In brief, Russia was a "have" nation with a stake in the global status quo, while China was a "have-not" nation proposing a radical redistribution of global benefits. Given these crucial differences in national perspective and interest, a parting of the ways in foreign policy was almost inevitable.

The latent tension between the two countries was compounded by their incompatible traditional views of themselves. As mentioned previously, the Russia of the Czars conceived of itself as the Third Rome, and much as the ancient caesars had united in their persons both the secular government and the state religion, the Czars assumed the sacramental role of defender of the Orthodox Church. The continual expansion of the Czarist imperial domain was rationalized in terms of the historical and religious missionary obligations of the new Rome. The Bolshevik Revolution of 1917 superimposed one variety of ideological and universalist pretention upon another. The basic mold of Russian foreign policy was unchanged.

The Chinese claim to cultural and political superiority is much older than that of Russians. Modern China is the direct descendant of one of the oldest civilizations on earth. For some two thousand years, the Chinese saw themselves as the center of the universe—the Middle Kingdom—and considered all non-Chinese and non-Sinicized people barbarians. Isolated from the Western world, the Chinese established a vast tributary system which, at the height of their power, linked all the lands surrounding China under the suzerainty of the Middle Kingdom and its emperor, who was considered to be the Son of Heaven. But the scientific and industrial revolutions which brought western Europe into the modern age bypassed the Orient, and the vast increase in capabilities which the process of modernization entailed was to leave the middle Kingdom at the mercy of the barbarians who were to descend upon it in the nineteenth century.

With the defeat of China in the Opium War (1839–41) at the hands of Great Britain, the Middle Kingdom's self-imposed isolation was shattered and its military weakness made all too evident to prospective imperialists, especially the eager Russians. With China then being divided up into foreign spheres of influence, Russia took more than her share in Manchuria, Mongolia and Turkestan. By the Treaty of Peking (1860), China was forced to cede a half-million square miles of territory in the Far East and central Asia to Czarist Russia. On the eve of the Bolshevik

Revolution, the Russian sphere represented some two-fifths of China's remaining land area.[30]

Communist Russia's China policy began with a renunciation of Czarist imperialist acquisitions but ended with a revival of the old Russian theme. Though the Bolshevik regime agreed by treaty (1924) to renounce past infractions on Chinese sovereignty, Outer Mongolia soon became a Soviet satellite and the Russians reasserted control over Sinkiang. Though Moscow aided in the formation of a Chinese Communist party, by the early 1930s, Mao Tse-tung had reorganized the Chinese Communists in the rural areas of the south. Unlike the Comintern- (i.e., Moscow-) dominated party of the 1920s, Mao's army was not urban, not proletarian and less dependent on the Soviet Union. Moreover, Stalin was now preoccupied in securing the eastern borders of Russia against a restless Japan and so supplied Mao's arch-enemy, Chiang Kai-shek, with military supplies and advisors. In addition, he concluded a nonaggression pact with the Japanese and directed the Chinese Communists to seek a united front with Chiang's government.

At the Yalta Conference, Stalin exacted from Churchill and Roosevelt concessions in China as the price for renouncing his nonaggression pact with Tokyo and entering the war in the Far East.* In all likelihood, Stalin did not expect a Communist victory in the Chinese civil war and was prepared to reinforce the Russian position in the Far East at Mao's expense. Indeed, there is reason to believe that Stalin did not want a Communist victory but rather a weak and divided China vulnerable to Soviet penetration and incapable of pursuing an independent course. But the tide of events in China was moving swiftly and was beyond the control of outsiders—American or Russian.

Upon securing the mainland, the Chinese Communists set out to liquidate a century of humiliation and degradation at the hands of the European colonial powers. But the unification and moderniza-

*The Americans and British agreed to the following: (1) preservation of the status quo (i.e., a Soviet satellite state) in Mongolia; (2) recognition of the "preeminent interests" of the Soviet Union in the port of Darien and the leasing of Port Arthur to Russia as a military base; (3) annexation of the Kuriles and the southern part of Sahkalin Island by the U.S.S.R.; (4) restoration of Soviet interests in the South Manchurian and Chinese Eastern Railroads.

tion of the devastated and backward China they inherited would require outside assistance and protection, and in return for Soviet help, Mao was willing temporarily to assume subordinate status. With the world dividing between East and West, Mao naturally decided to "lean to one side" and allied himself with the dominant (and, until recently, the only) Communist power in the global system. Yet Mao was forced to make concessions for the promise of Soviet aid—painful concessions which violated the principles of sovereignty and nationalism and smacked of previous unequal treaties: He would recognize the loss of Mongolia and allow continued Soviet exploitation of the mineral wealth of Sinkiang. For an ardent nationalist such as Mao, this kowtowing before Stalin's imperial designs was no doubt distasteful; yet a degree of subservience was the price for Soviet economic assistance and military protection in a bipolar world.

Thousands of Soviet technicians descended on China in the 1950s, bringing with them complete industrial plants and crucial technology. For a country trapped in a straightjacket of underdevelopment and aiming to become an independent world power, such an infusion of equipment and technology was of the highest importance. However, it soon became apparent to the Chinese that their payoff for Russia's assistance would be a good deal less than anticipated. Despite China's virtually limitless needs, the amount of Soviet economic assistance was small. Nevertheless, it was China's only foreign source and important to its development plans.

The Chinese came to believe that the Soviets had no desire to create a powerful and independent actor on their Far Eastern and central Asian borders or govern the worldwide Communist movement on behalf of any interest other than Russian national interest. As far as the Chinese were concerned, their great civil war remained unfinished owing to the United States' intervention, and yet the U.S.S.R. gradually moved toward a relaxation of tensions with Washington and seemed oblivious to the irredentist claims of its junior partner. In his address to the twentieth party congress in early 1956, Khrushchev showed a lack of militancy in the ideological struggle with the capitalist world by proclaiming a major departure in Russian theoretical doctrine concerning the likelihood of war. While the old Leninist-Stalinist principle steadfastly maintained that military confrontation would eventually be thrust upon the Communist camp by capitalist imperialism, Khrushchev now maintained that "war is not fatalistically inevitable" because the Soviet Union was now able effectively to deter aggression from the West. This line of reasoning antagonized the Chinese and reinforced their conviction that the Soviets would be willing to sacrifice the interests of loyal Communists in other lands—especially China—on the altar of Russian national interest. The Soviet Union, now a "have" nation, was acting more and more like a status quo, and not a revolutionary, power and was looking out for itself and not the international Communist movement. Mao severely criticized Soviet policies before the Chinese Politburo in the spring of 1956 and has been quoted as stating: "If we are not to be bullied in the present-day world, we cannot do without the bomb." [13]

To shore up the faltering Sino-Soviet alliance and preserve Chinese subservience, Khrushchev moved to placate the Chinese. In the fall of 1957, he agreed to supply the Chinese military with a "sample" atomic bomb and the technical data for nuclear-weapon construction. Simultaneously, he initiated his campaign of Sputnik diplomacy and rocket rattling against the West, hoping to prevent the Chinese from striking out on their own and challenging the ideological leadership of the U.S.S.R. The strategy backfired. Mao took Khrushchev's bold rhetoric seriously and, declaring that "the East wind prevails over the West wind," advocated a tough revolutionary push throughout the world. The Soviets, on the other hand, displayed a good deal of caution in their relations with the United States and had not abandoned their hopes of reaching an accommodation with the West. By the fall of the following year, Mao was to discover how incompatible Russian and Chinese strategies really were.

Chinese Communist shelling of the offshore islands of Quemoy and Matsu (still garrisoned by Nationalist troops) brought them into confrontation with the United States. The Russians, hardly eager to be drawn into a nuclear war over the fate of some barren Chinese islets, refused to give the People's Republic a blank check. The Chinese were forced to withdraw from the brink, but the crisis of confidence in Soviet leadership had reached a critical stage.[32]

In 1959, the Sino-Soviet rift widened significantly. In June of that year, the Soviet Union abruptly canceled its agreement to supply the Chinese with nuclear weapons. In August, Chinese and Indian troops clashed along their disputed frontier, and Moscow declared its neutrality in the conflict. Meanwhile, in Peking, a revolt was underway against Mao's leadership, apparently with the support of the Kremlin. In 1960, Peking decided to go public with its criticism of the U.S.S.R. in order to mobilize support within the international Communist movement.

The Chinese publicly accused Russia of "helping imperialism headed by the United States to dupe the people throughout the world." [33] In response, Khrushchev moved to isolate the Peking regime by attacking its "dogmatic" views on war and peace, and soon afterward withdrew all Soviet technicians stationed in China. Rather than cave in before this pressure, Peking suggested that the Russian Communists were guilty of the sin of "revisionism," a heresy previously charged only to the excommunicated Tito regime of Yugoslavia. Moscow, determined to assert the ideological and political dominance of the Soviet Union, denounced the Chinese as reckless warmongers and "Trotskyites" (as bad an insult as "revisionist" in the Communist lexicon). Though expressed in ideological language, the Sino-Soviet dispute was rooted in more mundane soil—competing national interests. In 1963, some of the ideological trappings were stripped away and the Chinese accused the Russians of "great-power chauvinism" in that they had sacrificed the interests of the international Communist movement (meaning, of course, China) to a "reactionary alliance with U.S. imperialism." In a move that underscored the fundamentally nonideological roots of the conflict, the Chinese threatened to raise with the Soviet Union the potentially explosive issue of its borders which, it correctly reminded the Russians, were the result of unequal treaties imposed by Czarist governments on a weak and prostrate China. In the following year, the People's Republic detonated its first atomic bomb, revealing to all that the days of a weak and prostrate China were no more, and described the "revisionist clique" in the Kremlin as "phony" Communists who were "leading the Soviet Union onto the path of the restoration of capitalism" and "seeking a partnership with U.S. imperialism for the partition of the world." [34]

By the mid-1960s, the rift between the former allies had developed into an unbridgeable chasm. Even after American intervention in Indochina, they continued their vituperative exchanges. In 1965, Peking elaborated its own strategy for world revolution ("the people's war"), wherein the "rural areas of the world" (the developing countries) would unite and, under Chinese leadership, defeat "the cities of the world" (the developed countries.)[35] The Chinese Communists had finally established themselves as the alternative doctrinal center of the international Communist movement. The Great Proletarian Cultural Revolution, which engulfed China in 1966, further exacerbated relations with the Soviet Union, and reconciliation with the U.S.S.R. was ruled out for the foreseeable future.

In 1969, the Sino-Soviet war of words erupted into armed conflict along their seven-thousand-mile border. There were over four hundred border skirmishes, culminating in a major battle along the Ussuri River. With the two antagonists poised on the brink of war, the Chinese leadership braced itself and issued a historical admonition:

> We warn the Soviet revisionist clique: We will never allow anybody to encroach upon China's territorial integrity and sovereignty.... Gone for ever are the days when the Chinese people were bullied by others. You are utterly blind and day-dreaming if you think you can deal with the Chinese people by resorting to the same old tricks used by tsarist Russia....
>
> Down with the new tsars! Down with the Soviet revisionists' social imperialism! *[36]

That same year the United States announced the Nixon Doctrine, foreshadowing American military retrenchment in the Far East and a lessening of tension between China and the United States.

* Following their invasion of Czechoslovakia in August of 1968, the Soviets announced the "Brezhnev Doctrine," by which they claimed the prerogative to intervene in the affairs of any Communist country which they felt was threatened with counterrevolution. The Chinese felt that this doctrine might be a prelude to an attack upon China itself and denounced the Russians for their new brand of imperialism (termed by the

The Soviet Union had clearly emerged as the primary threat to Chinese security.

During the two decades following the victory of Mao's forces on the mainland, Chinese-Russian relations had moved from ideological harmony and military alliance to ideological warfare and military confrontation. In 1971, Henry Kissinger would secretly travel to Peking to arrange for President Nixon's journey to China the following year. The split between China and the Soviet Union had led to a triangulation of power in the international system, undermining the bipolar distribution of capabilities and the single East-West axis of conflict which had dominated the postwar era. Two great and powerful nations like Russia and China, in different stages of economic development, sharing a long and disputed frontier, with a long history of cultural and political confrontation, were bound to part company in foreign policy. Though framed in ideological terms, the schism represented a fundamental divergence of national interest. The Chinese Communists were willing to accept second-class citizenship in the Communist bloc for the interim provided that there was a payoff—provided that the Soviets conducted the affairs of the Communist world so as to maximize China's objectives and aid her in becoming a major world power in her own right. When it became apparent that Russia had no intention of sharing power and envisioned a permanently inferior status for China, they concluded that there was no point in continued collaboration. Thus the imposing Communist monolith which confronted the West in the early 1950s proved to be a rather short-lived aberration in the history of world politics.

Whatever Happened to the "Free World": The West-West Axis of Conflict

The era that witnessed the dissolution of the Sino-Soviet alliance also saw the gradual dismantling of the Atlantic Alliance. The issues were fundamentally of the same nature: security, status and welfare. As long as the threat from the opposing coalition was perceived to be a clear and present danger, and as long as the

---

Chinese *social imperialism* to distinguish it from *capitalist imperialism).* Later, the Chinese would condemn the Brezhnev Doctrine as "imperialism with a 'socialist' label" and "naked neo-colonialism."

distribution of capabilities within each camp was overwhelmingly in favor of the dominant superpower, interbloc strife was eclipsed by the overriding necessity of defense against a common enemy. However, as the initial war scare of the cold war subsided, and as the junior partners in the Soviet and American empires regained a measure of economic and political vitality, the previously unchallenged hegemony of the superpowers was called into question. By the late 1950s, the countries of western Europe, as well as China, were chafing under superpower leadership and reassessing their status in the hierarchy of world power.

Following the Second World War, the western Europeans were, by and large, willing to place themselves under the temporary tutelage of the United States in order to avoid domination by the Soviet Union. Lacking the military strength to deter or defeat a Russian thrust to the Atlantic (which many believed to be a real possibility), and unable to dig themselves out of the economic morass of wartime destruction and dislocation, the major capitals of the Continent opted for the lesser of the evils: a tributary relationship to North America. Unscathed by foreign invasion or attack, the United States emerged from the war with a monopoly of nuclear weapons and a burgeoning economy which accounted for something like half of the gross world product in the immediate postwar period. Unlike their neighbors to the east, the western European nations voluntarily placed themselves under the wing of their superpower patron, and thus became military protectorates and economic client-states of the American colossus. The North Atlantic Treaty, though framed in the language of a mutual-defense arrangement, in reality was a unilateral pledge by the United States to contain Russian military expansion, and the subsequent stationing of a few hundred thousand American troops in central Europe was a guarantee of the American intention to wage war, if necessary, to that end. The European Recovery Program (or Marshall plan) represented the Europeans' welfare payoff for recognizing the primacy of American interests and objectives in the cold war. Thus the proud and historic nation-states of western Europe, which, until recently, had ruled most of the world, (at the height of its global power, Great Britain alone claimed two-fifths of mankind as subjects of Queen Victoria; by 1945, however, the sun was finally setting on the British Empire), were reduced to the station of vassals of an upstart peripheral power. This was brought home to the Europeans by the Suez crisis of 1956, when America crudely disciplined Britain and France for attempting to reassert their influence in the Middle East. The days of European supremacy, symbolized by "gunboat diplomacy" against recalcitrant princes in the non-Western world, were irretrievably lost, the casuality of a bipolar international system. Europe seemed no longer to exist as an autonomous, let alone central, actor in global affairs.

Much as he had been the symbol of French resistance to Nazi Germany ("I rebel, therefore France exists"), General Charles de Gaulle emerged in the late 1950s to challenge the American postwar imperium. Sensitive to France's wartime and postwar humiliation, at the conference table, as well as on the battlefield, de Gaulle was intent on rekindling the flame of French glory and leading the heirs of Charlemagne and Napolean to their just place in the sun. During World War II, de Gaulle had been snubbed by Roosevelt and Churchill. He had been refused entrance to the wartime conferences and he was not allowed to join in the deliberations shaping the postwar order. His all-consuming passion and ultimate mission was to erase these stains on French pride and lift France into the ranks of the major world powers.

Standing in the way was what he perceived to be collusion between the Anglo-Saxon powers. Of the western European states, only Britain maintained a "special relationship" with Washington, and only Britain was accorded the status of junior partner in the Atlantic Alliance. France was relegated to the ranks of the associates, along with Greece and Turkey. Such a state of affairs was simply intolerable for a man of de Gaulle's temperament. The symbol of Great Britain's special status was its position as the world's third nuclear power and the close nuclear relationship which existed between London and Washington (in 1958, the MacMahon Act prohibiting assistance to all states in the development of nuclear weapons was amended to permit the transfer of American nuclear information and material to Great Britain, which had already developed the bomb on its own). The French, who had yet to detonate their first atomic bomb, were still denied access to American technology. This was an affront to France. Upon obtaining power in France in 1958, de Gaulle immediately set out to rectify this imbalance in the Western coalition. Accordingly, he proposed to President Eisenhower (and later to President Kennedy) that a triumvirate be established within NATO; that is, that a political directorate of the United States, Britain and France be charged with the joint administration of the affairs of the Western camp and the development of a unified global strategy. In effect, de Gaulle was seeking from Washington what Mao was demanding from Moscow, namely, a voice in framing the foreign policy of the bloc. However, instead of disguising his ends with ideological rhetoric, de Gaulle appealed to the logic of national interest. Denied access to the inner circles of NATO, he warned that his only alternative was to develop an autonomous strategy in world politics based upon an independent French nuclear capability. But the Americans proved no more interested in sharing power with the French than the Russians were in sharing power with the Chinese.

De Gaulle evolved an alternative strategy. If the Anglo-Saxons would not accord France the global status to which she was entitled, then why not strike out on one's own, leading a "third force" capable of playing off one superpower against the other. (China developed a similar tactic; the doctrine of "the people's war" mentioned in the previous section was an attempt to establish China as the center of global revolutionary activity and the primary anti–status quo country. Opposing both the United States and its own former suzerain, China hoped to emerge as the acknowledged leader of the Third World.) The Gaullist design envisioned a Europe independent of the conflicting hegemonies of America and Russia—but a Europe in which France would predominate.

The general concentrated French resources and energies on the rapid development of a nuclear *force de frappe,* which would make France the sole atomic power situated on the Continent. (De Gaulle emphasized again and again that neither Britain nor Soviet Russia was a truly European power, the former being traditionally aloof from the Continent and the latter having a predominantly Eurasian empire.) Though he recognized that the European Common Market, consisting of France, West Germany, Italy and the Benelux countries, would have to be the nucleus of a united Europe, he actively opposed the plans of the Europeanists, who saw economic integration as a prelude to political union. A vigorous partisan of the French nation and its culture, de Gaulle had no intention of allowing France's historic civilization to drown in a polyglot federal union and adamantly opposed the evolution of supranational institutions in the European Community. Nor would he permit the Common Market to include the United Kingdom, which he viewed as a threat to French hegemony, given its nuclear capabilities and special relationship with the United States (he vetoed the British application for membership in the Common Market in 1963). As an alternative to a politically integrated Europe or a Europe including the English and the Americans he proposed a "Europe of the fatherlands," increasing cooperation among the sovereign states of the Continent from Gibraltar to the Urals. A Europe independent of the superpowers might eventually evolve into a loose confederation of states protected by the French nuclear umbrella and guided by the political genius of France itself. The Gaullist vision was not of a federation of European nations which would entail the eclipse of state sovereignty but of a new configuration of power, with Paris at the vortex. Shortly after blocking Britain's entry into the Common Market, France concluded an alliance with West Germany, hoping to consolidate French mastery on the Continent by drawing the highly productive (but nonnuclear) German economy into its political orbit. Then de Gaulle undertook independent diplomatic initiatives with both Soviet Russia and China, in order to gain recognition as an autonomous spokesman for western Europe. Finally, in 1966, he announced that the armed forces of France would be withdrawn from the integrated command structure of NATO and that the Western allies would have until the following year to remove NATO headquarters from French soil. Nevertheless, he stressed his continued adherence to the mutual defense obligations of the North Atlantic Treaty.

In addition to undermining the American military and diplomatic monopoly in western Europe, de Gaulle sought to topple the United States from its privileged economic position in the global economy.

Toward the end of the Second World War, policy makers in Washington became convinced that a prosperous and peaceful postwar international order would hinge on avoiding the division of the world into self-contained and competing economic spheres of influence. The disarray that marked international economic relations in the 1930s reinforced the American conviction that only a liberal economic system could contain the divisive and potentially explosive forces of economic nationalism. In short, if the governments of the world accepted free trade, the free movement of capital and a stable monetary system, all nations would share in the rapid increase in the planetary product made possible by economic efficiency.[37] To be sure, the productive and technologically advanced American economy would benefit at least as much as any other if the principle of comparative advantage were the central organizing concept of a liberal global economic order. The desired liberal economic system was known as the Bretton Woods system. The International Monetary Fund (IMF) was established to oversee the smooth functioning of international monetary transactions and lay the foundations for trade liberalization under the General Agreement on Tarriffs and Trade (GATT).

As a consequence of these American initiatives, international trade expanded to an unprecendented degree during the postwar period, as did the gross world product. Because of the perception of a common threat from the Soviet bloc (which was not a participant in the Bretton Woods system), not to mention the unchallengeable predominance of the American economy, economic issues did not emerge as a source of conflict among the developed Western countries. Nor was the privileged position of the United States questioned. The U.S. Dollar became the prime international currency, and the American economy was permitted to accumulate mounting balance-of-payments deficits, a right accorded no other state.[38] The role of the United States as, in effect, the world's banker enabled its government to maintain a vast military presence abroad and its business community to continue a virtually unhindered export of capital overseas (especially to western Europe). This economic and military presence of the United States abroad was responsible for the outflow of dollars and the chronic balance-of-payments problems. Yet the special role of the dollar in global economic transactions allowed this fundamental disequilibrium to continue. In effect, the rest of the Western world was subsidizing the American economic and military imperium by accepting dollars and not redeeming them in gold. The whole Bretton Woods system became increasingly fragile because it would be only a matter of time before American foreign indebtedness would far outstrip the ability to pay; that is, the value of the dollars in the hands of foreigners would be much greater than the value of the United States' gold reserves.

President de Gaulle was quick to exploit this weakness in the 1960s. In a way, he declared war on the dollar, seeing its precarious position as America's Achilles' heel. He particularly resented the growing dominance of American-based multinational corporations in Europe, fearing that their increasing presence in key sectors of European national economies would reduce the Continent to a mere economic appendage of the North American economy.[39] The volume of dollars in the world having mounted to a level several times the value of the gold in Fort Knox, de Gaulle announced that henceforth France would refuse to hold dollars and would instead demand payment in gold from the United States. Though France had not been able to pull the monetary rug out from under the United States by the time de Gaulle removed himself from the political scene in 1968, the huge American war effort in Indochina (and the new outflow of dollars it entailed) pushed the world monetary system over the brink. By the early 1970s, speculation against the dollar was causing periodic monetary crises. Finally, the run on the dollar precipitated devaluation by the Nixon Administration in 1971, and with this unilateral action, the Bretton Woods system collapsed.

The postwar economic miracles in western Europe and Japan, which were fostered by the liberal economic order established at Bretton Woods, eventually brought about the demise of that order. The whole international economic system had been premised on the continued dominance of the United States economy; the resurgence of other centers of wealth led to a progressive deterioration in the American position. With this development, coupled with the diminishing threat from the Soviet Union, economic issues gradually assumed a more conspicuous place on the Western diplomatic agenda. Increasingly, the western Europeans and the Japanese (led by the French) challenged the supremacy of the United States in monetary affairs. At the same time, America became less willing to accept the protectionist policies of its former clients. To ensure Japanese economic recovery from the ravages of war and integrate Japan into the Western community, the United States had been willing to overlook her neomercantile policies of subsidizing exports and restricting foreign investment. Succeeding administrations had permitted the Japanese to increase their exports to the United States, especially since the western Europeans, fearful of the competition, had erected barriers against Japanese goods. As for the Europeans, the United States disliked a number of policies set by the European Economic Community (EEC) which discriminated against American goods. Though originally the prime mover behind European integration (mainly as part of its strategy to contain the Soviet Union), the United States came to fear that the Common Market was turning increasingly inward, to the detriment of liberal economic relations with North America. Specifically, American policy makers attacked the EEC's Common Agricultural Policy (CAP), which was intended to restrict American agricultural exports to Europe. Moreover, the Common Market expanded its membership to include Britain, Ireland and Denmark and concluded a network of preferential trading agreements with a host of countries in Europe, Africa and the Caribbean. More and more, Western industrial societies came to view one another as competitors in the global economy, and economic tensions supplanted the common security fears that had bound them together during the postwar period.

In the West, as in the East, the bipolar distribution of power and dominance of a single axis of conflict were becoming the attributes of an earlier age.

The Struggle for a New Global Economic Order: The North-South Axis of Conflict

The fourth axis of world conflict is the confrontation between the developed countries (DCs) of the Northern Hemisphere and the less-developed countries (LDCs) of the southern portion of the globe. The stakes in the conflict between the global rich and the global poor involve neither security nor ideology; they revolve around a struggle for redistribution of the planetary product. This new cold war is being waged over the most fundamental of bread-and-butter issues.[40]

The dilemma confronting mankind stems from the gross disparities in income among the nations of the world. The international system is stratified into a small minority of "haves" and a vast majority of "have-nots," and the gulf separating these two worlds is great and continually widening. Between 1960 and 1974, the per capita output of the economies of the poorest countries of the Third World (compromising some one billion people) stagnated and, in some cases, actually declined. At the same time, the per capita output of the already affluent states rose dramatically from $2,768 to $4,500.[41] (By way of comparison, the per capita income of Bangladesh was $55 in 1974.) Robert S. McNamara, president of the World Bank, has described the wretched life of the global poor:

> But what is beyond the power of any set of statistics to illustrate is the inhuman degradation the vast majority of these individuals are condemned to because of poverty.
>
> Malnutrition saps their energy, stunts their bodies, and shortens their lives. Illiteracy darkens their minds, and forecloses their futures. Simple, preventable diseases maim and kill their children. Squalor and ugliness pollute and poison their surroundings.
>
> The miraculous gift of life itself, and all its intrinsic potential—so promising and rewarding for us—is eroded and reduced for them to a desperate effort to survive.[42]

The income gap between north and south (see Figure 14) is the result of the differential spread of modernization. Having begun in western Europe during the Renaissance, the process of modernization reached the rest of the world as European civilization expanded across the Americas, Asia and Africa. The initial impetus for this expansion was the dynamism of modernization itself.[43] Imperialism, which was the primary vehicle for the diffusion of Western values and know-how to traditional societies, is the natural outcome when power confronts weakness. Though Marxist commentators have attempted to define imperialism strictly as a by-product of capitalism, imperial relationships existed long before the emergence of modern capitalist societies.[44] To be sure, economic gain has always been a strong, if not dominant, motive for colonial expansion; however, the economic motive predates cap-

Figure 14

The Development Gap, 1976

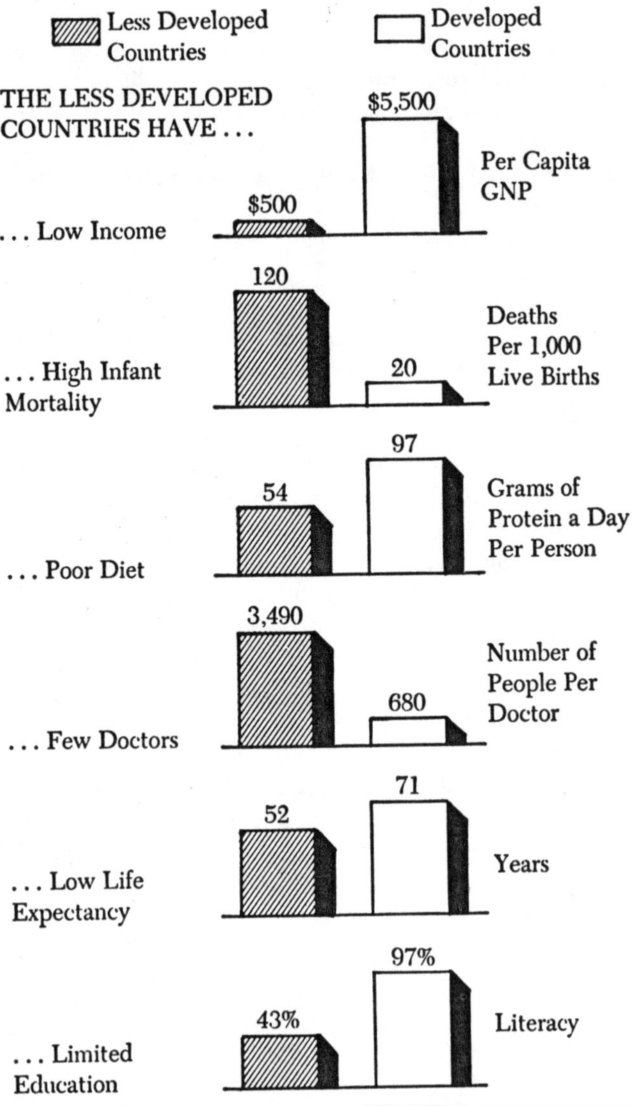

SOURCE: U.S. Agency for International Development.

italism and can be found in the contemporary foreign policy of the U.S.S.R. Moreover, imperial quests have had numerous non-economic causes, such as religious or ideological zeal, adventurism, security and glory. Regardless of the historical era and economic system of the countries involved, imperialism is the rule of one group by another group for the primary purpose of benefiting the latter.

Regardless of its motivations or subsequent rationalizations, imperialism's root cause is to be found in the disparities in capabilities between mother country and colony. The scientific and industrial revolutions allowed Europeans to subjugate the premodern societies with which they came in contact. By the end of the nineteenth century, the advanced states of Europe had succeeded in dividing among themselves the non-Western and premodern societies of the world and had begun the process of transforming them into the periphery of the developed world. Because modernization had destroyed their economic self-sufficiency, the imperial states needed the colonies as sources of raw materials ("hewers of wood and drawers of water") and also used them as markets for their manufactured products. The north disrupted the traditional societies of the south, but failed to spread modernization fully. Instead of benefiting from broad economic and political development, the south was to remain backward except for imperial enclaves necessary to produce and export the primary products demanded by the developed countries.

After the Second World War, the countries of the south regained a measure of political autonomy by ridding themselves of direct political rule from the metropole; however, the fundamental economic relationship between dominant economy and tributary economy remained. In short, because of the continuing disparity in power and wealth between the developed and developing states, the former colonial relationship was replaced by a neocolonial relationship.

The essence of underdevelopment is a low level of productivity, symbolized by the per capita GNP figures of the less-developed countries. Underlying this low per capita output is scarcity of capital and technology. But, more fundamentally, the poor countries are poor because they lack the most advanced methods of organizing human effort for the common purpose of creating wealth. By definition, premodern or modernizing societies have yet to evolve the organizational forms necessary for effective control over their environments. Political development (bureaucratic differentiation and administrative control) tends to be minimal, with governments incapable of efficiently mobilizing both human and natural resources; consequently, economic development also suffers. The root causes of underdevelopment are to be found in the developing countries themselves; the developed countries do not bear primary responsibility for the rest of the world's poverty.[45] Nevertheless, the leaders of the Third World are convinced that the global economic order created by the rich and powerful states perpetuates the backwardness of the vast majority of developing societies. While the West views the liberal postwar economic system as beneficial to rich and poor alike, spokesmen for the LDCs denounce the present order as a vestige of colonial exploitation that is inherently biased against the poor and powerless.[46]

The symbol of the structural inequalities in the present international economic order, as far as the Third World is concerned, is the relationship of trade. Foreign trade accounts for nearly 80 percent of the LDCs' foreign-exchange earnings, dwarfing private investment and governmental aid as a source of the foreign currencies necessary to finance development. Economic modernization requires an increase in the LDCs' share of world trade, but unfortunately, their share has progressively decreased from 32 percent in 1950 to 17 percent in 1970.[47] These countries are primarily exporters of basic commodities and importers of manufactured products. (Indeed, some seventeen agricultural and mineral commodities account for four-fifths of the south's exports.[48]) The "terms of trade"—the ratio of prices between what they export and what they import—are crucial to them. The raw materials that make up the bulk of their exports tend to rise in price at a slower rate than the manufactured goods exported by the north. For example, in 1974 alone, the LDCs' imports increased in price by some 40 percent.[49] The terms of trade are deteriorating; the LDCs must export more and more primary commodities to earn the foreign currency necessary to buy a certain volume of manufactured goods. In 1960, for instance, twenty-five tons of raw rubber earned enough on the world market to purchase six tractors; in 1975, the same amount of rubber bought only two tractors.[50] In addition, these countries are damaged by sharply fluctuating world prices for raw materials.[51] About half of all the developing countries obtain more than 50 percent of their export earnings from the sale of a single commodity and are, therefore, at the mercy of the vagaries of international supply and demand.[52] The African state of Zambia, for example, depends upon copper for 95 percent of its export earnings; between 1974 and 1976, the price of copper fell by two-thirds.[53] Bad terms of trade and unpredictable raw-material prices make it difficult for developing countries to modernize and plan for the future.

Deteriorating terms of trade have led to chronic foreign-exchange shortages in the LDCs and to mounting balance-of-payments deficits, which were severely aggravated by the steep rise in petroleum and food prices in the early 1970s.[54] By 1976, the total foreign indebtedness of the LDCs reached more than $170 billion (half of which had been financed through commercial banking institutions), raising doubts about whether a number of countries would be able to maintain their international solvency. Even if the poor countries did not default on their foreign debts, servicing the debt (interest payments and amortization) was placing a severe strain on many fragile economies in the Third World. In some cases, the inflow of foreign grants from the north was more than offset by the outflow of debt-service payments; moreover, the foreign exchange necessary to service the Third World's debt was consuming over ten percent of its meager and vital export earnings.[55] (In individual cases of course, the situation was much worse. By 1976, Pakistan's annual debt-service burden was siphoning off one-quarter of its export earnings.[56])

Foreign investment and governmental aid provide twenty percent of the Third World's foreign exchange. The development assistance provided by the north has been considerable: From 1960 to 1975, nonmilitary grants and concessionary loans totaled over $140 billion, and by the second half of the 1970s, the total flow of official assistance was over $30 billion annually. Nevertheless, foreign aid has never been able to bridge the development gap, and since 1960, the developed countries have appropriated progressively smaller portions of their national wealth for the purpose of assisting the LDCs. (For example, the United States' development assistance amounted to 0.53 percent of its GNP in 1960, but had diminished to 0.27 percent by 1975.[57]) The history of foreign aid leads one to the inescapable conclusion that, without outside pressure, the developed countries will be unwilling to make the sacrifices necessary for a major redistribution of income in the world. Given the logic of narrow self-interest in the primitive global system, this is not at all surprising.

The beginning of a united front among the Third World nations came in 1955 with the Bandung Conference. Though little of substance came from this summit meeting of the developing countries' leaders, the groundwork was laid for cooperation in the pursuit of decolonialization and economic development. By the 1960s, the number of independent states in the south had increased dramatically, and mounting disenchantment with the northern-dominated General Agreement on Tariffs and Trade (GATT) led in 1964 to the birth of a permanent United Nations Conference on Trade and Development (UNCTAD). Gradually the LDCs coalesced around central issues and mobilized support for major changes in the global economic order. To rectify what were seen as structural inequalities in international trade arrangements, the poor nations demanded international commodity agreements to guarantee just (that is, higher) and stable prices for the primary products they exported, free access for their manufactured goods to the markets of the north and "compensatory finance"—that is, subsidy from the developed countries for those with lagging export earnings. In short, the LDCs demanded a reallocation of global income through preferential treatment by the economically privileged countries.

Despite this impressive beginning, the Third World's platform made little progress. The developed countries put up a stubborn resistance to overhauling existing economic relations until 1973, when the Arab oil producers successfully employed the weapon of oil against the Western powers and the OPEC states simultaneously raised world petroleum prices (see Chapter 4). The oil embargo and resulting price rise became a rallying point for the Third World (despite the economic burden inflicted on the majority of poor countries) and a signal that a successful assault could now be mounted. Shortly afterward, the so-called Group of 77 (some 116 states by 1977), with an automatic two-thirds majority in the UN General Assembly, passed two resolutions which had the effect of delegitimizing the international economic order. They called for a new world economic order which would include the cancelation of Third World debt, compensation for past exploitation of their mineral resources, expanded participation in international economic institutions and a general rise in raw-material prices.[58]

At this juncture, the demands of the Third World could no longer be ignored by the developed nations. The international monetary system was in a state of disarray because of the downfall of the dollar, the subsequent "floating" of national currencies and the problems inherent in recycling the billions of "petrodollars" in the hands of the Persian Gulf oil-producing countries. The Western world was having its worst recession since the Great Depression of the 1930s and was plagued by spiraling inflation. The dilemma for the north (and the opportunity for the south) was that the concurrence of the developing states was necessary for construction of a new monetary order. The "have-nots" exercised genuine influence in monetary matters for the first time, and, by threatening to block a new financial system, the south secured a new agreement (the Jamaica Accord of 1976), which increased the availability of credit through the IMF and set an important precedent by providing for the sale of a portion of the fund's gold stock, with the proceeds going to the poorest countries.[59]

At the fourth UNCTAD conference, held in 1976, the LDCs called for a global version of the American New Deal: price supports for their primary commodities through indexed commodity prices and creation of buffer stocks. For the first time, the Western powers conceded that it was necessary to moderate price fluctuations and agreed to hold a special conference to discuss a common fund.[60] The rich countries' recognition of their growing dependence upon the developing world (especially in the areas of energy and raw materials) also led them to sit down with representatives of the Third World and consider the broad problems of energy, raw materials and development. This Conference on International Economic Cooperation was held during 1976 and 1977.

Nevertheless, as the decade entered its final years, the objectives of the south were still elusive. For the first time, the north was listening and even talking, but the slow pace of negotiations was leading to increasing frustration among the LDCs, who saw their vision of modernization fading.[61] Without genuine progress in negotiations for a new, more equitable—and thus legitimate—global economic order, the likelihood for increasing conflict along the north-south axis remains. As Tanzania's President Julius K. Nyerere has warned: "We demand change, and the only question is whether it comes by dialogue or confrontation." [62]

NOTES
Chapter 7

1. Arthur M. Schlesinger, Jr., "Origins of the Cold War," *Foreign Affairs* 46 (October 1967): 42.
2. Hans J. Morgenthau, in Lloyd C. Gardner, Arthur Schlesinger, Jr., and Hans J. Morgenthau, *The Origins of the Cold War* (Waltham, Mass.: Ginn, 1970), p. 79.
3. Ibid., p. 80.
4. See, for example, Samuel Flagg Bemis, *A Diplomatic History of the United States,* 5th ed. (New York; Holt, Rinehart & Winston, 1965); Julius W. Pratt, *A History of United States Foreign Policy,* 2nd ed. (Englewood Cliffs, N.J.: Prentice-Hall, 1965); Joseph M. Jones, *The Fifteen Weeks: An Inside Account of the Genesis of the Marshall Plan* (New York: Harcourt, Brace & World, 1955); John W. Spanier, *American Foreign Policy Since World War II* (New York: Praeger, 1960); Paul Y. Hammond, *The Cold War Years: American Foreign Policy Since 1945* (New York: Harcourt, Brace and World, 1969); David Rees, *The Age of Containment: The Cold War, 1945–1965* (New York: St. Martin's, 1967); Adam B. Ulam, *The Rivals: America and Russia Since World War II* (New York: Viking, 1971); Raymond Aron, *The Century of Total War* (Boston: Beach, 1955); George F. Kennan, *Russia and the West Under Lenin and Stalin* (Boston: Little, Brown, 1960); Herbert Feis, *Churchill, Roosevelt and Stalin: The War They Waged and Peace They Sought* (Princeton, N.J.: Princeton University Press, 1957); Schlesinger, "Origins," p. 42.
5. Representative of this school of historiography are D. F.

Fleming, *The Cold War and Its Origins, 1917-1960,* 2 vols. (Garden City, N. Y.: Doubleday, 1961); David Horowitz, *The Free World Colossus* (New Yrok: Hill & Wang, 1965); Gar Alperovitz, *Atomic Diplomacy: Hiroshima and Potsdam* (New York: Vintage, 1965); William Appleman Williams, *The Tragedy of American Diplomacy* (New York: Dell, 1962); Frederick L. Schuman, *Cold War: Retrospect and Prospect* (Baton Rouge: Louisiana State University Press, 1962); David Horowitz, ed., *Containment and Revolution* (Boston: Beacon, 1967); John M. Swomley, *American Empire: The Political Ethos of Twentieth Century Conquest* (New York: Macmillan, 1970); Joyce and Gabriel Kolko, *The Limits of Power: The World and United States Foreign Policy, 1945–1954* (New York: Harper & Row, 1972).

6. Schlesinger, "Origins," p. 52.

7. Walter Lippmann, *U.S. Foreign Policy: Shield of the Republic* (Boston: Little, Brown, 1943).

8. Walter Lippmann, *The Cold War* (New York: Harper & Brothers, 1947).

9. Lippmann, *U.S. Foreign Policy,* p. 94.

10. Ibid., p. 111.

11. Ibid., p. 51.

12. Ibid., p. 144.

13. Ibid., pp. 145–46.

14. Ibid., p. 148.

15. Fleming, *The Cold War,* p. 252.

16. Schuman, *Cold War,* p. 15.

17. Louis J. Halle, *The Cold War as History* (New York: Harper & Row, 1967), p. 12.

18. Quoted in Ulam, *The Rivals,* p. 11.

19. Schuman, *Cold War,* pp. 16–30.

20. Halle, *Cold War,* p. 17.

21. Lippmann, *U.S. Foreign Policy,* p. 118.

22. Adam B. Ulam, *Expansion and Coexistence: The History of Soviet Foreign Policy, 1917–1967* (New York: Praeger, 1968), p. 268.

23. See the discussion by Jones, *The Fifteen Weeks,* chapter 2.

24. Ibid., p. 151.

25. See Marshall D. Shulman, *Stalin's Foreign Policy Reappraised* (Cambridge, Mass.: Harvard University Press, 1963).

26. Alexis de Tocqueville, *Democracy in America*, vol. 1 (New York: Random House, 1945), p. 452.

27. U.S. Arms Control and Disarmament Agency, *Arms Control Report*, Publication 89 (Washington, D.C.: ACDA, 1976), pp. 18–19.

28. The discussion in this section draws upon the insights of Harry Schwartz, *Tsars, Mandarins, and Commissars: A History of Chinese-Russian Relations*, rev. ed. (New York: Doubleday, 1973). Of equal significance are Harold C. Hinton, *The Bear at the Gate: Chinese Policymaking Under Soviet Pressure* (Washington, D.C.: American Enterprise Institute for Public Policy Research, 1971); G. F. Hudson, et al., *The Sino-Soviet Dispute* (New York: Praeger, 1961); Donald S. Zagoria, *The Sino-Soviet Conflict, 1956–1961* (Princeton, N.J.: Princeton University Press, 1962); William E. Griffith, ed., *The Sino-Soviet Rift* (Cambridge, Mass.: M.I.T., 1964); Clement J. Zablocki, ed., *Sino-Soviet Rivalry: Implications for United States Policy* (New York: Praeger, 1966); Henry Wei, *China and Soviet Russia* (Princeton, N.J.: Van Nostrand, 1956); David J. Dallin, *The Rise of Russia in Asia* (New Haven, Conn.: Yale University Press, 1949); Harrison E. Salisbury, *War Between Russia and China* (New York: Bantam, 1970); Au Tai-Sung, *The Sino-Soviet Territorial Dispute* (Philadelphia: Westminster, 1973); Donald F. Lach and Edmund S. Wehrle, *International Politics in East Asia Since World War II* (New York: Praeger, 1975).

29. Schwartz, *Tsars, Mandarins, and Commissars*, chapter 1.

30. Ibid., p. 94.

31. The report was made public in December 1976 by the official Chinese news agency, Hsinhua. See the *New York Times*, December 26, 1976, p. 14.

32. Lach and Wehrle, *International Politics*, p. 187; also see Ulam, *Expansion and Coexistence*, p. 618.

33. Quoted in Schwartz, *Tsars, Mandarins, and Commissars*, p. 196.

34. Reprinted in Winberg Chai, ed., *The Foreign Relations of the People's Republic of China* (New York: Capricorn, 1972), pp. 138–50.

35. Lin Piao, "Long Live the Victory of the People's War," ibid., pp. 346–54.

36. Ibid., pp. 153–54.

37. For an excellent discussion of the American-sponsored global

economic order and its subsequent downfall, see David P. Calleo and Benjamin M. Rowland, *America and the World Political Economy: Atlantic Dreams and National Realities* (Bloomington: Indiana University Press, 1973).

38. For a solid study of international economic issues intended for the student of international politics, see David H. Blake and Robert S. Walters, *The Politics of Global Economic Relations* (Englewood Cliffs, N.J.: Prentice-Hall, 1976).

39. See, for example, J. J. Servan-Schreiber, *The American Challenge* (New York: Avon, 1969).

40. The north-south struggle has been aptly designated the "new Cold War" by Irving Kristol, "The New Cold War," *The Wall Street Journal,* July 17, 1975. See also the discussion in Jahangir Amuzegar, "The North-South Dialogue: From Conflict to Compromise," *Foreign Affairs* 54 (April 1976): 547–62.

41. *New York Times,* September 28, 1975, part IV, p. 1; and December 21, 1975, p. 16.

42. Robert S. McNamara, *Address to the Board of Governors of the World Bank Group,* Manila, Philippines, October 4, 1976 (Washington, D.C., IBRD, 1976), pp. 35–36.

43. See C. E. Black, *The Dynamics of Modernization: A Study in Comparative History* (New York: Harper & Row, 1966).

44. The classical Marxist critique is to be found, of course, in V. I. Lenin, *Imperialism, the Highest Stage of Capitalism* (Moscow: Foreign Languages Publishing House, 1950), originally published in 1916. Lenin, in turn, built upon the insights of J. A. Hobson, *Imperialism: A Study* (Ann Arbor: Univ. of Michigan Press, 1965), originally published in 1902. For two recent applications of this thesis, see Harry Magdoff, *The Age of Imperialism: The Economic of U.S. Foreign Policy* (New York: Monthly Review Press, 1969); and Gabriel Kolko, *The Roots of American Foreign Policy: An Analysis of Power and Purpose* (Boston: Beacon, 1969).

45. For an interesting argument contrary to the widespread belief that the global rich are responsible for world poverty, see Max Singer and Paul Bracken, "Don't Blame the U.S.," *New York Times Magazine,* November 7, 1976, pp. 34 ff.

46. For a concise contrast of the liberal-radical interpretations of global economic relations, see Blake and Walters, *Global Economic Relations.*

47. Ibid., p. 29.

48. *New York Times,* May 17, 1976, p. 14.

49. Robert S. McNamara, *Address to the Board of Governors of the World Bank Group,* Washington, D.C., September 1, 1976 (Washington, D.C.: IBRD, 1975), p. 3.

50. *New York Times,* October 13, 1975, p. 4.

51. A contentious United Nations study concluded in 1975 questioned popular assumptions concerning the deterioration of the terms of trade (ibid., May 25, 1975, p. 1).

52. Lester B. Pearson, *Partners in Development: Report of the Commission on International Development of the World Bank* (New York: Praeger, 1969), p. 81.

53. *New York Times,* May 17, 1976, p. 14; and July 19, 1976, p. 12.

54. Hollis B. Chenery, "Restructuring the World Economy," *Foreign Affairs* 53 (January 1975): 246.

55. Ibid., October 13, 1975, p. 14.

56. *Christian Science Monitor,* July 30, 1976, p. 11.

57. McNamara, *Address,* October 4, 1976, p. 40.

58. Thierry de Montbrial, "For a New World Economic Order," *Foreign Affairs* 54; (October 1975) 61–78.

59. *Christian Science Monitor,* February 9, 1976, p. 3. See also Tom de Vries, "Jamaica, or the Non-Reform of the International Monetary System," *Foreign Affairs* 54 (April 1976): 577–605.

60. *New York Times,* June 1, 1976, p. 11; *Christian Science Monitor,* June 1, 1976, p. 11.

61. *New York Times,* May 28, 1976, p. 14, and July 19, 1976, p. 1.

62. Ibid., September 5, 1975, section 4, p. 2.

PART IV

PROSPECTS

All the Dons spoke. All of them deplored the traffic in drugs as a bad thing that could cause trouble but agreed there was no way to control it. There was, simply, too much money to be made in the business, therefore it followed that there would be men who would dare to dabble in it. That was human nature.

—Mario Puzo, *The Godfather*

Chapter 8

The Crisis of World Power

"I'll reason with him," Vito Corleone said. It was to become a famous phrase in the years to come. It was to become a warning rattle before a deadly strike. When he became Don and asked opponents to sit down and reason with him, they understood it was the last chance to resolve an affair without bloodshed and murder.

—MARIO PUZO, *The Godfather*

POLITICS WITHOUT GOVERNMENT

As we have seen, politics is the process whereby men and states contend for influence and marshall the instruments for power on behalf of their differing versions of the just allocation of values. The essence of world politics is to be found in its anarchy. In national political systems, the struggle for power has been harnessed by the authority of the territorial state, stripped of its most destructive and divisive manifestations and redirected toward a commonly perceived public good. But on the international level, we still have politics without government—fragmentation of authority, diffusion of capabilities and influence and absence of orderly procedures for the reconciliation of conflicting views of distributive justice. To use Hobbesian terminology, men found the state of nature intolerable, but instead of creating a single and universal Leviathan, they brought forth a primitive society composed of many states, each with its tribal god, each claiming to be the sovereign judge of its interests and the sole custodian of its destiny. Lacking overall governmental organization to restrain national egoism, the international system forces each actor to provide for its security and welfare in a perpetually threatening environment. Though numerous aspects of international relations are not fundamentally conflictual, and though there do exist mechanisms for the amelioration of the competition for power, the principle of self-help is the logical concomitant of international anarchy. It is the very nature of global political society that condemns the territorial state to a competitive existence and propels it toward the defense of its exclusive and parochial goals.

From time to time in our study, we have alluded to organized crime syndicates struggling for unilateral gain in a decentralized system. If the behavior of states is sometimes analogous, this is because each set of actors is involved in a primitive environment where recourse to force and fraud are commonplace; indeed, where the threat and use of violence are inherent in the circumstances. If the nation-state resorts to duplicity, subversion, economic coercion and physical extortion, it is not because it is no better than a criminal association. Quite the contrary: The most powerful nations are often motivated by noble intentions and justify the acquisition and expansion of power and wealth in terms of the interests of mankind as a whole. Those who lead great nations invariably see themselves as the champions of divine destiny or the guardians of historical necessity. They are self-ordained prophets of progress, not purveyors of purposeless cruelty and atrocity. Hence the appearance of political figures like Cardinal Richelieu's accomplice, Father Joseph of Paris (see chapter 2). Or, to use a more contemporary example, consider the following passage from John G. Stoessinger's study of Secretary of State Henry Kissinger:

> . . . Kissinger made the pursuit of a stable world order the categorical imperative of his foreign policy. If, in the process, the human element had to be sacrificed at times on the altar of stability or a larger strategic vision, so be it, because, without stability, peace could not be born at all and justice,

> too, would be extinguished. He felt that, in a tragic world, a statesman was not able to choose between good and evil. Indeed, whatever decision he would make, *some* evil consequences were bound to flow from it. All that a realistic statesman could do in such a world was to choose the lesser evil.[1]

Despite the "Godfather" image of world politics, there is really no "crime" of world power in the sense that there exists among national elites a conscious design to cause human suffering. If statesmen do "evil," it is not because they are immoral by nature but because they are constrained to do so by the very structure of the primitive global system. The anarchic environment of world politics is not the result of the immoral acts committed by states. Rather, those acts are the inevitable product of that anarchic environment.

In the pursuit of influence and wealth, territorial states use any and all expedient means, including negotiation, subversion, economic sanctions or the threat or use of force. Yet, for a crime to exist, there must be a violation of the law and (usually) an intention to violate the law. States pursue their national interests often without regard for law because of the incomplete development of a global legal order. Where there is no law to break, there can be no illegal act. The international law that does exist is law by analogy only. It is not a hierarchical law backed by the sanctions of a higher authority. World politics is lacking anything resembling "constitutional" law—that is, the designation of a generally recognized and legitimate allocation mechanism—and the rules that do exist and that are regularly observed tend to be peripheral to the central problems of global order. More important, there is generally no intention on the part of statesmen to commit wrongs against humanity. To be sure, there occasionally appear national leaders with the power, motivation and desire to inflict mass misery and human suffering. But, by and large, these are aberrations, the exceptions as opposed to the rule.

International politics is akin to a Greek tragedy. As Arthur M. Schlesinger, Jr., writes concerning the tragic elements in the origins of the cold war:

> The question remains whether it was an instance of a Greek tragedy—as Auden called it, "the tragedy of necessity," where the feeling aroused in the spectator is "What a pity it had to be this way"—or of Christian tragedy, "the tragedy of possibility," where the feeling aroused is "What a pity it was this way when it might have been otherwise." [2]

Much as we concluded in the last chapter that the Soviet-American struggle for mastery of the European continent was a tragedy in the Greek sense of the term—a tragedy of necessity—so now we are led to the possibility that the present dilemma of world politics revolves around the same unavoidable kind of tragedy. In a primitive system, environmental constraints are paramount. The dynamics of competition seem to compel each participant to make decisions and undertake policies which will enable it to avoid what it interprets as the worst possible contingency, but all end up worse off than they would have been had they cooperated for the common good. The intersection of men's ambitions and dreams has resulted in the institutionalization of mutually disadvantageous and destructive modes of behavior. If the "realist" interpretation of politics behooves us to judge the morality of politics in its own terms—on the basis of consequences and not intentions—then we are justified in lamenting the "crime" of world power. And yet if it is true, as Francis Bacon once wrote, that "the mold of man's fortune is in his own hands," then it is still possible for us to avoid the ultimate consequences of anarchy.

WORLD POLITICS IN TRANSITION

The Peace of Westphalia bequeathed mankind a primitive political system which is becoming more and more deficient in the ability to provide order and justice in the world. The Westphalia system, a multitude of sovereign territorial states competing for power and pursuing separate and conflicting interests, may have been acceptable in the seventeenth century, before the process of modernization had made national autarchy untenable. But today, in an age of mounting interdependence in numerous fields of activity, a truly independent national existence based upon self-sufficiency and political autonomy is fast becoming—if it is not already—an anachronism. Ever since the beginning of the scientific and industrial revolutions, the peoples of the world have been gradually integrated into a truly global ecologic, economic and technologic—but not political—community. Despite their pretensions to sovereignty, national leaders are unable to ensure either domestic security or social welfare, both of which were the original *raisons d'être* of the postfeudal territorial state. Physical survival has come to depend upon mutual nuclear deterrence, which means that governments can no longer hope to defend their populations against foreign attack, but rather must base their safety upon the rationality of potential enemies. No longer can the state guarantee the economic prosperity and social well-being of its members. In an environment characterized by increasing scarcity and interdependence, the developed countries have become more and more reliant upon the developing world for their necessary supplies of energy and nonfuel resources; by the same token, the poorer nations must pin their hopes for a greater share of the fruits of modernization on the willingness of the industrial states to allow them access to investment capital, technology, aid and a growing share of world exports. Toward the end of the 1970s, each side was trying to accommodate the other at the least cost to itself, and both were experiencing mounting frustration. If the world is, indeed, approaching the limits of growth, as some suggest, the resulting resource scarcity is likely to aggravate international tension. When global wealth ceases to expand, or grows at an appreciably slower rate, there will inevitably ensue an intensified struggle for shares in the more-or-less fixed supply of benefits.

Since the inauguration of the modern state system, when the level of technology more or less coincided with the level of political development, the progress of modernization has far outstripped the marginal modifications which have been made in global organization. The global system is in a profound state of disequilibrium, caused by the ever-widening gap between social and political realities. The demands a modern society places upon its inadequate, primitive political system may well result, sooner or later, in overload and a resulting breakdown in the precarious order which thus far has been painstakingly maintained. If present trends are not arrested, it is likely that there will be a crisis of world power, resulting from acute scarcity of resources brought about by ecological stress and the depletion of natural resources. Such a conflict-generating situation will be exacerbated by a primitive political system characterized by the proliferation of weapons of mass destruction.

THE TRAGEDY OF THE GLOBAL "COMMONS"

Few informed observers would disagree with the argument that mankind has yet to evolve a stable relationship with its physical environment, the fragile biosphere that sustains and nourishes all life on this planet. Industrialization, coupled with unchecked population growth, has brought about exponential increases in environmental pollution; consumption of food, energy, and nonfuel raw materials; and general stripping of the earth's surface. As a result of the progress of technological civilization, more and more of the things men value (clean air, fresh water, space) are being transformed from free goods (in the economic sense) to increasingly scarce commodities. In addition, those resources which have always been in more or less short supply, and therefore in need of allocation, are becoming scarcer yet.

The quasi-anarchic international system creates the dilemma where what is rational and advantageous for the individual actor becomes detrimental to the good of the whole community. Richard Falk refers to this as the "paradox of aggregation." The conflict between short-term private benefits and long-term public benefit is vividly portrayed in the metaphor of the English commons. The common pasturelands of the English countryside were destroyed during the eighteenth century because of the overgrazing of private herds of sheep and cattle. As Falk relates:

> "The tragedy of the commons" occurs because each farmer calculates his own advantage by reference to the enlargement of his own herd. The gain that results from each additional animal added to the herd is a definite increment to the farmer's wealth and profits. When the sum of the separate herds pushes up against the carrying capacity of the

> land, the paradox of aggregation takes over. It does not help much even to crystallize the community interest and appeal to the conscience of farmers. . . . Unless the appeal is uniformly successful, a very unlikely outcome as it requires farmers of unequal wealth to forgo immediate private gain, then its results are merely to reward the less socially responsible members of the community at the expense of the more socially responsible. In this kind of setting, the temptation to maintain or enlarge one's own share of the pie is difficult to resist. . . . The typical outcome in such a situation then is . . . the exhaustion of the common resource by overuse to the detriment of *all* users. Only a common plan of conservation that allocates quotas and effectively punishes violations can hope to protect the collective interests under conditions of scarcity.[3]

The paradox of aggregation is increasingly visible in the contemporary world: The poor in developing societies continue to procreate despite overpopulation, convinced that their individual lot will be bettered by additional offspring; corporations struggle to avoid troublesome antipollution regulations by transferring production to friendlier jurisdictions, knowing full well that new waste-disposal methods will reduce their profits; national fishing fleets continue to overfish the oceans, fearing that they will be outdone by their competitors; industrial states strive to increase their share of the world arms market knowing only too well that a voluntary cutback in the export of weapons by any one nation will simply mean more business for less scrupulous adversaries.

Without centralized regulation of the competition for influence and wealth, the prospect is one of acute scarcity and resulting intensification of international conflict. The increase in global tensions which has accompanied the energy crisis is but a harbinger of things to come. According to a CIA study made public in 1977, world demand for petroleum will outstrip supply by the mid-1980s.[4] In the same year, President Carter warned the American people (who consume over 30 percent of the world's oil): "Within ten years, we will not be able to import enough oil—from any country, at any price." [5] The Soviet Union might well become a major oil importer by 1985, placing the energy dilemma firmly within the East-West axis of conflict.[6] A study sponsored by the Massachusetts Institute of Technology has predicted soaring oil prices and economic depression in the developed countries by the end of the 1980s.[7] This report warned that the critical interdependence in energy would require unprecedented international collaboration and that energy could "become a focus for confrontation and conflict" in the near future.

What is true for oil is also becoming true for mineral resources. The major industrial nations have long pinned their economic well-being on continued and secure access to relatively cheap, high-grade metallic ores beyond their borders. With global industrial activity doubling every decade and a half, it is already becoming necessary to process relatively low-grade ores by the use of progressively large amounts of energy. If present trends continue, within a half-century, the volume of raw materials extracted will be over thirty times greater than today's needs.[8] The days of inexpensive mineral resources, as well as cheap energy, are gone, and the costs of needed resources may become prohibitive in coming decades. Again, the likelihood of mounting scarcity appears, together with intense competition for what resources remain.

The scramble for resources will be taking place in a complex and delicate ecosystem highly sensitive to man-made disruption. As more and more energy is expended in the search for, extraction and processing of mineral resources, the danger exists that still greater damage will be done to an already strained environment. In addition to air and water pollution, there is the danger of thermal pollution, the inadvertent but irreversible warming of the earth's atmosphere. Continuing ecological damage, as well as the specter of ecological catastrophe, can serve only to aggravate global political tensions.

THE NEW SECURITY DILEMMA

Scarcity is endemic to all political situations and elicits competition for power in the conflict over distribution. But in an environment of chronic and acute scarcity, conflict will be even more intense. Consequently, if present trends continue, the international system during the next several decades will be marked by increasingly tense political relationships; simultaneously, the ability to inflict harm on adversaries can be expected to increase substantially with an increasingly interdependent global economy and the proliferation of nuclear weapons. More and more countries are seeking nuclear-power plants and reprocessing facilities that will provide secure sources of atomic fuel. The diffusion of weapons-grade plutonium will be an inevitable by-product of this development and, in a world where the technical know-how to produce nuclear bombs is already widespread, perhaps dozens of presently nonnuclear states will decide on a nuclear option.

In addition to the present five nuclear-weapons states (seven if we include India and Israel), at least fifteen nations have nuclear-power reactors, and no less than sixteen others plan to build them or are actually constructing them. As Senator John Glenn has warned: "Nearly half of all non-weapons states have not signed the Non-Proliferation Treaty. . . . By the year 2000 the world may be producing enough plutonium in power reactors for 200,000 bombs per year."[9] In a primitive international system, the inhibitions against proliferation are minimal. Though several nuclear powers (including the United States) recognize the potential danger in the spread of atomic bombs, others fear that a halt in nuclear sales will cause economic hardship and stifle their own nuclear industries. Here we see a classical instance of the *paradox of aggregation.* As for the nuclear have-nots, though many (if not most) might prefer a world free of the danger of nuclear plenty, here, too, the paradox of aggregation is operative. As long as world politics remains fundamentally anarchic, to forgo unilaterally the nuclear option is to place oneself at the mercy of less scrupulous adversaries. As an editorial in a Brazilian newspaper recently put it: "If other emerging powers have an instrument of intimidation at their disposal, we should have ours. If others can have it, it is not morally just for us not to have the bomb."

It is highly unlikely that the world will be safer when a host of governments, including many dissatisfied with the global status quo, have access to the nuclear trigger. It is true that a balance of terror has evolved in the superpower relationship, but the evolution of balanced forces, theoretical doctrines and myriad channels of communication between the United States and the Soviet Union will not be repeated in less stable relationships between inferior powers. Consider the situation in the Middle East. In this volatile region, Israel and its Arab enemies have been in a constant state of war—not cold war—for some thirty years and lack even informal diplomatic contacts. For a generation, the adversaries have failed to develop either the rhetoric or practice of deterrence, even on a conventional level. As two students of the problem acknowledge: "It may well be that nuclear weapons will be used in the Middle East in the near future, perhaps even in the next round of fighting, should there be another war."[10] If this were to happen, the prospect of local nuclear war among third parties escalating into a confrontation between opposing superpower patrons would be great. And there are numerous other trouble spots around the world capable of igniting a major conflagration. Even if nuclear war by conscious design is avoided and miniature balances of terror established in various regions, the possibility of war by miscalculation or accident would forever loom in the foreground of international relations. Simply stated, the more states in possession of weapons of mass destruction, the greater the mathematical probability that they will be used.

Dissatisfied territorial states may not be the only international actors in possession of nuclear bombs in the near future. The alarming incidence of transnational terrorist activity in the last decade raises the possibility of nongovernmental actors coming into possession of nuclear explosives, either by hijacking the plutonium and building a bomb, stealing a weapon from a national stockpile or being supplied with such a device by a sympathetic government. All that is needed for the fabrication of a nuclear weapon is fissile material, technological expertise and the motivation to go nuclear. The last two ingredients are presently available, and the proliferation of nuclear-power reactors will soon supply the first. It has been estimated that a mere half-dozen or so skilled technicians could put together a crude nuclear bomb,[11] and that a million people might die were a 20-kiloton weapon exploded on Wall Street in New York City during business hours. Disturbing facts like these combine to create frightening possibilities of nuclear blackmail by dedicated bands of terrorists or nuclear extortion by criminal associations. And unlike territorial states, transnational terrorists cannot be deterred by the threat of nuclear retaliation.[12]

There can be little doubt that a world of heightened scarcity, perceived injustices and nuclear plenty would be a world where peace and survival will be in danger. We are on the verge of a new security dilemma.

THE STRUGGLE FOR POWER AND ORDER IN AN ANARCHIC WORLD

The challenges mankind faces are, as Heilbroner correctly points out, "*social* problems, originating in human behavior and capable of amelioration by the alteration of that behavior."[13] The interrelated threats of scarcity and insecurity could be dealt with effectively if the ultimate problem were simply technological. However, the real threat to man's future well-being and survival stems from the primitive state of political organization, not from deficiencies in human knowledge. Only the evolution of supranational institutions and arrangements can address the global dilemmas of a crowded and finite world. Only the eclipse of state sovereignty can stem the tide of nuclear proliferation and prevent international competition from crossing the threshold into violent conflict and escalating global instability.

The ultimate challenge for the future of international politics revolves around the ability of national elites to react positively to the growing symptoms of a crisis of world power. Ideally, these signs of mounting stress will cause them to focus their attention and energy on the establishment of a new, more centralized global order capable of surmounting both the prisoners' dilemma and the paradox of aggregation. In principle, the urgent problems on the international agenda can be solved if a new locus of global authority is created. But reality is more complex, and we must guard against excessive optimism. As Falk notes, "we find ourselves caught within a vicious circle. The character of sovereignty is such that it contradicts efforts to circumvent it." [14] If the past is a guide to the future, we must bear in mind that

> the history of governments is one long record of failure by political leaders to take curative action in time to safeguard an endangered society or civilization. Political leaders are often beholden to the wrongdoers and are certainly hemmed in by an assortment of pressures, interests, and traditions; resistance to change is fierce, especially on the part of those who expect to bear its main burdens.[15]

If the present international system does indeed prove resistant to fundamental change, then it is likely that the symptoms of breakdown will be insufficient to kindle a reorientation in global organization. Should this be the case, then the prospect for humankind would be traumatic change wrought by disaster and breakdown. Only then, when the whole edifice of the Westphalia system comes tumbling down under its own weight, when the last opportunity for choice has been allowed to slip away, will supranational organization find acceptance as the only remaining alternative. Even if disaster is averted and survival assured, the quality of life is bound to be affected by increasing political turmoil and scarcity of values. In a pioneering study of the effects of man on his ecological system, published long before such topics became fashionable, Harrison Brown warned that the logic of industrial civilization would lead it either to Armageddon and a reversion to agrarian existence or, more likely, toward the extension of state authority and the extinction of individual freedom. Pointing to the interrelationship between scarcity and political organization, he concluded:

> With increasing necessity and demand for efficiency, integration, and minimizing of waste in the economic world, there will be increasing demand for efficiency, integration, and minimizing of waste in the social world. These changes will have marked effects upon the ways in which men live. It seems clear that the first major penalty man will have to pay for his rapid consumption of the earth's non-renewable resources will be that of having to live in a world where his thoughts and actions are ever more strongly limited, where social organization has become all-pervasive, complex, and

> inflexible, and where the state completely dominates the actions of the individual.[15]

The prospects may seem grim indeed, but man's lot is by no means a hopeless one. Doomsday scenarios are discomforting, and we must take care to remember that such predictions project past performance and present trends into the future. Nothing is inevitable in the social world, provided that behavior patterns which have persisted for centuries are transcended and replaced by new survival policies.

As we have seen in Chapter 5, the contemporary global order is not simply a static reply of the eighteenth-century balance-of-power system. Numerous processes and structures have evolved to ameliorate the competition for power. Moreover, however many examples of intransigence and selfishness one can find in the history of international relations, one can also point to instances in which the logic of self-interest has led to cooperation in the pursuit of a mutually advantageous outcome. The whole history of the post–World War II era—the transformation of the superpower rivalry from cold war to détente, the reconciliation of France and West Germany and the formation of the European Community, the Sino-American rapprochement, the relatively peaceful liquidation of European colonialism, the north-south dialogue—suggests that the territorial state is indeed capable of adapting to a rapidly changing environment and that the state system may be becoming gradually less primitive.

Darwin taught us long ago that creatures that fail to adapt to their changing environments are doomed to extinction. The territorial state is approaching the crossroad. Unlike lower forms of animal life which have long since passed into oblivion, man has the ability to decide his fate. If he acts to reorder his priorities and gradually evolves global structures to deal with the challenges which threaten nation-state civilization, he can salvage both his survival and his freedom. But if he fails to act and allows the symptoms of breakdown to mount and multiply in a primitive system, he may someday be faced with the uneviable choice between survival and freedom.

Notes
Chapter 8

1. John G. Stoessinger, *Henry Kissinger: The Anguish of Power* (New York: Norton, 1976), p. 224. (Emphasis in the original.)
2. Arthur M. Schlesinger, Jr., "Origins of the Cold War," *Foreign Affairs* 46 (October 1967): 52.
3. Richard A. Falk, *This Endangered Planet: Prospects and Proposals for Human Survival* (New York: Vintage, 1972), pp. 48–49. (Emphasis in the original.)
4. *Christian Science Monitor,* April 20, 1977, p. 1.
5. *New York Times,* April 16, 1977, p. 11.
6. Ibid., April 4, 1977, p. 24.
7. Carroll L. Wilson, et al., *Energy: Global Prospects, 1985–2000* (New York: McGraw-Hill, 1977). The timing, but not the fact, of the crisis will depend upon the willingness of Saudi Arabia to increase oil production. See Dankwart A. Rustow, "U.S.–Saudi Relations and the Oil Crisis of the 1980s," *Foreign Affairs* 55 (April 1977): 494–576.
8. Robert L. Heilbroner, *An Inquiry into the Human Prospect* (New York: Norton, 1974), pp. 47–48.
9. *Christian Science Monitor,* May 24, 1977, p. 6.
10. Robert J. Pranger and Dale R. Tahtinen, *Nuclear Threat in the Middle East* (Washington, D.C.: American Enterprise Institute, 1975), p. 3.
11. See Thomas C. Schelling, "Who Will Have the Bomb?" *International Security* 1 (Summer 1976): 78.
12. See David Rosenbaum, "Nuclear Terror," *International Security* 1 (Winter 1977): 145.
13. Heilbroner, *An Inquiry,* p. 61 (Emphasis in the original.)
14. Falk, *This Endangered Planet,* p. 417.
15. Harrison Brown, *The Challenges of Man's Future* (New York: Viking, 1954), pp. 218–19. See also Roderick Seidenberg, *Post-Historic Man* (Durham: University of North Carolina Press, 1950).

Appendix

STRATEGIC NUCLEAR FORCES, 1976

UNITED STATES	656 SLBMs on 41 submarines 1054 ICBMs 453 long-range bombers
U. S. S. R.	845 SLBMs on 78 submarines 1527 ICBMs 600 IRBMs and MRBMs 135 long-range bombers 650 medium-range bombers
CHINA	20-30 IRBMs 30-50 MRBMs 65 medium-range bombers only a few ICBMs deployed
FRANCE	64 SLBMs on 4 submarines 18 IRBMs 36 Mirage bombers (with 14 in reserve)
UNITED KINGDOM	64 SLBMs on 4 submarines

abbreviations: ICBMs: intercontinental ballistic missiles
SLBMs: submarine-launched ballistic missiles
IRBMs: intermediate-range ballistic missiles
MRBMs: medium-range ballistic missiles

SOURCE: London Institute for Strategic Studies

Index